MARY WARNOCK

Mary Warnock

Ethics, Education and Public Policy in Post-War Britain

Philip Graham

OpenBook
Publishers

https://www.openbookpublishers.com

© 2021 Philip Graham

ISBN Paperback: 9781800643383
ISBN Hardback: 9781800643390
ISBN Digital (PDF): 9781800643406
ISBN Digital ebook (epub): 9781800643413
ISBN Digital ebook (mobi): 9781800643420
ISBN XML: 9781800643437
DOI: 10.11647/OBP.0278

Cover image: © Barbara Robinson. Photo credit: Girton College, University of Cambridge, https://artuk.org/discover/artworks/mary-warnock-195224
Cover design by Anna Gatti.

Contents

Preface

'Order! Order!' These were the first words I heard Mary Warnock utter. They could not have been more appropriate. For the next twenty-five years, in one field after another, she was to bring order into the too often disordered thinking that had resulted in confused and uncertain public policy. The occasion of this first encounter in September 1974 was the first meeting of the Committee of Enquiry into the Education of Handicapped Children and Young People. I was sitting with the other twenty-five members of the Committee, most of whom had not met each other before. There was a hubbub of noise as people round the large table introduced themselves to their neighbours, realised they had friends and colleagues in common and began to chat about them. Then came the call for silence. I noticed for the first time the slight, thickly bespectacled woman at one end of the table who, in her no-nonsense, North Oxford accent, had spoken. It was a voice that was already familiar and would become more so to listeners to BBC Radio Four discussion programmes.

The Committee presented its Report in March 1978. During the meetings, Mary and I realised we thought similarly on many issues. During a visit that a small sub-group of the Committee made to look at special educational units and schools in New York and Boston, we got to know each other better. After the Report was published, we became friends, corresponded and occasionally lunched together. As Mary, in her own account of our lunches, wrote some twenty-five years later, there was always 'an immense amount to talk about.'

Over those twenty-five years, bringing the clarity of thought with which her training as a moral philosopher had brought her, Mary contributed to the framing of public policy in an astonishing variety of fields. She is probably best known for chairing the government committee on Human Fertilisation and Embryology, whose Report was to guide public policy on the clinical care of infertility and experimentation on

© 2021 Philip Graham, CC BY 4.0   https://doi.org/10.11647/OBP.0278.12

embryos until the present day. It is less well known that, as well as the Committee of Enquiry into Children with Special Needs, she chaired a Home Office Committee on Animal Experimentation, was a member of the Independent Broadcasting Authority and of the Royal Commission on Environmental Pollution, chaired an Arts Council working party on the administration of the Royal Opera House and was an articulate member of the House of Lords. In the meantime, she wrote twenty books, some purely philosophical in content, but mostly relating to public policy in education and other fields.

Five months after Mary died in March 2019, I approached her executors, her two older children, Kitty and Felix Warnock, to ask if I might write her biography. They were not only kind enough to agree but have been most generous with their time in helping me along the way, not least with their editing skills. I should also like to thank for their assistance in many different ways: Michael Barton, Gillian Beer, Kenneth Blyth, Virginia Bottomley, Alan Budd, Susan Budd, Juliet Campbell, Robert Cassen, Tim Chambers, Ruth Cigman, Maggie Cohen, Sarah Curtis, David Davies, Bernard Donoughue, Martin Doyle, Juliet Dusinberre, Paul Ennals, Martin Ennis, Edmund Fawcett, Anne Fernihough, Sarah Franklin, Susan Golombok, Sara Graham, Judy Hague, Jeremy Isaacs, Gillian Jondorf, Nancy Lee-Perham, Robin Lovell-Badge, Martin Levy, Julia Lloyd, Nick Maurice, Hilary Maxwell-Hyslop, Molly Meacher, Jeremy Metters, Alison Murdoch, Elaine Murphy, Brahm Norwich, Caroline Raby, Jane Ridley, Gerry Robinson, Philippa Russell, Lucy Rutherford, Liz Sayce, Norma Scott, Lisa Sears, Jean Smith, Sarah Smith, Michelle Stanley, Andrew Steptoe, Ann Strawson, Gill Sutherland, Mark Wallinger, James Warnock, Maria Warnock, Hannah Westall, Sam Weisselberg, David Wiggins, Lucy Wood, Susan Wood and Susan Woollacott.

Finally, I should like to thank the extremely helpful editorial staff of Open Book Publishers.

1. Changing Times for Women (1950–2000)

Two Views from the Top

Two undergraduates, young women born eighteen months apart, studied at the University of Oxford during and immediately after World War Two. Though they both sang in the University Bach Choir, they probably never exchanged a word for they attended different women's colleges and, while one was reading 'Greats' or classical history, literature and philosophy, the other was studying Chemistry. Mary Warnock and Margaret Thatcher were both 'top women' who began their careers in the late 1940s when it was unusual for women to be successful in a man's world. After graduation, their careers diverged. Margaret Thatcher worked briefly as a chemist in industry but rapidly moved on to a stellar career in politics, making a massive impact both nationally and internationally and winning three general elections as Britain's first woman Prime Minister.

In the late 1940s, Mary, the subject of this biography, was appointed a philosophy don, a fellow of St. Hugh's College, Oxford. She spent the next sixteen years, while bringing up her five children, teaching philosophy to undergraduates and postgraduates as well as writing books and articles on philosophical topics. In 1966, she left university teaching on her appointment as headmistress of Oxford High School, an independent school for girls, remaining in this post for six years. In 1984, after a long period without a full-time job during which she chaired two important and highly influential government committees, she was appointed Mistress of Girton College, Cambridge, her last paid employment. Both while in full-time work and between the times when

   https://doi.org/10.11647/OBP.0278.06

she was holding these posts, Mary continued to publish philosophical books and articles on philosophical topics.

Her first book, *Ethics since 1900*, published first in 1960 but going into several editions, was a historical review of philosophical approaches to ethics.[1] The last chapter of this book discussed existentialism, a topic then largely ignored by the best-known British philosophers who were preoccupied with the analysis of language. Mary became the British authority on existentialist ethics and during the late 1960s and early 1970s authored three books on existentialism and edited another.[2] After she left the Oxford High School in 1972, she wrote *Imagination*, which might be regarded as the first of her books which went beyond a historical approach and expressed her own views on a subject.[3] Her experiences in both higher and secondary education then led her to write *Schools of Thought*, a series of reflections on the way education should enable students to lead what she herself regarded as a 'good life.'[4] In 1986, while at Girton, she wrote and published *Memory*,[5] in a sense a companion volume to *Imagination*, in which she explored the relationship between our imaginations and the way we recollect the past. She brought her thoughts on imagination and memory together in another book, *Imagination and Time*, published in 1994.[6] In 1999, she returned to the subject of her first book with *An Intelligent Person's Guide to Ethics*, this time drawing heavily on her experiences as a medical ethicist.[7] After the distressing death of her husband, Geoffrey, Mary developed radical ideas around euthanasia, and, jointly with an oncologist, wrote *Easeful Death* to which she contributed the philosophical chapters.[8] Finally, when just over ninety, she wrote *Critical Reflections on Ownership*, in which she discussed the way our sense of possession affects the way we regard both our own personal environment and the wider world.[9]

While, as we shall see, Mary Warnock did not regard herself as capable of generating truly original philosophical ideas, in 2003 she was described as 'probably the most famous philosopher in Britain.'[10] This judgement was based partly on her considerable published philosophical work for she published a number of other books as well as those listed above, but more because she brought the clarity of thought of a trained philosopher to the development of government policy in a number of different areas of public life. Further, as what is now known as a 'public intellectual,' she commented influentially throughout her life in the media on a very wide range of subjects, mostly but by no means only of educational interest.

* * *

The fifty years of the most active period of Mary's life, the whole of the second half of the twentieth century, were, as it happened, notable for considerable social, economic and political changes. Of these, the improvement in virtually all aspects of the lives of women, particularly middle-class women, stands out as one of the most striking. By the end of the twentieth century, women had by no means achieved parity. Indeed, at the time of writing in the early 2020s, not only do male Members of Parliament outnumber female MPs by two to one, but a number of prominent women have left politics because they have been exposed to intolerable abuse on social media. All the same, a brief description of the changing context of women's lives during Mary's active adult life helps us to understand her life, the contributions she made to British society and her own attitudes to feminism.

After the end of World War Two in 1945, when Mary was still an undergraduate, the raising of the school leaving age from fourteen to fifteen in 1947, followed a little later by the increases in the number of children as a result of the rising number of post-war births, meant there was an immediate need for many more schoolteachers. The gap was largely filled by young women. The 1944 Education Act abolished the ban on married women teachers opening the door for many more women, both married and unmarried, to enter the profession. Then, in the 1960s a number of new universities were founded. In contrast to the older universities, women filled much larger numbers of the undergraduate places that became available and were then more often appointed to the academic staff to posts previously filled almost entirely by men. In 1950, a tiny fraction of the female population graduated from English and Welsh universities, with very few going on to postgraduate study. By 2000, there had been a thirty-fold increase in the number of women graduating from university and tens of thousands studied for higher degrees.[11] Thus by the end of the century a very large number of mainly middle-class girls and young women were studying up to degree level. This meant that over this period, the numbers of educated women well-qualified to work in the professions and in other forms of middle-class employment greatly increased.

These changes were reflected in the gender balance in all the professions and other middle-class occupations. The marriage bar for entry into the civil service was lifted in 1946 though it was not until 1973 that women could enter the Foreign Service. By the early 2000s, around half of UK civil servants were women. There were more women than men working as administrative officers or assistants, but fewer as senior civil servants: the number of senior civil servants who were women increased from a tiny number in 1950 to one in five in 2000.[12] In the legal profession, only two women barristers had achieved the seniority of KCs (King's Counsel) in 1949 and the first woman judge was not appointed until 1956. Subsequently, however, there was a gradual rise in the number of women barristers so that by 2015, over a third of barristers were women.[13] In national politics, in the 1945 Parliament, only twenty-four Members of Parliament were women. In the late 1950s, though clearly a politician with outstanding potential for a successful parliamentary career, Margaret Thatcher was unsuccessful in several attempts to secure adoption as a candidate by a Conservative constituency.[14] By 1997 the proportion of women MPs had risen to about 20%. In medicine, in the 1950s about one in four medical students were women. By the end of the century, there were more female medical students than male. Many more women became consultants, but at the most competitive level in this field, clinical academic medicine, only one in ten of the posts were held by women and there were even fewer female professors.[15] In the Anglican Church, women have only been ordained as priests since 1994, and the first woman bishop was appointed in 2014. Many more women were employed in the media, but it was not until 1995 that the first woman editor of a national newspaper was appointed. Progress has been slower in the higher echelons of business. Women were only allowed to be members of the London Stock Exchange in 1973 and the first CEO of a FTSE 100 company was not appointed until 1997.

The second half of the twentieth century saw smaller but also remarkable changes in the lives of working-class women. Labour-saving inventions such as dishwashers and washing machines meant that less of their time was spent at the kitchen sink. Their marriages changed to become more companionate. The substantial rise in female employment meant that more women gained control of their own income and expenditure. For all social classes, the possibility of foreign travel greatly increased. But these positive changes were clouded by the persistence of class inequalities in virtually all areas of life. Most strikingly, by the end of the century, the expectation of life was seven years less for women in the lowest income decile compared to the highest.

How did this reduction in gender inequality come about? As well as the increasing numbers of highly educated women there were other reasons. Among the most important was the increasing degree to which women could take control of their own fertility. The birth rate reached a peak in around 1961 when the average number of births per fertile woman was around 3.0. But following the availability of the contraceptive pill in the early 1960s, by 1971 it had fallen below 2.0. From then onwards, women spent many fewer years bringing up children and were more often looking for employment. What did not change or changed only to an insignificant degree was the career disadvantage experienced by women because of their need to take time off while their children were young. This did not affect women like Mary Warnock and Margaret Thatcher who were able to afford childcare but there were very large numbers of women who were not in this fortunate position and the state did not step up to help them financially.

Whatever the cause of the difference in the position of women in the two halves of the twentieth century, there can be no doubt of its size. In 1995 Margaret Forster described the way the lives of a number of women who had lived in the first half of that century had been constricted. She concludes her book *Hidden Lives* with the words:

> Let no one say that nothing has changed, that women have it as bad as ever. They do not [...] I am glad, glad not to have been born a working-class girl in 1869 or 1901. Everything for a woman is better now even if it is still not as good as it should be. To forget or deny that is an insult to the women who have gone before.[16]

A highly significant feature of the second half of the twentieth century was the resurgence of feminism as a political movement to promote the rights of women. This occurred first in the mid-1960s in the United States and then, by the end of the decade in the UK. Feminism as a political movement had been relatively quiescent from the end of the First World War when women over thirty were given the vote until the mid- to late 1960s. Second Wave feminism, so-called to distinguish it from First Wave (late Victorian and Edwardian) feminism which focussed especially on votes for women, is usually seen to have had its starting point with the publication in 1963 of Betty Friedan's *The Feminine Mystique*[17] and then in Britain in 1970 with Germaine Greer's *The Female Eunuch*.[18] Mary played no part in this new radical movement, but by the mid-1980s she had articulated a set of positions in relation to it. These views, which she expressed clearly in her memoir, published in 2000, were similar to those of many, perhaps most women of her generation.[19] These women, who constituted what might be regarded as a silent majority, saw no reason to rewrite history or philosophy or other academic subjects with a gendered perspective, but nevertheless felt strongly that women were unfairly treated in many areas of life and that legal reforms were needed to remove such unfairness.

Interviewed for *The Sunday Telegraph* in June 1984, Mary described herself as a 'conservative feminist.'[20] She expanded on this term two years later in an article in *St. Hugh's: One Hundred Years of Women's Education in Oxford* (1986)[21] marking the centenary of the foundation of St. Hugh's, the Oxford college to which she had been appointed as a research fellow in 1949 and where she was still an Honorary Fellow. She asked herself what the next hundred years would bring for the position of women in society. She saw the central message of Second Wave feminism or what she called radical feminism as the separateness of women from men. She wrote: 'The radical feminist argues that, once the consciousness of women in general is raised, they will see not only that they are exploited and used by men, but that the standards of success and failure, the criteria of what is and what is not worth doing, are all of them established by men.'[22] Any suggestion that the standards of success in subjects such as biology and mathematics are absolute is countered by radical feminists with the unanswerable objection that such standards are always set by men. If and when such standards are set by women, these subjects will be transformed, and new insights will emerge.[23]

Mary points out that while in the late-nineteenth century women had fought to be allowed to study the same subjects and take the same examinations as men, that battle had long ago been won. Now, she suggests, the claims of radical feminists that women had a separate contribution to make in advancing knowledge put in jeopardy the success of those who had won equal university rights for women.

The proposals that universities should run Women's Studies courses, for example, risked fighting old battles quite unnecessarily. She notes that, where these courses exist, they are mainly historical in content, exploring the role of women in the past when they had been overlooked. The danger is that the very name, 'Women's Studies' suggests these courses are mainly not about women, but *for* women. She sees this as the thin edge of a wedge leading on to Women's Physics, Women's Philosophy separate from 'proper' Physics and Philosophy.[24] She quotes from a then recently published book by Dale Spender, *Invisible Women* (1982) which proposed that every true proposition should be seen as relative to the gender of the person who utters it. This might seem a fantastic suggestion, but Mary thought it followed logically from the current idea that women have their own gendered way of thinking which is different from that of men. Such ideas present women with an impossible dilemma. If they resist separatism, they are betraying one another; if they support separatism, they are betraying the standards of scholarship. Mary hoped that this form of radical feminism would be rejected.[25]

She characterised the 'conservative feminism' of the type she herself espoused as embodying a very simple principle. It holds that no one should be at an educational disadvantage. 'Women are human; and if higher education is among those good things from which humans benefit, and to which they may even be thought entitled, then women should have as much of it as men.'[26] At the time she was writing, Mary saw the goal of genuine justice for girls and women in education as still some way from being achieved. Particularly at secondary schools there was still pressure on girls, encouraged by magazines and television, to have as their main aim to be attractive. They should make sure they seldom spoke in class as, by definition, a clever girl was unattractive and the lowest in the hierarchy of popularity. This had led to many girls giving up all academic aspirations. Mary saw one of the positive outcomes of feminism, whatever its type, as the undermining of the widely spread idea, popularised in comics for girls and in women's magazines, that a girl should think of little else but making herself desirable to the male sex. Girls must make sure they never answered up in class as, by definition, a clever girl was unattractive.[27] As we shall see, Mary loved clothes but their attractiveness to men was never important to her.

Instead, she thought what was needed was a societal change in women's beliefs about themselves and in their ability to master and control the physical universe.[28] Conservative feminists begin by affirming that true education and learning is a common ideal. Truths may be discovered by any student. 'The female ghetto of the radical feminists runs wholly counter to the spirit of a common learning.'[29]

Increasingly, Mary thought, girls should be thinking of themselves as educational equals to boys, whatever subject they were reading, and she was worried by the tendency for girls to choose the 'soft' subjects such as English or a foreign language. Such tendencies must be resisted, especially while the then recently established polytechnics were increasingly offering subjects such as biotechnology and information technology. Universities should be proactive in encouraging schools to ensure girls are as well prepared for these subjects as boys. She looked at the future world of employment and presciently saw that there was going to be more part-time employment with more opportunities for leisure. 'Women,' she thought, 'were peculiarly well-fitted to open the eyes of politicians and educationists to the new world of mixed employment.'[30] Given that the demands of child-bearing and raising continue inevitably to bear most heavily on women, they would be well placed to lead the way in the increasing demand for adult or later-life education. Thus the conservative feminist would have several roles to play in the future of education.

The dichotomy between radical and conservative feminism that Mary proposed in this article has to be seen in the context of the state of the feminist movement at the time she was writing in the mid-1980s. It had moved on. After twenty years, feminism was in no way losing momentum but the focus of political activity had changed. In Britain, so-called radical feminists were more likely by the 1980s to be engaged in left-wing political activism such as support for the miners' strike and protests against the existence of American nuclear weapons at RAF Greenham Common than in staking out a claim for the exclusivity of women's role in education.[31] In university education, the field of women's studies had been at least partly replaced by 'gender studies' which gave greater weight to relationships between the sexes and societal pressures on men. To some degree therefore, Mary's conservative feminist position had already achieved dominance in debates on education. All the same, conservative feminists, as Mary pointed out, still had many gross injustices to women to overcome.

True to her view that there was no specifically gendered approach to scholarship, when Mary was asked to edit a selection of writings by women philosophers, she specifically refuted the idea that women had a special contribution to make to her own subject. She concludes her introduction to the book, *Women Philosophers*, with the observation:

> In the end, I have not found any clear 'voice' shared by women philosophers. I have enjoyed reading their works, some more than others, and I have been filled with admiration for the leisured women who, before they had access to any university, took up philosophy as a hobby and became so relatively expert. But it would have been very unrealistic to find, among such determined and individualistic women, anything shared except these qualities of character. As for the professionals, they turn out, unsurprisingly, to be as various as their male colleagues. I believe this to be a matter not for disappointment, but for pride.[32]

There is a sense in which radical feminists, as Mary described them, were the natural heirs to the late Victorian and Edwardian suffragettes, the militant women who had taken violent action to advance the cause of votes for women. Conservative feminists such as Mary were in the tradition of the suffragists who had aimed to achieve the vote by traditional, constitutionally acceptable political activity. Who should take credit for the outcome? Writer and historian of the early feminist movement in Britain, Katherine Connelly argues 'the suffragettes were inspired by the suffragists, but (that) ultimately both movements played their part in winning the vote by organising women *en masse* in so many different ways.'[33] Similarly, both conservative and radical feminists can take credit for the significant advances made by women in the second half of the twentieth century. Mary was in no doubt where her allegiance lay. In a review written in 1983 of Barbara Taylor's *Eve and the New Jerusalem*, she wrote that feminists had two choices: 'Do we try within the framework of existing institutions to improve piecemeal the chances of women genuinely to compete with men on equal terms or march to revolution? [...] my own belief is that the first way, though slow is both possible and practical.'[34] She thought this process should begin with primary school reading books in which boys and girls should be seen as having similar careers ahead of them and in secondary school classrooms which should all be mixed.[35]

Mary's position as a 'conservative feminist' did not change as she got older. If anything, her hostility to 'radical feminism' hardened. In an interview she gave shortly before her death, she expressed her loathing for the #MeToo movement, a surely not very radical response to well-validated reports of the sexual abuse of celebrities.[36] As we shall see, as an undergraduate, Mary had herself been sexually harassed by one of her Oxford teachers, a man some thirty years older than herself. Her diary entries reveal she had been deeply distressed by this at the time but had come to view her experience as trivial in comparison with the brilliant teaching she had had from the man in question.

How do Mary's views on feminism compare with those of her Oxford contemporary, Margaret Thatcher? Thatcher shared with Mary the distinction of being a woman at the top of her profession and the two were very similar in their expressed views about the role of women in society. A previous comparison of the two women points to similarities in that both were supremely successful in their respective fields but were pariahs among some feminists because of their rejection of radical feminism.[37] Margaret Thatcher would have had no problem with being labelled a 'conservative feminist.' When in 1982, she gave the first Pankhurst Lecture to the 300 Group (an organisation aiming to achieve 300 women Members of Parliament),[38] she pointed to the special talents and experiences that women brought to public life.[39] This was a different form of conservative feminism from that of Mary Warnock who saw women as bringing identical gifts to scholarship as did men. More significantly, the two women differed greatly in their behaviour towards other women. Margaret Thatcher, despite her powerful position, did nothing to promote the careers of women in politics. Of the fifty-eight members who served in her cabinets during her eleven-year prime ministership, only one was a woman and she served for a very short time.[40] There was one undeniable way in which her prime ministership advanced the cause of women: for the very first time in the history of Britain, ambitious girls and young women could see that the sky was the limit for the achievement of a successful career for a woman. In this respect, she was a very significant role model.

Mary Warnock was a very different role model. As a young, married don with a family, she was seen by undergraduates as having a lifestyle they could emulate. As headmistress of a girls' secondary school, she strongly supported sixth-form girls to aim high academically and think in terms of careers in science and business, as well as in the professions. Disarmingly, in her memoir, she admits to loving being 'the only woman' when, for example, she appeared in the media,[41] but, throughout her life, she befriended, encouraged and helped women in their careers whenever she could.

There were more fundamental differences between the two women in the values they held important. Mary devotes a chapter in her memoir to a critique of Thatcherite policies and of Margaret Thatcher herself.[42] After strongly criticising Thatcherite policies towards both school and university education on grounds discussed later in this book, she goes on to make a much broader attack:

> Education is only one field in which the Thatcherite values became predominant. Any government must attempt as far as possible to eliminate the waste of resources, spending, as we are frequently told, taxpayers' money on things that do them no good. But perhaps of all the legacies of Margaret Thatcher, the most pervasive was the assumption that nothing matters except the non-squandering of money, and that no positive value exists except to save and prosper. The worst effect of such a scale of values was that people began to adopt it not simply with regard to the state, but with regard to themselves as individuals [...] If personal wealth is generally seen as the highest value, then the means to attain it may gradually become a matter of indifference [...] The idea of the common good, which genuinely lay behind the welfarism of the 1940s and 1950s, has simply got lost.

Mary goes on to suggest that out of Margaret Thatcher's 'character and taste arose a kind of generalised selfishness hard to reconcile with a truly civilised society.'[43] It cannot have helped that Margaret Thatcher frequently attributed her preoccupation with getting good value for money to her experience as a woman and a housewife buying groceries for her family.

Mary's personal dislike of Margaret Thatcher is strongly reflected in the chapter in her memoir devoted to her. She prefaces it with what she calls a 'skipping rhyme.'

> Missis Thatcher
> Stick her in the bin
> Put the lid on
> Sellotape her in.[44]

The rhyme sets the tone for the rest of the chapter. Mary had not always shown such deep hostility. At times, she had been prepared to defend Thatcher. In 1984, in an interview with Anthea Hall, Mary had criticised radical feminists for treating Margaret Thatcher as if she were 'the symbol of all that is evil because she has climbed to the top of a male-dominated profession, whereas I think she has done very well.'[45] Further, when Margaret Thatcher's name was put forward unsuccessfully for the award of an honorary degree in the University of Oxford, both Mary and her husband tried to canvass support for her.[46]

The two women encountered each other on rather few occasions. They met very briefly in 1977, while Mary was chairing a government committee on special education, a position to which Thatcher, as Secretary of State for Education, had appointed her. Their next encounter was in December 1980 on the occasion of a lunch meeting at the offices of the Independent Broadcasting Association (IBA) which was responsible for commercial television and radio. Mary was a member. Usually, these lunches were enjoyably informal and the time when Margaret Thatcher, by then Prime Minister, attended was the only such occasion which was thoroughly unpleasant. Mary's description is worth quoting:

> [Margaret Thatcher] spoke loudly, in a high-pitched and furious voice, and without drawing breath (or so it seemed, though she was able swiftly to eat up her lunch at the same time). Her theme was the appalling left-wing, anti-government bias of the independent television companies, and of the Authority itself. She spent a lot of time inveighing especially against Panorama, and there was no time, nor did it seem much to the purpose, to point out that this was a programme made and broadcast by the BBC. Indeed, all the specific programmes she mentioned were BBC programmes, but it was possible, we judged afterwards, that she never watched anything but the BBC, and in any case, we were perfectly used to people who never noticed who made a programme, or on what channel it was shown. Her new plan, she stated, was to curb the media, and compel them to present news and current affairs in accordance with government wishes.

Brian Young (the Director of the IBA)

> managed to say that perhaps such a policy would be damaging to the
> freedom of the press. It was the first time that any of us had spoken, and
> it sounded, and was, banal. In any case, she swept it aside, and declared
> that the People were not interested in the freedom of the press, but only
> in having Choice (it was the first time I had heard this formula) and
> choice meant having available a variety of channels, all of which were
> truthful and encouraging. Nobody mentioned Stalin, but he was in
> everyone's mind...'[47]

Geoffrey, Mary's husband, met Margaret Thatcher when, in 1981,
he was elected Vice-Chancellor of the University of Oxford. Within a
year of his appointment, he attended a meeting of Vice-Chancellors in
London, which was addressed by the Prime Minister. Almost as soon as
she arrived, she 'began to rant against the universities, their arrogance,
elitism, remoteness from the People, their indifference to the economy,
their insistence on wasting time and public money on such subjects as
history, philosophy and classics. Again, she did not stop for two hours...'[48]

A more unfortunate episode involving the two women occurred in
1988, when Mary and her husband gave a lunch party to which they
had invited a journalist, Graham Turner. Conversation, initiated by the
US columnist George Will (a former pupil of Geoffrey's), turned to why
Thatcher could be so revered in the US and so despised at home. The
Warnocks were unwisely free with their views on Thatcher's personality
and appearance. Turner reported their remarks, which they thought they
had made in confidence, in an article in *The Sunday Telegraph* in which
he quoted them and members of what might be called the metropolitan
elite, including the opera and theatre director, Jonathan Miller. Mary
was quoted as referring to Thatcher's 'patronising elocution voice,'[49] her
rudeness and her choice of clothes. In her memoir she wrote that both
she and Geoffrey 'spoke with eloquence on the subject of her appalling
rudeness. We expanded this into a discussion of her style and taste (as
shown in her gaudy clothes and her now rampant hairdressing, and I
ended by saying, I think, that she simply did not know how to behave
and was in some way LOW.'[50] There was something 'unladylike' about
her behaviour.[51] Clothes, Mary claimed, reflect personality and Mrs.
Thatcher's electric blue suit with fitted jacket, metal buttons and big

lapels, expressed 'the crudity, philistinism, and aggression' that made up her personality.[52] In Graham Turner's article, she was quoted as saying that 'Mrs. Thatcher wouldn't lose a wink of sleep if Oxford and Cambridge were sold off to ICI, so long as they fetched a good price.'[53] Not unnaturally, this article provoked much unfavourable comment about the snobbishness of the privileged classes towards the grocer's daughter who had dared to confront their values, but there was no mention of the possibility that Mary's dislike of Mrs. Thatcher was secondary to her objection to her policies. It should be added that some of the criticism of Margaret Thatcher was unfair. For example, she had a reputation for lacking generosity of spirit and harbouring grudges. In fact, she was immensely caring towards her personal staff. Her close friend, Carla Powell, reported 'She bestowed and received loyalty. She gave everyone love.'[54] Further it is notable that one month after Oxford dons voted in January 1985 to reject a proposal for Margaret Thatcher to be awarded an honorary degree, Mary was made a life peer and a year later her husband, Geoffrey was knighted.

Mary's stories about Margaret Thatcher reflect another important difference between the two women. Margaret Thatcher never really listened to those who took an opposing view to her. Mary took particular interest and listened most carefully when she was exposed to views that did not accord with her own. Indeed, sometimes listening to opposing views led her to change her mind, possibly, as we shall see in Chapter Seven, unnecessarily.

Mary's dislike of Margaret Thatcher was, at least to some degree, reciprocated. The author himself had a brief insight into her lack of ability to listen when, in April 1987, he was one of a group of about a dozen academics, administrators and educational and health professionals who formed a delegation invited to meet Margaret Thatcher. We were there to protest about the lack of coordination between government departments in the development of policies concerning children. We were each given about three minutes to say our pieces and then Tony Newton, a junior minister in the Department of Health and Social Security who had been asked to attend, was asked to comment. He, as doubtless briefed, denied there was a problem. The Prime Minister then lectured us for about an hour attacking first primary school teachers and then scientists for reasons that did not seem in any way relevant to the issue we had come to discuss. She then indicated the meeting was over. I said at this point: 'Well, Prime Minister, my colleagues here are really knowledgeable, experienced people and they think there *is* a problem.' I then quoted in support of our position some observation Mary Warnock had made to me. Mrs. Thatcher responded, with heavy sarcasm. 'Lady Warnock is a *very* clever woman. But she doesn't always get everything right.' She went on: 'Well, we've talked for quite a long time about this and I've other things to do. (Pause). Professor Graham, I'm sure your patients are missing you. So, I think we'll call it a day now.' I said: 'I think if my patients knew where I was (in the cabinet room of 10, Downing Street) they would be happy to wait a little longer.' But the meeting ended shortly afterwards. The Prime Minister said we would meet again after the forthcoming election, but of course, we never did. Lack of communication between government departments on policies concerning children remains an issue of concern.

* * *

In 2013, Margaret Thatcher died of a stroke, aged eighty-seven, in the Ritz Hotel, London. She was internationally famous. She had been suffering from dementia for nearly ten years. Had she not been demented she would have known that her name, in the words of one of her successors as prime minister, Boris Johnson, writing in 2009, had become 'a boo-word in British politics, a shorthand for selfishness and me-first-ism, and devil-take-the-hindmost and grinding the faces of the poor.'[55] Johnson lamented this decline in Thatcher's reputation which he saw as undeserved. Nevertheless, the foremost British authorities on inequality claim that 'Margaret Thatcher's most important long-term legacy is likely to be the huge rise in inequality that she caused. The widening of income differences between rich and poor that took place during the 1980s (particularly from 1985) is the most rapid ever recorded.'[56] Her policies led to immense suffering in large sections of the United Kingdom, particularly, but not only, in the industrial heartlands of the North of England and Scotland. Though the inept leadership of the National Union of Miners was significantly responsible, the heart-breaking stories of the suffering of the wives and children of striking miners during the 1984–85 strike are testament to the distress caused to women by Thatcherite policies. It was a failure of imagination which meant that she did not foresee such suffering was inevitable unless other measures were taken.

Others of her policies similarly reflected her lack of imagination. Giving council tenants the right to buy the properties they were renting indirectly led to the dysfunctional housing market of the 2000s. The proposal to levy a poll tax though happily never implemented was perhaps the most striking example of an imaginative failure. The deregulating monetary policies of her governments, which ultimately allowed apparently unlimited credit to be given to consumers, led indirectly to the financial crash of 2007–08 that again, Thatcher's imaginative capacities did not allow her to predict. Her support was key to the growing hostility to the feeling against the EU which eventually led in due course to the decision to hold a referendum on British membership of the European Union.[57] Further, though doubtless other factors, such as the failure of the Blair Government either to curb immigration or to address the impact of deindustrialisation were also of great importance, yet her policies of deindustrialisation in the Midlands, the North of England and Scotland are widely seen as leading indirectly to the success of the Brexit campaign and an economic break with continental Europe just over twenty-five years after she had left office.

When Mary Warnock died in 2019 aged ninety-four, in the modest flat in south-east London where she lived, she had the satisfaction of knowing that the two reports she had written on widely different topics (special education and services for childless couples) had had an enduring positive impact both nationally and internationally. They had helped to create a more decent society. In her prolific contributions to educational policy, she had repeatedly stressed that the primary goal of education must be to promote the development of the imagination. In education, she wrote, 'we have a duty to educate the imagination above all else,'[58] and again, 'Human beings are linked to one another (much more widely) by sympathy, an imaginative understanding of other members of their species, based on what they have in common.'[59] In support of her belief in the importance of the imagination, she quoted the French philosopher, Jean-Paul Sartre. Though she had serious reservations about some aspects of Sartre's philosophical thought, she repeatedly returned to his definition of imagination as the faculty that enables us to envisage what is not. It was this faculty, leading to imaginative understanding, that Margaret Thatcher lacked with such disastrous results. As we shall see, Mary wrote in the tradition of British and continental European philosophers who, over the centuries, especially during the Enlightenment and in the mid-twentieth century, have drawn from each other's work to enrich their own. Fortunately, ideas know no borders and whatever effects the economic break with Europe may have in the 2020s, ideas will continue to flow unimpeded in both directions across the English Channel.

Margaret Thatcher's life has been chronicled in several voluminous biographies and two works of autobiography.[60] This is not surprising as she was internationally famous. In contrast, Mary Warnock's notable life and achievements are so far unrecorded except in the memoirs she wrote herself. This biography aims to repair an important omission.

Notes

1   Mary Warnock, 1960.

2   Mary Warnock, 1965; Mary Warnock, 1967; Mary Warnock, 1970; Mary Warnock, 1971.

3   Mary Warnock, 1976.

4   Mary Warnock, 1977.

5   Mary Warnock, 1987.

6   Mary Warnock, 1994.

7   Mary Warnock, 1999.

8   Mary Warnock and Elisabeth Macdonald, 2008.

9   Mary Warnock, 2015.

10   Baggini and Stangroom, p. 152.

11   Bolton, 2012, Table 8.

12   Institute of Government, 2019.

13   Richard Nicholson, 2005.

14   Moore, 2013, p. 133.

15   Jefferson et al., 2015.

16   Margaret Forster, 1995.

17   Betty Friedan, 1963.

18   Germaine Greer, 1970.

19   Mary Warnock, 2000, pp. 21–22.

20   Anthea Hall, 1984.

21   Mary Warnock, 1986.

22   Ibid., p. 285.

23   Ibid.

24   Ibid., p. 287.

25   Ibid., pp. 287–288.

26   Ibid., p. 290.

27   Ibid., pp. 291–292.

28   Ibid., pp. 292–293.

29   Ibid., p. 293.

30   Ibid., p. 297.

31   Sheila Rowbotham, 1997, pp. 480–482.

32   Mary Warnock, 1996, p. xlvii.

33   Katherine Connelly, 2018.

34   Mary Warnock, Girton Archive, 1/16/2/7.

35   Mary Warnock. Broadcast, Personal view, 29 April 1972, Girton Archive, 1/16/2/2.

36   Interview with Giles Fraser, *Confessions*, 9 February 2019.

37   Baggini and Stangroom, p. 153.

38   Pankhurst Lecture to the 300 Group, 18 July 1990, Margaret Thatcher Foundation.

39   Margaret Thatcher, 1982.

40   Baroness Janet Young, Chancellor of the Duchy of Lancaster, 1981–83.

41   Mary Warnock, 2000, p. 21.

42   Ibid., pp. 169–196.

43   Ibid., pp. 195–196.

44   Ibid., p. 169.

45   Anthea Hall, 1984.

46   Moore, 2015, 657n.

47   Mary Warnock, 2000, pp. 172–173.

48   Ibid., p. 174.

49   Graham Turner, *Sunday Telegraph*, 10 January 1988.

50   Mary Warnock, 2000, p. 176.

51   Ibid.

52   Ibid., p. 180.

53   Graham Turner, 1988.

54   Charles Moore, 2013, p. 665.

55   Jonathan Freedland, 2013.

56   Richard Wilkinson and Kate Pickett, 2013.

57   Charles Moore, 2019, p. 803.

58   Warnock, 1976, p. 10.

59   Warnock, 1999, p. 86.

60   Hugo Young, 1991; Charles Moore, 2013; Moore, 2015; Moore, 2019; Margaret Thatcher, 2011.

2. Blissful Beginnings

The poet Wordsworth, in lines loved and often quoted by Mary Warnock, wrote of his strong sense of identity with the child he once had been:

> Unfading recollections! At this hour
> The heart is almost mine with which I felt,
> From some hill-top on sunny afternoons,
> The paper-kite high among fleecy clouds
> Pull at her rein like an impetuous courser...[1]

In her later years, Mary recalled the sights and sounds of her own childhood. She lived in a large house on the outskirts of the cathedral city, Winchester. At the back of the house was a secondary school for boys and a railway line. The school had an active Corps band. All her childhood memories, she wrote, were against the background of the playing of bugles and the sound of shunting trains.[2] For Mary it was childhood when the imaginative possibilities of becoming whatever you chose seemed endless, while adulthood brought a narrowing of options with the responsibilities of work, of family and of day-to-day stresses which unavoidably moulded life into conventional conformity.

Mary was a diarist, making a single whole page entry in a diary every day of her life from her early teens until her early nineties.[3] At that point, just three or four years before she died, she burnt all her diaries apart from those for the years 1941 to 1948 (from when she was seventeen to when she was twenty-four) on a bonfire in her back garden.[4] After the author had once complained that he found it almost impossible to read the minuscule handwriting in the letters she wrote to him, she told him, and this was many years before he had any thought of writing her biography, she pitied anyone who was going to try to read her diaries. It is not clear why she destroyed them, perhaps out of compassion for a biographer or perhaps there were entries she would prefer others not

      https://doi.org/10.11647/OBP.0278.02

to read. She herself, when challenged, simply said that she had come to realise they were boring, full of banal records of daily domestic life interspersed with a fair amount of professional gossip and other such trivia.[5]

She herself did however write at some length about significant periods in her life. The introductory chapter of her *Memoir: People and Places*[6] gives much relevant information about her childhood and she also left an unfinished autobiography with a fuller account. This consists of seven chapters covering her childhood and early adult life. She abandoned this project because she found it too difficult to select what she should include, and it was becoming inordinately lengthy.[7] She left many other recollections. In *Nature and Mortality*,[8] she wrote an account of the government committees she had chaired and for whose reports she had been responsible. In addition, she took part in a number of radio programmes with titles like 'Meeting Myself Coming Back' and 'The House I Grew Up In,' which provide further recollections.

In her mid-sixties, she wrote *Memory*, a philosophical account of the nature of memories and how important they are to our sense of personal identity, the sense of who we are.[9] In this book she discusses the differences between biography and autobiography. She sees 'the gap between biography and autobiography, still more between autobiography and regular history' as 'immense.'[10] This is because she sees autobiography as intensely 'personal and nothing but personal.'[11] Although she does not analyse the nature of biography, it can clearly not be personal to the writer in the specific and original sense that she explores. Mary mainly discusses autobiography in relation to childhood experience, placing emphasis on the importance of understanding the inevitable limitations of a child's perspective when interpreting what is going on around him. She quotes with approval Stephen Spender's view of autobiography: 'The autobiographer is really writing a story of two lives: his life as it appears to himself, from his own position, when he looks out at the world from behind his eye-sockets, and his life as it appears from outside, in the eyes of others...'[12] The difference, as Mary points out, is between an 'interiorised' and an 'externalised' account of a life.[13] This book is, of course, an exteriorised account of Mary Warnock's life, but she herself provided plenty of interiorised material.

Mary's strong sense of identity, even as a child, was firmly grounded in the contrasting family backgrounds of her parents, Archibald (Archie) Edward Wilson and Ethel Mary Schuster. Both came from distinguished families. Both her grandfathers led successful lives in public service, for which they received significant public honours. Indeed, while Mary's own parents did not achieve high distinction, there were, on both sides of her family, a generation and further back numerous forebears who showed quite unusually high intelligence, ambition and considerable worldly success in a variety of different fields.

Archie's father, Sir Arthur Wilson, was born in Dublin in 1837 into a protestant Anglo-Irish family. He studied law at Trinity College, Dublin where he was Gold Medallist of his year, became a successful junior barrister and was appointed QC in 1862. In 1878 he was appointed Puisne Judge to the High Court of Calcutta. Like his granddaughter, he had a strong interest in education and served as Vice-Chancellor of the University of Calcutta. Eventually in 1892 he returned to Britain where he was appointed Legal Adviser and Solicitor to the India Office. In 1898 he was appointed a Knight Commander of the Order of the Indian Empire. He was made a Privy Councillor in 1902 and a month later was appointed to the Judicial Committee of the Privy Council, at that time the highest court of the Empire.[14] He died in 1915 nearly ten years before Mary was born.

Arthur's wife, Mary (née Bardgett), was born in Islington, London, in 1840. She could trace her ancestry back to Oliver Cromwell. Her mother was the elder daughter of Sir James Malcolm, one of four Scottish brothers who had been knighted for distinguished military service in the Napoleonic Wars and in the colonisation of India by the East India Company. Mary and Arthur had seven children most of whom did not fare well, with two dying in infancy. The eldest child, Malcolm was killed in the Ashanti rising in the Sudan in 1900 while another brother, George, was shipped off to Canada after being involved in a drunken brawl in Winchester, and then disappearing from view. The next brother, Robin or Robert, died of alcoholism in 1914. Archie, the youngest son and Mary's father, who died in his forties, was the longest surviving of their sons.[15] They also had a daughter, Jean, who survived her father but was a chronic invalid throughout her life. Mary's paternal grandmother died in 1926, two years after her birth. According to Jean, Mary's sister, this grandmother was very attached to her Scottish heritage and proud of her ancestors' achievements.[16]

Mary came from a very different lineage on her mother's side. Her mother's father, Sir Felix Otto Schuster, was born in 1854 in Frankfurt am Main, Germany.[17] His father, a Jewish merchant banker whose family had initially traded as cloth merchants, converted to Christianity in 1849, apparently as a result of religious conviction rather, as was more frequent in the German Jewish population at that time, than for convenience. Felix was baptised in 1856. Following Frankfurt's annexation by Prussia in 1866, his father made 'financial arrangements' to ensure that Arthur and his brothers became Swiss citizens, thereby avoiding the threat of service in the Prussian army.[18] In 1869, when Felix was fifteen, his father moved with his family to take up a position in the family textile business which had transferred to Manchester, then centre of the cotton trade, where some of the family had already settled. He and his siblings became British citizens in 1875. Felix was educated at Owens College, Manchester, from where he entered the family firm in London.[19] In 1879, he married Meta, the daughter of a Rhineland physician, Hermann Weber, who himself, having immigrated to Britain, was knighted in 1899 for his work on tuberculosis. Meta's sister married Felix's brother, a successful lawyer who was the grandfather of the poet, Stephen Spender. There were other distinguished men in the family. Felix's older brother, Ethel's uncle, was Sir Arthur Schuster, a physicist knighted for his services to science. He was a pioneer in the fields of spectroscopy and meteorology. Greatly honoured by the Royal Society, Arthur Schuster received honorary degrees from the universities of both Oxford and Cambridge.[20] Felix and Meta had one son and four daughters, the eldest being Ethel, Mary's mother. Another daughter was married to Rayner Goddard, a lawyer who rose to become Lord Chief Justice.[21]

In 1888, the Schuster family firm was taken over by the Union Bank of London. Felix became first a director of this bank, then in 1893 a deputy governor and finally in 1895, governor. Felix's regime as Governor of the Union Bank was marked by micro-management; he personally monitored every account and minutely scrutinised the activities of every branch. But by the beginning of the new century, he was taking on wider responsibilities—he had become a financial adviser to the Treasury. Made a baronet in 1906, in the same year he was appointed finance member of the Council of India. In 1918, the Union Bank, which had greatly expanded under his governorship, merged with the National Provincial and, although Schuster officially retired at this point, he attended his office daily. He remained a powerful influence not only on the bank's policy but on national financial affairs.[22]

Mary described Felix as 'a figure straight from Osbert Lancaster; he could have been the model for Sir Ephraim Kirsch Bt. from Draynefleet, who wore hairy tweeds in the country and incongruously attended shooting parties [...] with his pale, sad face, black beard and hooded eyes, he often said he wished he had been a musician and indeed played the piano as if his heart would break.'[23] As a boy, he had studied with Ernest Pauer, a noted Austrian pianist, and he remained an accomplished pianist throughout his life. He became a Liveryman of the Musicians' Company and a friend and benefactor of a number of musicians. His other great passion was mountaineering. He was a prominent member and, for some years, Vice-President of the Alpine Club, 'visited the Alps regularly and took formidable mountain walks when he became too old to climb.'[24] In 1914 at the outbreak of war, it was his misfortune to be the target of much anti-German feeling.

His considerable wealth (he left over £600,000 at his death in 1936,[25] the equivalent of about £42 million at 2020 valuation) enabled him to buy a substantial property, Verdley Place, a large country house near Fernhurst in West Sussex, where Mary spent some holidays. From the recollections of a gardener, Arthur Hooper, who worked on the estate in the 1920s, he was mean to his staff. Later in life, Arthur reported that when his employer decided to have an economy drive, he 'cut wages, the coal allowance, restricted the vegetables they could have and free fruit was not allowed at all.'[26] His wealth, as we shall see, financed an affluent lifestyle for Mary and her family during her childhood and adolescence.

Information about Mary's father, Archie's early life is sketchy, but Jean, Mary's older sister, was fifteen when he died and she wrote her recollections of him.[27] An obituary in the Winchester College magazine, *The Wykehamist*, published very shortly after his death, also provides some information.[28] Born in 1875, at eighteen, Archie went up to Balliol in Oxford, graduating in 1898, but subsequently failed the entrance examination for the Civil Service. Following this disappointment, he decided to spend some time in Germany learning the language, and it was during this period abroad that he first met his wife-to-be. Ethel Schuster was then nineteen and on a family holiday in the Swiss Alps. The young couple fell in love, but Ethel's parents would not allow her to marry until Archie was settled in satisfactory employment. He decided on a career in teaching and by autumn 1900 had found his first teaching job at Merchiston College in Edinburgh. Evidently this institution was insufficiently prestigious (or Archie's position within it too lowly) to meet Sir Felix Schuster's high expectations and Ethel returned to the family home in Sussex pining for Archie. So inconsolable was she that it was said her parents would lock her in her bedroom to prevent her from upsetting her brother and sisters by constant talk of her hopeless love. In 1906, perhaps as a result of his future father-in-law's influence, Archie was appointed to the staff of Winchester College. To be appointed a 'don' at Winchester was regarded, at least in the Schuster household, as almost the equivalent of a university post, so parental consent to Ethel's marriage was at last forthcoming, and the couple were married in style in London on 5 April 1906.[29] Archie largely taught in the Junior School to begin with but was also the Senior German Master.

Ten months after Archie and Ethel's grand marriage, their first son, Malcolm, was born. The family grew rapidly. Malcolm was followed two years later, by a daughter, Jean, then another son, Duncan, born in 1911. Next came Grizel in 1913 and Alexander (Sandie) in 1917, who only lived for four years, dying in 1921. Shortly after his death, a girl, Stephana, was born in 1921. Finally, on 14 April 1924, came Mary, the youngest therefore of seven children.[30] Tragically, Archie, her father, had died of diphtheria in a school epidemic on 14 September 1923, seven months before she was born.[31]

Malcolm, the oldest child, seems to have developed normally for about eighteen months, indeed was said to be very responsive to music, but then regressed, lost his skills and failed to progress. He had a specially trained governess while at home, but, at the age of nine he was placed in a special school and then in residential care. In the early 1960s he was diagnosed as autistic and transferred to a hospital. His mother visited him regularly until her death in 1953, after which he was visited monthly by his sister, Jean, who felt he was looked after well. In her own memoir, Jean records that Malcolm was 'taken for granted' while he was at home, but that his existence became an embarrassment (certainly not talked about), after he was sent away. There is no suggestion that his existence was a secret within the family and Mary was certainly told about him at some point. He died at the age of sixty-two in 1969.[32]

Mary's parents lived in a house bought by Ethel's wealthy father on the outskirts of St. Cross, on the edge of Winchester. To accommodate their growing family, in 1913 they moved to a larger house near the centre of the city in St. Thomas's Street. Then in 1915 Archie was appointed a Winchester College housemaster and took over Kingsgate House.[33] This involved a major change of lifestyle. A boarding house of this type was then run as a private business. The housemaster was given no extra salary for running the house. Fees were paid by the parents of the thirty-nine boarders. The school took a proportion of the income with the balance remaining with the housemaster to pay the expenses, including the wages of about ten domestic staff, and draw an additional salary. This meant the housemaster's wife had considerable responsibility for buying food, managing the staff and keeping the accounts.[34] Ethel's responsibilities for running the house came to an abrupt end when her husband died in 1923. Shortly before Mary was born the family had to leave Kingsgate House for a private dwelling.

From Archie Wilson's obituary one has the impression he was regarded as rather lazy and Mary confirmed this was indeed his reputation. She was told that he taught reclining on a chaise longue, smoking Turkish cigarettes. Jean, his oldest daughter who was fourteen when he died, described him as a 'reserved man by nature, he never allowed his feelings to show and made all too frequent use of the scathing remarks that are so humiliating to children.'[35] On the other hand, his colleagues seem to have found him more sympathetic: the same school obituarist describes him as a man 'easy of access and a delightful companion.'[36] This does not exonerate him of the charge of laziness but at least it suggests they liked him. A keen fisherman, he evidently had an intense love of Scotland, from where his mother's family came, an appreciation which Mary inherited. He and Ethel also appreciated stylish furniture, china, Chinese art (which was fashionable at the time) and oriental rugs.[37]

After the death of his son-in-law, Sir Felix set his daughter and her family up in some style. They lived in St. Cross on the edge of Winchester in Kelso House, which Mary described as a large 'Edwardian house, ugly from the outside but light and comfortable inside, with huge sash windows and great substantial doors. The drawing room, two rooms thrown into one, smelled delectably of wood fires in winter and flowers in summer. I quite consciously loved that room and indeed the whole house from the time I was conscious of anything.'[38] The house had a substantial garden. The family was serviced by a cook, a chauffeur, a chamber maid, a parlour maid and, to look after the children, a nanny and an under-nurse.

Mary's early childhood years were spent in this almost exclusively female household. Her four older brothers and sisters were largely absent from home. Jean, Duncan and Grizel, fifteen, thirteen and eleven years older than Mary, were all at boarding school, so Mary and Stephana were, in effect, the only two children constantly in the house, with the key figures in their lives being their widowed mother and crucially, their nanny, Emily Coleman. Always known as Nan, she had been hired in 1908 and had thus been primarily responsible for the upbringing of all the Wilson children and so a thoroughly established fixture in the household by the time Mary was born in 1924. Nan was to remain attached to the family until her death, having looked after all of Ethel's children and then, many years later, taking a part in the early upbringing of the children of Grizel and Stephana and Mary's own children. She then lived first with Grizel in Hampstead and afterwards with Stephana at the Cathedral Choir School in Ripon.

The children's life at Kelso House centred around the nursery, and this was Nan's domain. In her memoir, Mary describes her in some detail, as a 'person of great energy and imagination.'[39] She herself came from a large family, her father having been the head gardener of a large estate. She had left school at fourteen to become a nursery maid successively to two other wealthy families before employment by Mary's mother. 'It was impossible to be bored in her company,'[40] Mary wrote, and her description of her makes it easy to understand why this was the case. She had a great repertoire of songs and if she heard a new song could immediately commit it to memory. Gilbert and Sullivan operas, performed every year by the Winchester Operatic Society, were a favourite source but Nan also remembered First World War and old music hall songs as well as hymns from her childhood.[41]

She had a large fund of quotations and sayings which she would bring out on appropriate occasions. If she had tasks to perform, she would get up from her chair reluctantly and say 'Work, for the night is coming. When man works no more.' This was a saying Mary spoke to herself for the rest of her life when she had things to do. If someone expressed a view with which she disagreed, Nan would say 'Everyone to his liking, as the old woman said when she kissed her cow.' If she wanted to threaten punishment for wrongdoing, she might say 'If it wasn't for taking off my kid glove and exposing my lily-white hand to the air...' or 'I'll give you what Paddy gave the drum, two big thumps instead of one' (a saying which Mary learned many years later, came from an Army practice of giving a drum two loud beats to signal the beginning of a march). If someone seemed over-confident, Nan would say 'Nothing, they said, could be finer, but just as these words were spoken, the raft ran into a liner.'[42]

Mary was taught by Nan to knit, to sew, to iron, to cook and to whistle. On the daily walks she and Stephana took with her from the nursery, Nan instilled in her a great love and knowledge of the natural world, while at the same time insisting that the girls recite their multiplication tables. At the time, Mary thought that Nan strongly preferred Stephana to her, but she regarded this as perfectly appropriate as she saw her sister as prettier and more gifted, especially musically, than she was. Nevertheless, she and her sister were very close friends who 'bonded together in the nursery, in opposition to all grown-ups, and especially to our older siblings.'[43] They made up elaborate stories and sang together, particularly the hymns they both loved. And Nan, whether or not she favoured Stephana, was a hugely stimulating adult, who clearly loved Mary, encouraged her imagination and provided a model of intense curiosity about the world around her.

Nan had strongly negative feelings about men. In contrast to the rest of the grown-ups in the family and indeed at that time to most of the rest of the adult world, she much preferred girls to boys. She used to say 'Poor things, men' and hold them in contempt.[44] Mary's mother, in contrast, told her when she was about three years old, how disappointed she had been that her two youngest children had both been girls when she had so much wished for another boy. Not surprisingly, when Mary had nightmares, they were not about anything dreadful happening to her mother but to Nan, whom she dreamed falling off a cliff.[45]

Like other upper middle-class mothers, Ethel took only a limited part in the upbringing of her children.[46] Her own education had been typical for the daughters of rich men. She did not attend school but was tutored at home by a succession of French and German governesses. Mary described her mother as uneducated but cultured and their home was full of music and books. Mary wrote that she and Stephana saw their mother as 'a somewhat exotic figure connected with London, rich food, delicious smells. As time went on we grew to like her more and more, and find her more and more interesting, though we never ceased to be partly irritated by her.'[47] Imogen Wrong, Mary's closest friend in her mid- to late teens, described Mary's mother as making a striking entrance to Winchester Cathedral for the Sunday morning services—'a woman of tall, dignified deportment, dressed in rich-looking Edwardian clothes (this would have been in the 1930s) which flowed down almost to her large hand-made shoes.'[48] Mary admitted to being embarrassed by her mother's dated appearance until she was about fifteen years old, when she suddenly felt rather proud of her and said to herself, 'She's magnificent,' for being, so to speak, 'her own woman.'[49] Jean, the sister who was fifteen years older than Mary, clearly did not like her mother and wrote dismissively about her lack of self-confidence and the aura of helplessness she gave off. She had been the oldest of five children and the only one regarded as having no talent. Jean described her as 'floundering through the greater part of her life in a state of bewilderment mixed with self-pity.'[50] She was hopelessly impractical, sending back to the kitchen for help if presented with an unopened jar of marmalade.

Ethel would only occasionally drift into the nursery to see what her youngest children were up to. Sometimes Stephana and Mary would be allowed to go downstairs to the drawing room to have tea with her. They would descend in clean frocks and coral necklaces for about an hour, where they heard songs on the gramophone or played with mosaic bricks. They would be served bread and butter and delicious little triangular sugar cakes.[51] Their regular meals were brought up to them in the nursery by a parlour maid. Remote she may have been, but it was her mother who taught her and Stephana to read. Mary remembered her mother teaching Stephana, while she, Mary, sat under the table, listening and apparently absorbing enough so that she herself learned how to read in this fashion.[52]

Fig. 1 Stephana (left) and Mary (right) (c. 1927), provided by the Warnock family, CC BY-NC.

Of her other siblings, Duncan was by far the most important to Mary. He was (in the absence of her father and Malcolm) the only male figure in the family. As a scholar and Head Boy of Winchester College, then a scholar at Balliol College, he was a role model for Mary as her own academic ambitions began to develop. He was intensely musical, a lover of classical music and an accomplished pianist. During the holidays, he played the piano for hours on end. Some of Duncan's large collection of records of classical music became Mary's favourite pieces. She felt him to be 'the authority on music,' indeed the authority on virtually anything.[53] As we shall see in Chapter Ten, he played an important part in shaping Mary's musical taste. As one of the few boarders who lived in Winchester, he used to bring his friends home for Sunday lunch. Mary vividly describes these occasions which she clearly remembered from when she was very young. The other boys 'discarded their gowns, long-sleeved waistcoats and top hats to play games with us, or show us conjuring tricks, or came into the Nursery to talk with Nanny.'[54] Duncan himself kept apart from such childish behaviour and Mary found him more difficult to talk to than his friends. He had what Mary saw as a typically Wykehamist (and not particularly attractive) trait of making fun of people who couldn't decide whether what he and others said was meant as a joke or not. Mary had a lifelong fear of ridicule on this account.[55]

She had, of course, never known her father but she does not seem to have suffered from this loss. She describes how, as a young child, she knew that 'he was in heaven.' So, she writes, she did not think it in the least bit odd that in church everyone should address their prayers to him: 'Our Father, which art in heaven...'[56] Given the absence of a father, the presence of a remote mother for whom she was explicitly seen as the 'wrong' sex, and a sister who was preferred by her Nan, the person she most looked up to in the world, it might be thought that the stage would have been set for a life characterised by recurrent depressions. This did not happen. As we shall see, Mary went through most, if not all her life a cheerful optimist with a strong belief in her own self-worth. This might be regarded as a defence mechanism against low self-worth but there is not the slightest indication this was the case.[57] Looking back to the age of three years when her mother told her how disappointed she was that she was not a boy, she wrote 'I felt, if anything, a bit indignant that she should overlook the advantages of having me (ME) as a daughter.'[58] Mary goes on: 'I was, I think, a self-pleased child, perfectly content to be who I was, even if others wished me to be different, as they often did.' Much later Mary and Stephana confronted their mother over her rejection of them. Her diary entry for 12 December 1942, contains this account:

> Steph and I got together and had an indignation meeting about Mither not wanting the children and Nanny. Mither herself came and must have listened outside for ages we had to put the whole thing before her—almost for the first time in the most emphatic general terms, about how awful it was and how shaming to have been under the thumb of these women. I think for the first time she realised what hell it was for us, too...

It seems clear from this diary entry that both Mary and her sister at least into their late adolescence felt humiliated by the way their mother had expressed her disappointment in their very existence.

The nine years before Mary went to school were important in establishing her self-confidence and her other personality traits. They also provided her with a strong educational grounding. As well as learning to read from her mother and a large number of practical skills by Nan, she had a governess, a Miss Falwasser, whose most remembered saying was 'I don't like rude little girls,' perhaps a commentary on Mary's lifelong outspokenness.[59] Miss Falwasser made her learn the collect, the catechism, the creed and numerous texts from the Bible. These remained part of Mary's stock of knowledge for the rest of her life. She also had drawing lessons from a Miss Corfe 'who was very old and with whom we drew plaster casts with shading to be done with soft pencils.' In addition, there were piano lessons with a Miss Lunn 'who was extremely jolly.'[60]

At nine, in 1933, Mary started to attend St. Swithun's School in Winchester, first as a day girl and then, from about the age of thirteen, as a boarder. Mary's time as a day girl was unremarkable apart, as she put it in her unpublished autobiography, from when, at the age of eleven, she 'endured my first unrequited love-affair, a passion for the lead chorister at the Cathedral, whose name, I think was Stephen Morse.'[61] She was invited to a Guy Fawkes party at the Pilgrim's School, the Winchester Cathedral Choir School and she wrote that, dancing around the huge bonfire, 'I found myself holding the hand of Stephen Morse. This represents for me the height of romantic excitement, unfulfilled and briefly perfect.'[62] Thus, at about the age when both girls and boys first experience sexual attraction to someone of the same or opposite sex, Mary had her first heterosexual feelings; she was never to be ambivalent in this respect.

When she was twelve her mother decided that the following year she must go to boarding school, but not to Downe House, the boarding school which Stephana attended, because her mother had fallen out with the staff there. Mary was upset by this as she found Stephana's friends beautiful, funny and glamorous and the location of Downe House in the hills above Newbury delightful. She found the dress worn by the Downe House girls, 'uniform green djibbahs in the winter and brilliant-coloured linen tunics in the summer, much preferable to the St. Swithun's drab brown and dirty flesh-coloured tunics.' But she was told she could not go there and chose instead to board at St. Swithun's.[63]

As a boarder, she found herself drawn much more closely into an institution with a very clear ethos. The ideal St. Swithun's girl was modest, well-behaved, unassuming and certainly must not be too clever. The worst offences were questioning religious belief and breaking the school rules, in however minor a way. Mary's instinctive resistance to these academic strictures was shared by another girl, Imogen Wrong, (later Rose) with whom she formed a close friendship which was to endure throughout their lives. As Imogen's memoir *A Difficult Girl* puts it,[64] the housemistress, Miss Winckworth, early on remarked to Mary that she should have known that she and Imogen would 'unite and become a Noisy Pair: the two of us being so alike, being critical, energetic and talkative.'[65] Imogen describes how 'our excitability, our loud voices, our private vocabulary and jokes did not accord with the St. Swithun's ideal of order, calm, civility and graciousness.'[66] The school's motto was 'Caritas, Humilitas, Sinceritas.' As far as the first two of these were concerned, Mary's personality did not by any means fully accord. Lacking in Caritas, she and Imogen made merciless fun of other girls whom they took a dislike to and were uncharitable even to the teachers that they liked. One otherwise admirable member of staff they found ridiculous because she lived with her mother in Streatham, clearly a lower middle-class part of London. Neither was Humilitas one of Mary's strong points although there were to be several occasions when she contritely admitted she was more often given to self-doubt than perhaps she allowed herself to reveal in public. On the other hand, she certainly did not lack Sincerity, though her tendency to express openly her sincere thoughts about other girls and teachers meant that even this virtue had its dangers. Given the complete absence of opportunity to mix with the opposite sex, it is perhaps not surprising that the two girls seemed indifferent to any 'boys' issues. Revealingly, when Imogen recalls what she described at the time as 'lusts of the flesh,' they were 'oversleeping, overeating, dress, daintiness.'[67] Basically, St. Swithun's was aiming to turn out young women who would, after a spell perhaps working as secretaries, marry well and become dutiful wives and mothers. It did not cater for girls like Mary who in no way fitted its system. Fortunately, the often cruel criticism she received from her teachers there did not dent her solid self-esteem to the slightest degree.

The school seems to have had high hopes of Mary, at least to start with. There were five boarding houses, each with about thirty girls.[68] Mary was in High House, which regarded itself as superior to the others. The housemistress, Miss Winckworth, known as Wincks, had a close friendship with the headmistress, a Miss Finlay, who placed the most promising girls in High House. Wincks was tall, had short frizzy hair and dressed in Macclesfield silk shirts, tweed skirts, expensive brogues and had an upper-class (and old-fashioned) way of pronouncing certain words such as otel, yumour, larndry.[69] She elicited trust and veneration rather than affection. She was deeply religious and there were House prayers every evening after supper. Later in life, Mary recalled jokingly, 'We were never off our knees.' On Sunday morning, there was hymn practice before the girls formed up in crocodile line to walk to church. Every alternate Sunday the girls went to Winchester Cathedral and on the Sundays in between to a local church, the choice of church determined by whether they came from 'High' or 'Low' Church families. St. Swithun's itself was very definitely a High Anglican school, so the smell of incense was a feature of its chapel. In addition, girls were expected to have two quiet times in their individual bedroom cubicles, one before breakfast and the other before Lights Out. There was a pervasive sense in the House that everyone must strive to be good in a specifically Christian way. All was conformity and discretion. Any shouting, banging, or self-dramatising was firmly curbed. The maintenance of a calm and agreeable demeanour was the essence of good manners. At mealtimes, there were seven girls round each table. Conversation had to be made but only within the strictest guidelines: no personal remarks were permitted, no comments about life at school, one's classes, one's work, other teachers, religious services, the food one was eating, no 'I love' or 'I hate,' nothing addressed to another girl. But also, no silence. It was a challenge to keep conversation flowing, indeed it is something of a miracle it ever began.[70]

There was great emphasis on upholding the Honour of the House. This required every girl to demonstrate honesty, integrity, moral courage and, above all, trustworthiness. Girls were not only expected to tell the absolute truth, but to come forward to confess any wrongdoing.

Over the weekend, girls were not supposed to go to the cinema or the local skating rink. If they did, they were expected to confess to the headmistress on return to school. In fact, on Monday mornings, there was usually a queue of girls waiting to see her for this purpose. Any grave misdemeanour required an interview with Wincks at which she lectured the miscreant, who was then told to go away and reflect for a few days. After this period of reflection, the girl was expected to return to Wincks to apologise and receive a further lecture. The school hierarchy was strictly observed with staff at the top, then prefects, then working steadily down the ladder to the most recently arrived junior girl at the bottom. If someone of higher rank passed you in the corridor, you were expected to flatten yourself against the wall while they passed. Order in the hierarchy determined how vegetables were served at meals, where you were in the crocodile line to go to church, your choice of cubicle for the following term and where you sat at desks in the Common Room. The emphasis was not just on being good, but on being preternaturally good. Indeed, the House song went:

> Present girls, old girls
> Keep good as gold girls
> That is the High House way.[71]

Mary described life as a boarder at the school as 'exceptionally dramatic [...] because of the intensity of our failed attempts to live up to the standards of good behaviour in thought, word and deed that were demanded. A burden of guilt hung over us. We knew that the purpose of the school was to make us good and holy, and some of us knew that we could not attain, worse, did not even want to attain, such ideals.'[72] Surprisingly, Mary felt that she enjoyed herself at the school. This was the time when she began her diary, passionately recording the daily dramas and, despite all the rules, constraints and disapproval, she continued to feel 'extraordinarily free to be whatever I liked, to indulge in friendships, passions, secret metaphysical speculations that I would have been ashamed to indulge in at home...'[73] She was accused by her housemistress of being 'self-absorbed, never admitting I was in the wrong, always ready with excuses and both noisy and untidy.'[74] Later in life, she was often only too ready to admit she was in the wrong, though the untidiness persisted.

The only book permitted in her bedroom cubicle was the Bible but she succeeded in broadening her education considerably by smuggling in to read under her bedclothes an anthology of prose and poetry entitled *The Spirit of Man*, compiled by the poet Robert Bridges. She described this as the most educative book she ever possessed. From it, she read and learned Shakespeare's sonnets, poems by Gerard Manley Hopkins and extracts from, amongst others, Spinoza, Tolstoy and Plato. Later in life, she came to regard this type of solitary reading as the most valuable aspect of education.[75] She was also delighted to discover, after she married, that Geoffrey, her husband, had also treasured this anthology at school at Winchester. They might both have been under their respective sheets within a few miles of each other, reading the same verses.

Despite the non-academic ethos of St. Swithun's, Mary and Imogen Wrong had been studying Latin and Greek together since the age of twelve, but they had more in common than simply a boisterous temperament and an unusual mutual interest in classics. They had both been brought up in fatherless families, though Imogen's father had not died until she was four.[76] They made the most of this, mocking other girls who talked about their 'mummies and daddies.'[77] They were both ambitious to go to either Oxford or Cambridge as undergraduates. In personality they were similar too, both bright and with strong intellectual interests but also noisier and more extravert than most of the other girls. Nevertheless, there were important differences. Imogen's mother, a don herself, was from a distinguished line of Oxford academics, the Smiths. Her father had been a don at Magdalen and a Smith had been the Master of Balliol. But, in marked contrast to Mary's mother's, she was very stretched financially and had to live frugally, Further, though Mary's mother was supportive and affectionate to her daughter, Imogen's mother, much taken up with flirtations and affairs, found her children something of an irritation. When they came home from boarding school on holiday, she would ask how long it was before they were going back.[78]

Mary and Imogen's high spirits and impulsiveness led them into frequent trouble with the St. Swithun's staff. Much to the staff's disapproval, they used to walk 'around the school shrieking with laughter each with piles of books with a large Liddell and Scott (a

Greek lexicon) at the bottom of the pile.'[79] Mary's exuberance and lack of inhibition, two of her most outstanding characteristics, first became apparent at this time.

On one occasion, Imogen caught German measles and was confined to the school sanatorium. She was not supposed to send letters out of the sanatorium but, because she felt so deprived of contact with Mary, she smuggled letters out through a friend. Mary was hauled up before Wincks, who was furious with her. 'A friendship that does this sort of thing is rotten,' she was told. 'At the moment, I never want to see you again. Go now and God help us both.'[80] The next day, Miss Finlay, the headmistress told Mary she was 'thoroughly deceitful and a moral coward.' Wincks thought the 'whole house had been contaminated with dishonour.'[81] Imogen was stripped of her prefectship and the whole affair dragged on for several days with much insistence on the writing of letters of abject apology. The senior staff's hostility to both the girls persisted right up to the time they left, Wincks responding to a farewell letter that Mary wrote when she left the school by saying 'The realisation of failure is the best and only way of learning lessons; the great thing now is not to be downcast but to put this bitter experience to good use.'[82] It was not clear to either of the girls what this 'bitter experience' might be, but it was probably their friendship. Wincks' final letter to Imogen was no friendlier. It contained the sentence 'the real sadness of your days at St. Swithun's is not the trouble you may have caused me or any other member of the Staff, but the harm you have done to your friends.'[83]

Mary was mortified by all this criticism, but she later wrote that

> I somehow seemed to preserve my feeling that, deeply as it might be hidden, I was more musical, better read, more philosophical than the other girls. It was not an amiable characteristic, this inner self-assurance [...] but I think it sprang from my love of life at home, in Kelso House, and my feeling that everything truly worthwhile and exciting had its existence there.[84]

As for Imogen, she had her own source of self-esteem. When she was asked by one of her daughters, forty years after meeting Mary, why their friendship had meant so much to her, she replied without thinking 'Because she was the first person in my life who saw anything worthwhile in me.'[85] Imogen was possibly the first but was certainly not the last person to credit Mary with having bestowed on her the gift of self-worth.

The outbreak of war in September 1939 did not immediately change the pattern of Mary's school and home life, but the situation became quite different a year later. Southampton was the target of heavy bombing during the last months of 1940,[86] and, only twelve miles away, Winchester was thought to be at risk. The girls were spending most nights sleeping in the school basement where the lacrosse boots and other equipment were kept and it seemed likely the school would have to close. In the end, it was decided to keep the school open, but by that time, Mary's mother had decided she wanted a change of school for her. On the advice of a friend, she chose Prior's Field School. No sooner had the choice been made, than St. Swithun's decided they loved Mary after all. The headmistress and her classics teacher wrote to Mary making her feel 'a moral coward, a rat,' for deserting the school in such difficult times.[87] But the decision had been made. So, with another St. Swithun's girl, Anne Wakefield, with whom she spent much time in the holidays, she began her new school in January 1941.[88]

Prior's Field had been founded in 1902 by Julia Huxley who came from an intellectually distinguished family. She was the granddaughter of Thomas Arnold, headmaster of Rugby School and her uncle was the poet, Matthew Arnold. She had married Leonard Huxley, whose father was Sir Thomas Huxley, biologist and leading defender of the theory of evolution. Julia and Leonard's five children included Julian Huxley, a scientist who became the first head of UNESCO and Aldous Huxley the novelist.[89] The headmistress at the time of Mary's attendance and since 1927 was Beatrice Burton-Brown, known to Mary and others by her nickname, Bice. She was the daughter of the previous head and had herself been a pupil at Prior's Field before going on to Newnham College, Cambridge, to read Classics. She had then attended the British School of Archaeology in Rome. Like many women of her generation, she had lost a fiancé killed in World War One and she had never married. She was widely regarded as kind and generous with a strong sense of humour. When her mother died and she succeeded her as the headmistress, she was said to have blossomed, bought a lot of very short dresses and a car and become a livelier personality. In her mid-forties when Mary first came to know her, she was highly respected in the school as wise and scholarly.[90]

Mary's transfer to Prior's Field at the age of sixteen turned out to be an inspired choice. Here, her intellectual prowess was valued instead of being seen as something of an embarrassment. Academic achievement was no longer seen as incompatible with a woman leading a full life; indeed there was an altogether different vision of being a woman. Her teachers were more emancipated and worldly than those at St. Swithun's[91] and there were even some men amongst them, including a Mr. Tressler, recently retired from Charterhouse, who had the main responsibility for teaching her classics. The teaching staff had also been supplemented by a new classics teacher, Laura Le Maitre, who was appointed particularly to teach Greek, possibly specifically so that Mary could have tuition in this subject.[92]

This was also the point at which she began to enjoy some physical activities, which might previously have been frowned upon. There was dancing in the Common Room, with other girls as partners. She played tennis and, by this time, had also become a competent golfer. Finally, the school extended her horizons to include some political thought. There were numerous discussions between girls and teaching staff about socialism, the reconstruction of society to reduce inequalities and the sort of world that might exist after the war was over. Mary also records in her diary 'a wonderful debate about Intellectual or Domestic Women.' She does not record how she voted at the end of the debate, but it is not difficult to guess.[93]

Though Prior's Field was not regarded as in great danger from bombing, for a period the girls slept in their classrooms rather than in dormitories as it was felt safer. Sometimes, the summer skies were black with German bombers and, on one occasion, a German plane fired on a group of girls going to church on a Sunday morning.[94] Girls were taught first aid, how to deal with incendiary bombs, and how to communicate using Morse code and semaphore. Food was far from plentiful due to rationing, but there was plenty of fruit and vegetables from the garden. Clothes rationing meant there was a great deal of darning of socks and stockings, as well as running repairs to other clothes.[95]

After initial homesickness and some self-questioning about how she could have allowed herself to leave St. Swithun's, Mary settled down happily. She made many new friends while continuing her friendship with Anne Wakefield, with whom she had transferred. Her diary entries give some idea of how she spent her days. Included below are one from each of the three terms she attended Prior's Field. These entries provide a reasonably representative account of the way she spent her time. They do not include mention of tennis, nor her regular Sunday church attendance. She always commented on the quality of the sermons, often describing them with one of her favourite adjectives at that time and indeed subsequently—'ghastly.' It will be noted how each entry contains at least one harsh criticism of herself, reflecting a tendency that was to remain with her throughout her life.

Wednesday 26 March 1941

Woke up for some reason singing 'Sheep May Safely Graze' and went on singing in my bath to my own pleasure. Did Euripides and Virgil most of the morning and started some awful notes on Addison's prose style. It was a foul rainy day. After rest in which we had some quartet practice, had half an hour's lovely French conversation in which we talked about L'Art Pure [sic]. Talked to Anne who wanted me to play flute for her, so I did and played quite well for me. But she wouldn't leave and I wanted to practice viola so I did and no doubt drove her out. But it was good to practice again and I have truly mastered the third position though my vibrato is awful [...] How does anyone play the beastly instrument? Worked quite hard at Plato in the evening and practised again. After supper, Anne and I sat in the Library. No one else there except Joan Gidney who started to talk and was very nice and we read each other modern poetry. Great fun.

Wednesday 16 July 1941

Did Greek unseen before my lesson with Mr. Tressler. This was even worse than I had feared. The Greek prose I got back wasn't bad but the rest was too awful. Pliny was appalling and he enraged me by altering every translation I gave just a very little and then asking if I understood. This went on and on. But the Cicero was worse because in fact I'd prepared it badly but was ready to argue and argue and appear pig obstinate which of course infuriated him. When he'd gone at last turned to Thucydides with relief. [...] worked again at Cicero's letters. How ghastly to get such letters. It rained. Fooled around about doing a bit of gardening and about two words of Aristotle.

Saturday 18 October 1941

Bice's [her headmistress] unseen before breakfast. Then Mr. Tressler simply grim. He droned on and on and I felt sicker and sicker with hunger and boredom. He gave me an AB for Greek prose but then ruined that by saying it was only to encourage me. But at least it had no howlers. We finished Antigone and I managed to skate over all the bits I didn't know with a merry laugh and the same with Demosthenes. Letter from

Duncan [her brother]. Then did fair copy of prose. After lunch changed
in a rush and met Mrs. Western and we went to Guildford. Moiseiwitsch
marvellous. By far the best pianist I've ever heard. Tremendous energy
and passion. [...] Back at school did two unseens appallingly. Dreadful
supper then sat and wrote essay feverishly. Wrote nonsense quoting from
JW Turner's book on Beethoven and art, forgetting I was writing for Bice
and not just for myself. Came to dancing and had a nice dance with dear
Nell and terrifying one with Bice who asked me about the concert...

In late November and early December, Mary took the entrance
examination for Lady Margaret Hall College (LMH) in Oxford. After
the written papers she was called for an interview and recorded the
experience in her entry for 10 December. The examiners told her she
had done well in the written papers and made her aware that they knew
she was the sister both of Stephana (who was already at LMH) and
of Duncan, whom one of the dons had tutored at Balliol some years
earlier. On 16 December, she received a telegram informing her she had
won the top scholarship to the college. She found the news difficult
to believe. Later that morning she had her 'end of term' talk with the
headmistress who 'said a lot of stuff I liked to hear about humility and
gentleness and strength of character (ME?) and responsibility.' So her
major academic achievement was followed by a flattering appraisal of
her moral character.

Mary's Prior's Field experience was important for her in a number
of ways. For the first time, she had proper lessons in flute and piano.
Her musical skills and talent for musical appreciation grew greatly.[96]
She was expected to take in interest in current affairs and the need for
the abandonment of the existing social order. Her diary, she reports,
was 'full of socialism.'[97] The school's motto was 'We live by admiration,
hope and love.'[98] Mary felt that, in contrast to St. Swithun's, the teachers
really did admire her, had high hopes of her and, in a sense, did indeed
love her. The importance of encouragement from teachers as a powerful
motivator was a lesson never forgotten. Attitudes to religion provided
another stark contrast—at St. Swithun's the overwhelming emphasis had
been on sins and the need for repentance. In contrast, Mary recorded a
Divinity lesson with Bice in which she experienced enjoyment at 'seeing
a new and saner version of proper Christianity. Much more like the
Cathedral at home and I have developed an enormous interest in St.
John's Gospel.' Later she recorded reading a section of G. K. Chesterton,

the Anglo-Catholic writer about whom she wrote 'How wonderful to find all you want to say so brilliantly expressed.'[99] Almost until the time she left Prior's Field she continued to have conversations about religion with Bice. For example, on 9 December 1941, she recorded that 'I turned the conversation to Meredith and then to religion. I asked whether she believed what I do about the relation of Mind/Body/Soul and she agreed emphatically. Our conversation wandered between Browning and the resurrection. She disappointed me by saying "the resurrection means the survival of personality". But I don't know what that means, and I suspect she doesn't either. But she agreed that much of what we believe is wishful thinking. It was wonderful to talk like this anyway.' These reflections on religion first experienced at Prior's Field, foreshadow Mary's later religious beliefs.

Prior's Field was also the first time Mary was extended academically. Her diary entries make it clear that her teachers were difficult to satisfy and although this meant she was often in despair, in the event her grasp of a wide range of classical authors was impressive. At St. Swithun's her academic achievements had been satisfactory but in no way outstanding. In her School Certificate examination, taken in 1938, she achieved six credits, but no distinctions in the subjects she took. It is clear she cannot have been stretched there.

Mary resisted a temptation to stay on at Prior's Field for another couple of terms before going up to Oxford the following October. She could have concentrated on her music there, but instead decided to take a job in an evacuated preparatory school called Rosehill.[100] This was situated in a village in a beautiful area in rural Gloucestershire near Wootton-under-Edge. Her duties ranged from looking after nursery-aged schoolchildren, giving the smaller boys in the prep school their baths and teaching Latin to the headmaster's youngest son, preparing him for entry to Rugby School. She was given a room in the Old Rectory in the village. This had no electricity and she had to read by candlelight. Her first term, from the beginning of 1942 to Easter, was in many ways miserable as she suffered from painful chilblains on her hands and feet. Chilblains, which result from exposure to cold, are soothed by warm water, but Mary was only allowed hot water twice a week for a bath. She was sometimes reduced to tears by not being able to get warm when she went to bed.[101]

Despite the physical discomfort, Mary did a vast amount of reading in theology, history—including much of Gibbon's *Decline and Fall of the Roman Empire* (1776–89), as well as twentieth-century poetry.[102] Although the headmaster was a remote figure, the rest of the teaching staff, most of whom were retired teachers brought back to work because of the war, were kind to her. It was the first time she was in the company of adults doing a job like them. In fact, she lived partly in the world of teachers and partly 'downstairs' with the cooks and felt she got on equally well in both spheres of the institution.[103]

Her main new experience was a friendship with Tim, a boy her own age. He was the headmaster's oldest son, who had also won a scholarship to Oxford. Their friendship was complicated by the fact that a woman friend of the headmaster's family had marked Tim out as a future spouse for one of her own daughters.[104] This meant that Mary took care, as she wrote later, not to fall in love with him. Despite her 'hands off' message to Mary, this woman was friendly to her and indeed introduced her for the first time to alcohol. Mary instantly took to gin and lime, the fashionable tipple of the time, because of the releasing effect it had on her tongue.[105] In Mary's words: 'Tim and I taught each other a lot and he was the first contemporary male I had ever talked to at length or seriously, so conversation with him had, for me, an intrinsic excitement.'[106] They spent a great deal of time together, talking about books, reading poetry to each other and going for long rambles in the surrounding countryside, she on a lazy horse called Rufty and he riding alongside on a bicycle.[107] Tim introduced her to Racine and a number of other French authors. They each planned to write an anthology and discussed with each other what to include that would fit their respective themes. Mary's anthology was called 'Unfulfilment' and was intensely romantic in content. Although her relationship with Tim was not, on Mary's account, a romantic one, she never forgot it. Indeed, in a diary entry dated 11 April 1943, a year after she had left Rosehill, Mary remembered the summer she had spent with Tim with great warmth and pleasure and wondered if indeed she had not been in love with him. If she had ever felt awkward talking to young men, this relationship must have helped her to see that men could be good friends as well as potential romantic partners, an experience denied to many of her female contemporaries who attended single-sex schools. After she left the school, Tim joined the Army and was tragically killed in action only a year later.[108]

Mary had also been much taken with Tim's mother, the head's wife, a clever, outspoken woman with corn-coloured hair. She loved being close to her and was amazed when, on departure, she gave Mary a kiss on the forehead. As she travelled home, in an early demonstration of her capacity to relate her life experiences to her reading, she repeated to herself a line that Tim had taught her from a mid-nineteenth-century poem by Gérard de Nerval 'Ma front est rouge encore, Du baiser de la reine.'[109] Mary heard that soon after she left the school, this woman ran off with one of the younger masters.

Mary left Rosehill at the end of July 1942 and spent the summer holidays before she went up to Oxford at home in Winchester. She had a most enjoyable couple of months and the adjectives 'heavenly' and 'blissful' figure frequently in her diary entries. The weather was largely good. She went out on rides into the surrounding countryside on her horse, Dan, visited her older sister, Grizel, who by now had a baby, played music with Stephana and listened to a great deal of classical music with her sister and mother. Occasionally, she would go on a trip for three or four days to a friend's house and once, when the term had started there, she went back to Prior's Field for more talks with Bice. She travelled up to London alone and felt a sense of adventure even though she was doing little more than window-shopping in New Bond Street. She continued to read a great deal, including Virgil, Lucretius and Herodotus and attended the local church or cathedral regularly. She spent some time preparing the anthology of favourite poems and prose passages she had discussed with Tim. As for the war, then at a low point in the fortunes of the Allied Forces, it hardly features in her diary entries, but once she reports with sadness the death of the brother of one of her friends. Mostly her mood was buoyant and cheerful, but very occasionally, as happened throughout her life, she descended into depths of self-loathing, mainly as a result of guilt about the way she had treated one of her best friends.

On Friday 9 October 1942, with her friend, Jean Stanier, who had already spent a year at Somerville College, she took the train to Oxford and established herself in her room at Lady Margaret Hall.[110] The transition to Oxford seems to have been completely painless, unsurprising in view of the fact that she already had many friends there, her sister was in the same college and her status as the senior scholar immediately put her in a position of social advantage. She records in her diary that, on her very first evening, clearly already marked as an outstanding undergraduate, she was invited to sit at High Table between two of the college fellows.

Notes

1   William Wordsworth, *Collected Poems*, p. 759.

2   Unpublished autobiography (UA) 1, p. 1.

3   UA 2, p. 2.

4   Felix Warnock, personal communication.

5   Kitty Warnock, personal communication.

6   Mary Warnock, 2000.

7   Kitty Warnock, personal communication.

8   Mary Warnock, 2003.

9   Mary Warnock, 1987.

10   Ibid., p. 118.

11   Ibid.

12   Ibid., p. 121.

13   Ibid.

14   Jean Crossley, pp. 13–16.

15   Ibid., pp. 15–16.

16   Crossley, 2006, p. 15.

17   Richard Davenport-Hines, 2004.

18   Richard Howarth, 2004.

19   Richard Davenport-Hines, 2004.

20   Richard Howarth, 2004.

21   Crossley, 2006, pp. 18–20.

22   Richard Davenport-Hines, 2004.

23   Warnock, 2000, p. 2.

24   Richard Davenport-Hines, 2004.

25   Ibid.

26   Arthur Hooper, undated.

27   Crossley, 2006, p. 17.

28   Crossley, 1993, pp. 93–94.

29   Ibid.

30   Crossley, 2006, p. 26.

31   Ibid.

32   Crossley, 2006, pp. 33–34.

33   Ibid., p. 7.

34   Crossley, 2006, pp. 91–92.

35   Ibid, p. 17.

36   Crossley, 1993, pp. 91–92.

37   Crossley, 2006, p. 137.

38   UA 1, p. 1.

39   Warnock, 2000, p. 4.

40   Ibid.

41   Ibid.

42   Ibid., pp. 4–5.

43   Ibid., p. 6.

44   Ibid.

45   Ibid., p. 6.

46   Warnock, 2000, p. 3.

47   Warnock, 2000, p. 6.

48   Imogen Rose, p. 313.

49   UA, 2, p. 12.

50   Crossley, 2006, p. 22.

51   Warnock, 2000, p. 3.

52   UA, 1, p. 13.

53   Warnock, 2000, p. 200.

54   Ibid., p. 199.

55   Ibid., p. 201.

56   Ibid., p. 3.

57   UA, 2, p. 24.

58   Warnock, 2000, p. 3.

59   UA, 1, pp. 13–14.

60   Ibid., pp. 14–15.

61   UA, 1, p. 18.

62   Ibid.

63   Warnock, 2000, pp. 7–8.

64   Imogen Rose, 2002.

65   Ibid., p. 284.

66   Ibid., p. 285.

67   Ibid., p. 297.

68   Ibid., p. 169.

69   Ibid., p. 171.

70   Ibid., p. 173.

71   Ibid., p. 176.

72   Warnock, 2000, p. 8.

73   Ibid.

74   Ibid.

75   Warnock, 2000, p. 9.

76   Ibid., pp. 9–10.

77   UA, 2, p. 13.

78   Rose, p. 186.

79   Ibid., p. 285.

80   Ibid., p. 328.

81   Ibid., p. 329.

82   Ibid., p. 422.

83   Ibid., p. 423.

84   Warnock, 2000, pp. 10–11.

85   Rose, p. 284.

86   Ibid., p. 11.

87   UA, 2, p. 21.

88   Warnock, 2000, p. 12.

89   Margaret Elliott, 2002, pp. 9–20.

90   Ibid., pp. 36–37.

91   UA, 2, p. 23.

92   Ibid., p. 55.

93   UA. 2, p. 23.

94   Elliott, p. 56.

95   Ibid, pp. 56–57.

96   UA, 2, p. 23.

97   Ibid.

98   Ibid., p. 25.

99   Ibid., p. 24.

100   Ibid., 3, p. 1.

101   Ibid.

102   Ibid., p. 4.

103   Ibid., p. 2.

104   Ibid., pp. 2–3.

105   Ibid., p. 5.

106   Ibid., pp. 3–4.

107   Ibid., p. 4.

108   Warnock, 2000, p. 13.

109   UA, 3, p. 5.

110   Ibid.

3. Emerging

The physical conditions of Oxford undergraduate life on which Mary was embarking in October 1942 were bleak indeed. Food rationing was severe (one egg per week and tiny quantities of luxuries such as butter) and shortages of everything needed for basic comforts, especially fuel: for example, undergraduates received a single scuttle of coal per week to heat their rooms. Such privations applied across the whole university, of course, and in some respects the women's colleges fared better than the men's. Nearly all the younger male dons had been recruited either into one of the armed forces or into the intelligence services, and the greatly reduced number of male undergraduates comprised only those who had, for one reason or another, secured exemption from war service. The women's colleges were relatively unaffected by conscription, so Lady Margaret Hall (LMH), Mary's new college, maintained a much higher undergraduate intake than any of its male counterparts. Indeed, the predominantly male demographic of pre-war Oxford had been changed for ever; not only was the proportion of women undergraduates higher, but many more women were now working in the re-located government offices which had moved into the vacant spaces in the men's colleges.

LMH, one of the five women's colleges in the University of Oxford at the time, had been founded in 1879. Jointly with Somerville, it was the first woman's college in Oxford. At the time Mary went there about sixty women undergraduates entered each year. Men were admitted as undergraduates in 1979, a hundred years after its foundation. The college is situated in spacious grounds, backing onto the River Cherwell, about a mile from the centre of the city. At Oxford, the college rather than the university is responsible for undergraduate teaching. It also provides a home. 'A college is more than a hostel; it is more than just a private

   https://doi.org/10.11647/OBP.0278.03

society; it is a household, a very large one, of course, but a household all the same.'[1]

When it came to their studies, all undergraduates had a main tutor in their college whose responsibility was to ensure that their pupils had at least one and sometimes two weekly individual or very small group tutorials appropriate to their subject. The tutor would usually conduct these tutorials herself or sometimes, depending on the subject, would share her duties with tutors from other colleges. Mary was largely taught in her college by women and elderly male dons. In addition, the main tutor had a pastoral function, and was available for support if there were any problems.

Another consequence of war was that university degree courses had been reduced, so that undergraduates could only stay for five terms. They were then awarded a 'war degree' and given the right to return to complete a full degree after the war. This shortened degree did not, at first, have much impact on Mary's course: she was reading Classics, a course which was divided into Parts 1 and 2. Part 1 was, conveniently, arranged over five terms and known as 'Honour Moderations' or 'Mods' and was primarily concerned with knowing the languages of Latin and Greek, with exercises in translations and 'proses,' and knowledge of some of the core texts such as Homer's *Iliad*, Virgil's *Aeneid*, Cicero, Tacitus, Plato and Aristophanes. Mary's first goal was to pass the Mods examination successfully. At that point she would need to make a choice: the second part of the course, known as 'Greats,' would, in normal times, consist of seven terms preparing for 'Finals,' which consisted of eight papers ranging more widely across the ancient world, but essentially covering Greek and Roman history and philosophy. The Greats course had been pared down to a single year and Mary's choice, on completing Mods, would be whether to do the much-reduced version of Greats or to leave Oxford for the duration of the war, exercising her right to a post-war return to resume her studies on a full-length course.

Mary's diary gives a sometimes painfully clear picture of her undergraduate life and pre-occupations, many of which revolved around her work: she found translating prose passages from English into Latin or Greek frustratingly difficult, often spending one or two days a week on this exercise, sometimes being reduced to tears at her inability to achieve the expected standard. She claimed that even her best efforts contained gross grammatical errors. Nevertheless, she found her tutor, Martha Kneale, 'kind and encouraging.' She also had tutorials from a Somerville don, Mildred Hartley, whom she described as 'young, attractive and sarcastic.'[2] When Mildred temporarily left to join the Civil Service, her place was taken by a retired Balliol don, Cyril Bailey, who, from Mary's point of view, was a discomfiting presence as he had supervised her brilliant brother, Duncan, who had been a scholar at Balliol thirteen years earlier. Bailey couldn't believe, according to Mary, that Duncan's sister could perform so poorly in comparison.[3] Mary felt this comparison was unfair as she had not had the pre-university experience in classics that most public schoolboys like Duncan took for granted. Such boys had often been studying both Greek and Latin from the age of seven and, before arriving at the university, had already had vastly more practice in translation from original texts.

As well as the individual tutorials, Mary attended numerous university lectures, as many as fourteen in some weeks. Many of these lectures were eye-opening for her. Historically, classical studies were at the heart of Oxford activities. As the Oxford historian, José Harris, wrote:

> Oxford (in 1939) was dominated, both intellectually and numerically, by the traditional humanities disciplines [...] between the different arts faculties, however, there was a distinct hierarchy of academic esteem, and a number of very different academic traditions. At the apex of the hierarchy was the faculty of Literae Humaniores or Classics. The truth is, though, that high esteem accorded to those reading Mods and Greats was not based exactly on an admiration for scholarship, as such, but on a kind of societal knowledge that the cleverest boys at school were always those who did Classics, and graduates who had read Greats were therefore likely to be the best generalists in the country, equipped to become lawyers, civil servants, politicians or indeed any other profession to which society attached special value. The classicist would have, in today's language, the best transferable skills. The traditional Oxford belief was that education of the kind provided in the Classics, placing a high value on attention to detail, accuracy of expression, even pedantry, was a good in itself. It taught very particular skills which had the widest possible general application.[4]

Most pre-war Oxford dons had by now left either for active service or to work in various government departments dealing with war work.

Lectures were almost entirely given by Jewish refugees from central
or eastern Europe, mainly Germany and Austria, who brought new
insights to classical studies in Oxford.[5] Traditionally, such studies had
been largely a matter of uncritical transmission of accepted knowledge
of the texts. The refugees brought a much more questioning approach
to the subject. They were primarily interested in exploring more critical
readings of the texts. It was only after the war that the sort of postgraduate
study in which such research could be conducted was introduced
into the Oxford syllabus. Further, the refugees were more widely
cultured than their predecessors and made many more connections
with contemporary continental European writers and thinkers. Mary
found this inter-disciplinary approach exciting and stimulating. She
attended lectures by Rudi Pfeiffer, who taught from *The Oxford Book of
Greek Verse*, edited badly, according to him, by the eminent Oxford don,
Maurice Bowra, and Karl Oskar Levy, known as Charles Brink, lectured
on textual criticism.[6] But the most stimulating lectures were given by
Eduard Fraenkel, Professor of Latin in the university, but lecturing
predominantly on Greek subjects. Mary straightaway identified him as
an exotic, indeed inspiring presence in Oxford, bringing a wholly new
approach to classical scholarship.

   Born in 1888 into a wealthy Jewish family in Berlin, by his thirties
Fraenkel had become a distinguished classical scholar in Germany.
He obtained senior academic positions in classical studies first in
Göttingen and then in Freiburg. After the election of a Nazi government
in 1933, he was sacked from his Freiburg post and immediately began
negotiating for a move to England. Mary would not have known it
at the time, but Fraenkel's election to the professorship in 1935
had been bitterly opposed. This opposition was nothing to do with
antisemitism, from which academic life was relatively free, but rather
the consciousness that an entirely new approach to classical studies
would be unleashed and legitimised if he held the chair. Opponents of
Fraenkel's appointment were proved right to the extent that he and his
refugee colleagues did bring a radically new approach. For example,
he delivered a series of lectures on the *Oresteia* twice a week over the
course of three terms. Fraenkel also lectured once a week on either
Horace or Catullus and gave a class on Aristophanes' *Birds* to which
undergraduates were admitted only by invitation. Mary wrote later

of his astonishing breadth of scholarship, his ability to link one thing with another across a vast range of time and geography, to start with a detail and expand it to general insights, and his genuine passion to hand down to the next generation the same tradition of scholarship of which he was an exemplar:

> From Fraenkel, I learned about things that were miles from the Mods syllabus. I learned about prosody, both in Greek and Latin and much more about the transmission, not only of texts, but of styles, dramatic and poetic. There was nothing we read that was not given a literary and historical context, and this, one of the essentials of enjoying literature, had never been taught at school, whether about English or Classical literature [...] for the first time I started to think about what happened between, as it were, the end of Greek and the beginning of Latin. Even more exciting, he showed me how these conventions continued to have echoes in the operas of Monteverdi and even Mozart. Fraenkel was a true polymath.[7]

It was a shock for her to discover what real scholarship was about. Fraenkel, wide-ranging as were the connections he made, was no speculator, and no dealer in generalities. It was one small thing at a time. But the following of these sorts of clues ended, far more often than not, with a sense of astonished enlightenment.

Mary was not the only undergraduate to find Fraenkel's teaching outstanding. One undergraduate who attended a decade later noted that lectures were not compulsory but 'if you didn't go to Fraenkel on Aeschylus when you were doing Mods, you might as well not have been at Oxford.'[8] The best-known attendee was Iris Murdoch, the novelist, who attended three years before Mary. Twenty-five years afterwards she wrote a poem 'The Agamemnon Class, 1939' in which she conflated the dread of war with Germany with the Trojan War. It began:

> Do you remember Professor
> Eduard Fraenkel's endless
> Class on the *Agamemnon*?
> Between line eighty-three and line a thousand
> It seemed to us our innocence
> Was lost, our youth laid waste,
> In that pellucid, unforgiving air,
> The aftermath experienced before[9]

When this poem appeared, Mary wrote an appreciative letter to Iris, commenting 'that atmosphere of dread and apprehension brought it all back to me. One dread merging into another. How amazing.'[10]

Fraenkel was never officially one of Mary's tutors, but he was in the habit of selecting individual undergraduates, always female, for one-to-one teaching in his room in Corpus Christi, between eight o'clock and ten thirty in the evening (undergraduates had to be back in their own colleges by eleven o'clock). One of the earliest of 'Fraenkel's girls' was Iris Murdoch, whose Somerville tutor, Isobel Henderson, warned her that Fraenkel would probably 'paw her about a bit,' which indeed he did. Murdoch seems to have taken this in her stride, going on to have an affectionate relationship with him and writing about him in her novels. In 1942 Mary became another pupil-cum-victim.

Mary's grooming as a Fraenkel girl began as early as her first term. While he was talking to her, for example, about the ancient Greek poets and dramatists such as Pindar or Menander, Fraenkel would begin to fondle her thighs and breasts. Naturally, Mary found this sexual behaviour deeply upsetting. Her diary entry for 10 November 1942, when she had been at Oxford for just over a month and went to his room accompanied by another girl, reads: 'Went up to Fr.'s room afterwards. He was just nicer than one could believe possible. We had lots of lovely sherry and cigarettes to pluck us up [...] I really ceased to be frightened of him at all [...] He was v. funny and nice with me, always with his hand on my shoulder and calling us "dear children".' These sessions rapidly became individual and more intimate. On 17 November, after she had been to his lecture, she recorded: 'Then utter hell in his room till five to one. God, it was awful [...] He was in charming mood [...] I thought I was going to die or to weep he was very nice and comforting but God, it was hell. Had sherry but didn't appreciate it.' On 14 December, apparently *à propos* of nothing, there is a diary entry: 'Oh God, what a nightmare. I cld murder Fraenkel.'

The abuse continued over three terms, often including during the vacations, until the summer of 1943 at the end of her first undergraduate year. In order, as she hoped to continue to receive such wonderful teaching but without having to withstand Fraenkel's sexual advances, Mary decided to introduce him in the 1943 Easter vacation to her best friend from St. Swithun's, Imogen Wrong. Imogen was studying Classics at Newnham College, Cambridge but lived in Oxford and so was there during the vacations. Fraenkel, she predicted, would not be able to continue his behaviour if he was teaching the two of them. Fraenkel was delighted to meet Imogen, whom Mary described as 'scholarly, well-read, full of boundless curiosity,'[11] and 'extraordinarily attractive, with genuinely corn-coloured hair, brown eyes and a preference for wearing bright clear colours.'[12] The plan badly misfired. 'After one or perhaps two mornings of our being taught together, Fraenkel found it would be infinitely more satisfactory to teach us separately, our interests and knowledge being so different.'[13] Eventually, after a further term's abuse, these goings-on were revealed. This may have happened because Mary made no attempt to cover them up. In her diary entry for 26 August, she wrote: 'I seemed to be entertaining the whole of LMH with stories about Fr.' Mary's friends, Stephana, her sister, and her former Prior's Field headteacher, in all of whom she confided, told her she must report the matter to her Somerville tutor, Mildred Hartley. Hartley, in turn, asked Cyril Bailey, Mary's supervisor, to warn Fraenkel that his behaviour was now public knowledge and must stop. Mary herself in her memoir published decades later, had a different version derived from her diary. She reported:

> Fraenkel picked up another girl from Lady Margaret Hall, who was extremely pretty and wore a scholar's gown (a necessary condition for his interest), but who was neither particularly interested in classical studies nor anything like as naïve as I was. She briskly said 'no thanks' to his advances and that anyway her fiancé would not like it; and then revealed what had happened to her tutor.[14]

In her diary she wrote that 'Fraenkel was confronted. He implied this had never happened before. "This was a madness that overcame me, it shall never happen again." Mildred pointed out "I happen to know you have done it before." Fraenkel was "dumbfounded" and asked who had told her?' Hartley replied that she didn't think that made any difference. There was some discussion about how he was to conquer his behaviour. Mary noted in her diary that Fraenkel must be livid with her. At any rate, his sexualised behaviour stopped, and she completed the last two terms before the Honour Mods examinations in April 1944, unmolested by him, but also deprived of his individual teaching.

Mary's diary entries made after the abuse finished make distressing reading. For months afterwards, she was deeply disturbed and guilt-ridden by what had happened. In a diary entry dated 21 September 1943, a month after Fraenkel had been exposed and her visits to him had stopped, she wrote:

> I am still haunted by my sin, my particular sin with Fraenkel: not so much but the memory of it haunts me, but that even to think of it I was filled only with desire to have it back, admit it and so I can't repent of it (even I grant myself that take away all the associations, even Fraenkel's noxious personality, and I am glad to be rid of my own part in it. But what is that? I can't repent of conniving in Fraenkel's particular lechery). Also, by the fear that somehow I am different because of it and shan't be prepared to be so shocked by it in the future. (Im [Imogen] feels this too, I know). I know that by the end of the time I was waiting for it to happen and if it didn't, I was disappointed. Oh Lord, what a confusion, but what is the good of going back over the whole thing? I can't satisfy myself that I am forgiven, that is all. But I know that if I had a chance, I should still be behaving in just the same way. [...] I have been alone so much...

It is notable that she sees herself as a sinner colluding in what had happened. Yet there is ample evidence that she was in Fraenkel's power and made several attempts to stop him abusing her.

In her memoir, written in the late 1990s, some fifty-five years later, she reports that, for some years after the abuse stopped, when they met, she and Imogen, the friend she introduced to Fraenkel as a protection, but who became another victim, would 'spend hours, in Oxford and in Winchester, devising more protective clothing, re-enacting especially absurd scenes, where the furniture was knocked over, or books scattered to the ground in our fruitless efforts to escape. Together we found it immensely comic, a never-failing source of those "hysterics" of which my diary is so full.'[15] Elsewhere, Mary recorded that Imogen did 'not altogether share my feelings about Fraenkel. She found his behaviour, though comic, genuinely disgusting, and she told me recently [just prior to 2000] that she thought it had had a lasting and bad effect on her attitude to sex.'[16] Mary expresses a hope this was not true, although it is not clear why she thought Imogen might have made it up.

Writing about ten years later, around 2010, in her unpublished autobiography, Mary again made light of the whole episode, treating it as if it were an unfortunate event with its funny side but with massive benefits. In fact, at this time, she recorded accurately: 'What went on would today count as gross sexual harassment,' but 'the good side was that I had literally hours of teaching, mostly after dinner in the evenings in term and during the vacations almost every day I was in Oxford.'[17]

A few years later, about six months before she died, Mary was asked for her view on a protest that had been made by the undergraduates of Corpus Christi College, Oxford. The Junior Common Room had requested that, in the light of his now notorious sexual behaviour, a room named after Fraenkel should no longer bear his name. While the Governing Body was considering the matter, a number of people connected with the college and the relevant events were asked for their views. Mary was among them. On 23 January 2018, she wrote to the President of the College:[18]

> I was horrified to see last week that undergraduates at Corpus were agitating to have the Fraenkel Room dismantled, and memorials of him removed, on the grounds of sexism. I feel extremely guilty to think that it was partly my pages about Eduard Fraenkel that have been responsible for this nonsense. I have never in my life gained so much as I gained from being 'picked up' by Fraenkel from his Agamemnon lectures and taught especially about early Latin, and other things as well. It was my introduction to scholarship and learning and represented what was the most exciting and amazingly eye-opening experience I could ever have had. Of course, I complained about his mild mauling, but I need not have gone on going to him if I thought it worse than mildly awful (and a subject for a lot of jokes). I do very much hope that you can get some sense of proportion into the undergraduates—who seem to me to have no sense of history apart from anything else.
>
> Please forgive my terrible handwriting.
>
> Yours very sincerely,
>
> Mary Warnock.

This letter confirmed the fact that she had no recollection of the deep sense of shame and guilt she had experienced after her experiences with Fraenkel. In the event, the room was renamed The Refugee Scholars Room and now commemorates not only Fraenkel but a number of other eminent scholars who had been welcomed into Corpus over the years.[19]

A few weeks before she died, Mary was asked in an interview conducted in January 2019, what she thought of the #MeToo movement.[20] 'Oh God,' she replied,

I hate it [...] People are now prepared to think that they are always victims... Why don't they just go away or hit the person [...] It does seem to me that women, on the whole see themselves as potential victims and not as being in charge of what happens. But why not? There's no reason it seems to me why they cannot object to someone who paws them around or whatever they do. Why don't they just go away or tell them to stop?

For Mary, the intellectual excitement she had experienced from Fraenkel's teaching far outweighed the emotional distress that accompanied and followed her sessions with him. She wrote of the time after she stopped seeing Fraenkel: 'I deeply missed Fraenkel's teaching [...] but what appalled me was that I had never, after the beginning, minded his advances.'[21]

It is worth noting, as we leave this episode in Mary's life, that there is no evidence that Mary's own subsequent life was in any way, sexually or otherwise, significantly affected by this traumatic experience. There is a vast psychological literature on why, in the face of seriously distressing events, some people show resilience while others suffer throughout their lives. It is likely that Mary's optimistic personality and the open way she was able to talk about her experiences contributed to her emerging unscathed.

Returning now to her academic studies in her first year as an undergraduate, Mary found keeping up with the requirements of the Honour Mods syllabus highly demanding, but she nevertheless found time to read widely outside the curriculum. At the end of her 1942 diary there is an impressively wide-ranging list of books she had read that year including novels by Thomas Hardy and E. M. Forster, plays by Shakespeare, Ibsen, Racine and Molière, religious or semi-religious texts by Sir Thomas Browne and C. S. Lewis. She records no reading that might be regarded as light or frivolous.

Her social life, such as it was at this time, revolved around a few close women friends among the other undergraduates of her college. She recorded in later life that these friends were few in number because of an early social disaster. As senior scholar of the year she was expected to put on a play for the entertainment of fellow undergraduates in her first term. Mary had, with difficulty, written a musical play called *Soldier, Soldier*, for which her talented older sister, Stephana, had written the music. This was performed on 31 October, about three weeks into the term. Many years later, Mary recorded that it had been a terrible flop and that no one would talk to her after it.[22] She may have known it was not really very good but her diary tells a somewhat different story: '... it really went rather well. Music not so bad. People acted well.' Nowhere does she report criticism or ostracism as a result of its performance.

One close friend was Nancy Pym, who went on to become headmistress of two Girls Day School Trust schools,[23] and with whom she remained friends until Nancy's death in 1998. Nancy was the only other contemporary at LMH reading Classics and Mary bonded with her especially because they shared the serious disadvantage of having suffered from inadequate classics teaching at school before arriving in Oxford. Mary got to know Nancy's parents. Her father was an ex-chaplain of Balliol College who had taken early retirement as he suffered from multiple sclerosis. Her mother, known as Mrs. Pym even to her own children, was, according to Mary, 'a hugely tall, bony figure, also a classicist and a great teller of fantastic sagas.' She used to send and occasionally bring great parcels of food from which Mary benefited. Uninhibited, when she, her daughter and Mary got together, their loud voices and uncontrollable laughter would bring complaints from the fellow who had rooms next to Nancy. Mary often visited the Pym family at their home during the vacations.[24]

Her other close friend was Elisabeth de Gaulle, the daughter of Charles de Gaulle, then leader of the French resistance army in London, and later President of France. They met at their first breakfast in Hall (the college dining hall) and remained friends until, around 1949, they lost contact after Elisabeth's and her own marriage. Elisabeth felt neglected by her parents who gave greater attention to their severely mentally handicapped younger daughter.[25] When this girl died several years later, her father commented 'enfin, elle est comme les autres.' Her favourite book in English, above all others, was the children's book *Winnie the Pooh* by AA Milne and she named her friends after characters in the Pooh stories. Mary was Roo on account of her 'tendency to show off.' Mary wrote that 'she was the only outspokenly morally critical friend I ever had.'[26]

They generally got on well together (at least in part because Elisabeth was a reliable source of cigarettes, which were used to ward off hunger) but had occasional violent arguments when Elisabeth made comparisons, to the advantage of her own country, between political institutions in France and Britain. Mary thought that the fact that, since

1940, France had been occupied by an enemy power, made it ludicrous
for Elisabeth to be dismissive of British political life. She tried to hold
back from delivering the obvious riposte by pointing to the predicament
in which France now found itself. One suspects she was not always
successful as Elisabeth was frequently deeply offended by her, but
they seem to have made up their differences pretty rapidly. Sometimes
Mary found herself in the role of Elisabeth's protector. As part of the air
raid precautions, students were made to undergo all sorts of exercises,
including crawling through a gas-filled tent wearing their gas masks.
Elisabeth's father had forbidden her to do this when he had heard
about it. Mary found herself explaining her friend's predicament to
the intimidating officer in charge of the exercise. The ARP examination
was particularly difficult for Elisabeth as, 'although her English was
excellent, it tended to be in the language of Macauley or Gibbon, and
she was not strong on the names of gases or words like "musty hay"
which you were supposed to smell, nor was she adept at understanding
instructions relating to dragging people downstairs when their legs
appeared to be broken.'[27]

In the 1944 winter term of the Mods examinations, Mary later
recorded that she tried to brush Elisabeth off so that she could
concentrate entirely on her work, determined to achieve a first-class
degree. Later, she felt guilty about this, thinking she had been rude to her
friend, but the relationship seems to have continued by correspondence
in an entirely friendly manner. Mary, although she could not go, was
invited to Elisabeth's marriage. Although she saw little of her fellow
undergraduates, apart from Nancy Pym and Elisabeth, Mary saw rather
more of her tutor, Cyril Bailey who pressed her to join the University
Bach Choir. Once she agreed, he insisted on practicing with her. She was
an alto and he a bass, and they had difficulty in keeping time in passages
in which the soprano and tenor parts predominate. On one occasion,
Cyril invited her and the other LMH Classics undergraduate, Nancy
Pym, for lunch and a walk in the country near his home. Mary had
great difficulty communicating with his very deaf wife, an embarrassing
experience for her.[28] As well as seeing her two friends, Mary frequently
saw Stephana, who came up from London where she was now working
and corresponded with another sister, Jean. A few of her teachers from
her school days had become friends, and she was in regular contact with

Bice at Prior's Field and Tim at Rosehill. Over this period, Tim seems to have been her only male friend.

The war meant that the college was unable to find sufficient domestic staff to keep the place clean. The undergraduates were expected to do a certain number of hours a week domestic work and Mary took part in this. One of the earliest of these undergraduate 'war tasks' had been to dig up the college tennis courts so that the college could grow most of its own fruit and vegetables. She was supposed to help preparing meals and gardening. Peeling and chopping up onions 'under the eye of a terrible old woman called Emily' (who was in fact the college bursar), was no pleasure,[29] although it might have been preferable to peeling beetroots which left your hands indelibly stained. At the end of one term, she was told that she was twenty-four hours behind her quota of gardening and that she must make it up before she went down. There seemed nothing to do and she was revising for her Mods examinations, so she 'spent two or three days out of doors, inscribing broad iris leaves with as many of the poems of Horace, Catullus and the Greek lyric poets as I could remember using the point of a knife, and then floating the leaves down the river.'[30] Much of the rest of the time in the vegetable garden seems to have been spent gossiping and smoking.

The privations brought about by the war were lasting memories. When she was asked, about fifty years after leaving, what would most have improved her time at LMH, she wrote 'MORE FOOD AND MORE HEAT IN WINTER' (her use of capitals). 'My chief, overwhelming recollections are of hunger and cold.'[31] There was just not sufficient fuel to heat the rooms adequately and inefficient coal fires in student's rooms gave off little heat. When students arrived at the beginning of each term, they handed in their ration books. In return, they were given unappetising meals in Hall, a meagre ration of milk and a single pot of marmalade that had to last a whole term. Those who had the means could buy food outside in cafes and restaurants, but all the same, most, like Mary, felt hungry most of the time. The city itself was a bleak place. By day, the streets were filled not with undergraduates but with evacuees and refugees. In the evening and by night, the total blackout meant it was eerily dark and, to some, frightening to venture out.[32]

In her last term at Oxford, the term in which she was to sit the Mods exam, Mary attempted to describe her life goals. Her diary entry for 4 February 1944 records them as:

a) (To complete) my work here as much and as well as may be (NB it is of the nature of the service always to be dissatisfied with what you have done)

b) To work at German intelligently with all my energy and application

c) My goal is Oxford and as much success as possible there—from there to be prepared for anything

d) My life to be balanced with riding and poetry and the utmost energy and generosity towards my friends

All this in God's will

Her idea of a balanced life involving riding, poetry and friends seems to have no room for boyfriends or marriage. When she does mention marriage, elsewhere in her diary, as in the entry for 11 April 1943, it is in negative terms. She writes: 'And yet my theories about the disadvantages of marriage still hold. I should hate to get married.'

During the lengthy vacations (university terms occupied less than half the year), Mary continued to do some studying each day. But she also spent time talking to her mother and sisters, playing music with Stephana, listening to classical music and reading more widely. She went riding most days on her horse, Dan, but sometimes also went for walks in the countryside, alone or with friends. She wrote and received letters most days. Occasionally she would go on day trips lasting three or four days to visit her sister, Grizel, and her new baby, Alison. Overall, the vacations were a relaxed time, enabling Mary to recharge her batteries before facing the intensity of a new term at Oxford. In mid-March 1944 she sat for the Mods examinations, finding them of varying difficulty. Her own assessment, recorded in her diary entry for 17 March, was that she did the general paper 'damn badly,' the Pindar was 'grim,' but the Logic paper 'quite nice. I'd done all the questions before.'

When the results arrived at the end of that month, she learned that she had achieved the first class she had so much wanted, but only just. For this class of degree, one had to achieve a first-class mark in seven out of the fifteen papers. She had just scraped this number. Her reaction to the results was typical. On receiving the marks from Cyril Bailey, her supervisor, she noted in her diary entry of 31 March 'Appallingly bad. Only just managing a First.' 'But' she goes on, 'I'm rather glad the moderators picked on my great fault, being unable to translate anything at all.' Self-deprecation accompanying impressive achievement was always the hallmark of Mary's reactions to the tests she faced in life and this was no exception.

Mary now opted to leave Oxford in April 1944 to take up a so-called 'reserved' occupation. She did not want to do the compressed wartime version of Greats, so chose to complete her degree when the war ended, whenever that might be.[33] Many female undergraduates who were reading Classics, especially if they were high-fliers such as Mary, were recruited for work at Bletchley Park, the famous centre for Allied code-breaking. This was where some Oxford philosophy dons, such as Gilbert Ryle and Stuart Hampshire, also spent their war years. But there was a rumour that, if you went to Bletchley, you would only be able to leave when the war with Japan was ended and, in 1944, when the atom bomb was not yet envisaged, it was assumed that the war with Japan could last for years, with every Pacific island occupied by the Japanese having to be recaptured in hand-to-hand combat at enormous cost in lives. Other reserved occupation would probably end when the war in Europe ended. Mary wanted to return to Oxford as soon as possible, so, although she went to look at Bletchley, she decided to try to find a reserved occupation elsewhere. She also made a trip to the Careers Office in Southampton where, she recorded in her diary, she was told not to be choosy and asked why she wasn't trying to get married as soon as possible.

Mary's sister-in-law, Betty Fleming, whom Mary's older brother, Duncan, had married in 1937, had taught for a time at Sherborne Girls' School and had got on well with its charismatic head, Helen Stuart. A contact was made and, after a brief interview with the head in London, Mary was offered a job at the school. The main duties involved coaching sixth-formers in Latin which was at that time a compulsory subject for all applicants to Oxbridge. The girls she taught were all upper middle-class and, in her view, rather full of themselves. Mary described them as 'confident, sometimes arrogant goddesses.'[34] As a group, they had little interest in Latin, so Mary devised comic English sentences for them to translate, encouraging them to think up such sentences themselves.

The first essential of teaching, she learned at Sherborne, was not to bore one's pupils.[35]

Sherborne's location in north-west Dorset was sufficiently remote to be safe from bombing (though there had been several fatalities when a bomb had dropped on the nearby village of Sherborne in 1940, four years earlier),[36] but there were certainly other challenges in everyday life. Mary had a room in a rather primitive house across the road from the school which at least boasted a bathroom, although the bath was filled with coal when not in use. Food was rationed. One girl remembered later how the butter for one week consisted of 'little pieces of butter you could blow on two slices of bread or eke it out.'[37]

In her diary entries written during her two years at Sherborne, Mary begins to reflect, almost for the first time, on her views on love, friendship and marriage. She values friendship with women above everything else but does not want such friendship to result in loss of autonomy. She writes in her entry of 1 August 1944:

> I have a great desire to share but not to make myself into what I'm not that is I want very badly to entertain people to give to them, to make them happy but not to communicate with anyone so that we are one person instead of two. [...] Perhaps because with Virginia Woolf, in mockery, I say are not all women are nicer than any man and one is taught not to feel like a lover towards women. There are lots of women I love very much indeed, more than anything on earth probably but the essence of the joy of my relationship with them is twoness, not oneness.

As Mary moved through life, in each of the situations she found herself, she nearly always found a soul mate, someone with whom she could share confidences, gossip about mutual acquaintances, and, very importantly, laugh and have fun. Before going to school, this role had been filled by her sister, Stephana; at St. Swithun's, Imogen Wrong; at Prior's Field, Bice, her headmistress; at Lady Margaret Hall, Nancy Pym and, to a lesser extent, Elisabeth de Gaulle; and now, at Sherborne, she made another lifelong friend, Rachel Drever Smith. Rachel had a beautiful living room in the school building where Mary spent some of her evenings. She played duets with her and this led to her teaching the flute to some of the girls.[38] Rachel later became headmistress of St. Bride's Girls' School in Helensburgh, Scotland. She and Mary continued to see each other until her death in the 1990s, and indeed she was godmother to Kitty, Mary's oldest child. When she wasn't teaching, Mary read and went for long walks or bicycle rides in the surrounding country.

Her diary entries begin to look forward to possible post-war futures. For example, on 25 September 1944 she wrote: 'I would put aside anything to promote peace by working for the understanding of the outlook and desires of one other country (and, of course, before all countries, I would choose France) and second, that in the same way I would abandon anything for the sake of doing away with some of the present social abuses in England.' It is interesting that she has become so attached to France. Perhaps, she writes in the same entry '[...] it is because of having seen, in my last two terms' at Oxford, so much in Elisabeth that is beyond praise [...] An incredibly human and sensitive intelligence [...] A most marvellous control. Europe is not itself without a safe, active, creative France.'

She considers where she stands on the political spectrum and, in the same entry, on 25 September 1944, reflects: 'There is no political party to which I would attach myself [...] no choice except between capitalism and socialism [...] iniquitous capitalist system [...] and socialism seems to be a very poor alternative.' She is attracted to the political ideal of G. K. Chesteron and Hilaire Belloc which she calls the 'ChesterBelloc service state' but dismisses this as 'pure idealism.' Her criterion for political choice is compatibility with Christianity, but 'I don't even see which of the possible parties is most Christian.'

Her religious faith also raises issues for her possible future career. During the school holidays, at home in Winchester, Mary confided in Canon Lloyd, the member of the Winchester Cathedral clergy she knew best, that her intention to teach philosophy might not be compatible with her Christian faith, giving little opportunity to help and love other people. Lloyd appears to have successfully reassured her.

Following the end of the war in Europe in May 1945, Mary records that her jubilation is almost immediately superseded by fears of another war with Russia. She also writes about the discovery of the truth about the concentration camps, particularly Belsen which had been liberated by the British Army. She and Rachel speculated about whether they could have behaved as the Germans did and concluded they certainly could not. Mary was lucky in having no relatives killed in the war. There is only one reference to the involvement of a member of her own family.

This is to Duncan, her older brother, who is in Germany at the time she wrote. She had no idea what he was doing each day, but he survived unscathed.

A few months later, she is thinking of her own future, about the pleasures of teaching and of reading in order to improve her teaching. The only disadvantage of a scholarly life, she wrote, is that

> everyone (ie Jean and Mither) will expect me to get engaged this time or never, I feel sure, and will consider me a disappointed spinster when I come down without doing so. And if, for a moment, I let myself accept their standards, I shall begin to feel I am the one disappointed. I admit that I should get married if I met anyone who wished to marry me (almost impossible) and, in return, I wished to marry (very unlikely).

She goes on, in the same entry, to relate these thoughts about marriage to her Christian beliefs about the purpose of life. 'Otherwise,' she writes, 'I feel there are so many things to do and so many people to teach that there is no need to feel frustrated in the least. And in any case, for a Christian to feel frustrated simply from that would be ridiculous.' Both she and Stephana were coming under increasing pressure from their older sister Jean as well as their mother to find themselves boyfriends with a view to getting married. Jean, who herself had married early, separated and by now was divorced, 'was constantly trying to civilise us and make us grow up, both by urging make-up and hairdressers on us, and by trying to talk to us about her life, in what we thought was her "all men" style of conversation.' As Mary saw it, Jean's view was that what ought to rule their lives was to make themselves attractive.[39]

She left Sherborne at Easter 1946 and returned immediately to LMH to resume her studies. The Oxford to which Mary returned was very different from the one she had left two years earlier. During the war years, the university had lost its dominance in the city, but now it reasserted its position. Undergraduates were everywhere and they were much more diverse than they had been pre-war. Some were typically callow, inexperienced youths straight up from public school, but they were now joined by men coming back from the war, some in their early, but many in their mid- or even late, twenties. These men had mostly been on active service and seen friends killed or wounded. Many were now sexually experienced; some were married and some undoubtedly found the adjustment to civilian life difficult. This led to some division.

'Ex-majors with MCs, wives and moustaches had little in common with 17-year old boys who carried green ration books entitling them to extra bananas.'[40] There were also differences in the predominant political and religious value systems. During Mary's first stay in Oxford, young liberal and left-wing intellectual leaders tended to be away in the services, leaving an older and more conservative generation, such as C. S. Lewis and Charles Williams as guiding spirits for the Oxford young. As the younger dons returned, more politically radical and secular voices were increasingly heard.

More women came straight from school. A few had been in one of the armed forces, but even these were unlikely to have seen active service. The women who came up to Oxford would mostly have lived sheltered lives in single-sex schools, with little contact with the opposite sex and Mary, even though she was now twenty-two, fell into this inexperienced category. Apart from her brother, Duncan, and the headmaster's son, Tim, whom she had met at Rosehill and with whom she had had a platonic relationship, she had seldom had even as much as a conversation with a man her own age. As a consequence, she had little confidence in her ability to do so. Later in life she described how she felt 'ugly, clumsy and without any powers of conversation, being frequently overcome with horror at not being able to think of anything to say.' This resulted in her being 'intensely grateful to any man who seemed to like me. This made me prone to decide I was in love with him.'[41]

As we have seen, Jean would constantly try to advise her on how to make herself attractive, but Mary had very little interest in make-up or in having her hair done. She wrote: '[...] on the whole my appearance was something I preferred to draw a veil over.'[42] On the other hand, she was developing a love of clothes which was to last throughout her life but there were few opportunities immediately after the war to branch out in this respect. Jean gave her a hand-knitted purple jumper and a pink and white striped blouse. She also had a plain dark-green kilt which she greatly liked. Clothes rationing meant new clothes were largely impossible to buy. In her last year as an undergraduate, she bought a scarlet suede jacket from a friend, paying her in coupons for it. She continued to love this jacket even when it got old and shiny.

One essential difference between post- and pre-war Oxford was the great differences in the opportunities for women undergraduates to find partners, even if college rules did little to encourage this. All undergraduates had to be back in College by ten p.m. and any student found with a man in her room after seven p.m. was automatically 'sent down,' that is expelled. But the fact remained that there were now five or six times more male than female undergraduates.

Times were also very different politically. During Mary's first five terms in Oxford between 1942 and 1944, all the talk had been about the progress of the war. In 1945 a Labour government had been elected with a mandate to carry out sweeping social reforms. Mary, like most of her contemporaries, had no hesitation in voting Labour at this election. Women were becoming active in political clubs whose meetings were often addressed by prominent politicians. They could not be members of the Oxford Union, often the pathway to a political career, but they could be and often were active members of the Labour, Liberal and Conservative Clubs. Amateur dramatics flourished once again and OUDS (Oxford University Dramatic Society) which had closed during the war, opened again in 1947, giving opportunities for budding young actresses. More relevantly for Mary, the Jowett Society, the philosophy discussion group, now had many more men attending.

Soon after her arrival back in Oxford, Mary made a new LMH friend, Sheila Westbrook, who was also reading Greats. She had digs in a house owned by a don, Hilda Lorimer, a Homeric scholar. Mary spent a great deal of her time in Sheila's room which was lined with books, as it also served as Miss Lorimer's library. The two played tennis most mornings before breakfast and then, after breakfast, studied there until lunchtime. For many weeks, Mary studied Aristotle's *Nicomachean Ethics* in this room. From time to time, a maid would come in with cups of coffee, biscuits and fruit cake. This was great luxury[43] for at this point food rationing was at its most severe, with even bread and potatoes on the ration. Using Sheila's room also saved fuel; there was no central heating at LMH, and Mary only had one scuttle of coal each week for the fire in her college room. This made the particularly hard winter of 1947 extremely difficult. Dinners were meagre; at LMH the undergraduates often only had soup and bread for their supper.

Sheila was attached to an undergraduate at New College, whom she later married. She and Mary often had tea with this young man, whom Mary remembered as making 'the most delicious cucumber sandwiches.'[44] It was probably through him that she began to strike up friendships with New College undergraduates. At this point, Mary's views on her marriage prospects had not changed. At the beginning of her second term back, on 10 October 1946, she wrote in her diary:

> I see clearly that I shall be alone all my life [...] solitude has been my greatest satisfaction. It is only in the midst of people who can't bear the thought of a solitary life that non-marriage seems terrible and to be ashamed of. If I can only overcome my body, my mind will be all right [...] the greatest satisfaction that I shall ever have is to make other people feel that it is worth living.

She was, in any case, extremely busy. Her daily diary entry for 12 October begins 'The hecticness of this term is going to pass belief.' Perhaps not quite as hectic as this sounds, though, for the entry goes on, 'Woke late-ish and a long nice breakfast.' All the same, the schedule of work she set herself with the very explicit determination to achieve a first-class degree was highly demanding.

Despite the reservations expressed in her diary, it was not long before Mary began to forge romantic relationships with men. She describes the men with whom she had her first two romantic relationships as 'suitors' but it is clear from her diary that, at the start of both these relationships, she was more the pursuer than the pursued. In her unpublished biography, she writes of this phase of her life:

> I felt I was learning new things, seeing and understanding things I had missed before. [...] I always worked better if my emotional life was in ferment and now I was torn between two men who wanted to marry me. I had pursued each of them in turn relentlessly when I had first known them but when they began to show interest in me though I enjoyed the sense of power this gave me, my ardour cooled.[45]

Thus, by the end of her second term back at Oxford, she was in love with a man called Charles, whom she had known since the end of the previous term.[46] In her memoir, she describes Charles, both in appearance and manner, in ambivalent terms.

> He was an extremely good-looking man, in a melancholy way, his almost shaven short hair, brown eyes and bony face, with its remarkably short upper lip, merging into a kind of spiky unity. He treated me with unbending scorn, mixed with a kind of mocking affection, as if I were a slightly tiresome dog. (Later [...] he became the dog, his eyes fitting him well for the part).[47]

The relationship, which had many ups and downs, lasted about a year.

During the 1947 Easter holiday, while she was still in a relationship with Charles, Mary and her friend, Sheila Westbrook, crossed the English Channel with their bicycles, took the train to Paris, cycled across Paris and then took another train to Biarritz, in south-west France. When they got out of the train, they were met by dazzling sunshine, a marked contrast to the snowy weather they had left behind in England. They cycled across the Pyrenees into Spain 'where hoopoes were all around us' and pushed their bicycles up mountainous roads through villages where there had hardly been any English visitors since the war. They felt flattered because their accents made the Spaniards think they were Normans from the North of France.[48] This was Mary's first visit to continental Europe. A fortnight after her return, she wrote in her diary entry dated 18 April: 'I am full of the feeling of health and inexhaustible energy which I associate with home, especially here in the Spring and in September, and spring has started in England only now though I, of course, have cheated, and had some spring in France. [...] superb climbing up Mt. Louis [...]'

This diary entry includes some thoughts on her relationship with Charles:

> I want to get married [...] But I want to marry Charles and that is the second important thing [...] He, of course, is entirely indifferent to me. I dare say in four years-time I shall tell myself that I wasn't really in love with him at all and wouldn't have married him [...] If I give him up now I doubt if he would notice [...] I've no doubt that next term will bring more misery and a further realisation of how futile to hope for anything, even the continuation of what I've had.

Charles continued to make her miserable. By the end of that summer term, it is clear there are problems in the relationship. On 13 July 1947, she wrote: 'Life is certainly extraordinarily different from what it was. I don't think that I shall ever deny that I loved Charles [...] the self-absorbed recipient of unreciprocated love [...] a kind of self-consciousness which Elizabeth Anscombe [a Somerville don who had tutored her] calls priggishness [...]' Mary's mother had had high hopes of this relationship. Mary records: 'Mither [her mother] has considered him mine...'

The 1947 Long (Summer) Vacation was spent in her mother's house on the banks of the River Test in Romsey, Hampshire, where her mother had moved a year previously, having sold the family home in Winchester. The Romsey house had a large garden, an orchard where there were nightingales in the bushes and a lake nearby in which one could swim. During this holiday she spent a great deal of time with Stephana, riding and playing music, Stephana now having switched from a Chemistry to a Music degree at Oxford.[49] She also spent part of the vacation in Oxford, where she continued to see Charles.

On 21 August 1947, she records just after Charles has left her room:

> What shall I do? I could never have believed that one person could so utterly occupy me [...] And paralyse all my mental activity [...] He has left only 20 minutes ago and I feel hysterical. I love him too much to pester him. [...] the last three weeks have been important but only in showing me what I knew already, that is to do things for other people is the only way to do them and to do things for Charles is all I ask. It is entirely reprehensible to give myself up to this passionate outburst of Unrequited love.

But there was a problem. By 11 November, she had worked out what this was. Her diary entry for that date notes: 'I know intellectually that the real answer is his sexual απαθεια [It is not clear why Mary translated apathy into Greek]. He simply doesn't want to marry me and that is that. There is nothing I can do but go on loving him.' Whether Charles was under-sexed or homosexual or just did not find Mary physically attractive, is unclear but, whatever the reason for his lack of sexual interest in Mary, it gradually spelled the end of her relationship with him.

Four months later in the early months of 1948, she is deep into another relationship, this time a more physically intense one, with another undergraduate. She describes this second suitor, whom I shall call 'Ian,' as 'a dim and endearing man, easily amused and, contrary to his most deeply held principles, extremely emotional.' He had got a first in Classical Mods at the beginning of the war, served in the Army and then returned to the university from war service.[50] By 28 April 1948 she tells herself she must exercise more restraint in her behaviour with him. She writes in her diary of 'Resolutions that must be kept,' but then adds rather charmingly, 'Till June.' They are:

No more self-pity: no more wallowing in misery with Ian
Work
I. only on Saturdays.
No more talk of marriage
The minimum of kissing and dallying
No more forcing I. to consider the future
Keep stimulated about philosophy somehow
The obligation to be cheerful.

Initially Ian is reluctant to form a serious relationship with her, but gradually he too succumbs. By early July he is deeply in love with her and wants to marry her, but at this point Mary has fallen in love with another.

To understand Mary's change of heart regarding Ian, one needs to go back to the beginning of the 1947 Michaelmas (October to December) term when Mary was elected Secretary of the Jowett Society. This Society, which held weekly meetings on philosophical topics when the audience was addressed by eminent philosophers, was open to all members of the faculty and was attended both by dons and by undergraduates. By tradition, the Secretary of the Society was an outstanding undergraduate. It is a measure of Mary's academic status as an undergraduate that she was elected Secretary. Another tradition was that, after one term, the Secretary became President and had the duty to find a successor as Secretary. In Mary's words:

> I consulted Tim Miles, now President, whom he thought I should invite to be secretary. He said unhesitatingly 'Geoffrey Warnock. He is far the best philosopher around' [...] I knew Geoffrey Warnock by sight and had decided he was formidable. I had seen other undergraduates consulting him, for example, at Austin's Things class, and I thought he looked pleased with himself. However, I obediently wrote to him, asking him to serve. We were extremely formal in those days about how we addressed people we did not know. If I had been a man, I would have written 'Dear Warnock'. Most senior members addressed each other in this way, but women did not have this useful halfway between full title and Christian name. [...] In the end, I compromised. I wrote 'Dear Mr. Warnock (may I call you, Geoffrey?)'. He, disobligingly, I thought, wrote back 'Dear Mary (may I call you Miss Wilson?)'. It was a bad start. But at least he was willing to take on the job; and as soon as we started to meet in his room at the top of New College tower, in order to make lists of potential speakers and members and, increasingly, to go over the events of the previous meeting, I realized I had encountered someone who made me laugh and

with whom I got on as well as with my women friends, without self-consciousness and without anxiety.[51]

At the time she met Geoffrey for the first time, she had been in a romantic relationship with Charles for nearly a year. As we have seen, during the autumn of 1947, her relationship with Charles gradually cooled and was over by the end of the year. She and Geoffrey were often in touch over matters concerning the Jowett Society, but there was no romantic element to their relationship. Indeed, as we have seen, shortly after the beginning of 1948, she met Ian, with whom she had another, more purely physical relationship lasting six months until the middle of that year. But gradually over this period while she was seeing Ian, her relationship with Geoffrey developed romantically, so that by June 1948, she acknowledged to herself she was in love with him and would have to drop Ian. Mary's falling in love for the third time, on this occasion, was definitive, and so intense she did not care whether her love was reciprocated.

When they first met Geoffrey Warnock was twenty-four, just a year older than Mary but with considerably greater experience of life. Born in Leeds, the son of a successful general practitioner, himself raised in Ulster, Geoffrey won a scholarship to Winchester College. Then in 1940 he had won an Open Scholarship to read Politics, Philosophy and Economics at New College, Oxford. Instead of taking up his scholarship he volunteered to join the Irish Guards and, in December 1942, was commissioned as a second lieutenant. As a signals officer, after active service in Italy, he landed with his regiment on the Normandy beaches in June 1944. The regiment went on to fight at Caen, before joining the advance into Belgium and Holland. After joining other units to relieve the airborne troops at Arnhem, it then fought its way into Germany.[52] Later in life Geoffrey spoke of his experience as a signals officer. He had been appalled by the quality of military leadership and was especially unforgiving of an outbreak of squabbling amongst senior officers over who should take command when the general in charge of the campaign was captured. He described how on occasions when he thought transmitting a signal would lead to disaster, he just would not pass it on.[53] If he was inclined to insubordination in respect of his senior officers he was regarded as a leader by the other ranks in the regiment. Those who found themselves up before a court martial would often ask for him to be their advocate. His last posting, after the war with Germany ended, was in Hamburg where he spent some time educating his men and fellow officers in current affairs.[54] It was reported that under his tuition, even some of the most incorrigibly conservative officers in his very conservative Guards regiment emerged as committed socialists.

Mary's relationship with Geoffrey gradually deepened during the spring of 1948 while she was still in a relationship with Ian. Before they both took their final examinations, Geoffrey invited her to be his partner at the New College Commemoration Ball to be held in June. But before that Mary had to face the ordeal of the final examinations. Further, her Roman History tutor at Somerville had recommended that she put in for a one-year fellowship in Ancient History that she could take up the following year. She was successful in obtaining this fellowship and decided to use it to study for a newly devised postgraduate degree, the B.Phil. This degree was the brainchild of Gilbert Ryle, the *éminence grise* of the Philosophy Faculty, to enable Oxford to attract philosophy graduates from elsewhere to pursue postgraduate research in the subject after graduation. The degree, in contrast to similar degrees elsewhere, would only require a short dissertation, the main teaching taking place in small group seminars with marked written papers. This suited Mary extremely well, except for the fact that it was designed as a two-year course and she wanted to do it in one year. She persuaded Ryle she could do this.

Although she found the final examinations in Greats extremely stressful, she had some useful counselling beforehand about how to cope with the lack of sleep while the examinations were in progress. Lucy Sutherland, the Principal of LMH, gave a talk to all the candidates beforehand to suggest to them that lack of sleep was no barrier to a good performance. One should not worry about not sleeping.[55] Mary found this helpful advice that she subsequently passed on. In the event, she did well and obtained the first-class degree everyone expected of her. Geoffrey did equally well, so they had much to celebrate. During the ball, Geoffrey told her he had decided not to marry another LMH undergraduate to whom he had been attached. As is traditional, the couple stayed up the whole night of the ball, at the end of which Geoffrey took Mary to Oxford station so that she could catch the 6.25 train to Stockport to attend Sheila Westbrook's wedding.[56]

It did not take her long to realise that she found Geoffrey infinitely more attractive than either of the two men with whom she had previously had relationships. Her diary entry for 3 July 1948 reads:

> And now time has come and gone, and all that I made resolutions for is cracked and crumbled away, because I have forced Ian to love me, and now given him up, at least said I will not marry him [...] All that is wicked, I am wicked. I have used him bodily and still could, if it were not that I love Geoffrey [...] I feel as if I have fallen in love finally and for all time. But I have felt that before [...] I feel that though he won't marry me, I shall survive that. I shall be content in some way to say, when I am old [...] I did love Geoffrey [...] there are aspects of what I feel about Geoffrey that are totally unlike love of Charles or love of Ian [...] If he wanted to marry me, I should say yes and worry no more. [...] our most heavenly evening at the New College Ball [...]. I really think, except that I should not be good enough and too dull for him [...] thus although I am right to say I feel adolescent because of Geoffrey (romantic irresponsibility), I also feel non-hysterical and this <u>must</u> be more grown-up than last year or even before.

She goes on castigating herself about the way she has treated Ian: 'I have undoubtedly behaved shockingly badly towards Ian, even after I knew I was not going to marry him [...] it was so much easier to give in, physically [...] that I was horrible to him and let him practically possess me physically [...] now I look back on July with distaste' and finally, she admits to herself: 'I admit unashamedly that I want to marry Geoffrey.' So, while in her published memoir she gives no reason for the breakdown of her relationship with Charles, it is clear from her diary that it stopped because he was 'sexually apathetic.' Further, while in her unpublished autobiography, she claims that the relationship with Ian broke down because she realised he was intellectually inferior to her,[57] it is apparent from her diary that as soon as she met Geoffrey, she realised she would most definitely prefer to marry him. Thus her diary reveals her to be, even as an undergraduate, what she was to remain all her life, a woman with enormous energy, drive and determination accompanied very occasionally by a certain ruthless streak.

The first half of the 1948 summer vacation was, to put it mildly, emotionally complicated for Mary. By early August, she had more or less detached herself from Ian and cemented her relationship with

Geoffrey who had then gone back home to Leeds. Her diary entry for 11 August reads:

> The more immediate problem is how to wait until October when I can see him again. [...] lying looking at the view into Salisbury in a pool of blue mist while he talked, brilliantly, about France and the Dreyfus affair and then read To the Lighthouse, that was perfect [...] and half slept and talked foolishly and laughed a good deal and removed insects and leaves and bits of things from each other's bodies. He looked beautiful and very small and thin, but exquisitely made and shaped and very strong. [...] I admit unashamedly that I want to marry Geoffrey. It's no longer true that I could see him marry someone else with equanimity.'

Her abiding memory of the long summer she spent with her mother in Romsey is of 'sitting in Mither's garden, wondering whether the second post would bring a letter from Leeds, reading Proust, and listening to Verdi opera on the gramophone, a new passion to which Geoffrey had introduced me. It was an absurdly happy and carefree time.'[58] As an example of their common views, they shared their absorption in Proust. Unlike most readers of Proust who fail to get past the first of the twelve volumes of his *chef d'oeuvre*, Geoffrey notes that they both loved volume eleven.

Geoffrey's letters reveal it was not quite as uncomplicated a time as Mary suggests. She had not altogether disentangled herself from Ian who was still pining for her and Charles, her first suitor, actually stayed with her at her mother's home for a short time. When Geoffrey whom she had also invited to stay, heard of this, he had wise advice to offer her about how to end these relationships.[59] In the meantime, he described to her how he had ended his own relationship with the LMH girl to whom he himself had been attached. Clearly Mary had been anxious about how this fellow undergraduate would react to being told her relationship with Geoffrey must end for Geoffrey writes '[...] X is far too sensible and sane to do anything silly,' but clearly 'X' had been very upset and tearful. Mary must also have expressed some concern that she might become too reliant on Geoffrey. He tried to reassure her.[60] As their relationship deepened, he became more open in his affection for her. 'I do love you a ridiculous lot [...],' he writes in the restrained language of the time. After a misunderstanding between them, he writes: 'I am fantastically glad that nothing is wrong and I don't see how you could be Nicer, either in yourself or to me. Therefore (and also because) Love, Geoffrey.'[61]

During the following year, Mary left her college room and shared a flat with Anne Wakefield, her friend from school. Geoffrey arranged to stay on at New College to study Ancient History with a view to taking the Greats examination. Mary was able to help him by lending him her essays and, according to her, he virtually wrote her dissertation for the B.Phil degree.[62] They had an agreeable year planning their future, having decided to marry even if neither of them had a job. However, after Christmas 1948, Geoffrey took the Prize Fellowship examination at Magdalen, was successful and was duly appointed a fellow there. He was advised not to pursue his idea of taking the Greats examination as it would be embarrassing for a fellow of Magdalen not to achieve a first-class degree. Later in the year, Mary was appointed to a lectureship in philosophy at St. Hugh's College so, in the event, they not only both had jobs, but had avoided any difficulty over whose career would take precedence. They were now both in academic employment with virtually lifelong tenure.[63]

The couple were married in Winchester College Chapel with music arranged by Stephana and played by her and her friends. Mary claimed that all she could remember of the ceremony was the music and the fact that, as she was proceeding up the aisle, Geoffrey trod on the back of her dress (borrowed from Sheila Westbrook, who had been married in it the year before). Mary had shouted at him 'Get off, you clown!' to prevent further damage.[64] After the wedding and the party that followed, they honeymooned in Edinburgh, attending the Festival (described in the next chapter) and then went straight back to Oxford, because Geoffrey was teaching at an American summer school.

During the three years from her arrival back in Oxford in April 1946 to her marriage in August 1949, both Mary's personality and her most fundamental beliefs had drastically changed. Although she saw her academic ability as inferior to Geoffrey, she was not in any doubt that she could teach philosophy at an undergraduate level and contribute to the subject. Now confident in her relationships with men, she was accepting of her own physical desires and no longer saw them as best suppressed. Her political views had crystallised, so that she was a strong supporter of the Labour government and socially liberal in her opinions on the issues of the day. There had also been a significant change in her religious views. While still seeing herself as a Christian and a member of the Anglican Church, she was no longer imbued with a sense of her own sinfulness. When she felt she had behaved badly, as was not infrequently the case, she did not hesitate to admit the fact, but she no longer looked to Christian beliefs to justify her self-castigation. She was now taking full responsibility for her actions. So, she began what she called her 'real life,' having indeed emerged her own woman.

Notes

1   Thomas, p. 179.

2   Unpublished autobiography (UA), 3, p. 20.

3   UA, 3, p. 21.

4   José Harris, 1994.

5   UA, 3, p. 23.

6   Ibid., 3, pp. 23–27.

7   Ibid., 3, p. 30.

8   Robert Cassen, personal communication, September 2020.

9   Conradi, pp. 121–122.

10   Ibid., p. 122.

11   UA, 3, p. 32.

12   Ibid.

13   UA, 3, p. 33.

14   Warnock, 2000, p. 82.

15   Ibid., 3, p. 33.

16   Warnock, 2000, p. 84.

17   UA, 3, p. 30.

18   Jas Elsner, 2021, pp. 328–329.

19   Ibid.

20   Interview with Giles Fraser, *Confessions*, 10 February 2019.

21   Ibid.

22 UA, 3, p. 6.

23 Ibid., p. 7.

24 Ibid.

25 Ibid., pp. 7–12.

26 Ibid., p. 9.

27 Ibid., p. 14.

28 Ibid., p. 21.

29 Ibid., p. 5.

30 Ibid., p. 16.

31 Archive, LMH, *Your memories of Lady Margaret Hall*, 2015.

32 Addison, p. 177.

33 Ibid., p. 172.

34 UA, 3, p. 2.

35 Ibid.

36 Williams, 1998, p. 69.

37 Ibid.

38 Ibid., 3, p. 4.

39 UA 5, p. 4.

40 Thomas, p. 208.

41 UA, 5, p. 3.

42 Ibid., p. 6.

43 Ibid., pp. 7–9.

44 Ibid., p. 20.

45 Ibid., p. 18.

46 Charles Salter was a brilliant undergraduate, who won many prizes. His career did not prosper after he left Oxford. He died in 2008 following retirement as Lecturer in Humanities in the University of Glasgow.

47 Warnock, 2000, p. 76.

48 UA, 5, p. 9.

49 Ibid., pp. 15–16.

50   Ibid., pp. 18–19.

51   Ibid., pp. 10–11.

52   Strawson, 2004.

53   Felix Warnock, personal communication.

54   Ibid.

55   UA, 5, pp. 20–21.

56   Ibid., p. 23.

57   Ibid., p. 19.

58   Warnock, 2000, p. 16.

59   Letter, GW to MW, 5 July 1948.

60   Ibid.

61   Ibid., 9 September 1948.

62   UA, 5, p. 24.

63   Warnock, 2000, p. 16.

64   UA, 5, p. 25.

4. The Good Life

'Bliss it was in that dawn to be alive, but to be young was very heaven.' With this quotation from William Wordsworth, John Searle, an American undergraduate and postgraduate student in the Oxford Faculty of Philosophy between 1952 and 1959, concludes his account of his years in Oxford. Searle, a Rhodes scholar, claims that he was exposed to 'one of the greatest collections of philosophers in one place since Athens in the fifth century B. C.'[1] There was, he writes, no giant of the stature of Aristotle or Plato, but he lists twenty-three Oxford philosophers of the time, including Mary Warnock, who published prolifically and had international reputations.[2]

The pre-eminence of Oxford in the study of philosophy which Searle described was, at the time Mary became part of the faculty, relatively new. Until the Second World War, Cambridge, where G. E. Moore, Bertrand Russell and Ludwig Wittgenstein taught, had held this position. The turning point came with the Oxford philosophy school's response to the publication in 1936 of A. J. Ayer's book *Language, Truth and Logic*.[3] Ayer had studied philosophy in Vienna where the so-called 'Vienna Circle' had developed the philosophical position known as logical positivism. This held that the only truthful statements were those that could be empirically confirmed. Logical positivism, a branch of linguistic philosophy, regarded the task of philosophy as the development of an ideal language that could be the basis of established truth. This could be derived from science and only from science, because only scientific propositions were verifiable. All other propositions, including all metaphysical statements and those that made statements of value as well as ethical, religious and aesthetic judgements, were essentially meaningless.[4] The way ordinary language was used was a barrier to the discovery of truth because it was so imprecise.

The Oxford analytic philosophers, who, apart from J. L. Austin, only began to contribute to the field after the end of World War Two, also

   https://doi.org/10.11647/OBP.0278.04

saw the study of language as the gateway to truth but, in contrast to the Logical Positivists, saw the attempt to establish an ideal language as unhelpful and the careful study of the way ordinary language was used to be a more profitable way to pursue truth. These Oxford philosophers, especially Gilbert Ryle and Peter Strawson, joined J. L. Austin in articulating what later became known as ordinary language philosophy. Austin, in particular, became a master of the study of the uses of language and of the nuanced ways in which the same words and phrases can be used differently. Thus, while the logical positivists saw language as having a 'truth' function, ordinary language philosophy regarded study of the 'use' function of language as far more productive. Wittgenstein's famous dictum: 'in most cases the meaning of a word is its use' may be seen as a concise formulation of this idea, though the Oxford school modified and elaborated on this concept in a variety of important ways.

Logical positivists, as we have seen, dismissed moral philosophy as meaningless and, although ordinary language philosophy did not take this position, inevitably as the most highly regarded analytic philosophers in Oxford were preoccupied with the analysis of ordinary language, other aspects of the subject received less attention. Mary wrote later: 'numerous and various as were the philosophers in Oxford, there was one characteristic they all shared, and that was a lack of interest in moral and political philosophy.'[5] These were, at that time, not fashionable subjects, and the ambitious men who dominated Oxford philosophy, with one or two exceptions such as R. M. Hare, were largely happy to leave it to their female colleagues such as Philippa Foot, whom Mary greatly admired. Mary studied ordinary-language or analytic philosophy intensely but was more attracted to moral philosophy: the nature of the good, together with the political and ethical ramifications of what the good entailed.

Also out of fashion was continental European philosophy. In Oxford this was held in some degree of contempt and largely dismissed. The phenomenology of Edmund Husserl, for example, and the existentialism of Jean-Paul Sartre, both of great significance to continental European philosophers, were barely taught. At a meeting of British and French philosophers held in 1958 at Royaumont, a French abbey north of Paris, ostensibly for mutual intellectual enrichment, Gilbert Ryle, a leader of the Oxford school, gave great offence by brusquely dismissing Husserl's ideas.[6]

Like Cambridge, Oxford was much more than it is now, when research is of greater importance in its standing, an educational institution primarily dedicated to the teaching of undergraduates. The method of undergraduate teaching at Oxford, especially in humanities subjects, allowed a great deal of autonomy to the student. He or she might be expected to attend only three or four university lectures a week and, as we have seen from the description of Mary's experience, it was the college which was the centre of undergraduate life, both academic and social. The undergraduate would attend a weekly tutorial organised by his college, at which he would be expected to present an essay to his tutor.[7] The tutorial might be in a small group of two or three but often it was one to one. John Searle, the American Rhodes scholar quoted earlier, describes how the eminent philosopher, Peter Strawson, who saw him individually, required him to deliver his weekly essay a day before his supervision.[8] When he arrived Strawson would suggest to him what he had been trying to say in his essay but putting Searle's formulation far more powerfully than he had managed himself. Searle would agree this was exactly what he had been trying to convey. Strawson would say '"Well then, it does seem to me that that view is subject to the following four objections", whereupon he would simply demolish the theory step by step.'[9] This would be done with the utmost civility without any expression of hostility. Searle felt this was the best teaching he had ever had, or ever would have, in his life.

Mary's duties as a philosophy don at St. Hugh's were periodically, but only periodically, onerous. John Searle was undoubtedly right to marvel at the individual brilliance and international eminence of the members of the faculty, but at Oxford and Cambridge in particular, when a young academic such as Mary was elected to her first academic position, it was as a member of a college, as opposed to a university-wide faculty with which she was identified and her primary task was teaching undergraduates in her college rather than tackling thorny philosophical problems. During term-time, Mary would conduct eighteen or more tutorials a week with undergraduates and postgraduates as well as delivering two or three faculty lectures a term. Lecturing however only took place during term time and each of the three terms only lasted eight weeks. So, Mary's hectic teaching schedule lasted for less than half the year. Postgraduate teaching did go on during the vacations but did not make much of a call on Mary's time and, in any case, could be arranged to suit her own needs. There is no systematic evidence of the quality of Mary's teaching, but the reports of those who were her students suggest she made excellent rapport with them.

Sarah Curtis (née Myers), who later went on to work as one of the first women journalists on *The Times,* was an Exhibitioner at St. Hugh's and was tutored by Mary in moral philosophy from 1954 to 1958. Sarah thought Mary was not an original thinker but a marvellously lucid teacher.[10] She made the careful and subtle arguments of Hume and Kant, for example, understandable to her for the first time. Mary used examples from everyday life to illustrate moral problems. 'She taught me,' Sarah claimed, 'how to think. She made you feel you were wonderful.'[11] In addition, as her moral tutor, Mary helped to disentangle Sarah from difficulties in her relationships with boyfriends. Sarah came from a largely secular Jewish background and Mary, probably for personal reasons arising from her own background, was particularly interested in this aspect of Sarah's life. When it became clear that Sarah was going to marry a non-Jew, Mary helped her to sort out how she was going to deal with her family's attitude to her 'marrying out.' Towards the end of her time as an undergraduate, she and Mary became personal friends. Sarah had her first baby in the same week as Maria (Boz), Mary's youngest, was born and this was a bond between them. Occasionally, when the needs of Mary's young children made it necessary, Sarah had tutorials in the family home in Chadlington Road. Mary's children were largely out of sight, presumably being looked after by their nanny. Sarah stayed in contact with Mary after she graduated and found her helpful when, much later, she was working in the field of fostering and adoption. She was in no doubt of her debt to Mary. She called her 'the most formative person in my life. Love is a silly word, but I did love her.'[12] For some of the students at St. Hugh's, such as Sarah, she was a role model pointing to ways they themselves might be able to combine professional work and full family life. Another student recalled how Mary 'seemed to us to be constantly pregnant or involved with very small children [...] billowing up St. Giles on her bicycle, exasperated at the beginning of my tutorial because Kit (and Felix) had, to be helpful, just put into the bath all the clean clothes that had been put out for them to wear.'[13]

Fig. 2 St. Hugh's College members, taken during Mary's time there (1949–66), with Mary Warnock front row, ninth from the right. Photograph provided by kind permission of the Principal and Fellows of St. Hugh's College, Oxford, copyright Gillman & Soame.

A little later, in 1960, Onora O'Neill, who became a distinguished moral philosopher herself and a colleague of Mary's in the House of Lords, spent a month having tutorials with her, writing essays, and reading the works of Hobbes, Locke, Rousseau and Marx. Onora was struck by 'how much fun and how jolly she was.'[14] At about the same time, Adrian Whitfield, later a barrister and Treasurer of the Middle Temple, came into contact with Mary when she gave him tutorials. The text they studied in Greek, was Aristotle's *Organon*. He found it tough going, not 'because of the way in which Mary Warnock tutored me, but because of the inherent difficulty of the exercise. My memory of her as a tutor is one of a person of great patience and clarity of expression.'[15] Much later, in the early 1980s, Patrick Lawrence, who was studying Politics, Philosophy and Economics at Christ Church was sent to Mary by his college tutors. They had been unimpressed by his work in philosophy with, he now thinks, good reason. Mary prepared Lawrence for the paper on Aristotle, but her teaching and guidance extended well beyond

Aristotelian ethics. He found Mary's supervision far more stimulating than any he had previously experienced and started to work hard. After he had handed in a few essays, she was pleased. 'If your other subjects are as good as this, I think you could get a First,' she said. This he did, going on to become a successful barrister and member of the House of Lords.[16]

Mary was elected a Fellow of St. Hugh's in 1952, three years after her original lectureship appointment and, as a new fellow, she soon became more involved in the governance and politics of the college.[17] St. Hugh's was a relative newcomer, not accorded full college status, with the right of representation on the University Council until 1959.[18] From 1920, in contrast to Cambridge, women at Oxford had the right to be full members of the university, and to graduate with degrees equivalent to those of men. Generally, women's colleges were somewhat smaller than were those for men, their student numbers having been capped by the university authorities. Most had between 150 and 300 undergraduates (St. Hugh's had 180) while men's colleges ranged in size from 50 to 450 with most taking around 300 students.

At the time Mary was at St. Hugh's in the 1950s and 1960s, just over a quarter of Oxford undergraduates were women. They led restricted lives, not permitted to be members of the Oxford Union, the university debating society, until 1962, or to be full members of the leading drama society, the Oxford University Dramatic Society (OUDS) until 1964.[19] Men were not allowed in their rooms unless authorised and signed in until the 1980s.[20] They had greater academic demands on them, expected to write two essays a week rather than one as the men did. Their academic achievements were on a par with the men, with more first-class degrees than men in the five years from 1950 to 1973. All the same, they often were made to feel outsiders. Only one of ninety-seven university professors was female.[21] A woman undergraduate recalled of the late 1950s, 'in my days going to Oxford as a female was like being on the sidelines of a gigantic male public school.'[22]

Up to the time Mary was appointed, all but one of the fellows, the senior members of St. Hugh's, had been unmarried.[23] The fact that Mary was married was regarded with suspicion by the other fellows who doubted if she would be able to give the commitment to the college that full-time residence within its walls made possible. For the single fellows their college was not just the place they taught; it was their home. Their fellow dons were their family. Every day, they lunched and dined together and, after dinner, they retired to the Senior Common Room to converse and gossip together. Some of them almost certainly slept together as sexual partners. As Mary describes the atmosphere, when the fellows were gathered together, 'tension was never absent; jealousy, spite, passionate suppressed love, suspicion of the new [...] were all ingredients in the excitable atmosphere.'[24] Not surprisingly, groups of fellows with similar interests were formed. Susan Chenevix-Trench said her heart sank when, shortly after her appointment to St. Hugh's in 1950, she was asked if 'she would belong to the Bird faction or the Flower faction.'[25]

Although it was over twenty-five years since a major internal dispute known as 'The Row' had divided the members of the St. Hugh's Senior Common Room, the college atmosphere remained strained by this event.[26] In 1923, a history don, Cecilia Ady, had been summarily dismissed by the then Principal, Eleanor Jourdain, with whom she had a long-standing tense and difficult relationship having been accused of leaking information about the proposed appointment of a Vice-Principal. A number of the other fellows resigned in protest. Eventually, an enquiry carried out by Lord Curzon, the Vice-Chancellor, exonerated Ady, but Eleanor Jourdain died just before she was due to resign.

Jourdain was decidedly eccentric. Together with her close friend, Annie Moberley, she had written a best-selling book published in 1911, *An Adventure*, about a paranormal experience that had occurred to them when they were visiting Versailles in 1901. They reported having seen figures dressed in late eighteenth-century dress whom they supposed were spirits revisiting their old haunts.[27] By the time Mary arrived, Jourdain had long since been replaced as principal, but the atmosphere of wilfulness and irresponsibility she had helped create lingered in the St. Hugh's Senior Common Room. In the 1923 Adey affair many undergraduates had sided with her against Jourdain. It was an early revolt against old ways that presaged later changes. During the 1930s, women undergraduates obtained freedoms from restrictions that nowadays are difficult to imagine. They were, for example, allowed for the first time to attend lectures without a chaperone and to join the university's political societies.[28] Even in Mary's day, nevertheless, discriminations and old attitudes persisted.

Mary thought her married status was accepted only because her husband was also a don, a fellow of Magdalen College. Her tenuous hold on acceptability was, however, called seriously into question when she began to have children. Kitty's birth in 1950 was followed shortly afterwards by that of Felix. Mary wrote that their names were a piece of good luck because the other fellows could ask after them very much as they asked after each other's pets: cats, dogs and tortoises.[29] She recalled the experience of Susan Chenevix-Trench, appointed to a lectureship at about the same time she was. Susan had only been in post a few weeks, when she had to go to the then Principal, a Miss Procter, to say that she was shortly to be married. Like Mary, she was also marrying a don, Oscar Wood, a fellow of Christ Church, but even so, the Principal made her feel guiltily at fault. Mary waited for her outside the Principal's door and described her, on emerging, as 'shaken to the core.'[30] During the 1960s and 1970s, more and more married women were appointed as fellows and more began to live out of college, so that Mary's position became less anomalous.[31] Indeed she began to act as a role model in this respect. Besides, as time went on, and her profile beyond the confines of the college began to rise, fewer of her activities were centred on the college and more on the university and university societies. This was the case for a number of women dons as they looked more widely for professional and social relationships.[32]

Life at the college became much more enjoyable for Mary in 1954 when an English scholar, Rachel Trickett, was elected to a tutorship there.[33] Rachel, although not married, had a life of her own outside college. Most other fellows had moved directly from undergraduate study to research lectureships and then to fellowships and had virtually no experience outside the university. Before her arrival Rachel had worked as a curator in an art gallery, as a lecturer at a provincial university, Hull, and had written a highly acclaimed novel as well as a libretto for an opera.[34] She and Mary had been contemporaries at Lady Margaret Hall during the war and could reminisce happily about their equally dreadful wartime experiences. They could also discuss together the fraught and, in retrospect, hilariously eccentric meetings of the St.

Hugh's Governing Body.[35] Geoffrey would listen to these conversations and marvel at the contrast with the sedate method of conducting business at Magdalen, his own college.[36]

There was a small number of other St. Hugh's dons Mary found sympathetic. One was Olga Bickley, who, despite her surname was part Russian and part Italian.[37] In the Long Vacation she lived in a large palazzo near Genoa. She would sometimes arrive several days late for the beginning of the academic year, enraging the Principal with her excuse that she had been treading out the grapes. The other colleague whose company Mary enjoyed was Agnes Headlam-Morley, the Professor of International Relations.[38] Agnes was a devout Catholic and tried, unsuccessfully to convert Mary to her faith. It was through her and the Catholic connection that the Warnocks met Frank Longford, the prison reformer and member of the House of Lords. Longford often came to stay with the Warnocks when he was speaking at the Oxford Union.[39]

For some married people it is a relief to leave their work behind after a busy day. This was the reverse of how Mary felt. She wrote, 'I pity people who do not share a professional interest with their spouse.'[40] Academic stimulation for her began at home. Her husband, Geoffrey, was establishing a reputation as an outstanding philosopher. His book on the early eighteenth-century idealist, Bishop Berkeley, published in 1953 was highly regarded.[41] Mary particularly admired Geoffrey's prodigious memory which helped fill gaps in her knowledge of nineteenth- and twentieth-century political history. Through their separate work they got to know the leading philosophers in Oxford and many elsewhere. Between them, they developed a 'pattern of talk and entertaining' which lasted throughout their lives.[42]

The most stimulating philosophical events Mary attended were the Saturday morning meetings organised by John Austin (professionally known as J. L. Austin), as we have seen, one of the leaders of analytic philosophy.[43] Geoffrey was a regular attender at these meetings but, because they were all-male affairs, Mary was initially excluded. When Mary approached Austin to ask permission to attend, his response was that he would like to invite her but he didn't know if the rules permitted it. As he himself was the organiser and made up the rules as he went along, this did not make much sense. Shortly after Mary approached him, he called at the Warnock house in North Oxford and told her she might join.[44] She became the only woman participant.

After Austin died, Geoffrey edited his unpublished works and became a scholarly authority on his ideas, writing two books about them. Both he and Mary left personal reflections of these Saturday morning meetings. From Geoffrey's perspective, one remarkable feature of these occasions was the degree to which Austin exercised his authority, apparently effortlessly. Geoffrey believed Austin's motivation was to help his audience to see 'not only for our immediate group but for the sake of the subject, how desirable it was to get out of the "bogs and tracks" of familiar, time-hallowed philosophical campaigning.'[45] The meetings began with the selection of a philosophical work, sometimes classical such as Aristotles's *Nichomachean Ethics*, sometimes modern or even contemporary. The text would be analysed sentence by sentence using an 'ordinary language' approach around a theme chosen by Austin. So, for one term, discussion centred around the use of words such as 'tools.' Could words really be compared with using tools? How did tools differ from other things that were used, such as utensils and instruments? On another occasion, actual moral situations were discussed to examine the language people used to discuss them.[46] Austin's approach to problems was direct and straightforward. Mary recalled how R. M. Hare, the moral philosopher, whose theory of moral behaviour appealed to the idea of universally defensible principles, was asked how he would behave if he were offered a bribe by a candidate. He said he would say, 'I do not accept bribes on principle.' Austin interjected 'Would you, Hare? I'd just say "No, thanks."'[47]

Austin discouraged the use of any jargon and instead preferred to rely on the distinctions that could be made by examining the way language was normally used. His influence made his audience focus with great concentration on finding a solution to the problems that were being addressed. What Mary admired about him was his 'impressively direct, fresh and straightforward' approach. 'He seemed genuinely to want to go back to the beginning to cut away any philosophical jargon we might have picked up and use without thinking [...]'[48] These Saturday mornings were clearly the highlight of Mary's week. It was the feeling that what might happen was unpredictable, 'that light might be cast in unexpected ways which made these meetings, most of them so enlivening and such a strong defence against boredom, both for oneself and one's pupils.'[49] Indeed, Mary found these meetings very helpful in guiding the way she conducted her own tutorials with her pupils over the following weeks. She wrote: 'I was fully aware that what had been said and discussed on Saturday made a palpable difference to my teaching in the next week. It was extraordinary how often distinctions which had been apparently casually drawn proved relevant to whatever was the subject of a tutorial.'[50] Austin died prematurely of lung cancer in 1960 and attempts to revive Saturday morning meetings under other leadership failed.[51]

Although Mary managed to circumvent the rules against female attendance at Austin's meetings, she made no attempt to find her way into an all-male dining club of which Geoffrey was a member. This was simply called The Club. Its members were drawn from a variety of disciplines, particularly philosophy, economics and law. From what Mary gleaned from Geoffrey about the subjects discussed, a great deal of time was spent in deciding who should be invited to be a member. The criteria were unclear but some degree of social smartness, high intelligence and a capacity both for amusing others and being amused oneself were essential. The members dined twice a term in the college of one of its members.[52] A great deal of the rest of the time was spent in gossip about colleagues. Mary suspected that the reason why the distinguished philosopher Stuart Hampshire was never elected was because, if he had been, it would no longer have been possible to gossip about his personal life which was a rich source of amusement to the existing members. These called each other 'Brother.' Thus, 'Brother Warnock' called Isaiah 'Brother Berlin' so this in itself was a reason why a woman could never be a member. When eventually its members decided that a woman, not Mary, should be invited to join, there was consternation as to how she should be addressed. In the end she was also called 'Brother,' perhaps an early though not very politically correct example of gender blindness.

Through their separate work, Mary and Geoffrey were familiar with all the leading philosophers at Oxford and many elsewhere. Mary attended occasional lectures given by Stuart Hampshire, Isaiah Berlin, Gilbert Ryle, Bernard Williams and A. J. Ayer and sometimes attended the same social gatherings as they did. The presence of these

philosophers, some of whom were based in Oxford with others visiting
from time to time, made philosophy the exciting subject it was widely
seen to be. Analytic philosophy was not the only subject in which
there was outstanding teaching. For example, Bernard Williams ran a
seminar on Kant, H. L. A. Hart talked about freedom of the will from
the point of view of the philosophy of jurisprudence and Isaiah Berlin
lectured regularly on human rights. The only philosophers Mary saw
more frequently, indeed much more frequently, were Peter Strawson
and Marcus Dick. The Warnocks talked philosophy with them, but the
relationship was not primarily academic. As the next chapter will show,
Mary, Geoffrey and their children became close family friends with both
the Strawsons and the Dicks.

There were two women philosophers, both fellows at Somerville,
who impressed Mary. She greatly admired Philippa Foot's major
philosophical contribution: her insistence, contrary to current teaching
by logical positivists, that values could not be separated from facts.
Mary regarded Philippa, with whom she had little contact, as 'someone
infinitely above me, as one might regard a much older member of a
grand family.'[53] Elizabeth Anscombe, a strong champion and friend
of Ludwig Wittgenstein,[54] the Cambridge philosopher, taught Mary
as an undergraduate. She was unimpressed by Mary as a student and
told her she would never make an academic philosopher.[55] After Mary
graduated, they saw little of each other especially after Anscombe was
appointed to a chair in philosophy at Cambridge.[56]

Anscombe's devotion to Wittgenstein, an enthusiasm which Mary
found hard to share,[57] played a key role in one particularly memorable
meeting of the Jowett Society.[58] This had been an undergraduate society
but in the post-war period it became the custom for dons to attend and read
or reply to papers. Because everyone, dons as well as undergraduates,
had been away, all had papers to read and ideas to discuss. Anscombe
had spoken to the Jowett Society of the work Wittgenstein was doing
in Cambridge, a kind of philosophy very different from his *Tractatus
Logico-Philosophicus* (1921). In 1947 Mary, during her term as secretary
of the society, encouraged Anscombe to persuade Wittgenstein to attend
one of the Jowett meetings (though not to read a paper). The meeting
in Magdalen on 14 May 1947 had been eagerly awaited and was a
highly charged affair. The room was packed by the time Wittgenstein

arrived to take his place at a small table between Anscombe and the young Oscar Wood, then an undergraduate at Corpus Christi, who was to read a paper on whether Descartes' 'cogito ergo sum' is a valid argument. Wittgenstein was to reply but, according to Mary's account at the time, he struggled to say anything coherent at all. He began by saying, accusingly, that Mr. Wood had appeared to make two points, one about knowledge and one about substance, but Wittgenstein was almost inaudible and his sentences trailed off before he had finished, whereupon he would laboriously start again. Wood tried to steer him towards talking about knowledge, but Wittgenstein seemed 'in an agony of indecision.' There were long periods of silence when Wittgenstein tore his hair or buried his head in his hands, occasionally muttering to himself 'No, that's not right at all.' Mary declared herself familiar with 'this way of going on' because Anscombe had, as a true acolyte, adopted many of the same mannerisms.[59]

Amongst those present was an aged and eminent don H. A. Prichard, who had been Austin's tutor at Balliol before the war, sitting immediately beside the table where the main protagonists were placed. He was afflicted by a terrible cough which silenced everyone when a fit came on. Prichard was becoming more and more angry and tried to intervene three times to get Wittgenstein to address the question Oscar Wood had asked. At one stage, not in reply to Prichard, but more or less out of the blue, Wittgenstein said 'If a man looked up at the sky and said "I think it's going to rain therefore I am" I should not understand him.' This was too much for Prichard, who said: 'With respect to you and your colleagues, what Descartes said is of far more importance than anything you have said,' got up and 'tottered out, to everyone's acute embarrassment.' Shortly after this, Wittgenstein suggested an adjournment until the following afternoon, a proposal which was greeted with general relief as it was already past eleven p.m.

The next day there were fewer senior members of the university present and no Prichard. This time Wittgenstein made no pretence of responding to Oscar Wood's paper but embarked on an apparently directionless set of observations which began to take some suggestive shape as they developed, talking first about the difference between 'psychological' verbs describing experiences and others, then launching into a discourse on thinking of the different languages we use and keep ready to hand like tools in a box. This was unfamiliar territory for most of the undergraduates present, including Mary, who describes coming away exhausted, but feeling on the brink of understanding something completely new. It was not until a year later that Anscombe showed her some parts of her translation of what was to be the *Philosophical Investigation* (1953), and 'things began to fall into place.'

A third colleague who made a deep impression on Mary at the time was Iris Murdoch, then a fellow of St. Anne's, who was shortly to make another career as a celebrated novelist.[60] They first met in 1948 when Iris was twenty-nine, five years older than Mary, who found her 'a figure of enormous glamour and romance.'[61] Murdoch had travelled all over Europe working with UNRRA (the United Nations Relief and Rehabilitation Agency).[62] The man she had been in love with had been killed in the war, following which she had numerous, well-publicised romantic relationships. After a brilliant undergraduate career during which she had been sexually harassed by the same older don who had abused Mary (see Chapter Three) she had gone on to pursue careers first as a civil servant and then both as a novelist and as an academic philosopher. Mary reports that she had only one proper conversation with her,[63] but there were numerous similarities in their lives and values. Both married other Oxford dons. In 1956, Murdoch married John Bayley, an English don at New College. Both Murdoch and Mary wrote books about existentialism but were simultaneously fascinated and repelled by it. Iris's book dealt mainly with Sartre as novelist but had a chapter on his philosophy.[64] Mary's much more extensive work on existentialism is discussed later in this chapter. Both were, in an important sense, deeply religious but did not believe in God. Both were moral philosophers but there were considerable philosophical differences between them. Murdoch was a thoroughgoing Platonist, endorsing the Idea of the Good.[65] Mary reports that she loved Plato, but was more of an Aristotelian by temperament.[66]As they moved into middle and older age, they moved further apart in their approach to moral philosophy. While Mary's approach was rooted in the practical moral problems she confronted in her public life, Iris's philosophical ideas became more and more metaphysical, culminating in her book *Metaphysics as a Guide to Morals* (1992) which Mary, like many others, found virtually unreadable.[67]

In 1953, shortly after Geoffrey's book on Bishop Berkeley had been published, Mary met a BBC Talks Producer who was lunching at St. Hugh's. Mary suggested there might be some interest in Geoffrey giving a talk on the Third Programme about his book. The Third Programme, the precursor of Radio Three, was increasingly looking to Oxbridge dons to give talks on their subjects. They, in their turn, were delighted at the publicity that was offered to them for their work. So pleased were they that there was a story going the rounds about an Oxford philosopher who, on the suggestion he might give a broadcast talk, for which the fee would be twenty pounds, asked the producer if he should pay the twenty-pound fee by cash or cheque. The Warnocks were not as naïve as this and were simply content that broadcasting could provide them with at least a small, additional income.

Geoffrey gave his talk to great approval. It was then suggested by another BBC Talks Producer, T. S. Gregory, that there would be interest in a series of broadcast debates between philosophers on topics of general interest. Gregory came to Oxford, stayed with the Warnocks and drank much of their brandy and a format was agreed for a series of broadcast debates on philosophical topics. The Warnocks recruited Peter Strawson and David Pears, dons at University College and Christ Church respectively. So these four dons, Mary and Geoffrey Warnock, Peter Strawson and David Pears, sometimes joined by other philosophers, broadcast a number of debates in 1953 and 1954.[68] Topics included the nature of perception, personal identity and explanations of human behaviour. Although a perfunctory attempt was made to suggest the debates were spontaneous, they were carefully rehearsed. The four participants would first have an informal meeting with Gregory to work out the ground to be covered. They went away and each wrote a script for themselves. Then they would meet and mesh their prepared scripts together, with each taking a part, after which they would all go up to Broadcasting House in London for what might be termed their performance. Mary often played a secondary role as was still seen as generally appropriate for a woman. She asked questions because she didn't quite understand what was being said. She wrote later, 'my usual role was to play the silly-ass character, who didn't understand and needed something to be said again in different words.'[69] According to her, these performances were derided by the more professional performers among their academic colleagues such as Isaiah Berlin, Stuart Hampshire and Iris Murdoch. Mary felt that, for her, the discussions which preceded the broadcasts were highly educational and again, informed her teaching.

These broadcasts did little to enhance Mary's academic status. Such status in Oxford at that time depended particularly on two areas of achievement, principally the quality of one's teaching and lecturing. In the 1980s and 1990s, research output became virtually the only criterion of academic status but from the 1950s to the 1970s it was the quality of a don's teaching that marked him or her out as anything between outstanding and downright poor. Some historians such as Hugh Trevor-Roper and Alan (A. J. P.) Taylor developed national reputations by lecturing on their subject on television. Lecturers such as Isaiah Berlin attracted undergraduate audiences that went far beyond those studying for degrees in philosophy. But it was the don's capacity for engaging and inspiring undergraduates face-to-face, often in one-to-one supervision that made his or her reputation. As the social historian José Harris wrote of this period, 'Oxford continued to reserve the highest palm for the dedicated Socratic tutor who made overall guidance of the young a higher priority than his own or other people's learned publications.'[70] Mary was reckoned, as we have seen, to be an excellent supervisor, but as a don in a woman's college, specialising in a branch of philosophy that was not as fashionable as the analytic study of language, it was unlikely that she would be given the opportunity to supervise the brightest men.

The production of original work was the other criterion for academic status. In philosophy, this was measured especially by the publication of original articles in a prestigious philosophical academic journal such as *The Philosophical Review* or *Mind*. Highest status was won if the article produced major debate and controversy, stimulating other philosophers to disagree or expand on the original thesis. Second-best was publishing a book that had a similar effect. Mary reckoned that she did not have the capacity for such original thought as would be required for an article in a professional journal. For this, she wrote, one had to be, using a metaphor coined by her undergraduate tutor, Eduard Fraenkel, a 'blood and bones' philosopher, someone who lived and breathed philosophical ideas and arguments; she did not count herself as one of those, though Onora O'Neill disagrees.[71] All the same, she was ambitious to achieve in her field and the opportunity came to write books that were not in the first rank of original philosophical thinking but that served a useful purpose in articulating the thoughts of others, placing their work in the context of the history of ideas. It was in this way that Mary made her academic mark.

During the latter part of the 1950s, Mary was commissioned by J. L. Austin, the editor of a series of books of philosophical topics published by Oxford University Press, to write a book on recent philosophical contributions to moral philosophy.[72] Geoffrey had already published *English Ethics since 1900* (1957) in this series.[73] Mary's *Ethics since 1900* (1960) turned out to be a lucid survey of ethical thought in English-speaking philosophy since the late nineteenth century.[74] The main thrust of the book was dissatisfaction—by then quite widely shared—with deflationary mid-century attempts to deny moral judgments their authority in a science-minded world and so rob moral philosophy of its distinctive subject matter.

Mary's book begins with a brief account of F. H. Bradley's 'metaphysical ethics' and goes on to consider at greater length G. E. Moore's *Principia Ethica* (1903). She then discusses the work of the intuitionist and emotivist approaches to ethics and points to their indebtedness to Charles Stevenson, the American philosopher. She senses that moral philosophers are slowly beginning to realise the importance of the inter-relationships of persons as moral agents, making moral evaluations and facing practical moral problems.

Mary concluded *Ethics since 1900* with a rather negative judgement on those philosophers whose work she had discussed. The one common theme taken by moral philosophers over the period, she noted, is that they are all hostile to ethical naturalism, that is they all agree that defining the good cannot depend on an assumption, the 'naturalistic fallacy,' that the good is based on natural properties or features of the natural world.[75] Mary, who was herself unhappy with the naturalistic fallacy, nevertheless considered that the concentration of the philosophers who rejected it on the basis of linguistic analysis of ethical language had resulted in 'the increasing triviality of the subject.'[76] Most such philosophers of this period seemed determined to avoid expressing any moral opinions at all. In Ayer's view, this was desirable. He drew the distinction between moral philosophers who analyse moral judgements and moralists who elaborate moral codes or encourage their observance.[77] Mary felt that confining the scope of moral philosophy to such arid analysis was likely to condemn the subject to triviality and she expressed the hope that philosophers might turn their attention to 'how people actually decide, or what moral decisions are actually like.[78]

The critical reception of *Ethics since 1900* by contemporary philosophers was largely positive. Her account of the subject was repeatedly referred to as not only readable but lucid. Nevertheless, her rejection of the linguistic analysis of ethical language was questioned. A. C. Ewing, for example, thought it was of real practical importance to give a coherent (linguistic) account of ethics to defend against the charge that 'ethics is merely a subjective matter incapable of real justification.'[79] *Ethics since 1900* went into three editions and remained in print for many years. It was found by successive generations of undergraduates studying philosophy to be of invaluable assistance in preparation for their final examinations. One such Oxford student in the late 1960s recalled it fifty years later as 'immensely helpful as it was written so clearly.'[80]

Mary's book was nearing completion when, one morning, she was telephoned by Austin to request that she include a chapter on existentialism.[81] She described how she spent the whole of the following Long Vacation in 1959 reading works by Jean-Paul Sartre, existentialism's founding father. Indeed in his address at the memorial service held six months after Mary died, her son Felix recalled how, during the summer of 1959, when he was seven and had a sister one year older and a younger brother and sister, his mother 'simply cast us children loose on the beach, to sink or swim, or possibly just freeze to death, as we chose, while she took up position on an exposed rock armed with a battered copy of Sartre's *L'Etre et le néant* and a large French dictionary. In the midst of family chaos, she was at work on her first book.'[82]

Although, on her own account, she had no previous special interest in existentialism, Mary was by no means unqualified to write about it. She was already knowledgeable in one of its primary sources, German phenomenology, the influential school of which Husserl (dismissed by Ryle) was a leading thinker. She had studied Descartes, but she was far less familiar with the more recent French philosophical tradition. She did, however, speak reasonably fluent French and this was an advantage. When Mary came to write about Sartre, *L'Etre et le néant* (1943) had just been translated as *Being and Nothingness* (1957) into contorted English, which made Sartre's obscurity even worse than it was in the original.[83] Mary preferred to read Sartre's work in French without a translator as an intermediary.

There were, in fact, various reasons why Mary should have found writing about existentialism a congenial task. By mid-century, Germany had lost its earlier intellectual pre-eminence. In the nineteenth century, from Kant onwards, it had been in the forefront not only of philosophical ideas but in virtually all branches of scientific endeavour. It had lost ground after the First World War, and by the end of the Second World War the country was in ruins not only physically but culturally. Most of the leading German-speaking philosophers, many of them Jewish, had fled Germany in the 1930s. Indeed, as we have seen, Mary had been taught by some of them during her undergraduate days in Oxford. Instead of Germany, the world now looked to France for intellectual leadership in the humanities and to the United States and Britain in the sciences. With extraordinary speed, after 1945, for any young writer, artist or philosopher, Paris became the most exciting place in the world to be. Existentialism became a byword 'for the young and rebellious who took it on as a way of life and a trendy label.'[84]

Jean-Paul Sartre had become the undisputed leader of French philosophical thought. He was not just a philosopher, he was a novelist and dramatist who had become a cult hero, indeed a celebrity. In 1945, when Iris Murdoch went to hear him speak in Brussels where she was then based, she found that vast crowds larger than those that had been attracted at a recent visit by Chico, the Marx brother celebrity, had turned out to see him.[85] As we have seen, Iris was one of Mary's intellectual heroes in Oxford. Herself a philosopher and novelist, she had been deeply influenced by Sartre and had, as we have seen, published a book about him.[86] Mary was in awe of her. If Iris could take Sartre seriously, there was every reason why Mary should do so too. While in fact there is rather little similarity between what Iris Murdoch had to say about existentialism and what she herself wrote, Mary regarded the philosophical chapter in Iris's book as 'an indispensable and saving thread to guide me through the labyrinth of what seemed at first to be impenetrable prose that I had to make sense of [...]'[87] Later, Mary admitted that, having been brought up in the somewhat austere atmosphere at Oxford, one of the most amazing things about first reading Sartre was that he was prepared to talk philosophically about passion and love, sex and obesity, cooking and all sorts of domestic subjects. There is an amazing passage in *Being and Nothingness*, about the nature of the obscene, which would have been regarded in English philosophy as pornography.[88]

Sartre thus appealed to Mary's imaginative spirit, even though she was, at the same time, repelled by many aspects of his philosophy.

As Mary recounted, the basic concept on which existentialism rests is that 'existence precedes essence.'[89] What Sartre means by this is that human beings, in contrast to inanimate objects, are not made to certain specifications to fulfil a certain purpose. Instead, they first exist and what they become depends on what they choose to do. Sartre gives as an example a paper knife which is designed for a specific purpose. A cook, in contrast, is not born a cook, he chooses to become one.[90] Mary points out that people are not by any means perfectly free to choose to become whatever they want. This is indeed illustrated by the characters in Sartre's novels who are constrained, at least to some degree, by their circumstances. Sartre calls an inanimate object a 'being-in-itself.' Human beings, in contrast, are 'beings for themselves.'[91] In explaining human behaviour, Sartre suggests that 'beings-for-themselves' to fill a void strive to achieve a purpose for themselves and it is from this striving that much of their conscious life arises. One prominent feature of this conscious life common to human beings is *nausea*, experienced as a reaction to the senselessness, the absurdity of the world.[92] Another feature is the sense of *viscosity*, (stickiness), Sartre's general term for things that are neither clearly material nor clearly mental and so disturb us by being hard to categorise in ways that go beyond the sense of touch.[93] *Sliminess* is a good example. It is not strictly a physical property. It depends crucially on us. But nor is it purely mental like the thought of the Eiffel Tower or abstract, like the number five. The unpleasant sensations of nausea and viscosity are avoided, Sartre contends, by a mental process (what psychoanalysts would call a 'defence mechanism') that he calls *mauvoise foi* or *bad faith*.[94]

Sartre stretched this concept of bad faith to include other ways in which we deny our freedom, avoid making choices and take refuge in playing a role rather than in making a definite life choice. Mary quotes two examples from *Being and Nothingness* to illustrate this idea. The first is a woman who is being courted sexually by a man. She allows her hand to remain in his when he takes it, not as an active decision, but to postpone a decision about whether to allow a sexual relationship to develop.[95] The second example is of a waiter in a café who rather than really choosing to be a waiter, is playing the part of waiter. He performs the role of a waiter, speaking and moving in prescribed ways in order to avoid the many choices available to him as a human being. This, Sartre alleges, results in the waiter being in the mode of *'Being-what-I-am-not.'*[96] Mary suggests these examples of bad faith arise because of what Sartre would regard as the individual's wish to become an object, a being-in-itself, like a paper knife.[97]

Mary points out that the problem with these explanations of human behaviour, a problem shared by psychoanalytic explanations with some of which they have more than a passing resemblance, is that they cannot be refuted.[98] There is no way they could be shown to be wrong. She is more sympathetic to Sartre's well-known analysis of shame. He gives the example of a man who, out of perhaps curiosity or jealousy, is looking through a keyhole. Suddenly he hears footsteps and realises he is observed. The feelings this experience arouse in him such as guilt and shame reveal several important features about human relationships. First, the suggestion from sceptical philosophers that other people could be mere delusions—there may not even exist 'other minds'—is fatally undermined by experiences such as these. We could not experience such feelings of shame unless we knew that the observer of our shameful behaviour was 'essentially' the same as us and would disapprove or hold us in contempt.

There is a basic tension in Sartre's world between a person's actual freedom and his/her appearance as an object for the other. Mary finds this part of Sartre's theory fascinating. She says it 'has a kind of bewildering power which derives from the intensity of Sartre's imaginative vision of each of us forming his own interpretations of the world, and locked in a constant battle with other people, with whom we are obliged to recognise as possessing as much freedom as we do ourselves.'[99] However Mary remains critical of Sartre's overall metaphysics which, she says, is too vague and incoherent to lead to any definite conclusions. His supreme value is freedom, but 'it is not wholly clear to what a man is committed if he chooses freedom, or what his alternatives are.'[100] What is clear is that Sartre considers that it is not possible to distinguish moral from political questions, which is why for Sartre, the question of whether to join the Communist Party was so significant. But joining any party almost inevitably leads to a man compromising his values and therefore to demonstrating 'bad faith.' So, Sartre's beliefs, in Mary's view, only lead to the asking of difficult questions to which he fails to provide answers. Mary's main contribution in the chapter on existentialism in *Ethics since 1900* was to put Sartre's ideas into more precise historical context than had previously been attempted, confirming her own view of herself as less a philosopher than a historian of ideas.

Although there were attractions to writing about existentialism, there were serious challenges too. The most daunting and, to Mary, the most irritating of these was Sartre's prose. She wrote of his style

> His method of composition is cumulative. He often attempts three or four ways of conveying a certain impression, which do not necessarily stay exactly the same as, and may even contradict each other. Almost everything he says about, for instance, perception, could be discussed and quarrelled with. But if one did that one would mistake his purpose; for, regrettably perhaps, he does not want to be precise, nor to get things exactly right. He is interested in presenting a picture of what things are like, in bludgeoning his readers into accepting a certain view of the world and he does not much care what weapons he uses to do this.[101]

Mary describes *L'Etre et le néant*, the key to much of Sartre's thought, as 'written in an extraordinarily thick, obscure style, full of technical terms of a grotesque kind, derived from Hegel.'[102] Such a style is almost exactly the opposite of that to which Mary herself aspired. Those who comment on her style use words like 'lucid' and 'precise.' So, in her chapter in *Ethics since 1900* and in her books on existentialism, she did her best to translate Sartre's obscurities into understandable ideas that could be discussed by those who wished to know more about them. Mary regarded her task as not to replay or précis Sartre's dialectical oratory, but to analyse the arguments he deployed. It was not an easy task.

A further problem in explaining Sartre's ideas even to an informed readership, was that these underwent a radical change in the years following the Second World War. A central tenet of existentialism, as we have seen, is that men (Sartre, in line with then current usage, refers to 'men' when he means 'people') are free to choose between courses of action and it is in the choices they make that they demonstrate their humanity. He writes in 1945 'the first effect of existentialism is that it puts every man in possession of himself as he is and places the entire responsibility for his existence squarely upon his own shoulders.'[103] It would scarcely be possible to articulate a more individualist doctrine. But by 1960, and the move had been apparent long before then, in *The Critique of Dialectical Reason*, Sartre had undergone a radical conversion to Marxism. At this point he had become convinced of the significance of history in determining the action of individuals and, 'the agent of change in history turns out to be not the individual free revolutionary, but the group of which he is a member.'[104] By 1960, from Mary's point of view, though not that of Sartre, who unsuccessfully sought to modify Marxism by introducing existentialist ideas, Sartre had ceased to be an existentialist in its original sense. Necessarily therefore, in explaining Sartre's ideas, she turned to his earlier formulations, though she took trouble to describe his subsequent conversion.

After the chapter on existentialism in *Ethics since 1900*, Mary was commissioned to write three more books as well as edit another book on the subject. Her own books expand on the historical context which underpins Sartre's philosophical work. She begins *The Philosophy of Sartre* (1965) with a discussion of the influence of Descartes, concluding with a discussion of the problem of reconciling Sartre's earlier views on the defining importance of individual freedom with his subsequent radical conversion to Marxism in his latest book, the *Critique of Dialectical Reason* (1960).[105] This had only just appeared when the earlier chapter in *Ethics since 1900* was written.

In *Existentialist Ethics* (1967) and *Existentialism* (1970), Mary considers some of the other philosophers who had influenced Sartre, in particular Friedrich Nietzsche, Sören Kierkegaard and Maurice Merleau-Ponty. The common theme here is the rejection of the claim of science to objective truth, pointing the way to Sartre's conclusion that perception precedes knowledge. Mary then reconsiders Sartre's own work, concluding, as she had done many times before, 'The Existentialists have given us many particular insights, especially in their discussion of persons, and of perception, but if philosophy is to continue to exist, then it is necessary to reject the subjective dogmatism of their attempt to reveal the ultimate meaning of Existence.'[106]

Finally, in this connection, there is a collection of critical essays Mary edited under the title *Sartre* (1971) in a series titled Modern Studies in Philosophy. This consists of fourteen essays written by British and American academics on different aspects of existentialism. After a lengthy exposition of Sartre's thought by Alisdair Macintyre and a brief review of *Being and Nothingness* by Stuart Hampshire, there are contributions by other philosophers, literary critics, and sociologists on the way Sartre's particular brand of existentialism has illuminated their fields of study.[107]

Mary's extensive writings on existentialism attracted some interest from British and French philosophers, but most of the reviewers were unimpressed. A. C. Ewing noted the contents of the chapter on this subject in *Ethics since 1900* but confessed he remained as puzzled by Sartre's philosophy and its mode of expression after he had read it as he had been beforehand.[108] French philosophers were slightly but not much more sympathetic. Gérard Deledalle in *Les études philosophiques* noted that Mary almost felt the need to excuse herself for spending time on a philosopher whose metaphysical approach had been so firmly rejected by British philosophers.[109] In a review of the book published in the *Revue Internationale de Philosophie*, the reviewer chose not to mention the chapter on existentialism at all.[110] Van Marter, in a review of the book on Sartre published in *Ethics*, reported that 'during 1963–64, if Oxford philosophers were asked what they had to say about contemporary philosophy at Paris, they usually replied by smiling incredulously at the thought that anyone should take seriously what goes on south of the Channel. Usually too [...] they paused long enough to point out with great sobriety that Mary Warnock was writing a book on Sartre.'[111] He considered that Mary's treatment of Sartre, including his theory of imagination, was conducted in 'a stimulating and seminal fashion [...] Her gift for terse expression often achieves results in formulation that are incisive and lucid.'[112]

One might well ask why Mary wrote so much about a philosophy which, she repeatedly said, she regarded as leading nowhere other than blind alleys. Indeed, in the last interview she gave only a few weeks before she died, when asked about existentialism, she said with great feeling 'I loathed it,' and explained this deep dislike on the basis of Sartre's lack of concern for evidence.[113] The answer to the question of why she devoted so much time to it is not clear, so we should perhaps accept Mary's own explanation that she was simply responding to commissions. If she had not quite 'cornered the market' in existentialism, she was, at least, an obvious choice of author because she had already shown interest in the subject and wrote as clearly as it was possible to write on a topic known for its difficulty. It is also possible that Sartre's philosophy was rather more attractive to her than she admitted. Far more than most people, at different times of her life, she exercised her freedom of choice in ways that might not have been expected. This was partly because her background and social contacts put her into a highly privileged position in the making of choices but also because features of her personality, especially her intellectual restlessness, made her particularly open to new challenges. To some degree at least, she lived out Sartre's idea of a good life by choosing to explore areas of life previously almost completely unfamiliar to her. There is a further reason why Mary might have been attracted to Sartre's writing. He constantly pointed to the way people avoided freedom by adopting the roles expected of them by virtue of their occupation or social status. Perhaps more than can be said of most people, Mary did not adopt the false selves that might have been expected of her. She was an unconventional female don by virtue of being married and having children. Though she loved her children, she was, as we shall see, in no way a typical mother. So, like Iris Murdoch, the other philosopher who wrote about existentialism though deploring its intellectual incoherence, she led the life she wanted to, not the life she might have been expected to. Iris Murdoch, in an essay entitled "On 'God' and 'Good'" wrote 'To do philosophy is to explore one's own temperament and yet at the same time to discover the truth.'[114] Mary would have agreed.

What impact did Mary's formidable set of publications have on anglophone interest in existentialism? There is no information on the numbers of her books that were sold, but it is likely sales were modest. There is also no evidence that Mary's books found anything other than an academic readership. All the same, by 1966, according to Geoffrey Strickland, Sartre was no longer a writer of the *avant-garde*. As an 'established classic,' he was a 'prescribed author in most English universities and also for A level examinations.'[115] However, existentialist philosophy, though it found a place in some schools of therapy, never

achieved the importance in English-speaking universities that it did in
continental Europe. In English and Cultural Studies, it was soon replaced
by various forms of post-modernist thought. Finally, what impact did
such intense exposure to existentialist thought have on Mary's own
philosophical ideas? Every time she wrote on the subject, she concluded
with a negative, often a strongly negative appraisal of Sartre's work.
While she admired the force of Sartre's style and the theatricality
with which he illustrated his arguments, she persisted in her belief
that existentialism did not add up to a coherent philosophical system.
Nevertheless, she continued, for the rest of her life, to acknowledge the
impact it had made on moral philosophy. In the introduction to a set of
readings from women philosophers—*Women Philosophers* (1996)—she
wrote 'I have no doubt that existentialism changed moral philosophy in
this country and made it less arid and depressing than it had been in the
period after the Second World War.'[116] She goes on to contend that, from
the 1960s onwards, as a result of the arousal of political consciousness
by the Vietnam War, university students all over the developed world
began to look for more relevance to political and social issues in the
content of their curriculum. 'Something akin to the existentialist mode,
at any rate the application of philosophy to live issues, began to appear
in almost all philosophy departments [...]'[117] Whether such intense
reading of existentialist philosophy played any part in Mary's own life
is not clear, but it is hard to think it can have had no effect. Mary was
not alone in thinking that existentialism had an enduring appeal. Nearly
fifty years after it was written, Richard Eyre, the British theatre director,
who was excited by existentialism in the 1960s, referred to *Being and
Nothingness* as providing 'a topographical account—a moral template
that helps me navigate the more shadowy parts of my existence'[118]

Mary's description of Oxford moral philosophy as 'arid and
depressing' before the advent of existentialism is telling. José Harris,
in her account of Oxford University arts and social sciences over this
period reports that 'by the 1950s linguistic philosophy had little to say
about theoretical and moral issues.' Its approach was increasingly seen
as purely negative, a judgement typified by an accusation Ayer levelled
at Austin: '[...] you are like a greyhound that refuses to race but bites the
other greyhounds to prevent their racing either.'[119] Mary might well have
had some sympathy with this view as well as with the London-based

philosopher, Bernard Williams, who wrote: 'Contemporary moral philosophy has found an original way of being boring, which is by not discussing moral issues at all [...] [it] leaves an impression that all the important issues are off the page and that great caution and little imagination have been used in letting tiny corners of them appear.'[120]

By the early 1960s Mary was looking at the possibility of finding a way out of academic philosophy. Although she gave other reasons for quitting her fellowship of St. Hugh's College in 1966, it seems likely that a sense of disillusionment with analytic thought, not just in moral philosophy but in other, more mainstream branches of the subject may have played some part in her decision. If that were the case, she would not have been alone. Much earlier, in 1950, Mary Midgley, the distinguished philosopher who focused especially on science, nature and the moral status of non-human animals, had left Oxford, where she was a fellow of Somerville College, for the University of Newcastle. In her autobiography, *The Owl of Minerva* (2005), she describes how, before she left, she attended a meeting of the Jowett Society, the discussion group Mary had chaired when she was an undergraduate, deeply depressed by the feuding that accompanied the arguments and by the progressive narrowing of the subject. She was much happier in Newcastle.[121] Another probably more influential refugee from Oxford philosophy was her senior colleague, Iris Murdoch. Iris's reasons for resigning from her fellowship at St. Anne's College in 1962 were mixed. She had become emotionally entangled with a woman colleague to a degree that had earned the disapproval of the Principal, Lady Ogilvie. Some of her students were finding her supervisions less than helpful. One described Iris spending the statutory hour lying mutely on the floor with her eyes closed. Probably most importantly, she was now achieving significant success as a novelist and wanted to be able to spend more time writing.[122] Whatever the reasons, Mary could see that it was possible for a woman don to find another life for herself out of Oxford academe.

Besides, Oxford was increasingly being seen by its own as a narrow and inward-looking place to be. *Camford Observed*, a book written in 1964 by two Cambridge dons, Jasper Rose and John Ziman, though largely couched in language sympathetic to the ancient universities, was a penetrating critique of the Oxbridge system. It pointed to the privileges of the don's life, the freedom he or she enjoyed and the lack of evidence that this level of autonomy produced results especially in the education of undergraduates which most then saw as the main purpose of these universities. The book was widely reviewed and discussed. Further, in the 1960s, new universities were being created in Britain and many young Oxbridge academics were attracted to found new departments in their subjects. As we shall see, the Warnocks' philosopher friend, Marcus Dick became one of these and there were dozens of others. In an account of her friendship with Rachel Trickett, the English don who became head of St. Hugh's, Mary claims that Rachel's novel *The Elders* (1966) gave the best account she had read of the atmosphere of Oxford in the Long Vacation.[123] Trickett describes a group of highly intelligent dons who spend the ample amounts of free time at their disposal during their sixteen-week summer holiday in scheming and gossiping over an academic appointment of trivial importance to anyone outside the university itself.[124] Mary must have wondered whether it was not time to seek work which would give her a wider context in which to exercise her talents.

Notes

1   John Searle, p. 173.

2   John Searle himself became an internationally renowned philosopher who went on after leaving Oxford to make a major contribution to the philosophy of consciousness. In his eighties, however, he was found guilty of sexually harassing several much younger female colleagues and stripped of his emeritus status at the University of California, Berkeley.

3   Ayer, 2001.

4   Warnock, 2000, p. 46.

5   Ibid., p. 49.

6   Ibid., pp. 184–185.

7   Thomas, p. 215.

8   Searle, p. 190.

9   Ibid., p. 196.

10   Sarah Curtis, née Myers, personal communication, 27 January 2020.

11   Ibid.

12 Ibid.

13 Schwartz, 2011, p. 84.

14 Onora O'Neill, 'Mary Warnock remembered', *The Observer*, 14 December 2019.

15 Adrian Whitfield, personal communication, 21 May 2020.

16 Patrick Lawrence, personal communication, 22 October 2019.

17 Warnock, 2000, p. 16.

18 Howarth, p. 352.

19 Ibid., p. 356.

20 Ibid., p. 362.

21 Ibid., p. 353.

22 Ibid., p. 355.

23 Warnock, 2000, p. 112.

24 Ibid., p. 114.

25 Schwartz, p. 86.

26 Ibid., p. 70.

27 C. A. Moberley and E. Jourdain, 1911.

28 Schwartz, 2011, pp. 51–52.

29 Unpublished autobiography (UA), 6, p. 8.

30 Warnock, 2000, p. 112.

31 Thomas, p. 197.

32 Howarth, p. 368.

33 Warnock, 2000, pp. 103–133.

34 Ibid., p. 110.

35 Ibid., p. 114.

36 UA, 6, p. 4.

37 Ibid., p. 9.

38 Ibid., p. 9.

39 Ibid., p. 10.

40 Ibid., p. 4.

41   Geoffrey Warnock, 1953.

42   UA, 6, p. 4.

43   Ibid., p. 18.

44   Ibid.

45   Geoffrey Warnock, 1973, p. 43.

46   UA, 6, p. 15.

47   Ibid., p. 6.

48   Ibid., p. 16.

49   Ibid., p. 17.

50   Ibid.

51   Ibid.

52   Warnock, 2000, pp. 31–33.

53   Ibid., p. 55.

54   Ibid., p. 56.

55   Ibid., p. 73.

56   Ibid., p. 74.

57   Ibid., p. 69.

58   Ibid., p. 61.

59   Ibid., p. 60.

60   Peter Conradi, 2001.

61   Warnock, 2000, p. 76.

62   Ibid., p. 76.

63   Ibid., p. 77.

64   Iris Murdoch, 1953.

65   Warnock, 2000, p. 88.

66   Ibid., p. 90.

67   Iris Murdoch, 1992.

68   Warnock, 2000, pp. 115–116.

69   UA, 6, pp. 19–20.

70   José Harris, p. 247.

71   Onora O'Neill, 'Mary Warnock remembered', *The Observer*, 14 December 2019.

72   Warnock, 2000, p. 92.

73   Geoffrey Warnock, 1969.

74   Mary Warnock, 1960.

75   Ibid., p. 197.

76   Ibid., p. 202.

77   Ibid., p. 131.

78   Ibid., p. 206.

79   Ewing, 1961, p. 236.

80   Adrian Whitfield, personal communication, 21 May 2020.

81   Mary Warnock, 2000, p. 92.

82   Felix Warnock, Address at memorial service, 22 October 2020.

83   Jean-Paul Sartre, 1943; Jean-Paul Sartre, trans. by Hazel E. Barnes, 1957.

84   Bakewell, p. 12.

85   Conradi, p. 215.

86   Iris Murdoch, 1953.

87   Warnock, 2000, p. 92.

88   Mary Warnock, ed. by Pyle, 1999, p. 9.

89   Mary Warnock, 1960, p. 164.

90   Ibid., p. 165.

91   Ibid., p. 171.

92   Ibid., p. 172.

93   Ibid., p. 174.

94   Ibid., p. 176.

95   Ibid., pp. 177–178.

96   Ibid., pp. 178–180.

97   Ibid., p. 180.

98   Ibid., p. 182.

99   Ibid., p. 190.

100   Ibid., p. 195.

101   Warnock, 1965, pp. 9–10.

102   Warnock, 1960, p. 168.

103   Jean-Paul Sartre, 1948, p. 29.

104   Warnock, 1970, p. 129.

105   Ibid., pp. 136–181.

106   Ibid., p. 140.

107   Mary Warnock, 1971.

108   Ewing, 1961, p. 236.

109   Deledalle, 1961.

110   Issman, 1960, pp. 455–456.

111   Van Marter, 1966, p. 151.

112   Ibid., p. 152.

113   Interview with Giles Fraser, *Confessions*, 16 January 2019.

114   Murdoch, 1970.

115   Strickland, 1965–66, p. 198.

116   Warnock, 1996, pp. xliii–xliv.

117   Ibid., p. xliv.

118   Eyre, 2003, p. xliii–xliv.

119   Harris, p. 203.

120   Williams, p. x.

121   Midgley, p. 162.

122   Conradi, p. 457.

123   Warnock, 2000, p. 118.

124   Trickett, 1966.

Fig. 3 Geoffrey and Mary on their wedding day (1949), provided by the Warnock family, CC BY-NC.

5. Fitting It All In[1]

In 1986 and 1987, journalist Valerie Grove interviewed twenty women who, she claimed, 'had it all'—marriage, motherhood and career. The first interview in the resulting book *The Compleat Woman* (1988)[2] was with Mary Warnock, who was selected for this position because it was her name that was most familiar to the general public.[3] So, there was a sense in which Mary not only 'had it all' but had achieved some degree of fame as well. How had she done all this?

There was almost exactly a year between her marriage in August 1949 and the birth of her first child, Kathleen or Kitty, in July 1950. As things turned out, whether by luck or good management, Felix, the second child, was the only one of Mary's five children not born in the Long Vacation, the university summer holiday which lasted from mid-June to early October. Childbearing interfered little with Mary's academic life.

The year from her marriage to the birth of her first child could have been one of settling down to married life. But Mary didn't settle down. She explains her immediate feeling of restlessness (which she distinguishes sharply from discontent or unhappiness), on the grounds that she had 'so short a time, no more than three years, of mixed sexual and intellectual excitement, that [...] I was prone to hanker for such excitement to come again.'[4] Restlessness may have been a feature of Mary's internal life, but, from the start, she had a powerfully affectionate, solid relationship with Geoffrey. With remarkable frankness, in her unpublished autobiography, she described how their sex life was 'a marvellous revelation. On our very first night after our wedding, our predominant feeling was of relief, that this was now legitimate, and no one could properly interrupt us.'[5] She continued to 'be astonished that we could have this vast and, it seemed, infinite pleasure whenever we liked, though increasing demands both of work and of children made our ways more conventional as time went on.'[6]

 https://doi.org/10.11647/OBP.0278.05

The strongest reason for this close relationship lay, Mary felt, in their shared professional subject. She described their talk as 'drifting between philosophy and gossip, as academic conversations tend to.'[7] Their colleagues were a source of constant amusement and they shared private jokes about the way their married friends talked to each other, mockingly imitating their 'My dears' and 'Darlings' in their own conversation. It is notable that, in nearly every phase of her life, Mary had a different woman friend with whom she could gossip and laugh, but Geoffrey was her paramount soul mate throughout, in addition to his role as a sounding board for her philosophical ideas.

A 'pattern of talk and entertaining each other'[8] began early on and continued throughout their married life. Mary always admired what she saw as Geoffrey's high intelligence, judgement, rationality, sense of humour and air of detachment, all, in her eyes, typical Wykehamist traits that she had appreciated in her older brother, Duncan.[9] Mary was, of course, not alone in her admiration for her husband. Although he was seen by his colleagues as austere in manner, there was universal acknowledgement of his professional and political wisdom as well as his skill as an administrator. This was reflected in the various senior positions to which he was later appointed.

Geoffrey had little social ambition and cared less than Mary what people thought about him. As a Yorkshireman with an interest, unfashionable among the Oxford academic elite, in playing cricket and golf[10] (and indeed in boxing though as a spectator rather than a participant), he always felt and was content to be an outsider in relation to Oxford's smart set who regarded these sporting interests as beneath them. Mary, in contrast, wanted to be accepted by the wider world and was always interested in extending her social circle. While she admired the poetry Geoffrey wrote and published, she noted that it consisted in 'a melancholy analysis of things as they were, viewed from the outside.' She wrote 'I was frightened by this pervading melancholy, and by his lack of social ambition. I was far less prepared to allow people to take me or leave me alone.'[11]

Mary shared Geoffrey's love of golf, and both loved country walks. Differences in their political and religious opinions were not in themselves creative of tension. Mary remained an unorthodox Christian throughout her life, disbelieving in God and the miracles, but wedded to the Anglican liturgy and sacred music to a degree that made church attendance an important spiritual experience for her. Geoffrey's atheism meant he found it difficult when his duties obliged him to attend college chapel services. Politically, both were initially strong supporters of the Labour government that took office in 1945, but their views diverged when, in the 1960s, Labour's educational policy began to drive through the abolition of grammar schools and their replacement by a comprehensive system. Geoffrey remained centre-left in his politics while Mary stopped supporting the Labour Party in 1965. Later, they were united in their opposition to Conservative and particularly Mrs. Thatcher's policies towards the universities.

Further testimony to the strength of her marriage comes from the letters Geoffrey wrote to Mary between 1950 and 1967 when he spent three periods, lasting four or five months each, as a guest lecturer in different US universities.[12] (Her letters to him have not been preserved.) His letters are chatty, recounting what he has been doing. There is a great deal about his students, classes, seminars, lectures—whether people are 'any good,' whether his own output is good, where he has got to in the course he is teaching. He often responds to news she has sent about Oxford University affairs and there is much gossip about people in their social circle in Oxford, or people he was meeting in the United States. They shared attitudes to people, which friends were dreary, which 'impossible' (but, despite the sometimes sharp judgements in this private correspondence, both in practice went out of their way to help people with problems). On each of his trips to the United States he seems to have had a very sociable time. He reports being pursued by women: though he describes them as 'crazy' this didn't seem to stop him having drinks or dinners with them. In return, he jokes about the men she would find attractive—'You would love him, though he's not huge and ugly'. (Mary's taste in men was a family joke.) He asks regularly after or refers to the children, especially in the letters he wrote in 1966, when Kitty had just started at a new school, James had started as a boarder at Winchester, and Mary had to find a new nanny for the five-year-old Maria. He is also concerned about his mother, who seems to have objected to his going away on this occasion and he worries about how she and Mary get on without him as a buffer. In this set of letters, Mary has just started as the headmistress of Oxford High School. She must have said to him she felt she had 'found her destiny'—he refers to this several times. He frequently urges her not to work too hard and makes suggestions about how she should deal with difficult school staff. He also jokes about her 'carrying on becoming famous'—it was another family joke, that what she wanted above all was fame or, even better, power. Thus, the letters reveal a rich private code of attitudes, words, jokes and nicknames, a strong intimate relationship with many shared interests and acquaintances. They also reveal Geoffrey to be a supportive husband, though occasionally mildly mocking of his wife's ambition, as well as a concerned and involved father.

The one area of life in which they markedly differed, and which might have tested their mutual tolerance, was household cleanliness and neatness. Geoffrey is quoted by Valerie Grove, in *The Compleat Woman* interview: 'Mary has a little study which is a pigsty, and I have a study which is neat and tidy. In shared quarters, I am constantly picking things off the floor. But I don't mind doing that.'[13] So even here they achieved a satisfactory *modus vivendi*. Although Mary was always there to cook and look after the house, she was never at all interested in things being spotlessly clean. Geoffrey used to follow her around doing such things as wiping the sink after washing up, and 'all those little things which are so easily overlooked,' a phrase he used in mockery, though without malice. The children do not recall their parents having actual rows but were in no doubt that many of their mother's habits must have been exasperating for their father.

Thirty years after the event, Mary wrote an affectionate account of their first 'terrible quarrel.' It appears in an article written for a series entitled 'My honeymoon in...' for a women's magazine (possibly *Woman's Weekly*, although the back issues do not survive). Following their wedding Mary and Geoffrey were both keen to get on with their new lives in Oxford, he as a young fellow of Magdalen and she at St. Hugh's, but

> my mother had the perfectly erroneous idea that I could not live without holidays (in fact, after childhood, I have nearly always begun counting the days after about twenty-four hours of a holiday). She therefore bought, on our behalf, a vast number of tickets for the Edinburgh Festival. [...] we were by far the youngest people at the festival, or so it seemed. There was no Fringe in those days, and the visitors were stately and, some of them, distinguished. One day in Prince's Street, Geoffrey said

'Look, there's Louis MacNeice'. I did look and walked straight into the largest man I have ever seen. It was the great Italian singer Paolo Silveri, who was singing in the Festival opera. We went four times to the opera, twice to *Cosi fan Tutte*, and twice to Verdi's *Un Ballo in Maschera*. All these performances were superb; but the last was spoiled for me by our having had a terrible quarrel, about whether or not we should change into evening dress for the performance, as was then the normal custom. I was for it, Geoffrey against. I had a wonderful long stripey skirt, newly made by my mother's dressmaker out of Italian silk, and I knew with complete certainty that if I did not wear it that night, I would never wear it again. Equally I knew that the disagreement which arose (Geoffrey's correct point being that it was deluging with rain, and the skirt would be ruined) spelled the final and irrevocable end of our marriage. However, by the morning, it was clear that that wasn't so [...].[14]

Having survived their honeymoon, the Warnocks returned to Oxford and began to look around for their first house. They were both on low salaries. University lecturers at that time earned relatively little compared to other middle-class people, based on the assumption that dons would be bachelors, live in university lodgings and have all their meals provided. Fortunately, Geoffrey's father, James, a retired general practitioner, was able to offer them an interest-free loan to buy a small house in Summertown, a mixed residential district in North Oxford, where they moved from their college rooms in January 1950.[15] Initially they had unrealistically high standards. Mary, recalling these days with astonishment, wrote that they thought they had to clean the whole house every day and that she had to serve two cooked meals a day as well as afternoon tea.[16] These assumptions were derived from their own pre-war childhoods, when they both had servants to clean and cook for them. It rapidly became apparent that such a lifestyle could not be sustained when both members of the couple had full-time jobs and there were no servants.

A month before the first baby, Kitty was born in July 1950, Emily Coleman (Nan) came to stay and help. It was she who, twenty-five years earlier had been responsible for bringing up Mary and her sister Stephana for the first six or seven years of their lives. Now her arrival would be a mixed blessing although Mary was undoubtedly very grateful for her help. She had firm and settled views about everything to do with babies, derived from bringing up babies in wealthy households. She insisted on expenditure the Warnocks, on their low salaries, could not really afford. Mary was 'appalled at the expense of buying two prams, dozens of muslin and towelling nappies, summer vests, winter vests and innumerable other items.' Further, Nan expected Mary to join her in endless sewing and knitting of the children's clothes. Thus, Mary was unwillingly trapped by her demanding nanny into a level of domesticity for which she did not have the time, the inclination, nor particular skills.[17]

University term began when Kitty was less than two months old, Nan returned to her home with Mary's sister, Grizel, in London, and Mary had to juggle hoovering and breast-feeding on the one hand and tutorials with her students on the other. For spare time reading, she was absorbed in the world of women's magazines, especially a weekly that appeared in small book form called *Housewife*,[18] in the hope of equalling Nan's skills in baby care. There were times when she thought of giving up academic life to devote herself to the children, but Geoffrey would not hear of this. According to Mary,

> Geoffrey never doubted for a moment that I should carry on with the job when we began having children. After Kitty was born, I used to get into despair every now and then and say I couldn't manage, and should I give up my job. But Geoffrey's reaction always was: 'Don't be an idiot. Let's spend more money getting more help.'

Felix was born eighteen months after Kitty in January 1952, followed by James in August 1953 and Stephana or Fanny in July 1956. The youngest, Grizel Maria (after Mary's sister) but very soon nicknamed Boz, was born after a five-year gap in July 1961. Despite, on her own account, being sick all the time and permanently exhausted especially when there were other small children around, Mary worked throughout her pregnancies. Childbirth was no problem for her; indeed she recalled 'I do so love the moment of giving birth to a new child, this new person, to whom you can attach a new name, it's something for ever, to have fixed a name and possibly a character for the rest of their lives.'[19] When Mary was asked by Valerie Grove why she had *five* children, she replied

> By the time you've got one, the argument for having more is very strong indeed. Geoffrey thought that was enough—he very reasonably thought that three was a decent family, and more than he'd come from (two), and it was really all we could manage, and he increasingly disliked the commotion the children caused. But I was by then addicted to the idea of four and desperate to have another.'[20]

Mary wrote elsewhere that she believed the middle child of three would always be disadvantaged, and, from her own experience she felt a large family was part of the natural order.

The Warnocks were able to afford a live-in nanny and after some bad initial experiences Mary found three in succession who each stayed four years. The last in particular was dearly loved by the family. She became pregnant before her wedding, and, Mary reported, 'she came to me to confess and I astonished her by saying "How wonderful."'[21] Mary's youngest child, Maria, was growing up by now, and this nanny was followed by a series of less full-time au pairs, sometimes students and sixth formers who had accommodation free in exchange for looking after her. Maria remembers all these women with fondness.

With Nan around, Mary had no need of child-rearing manuals. The best-selling baby book ever, *Baby and Child Care* by American paediatrician Benjamin Spock, had appeared in 1946[22] but Nan would not have been impressed by Spock's *laissez-faire* approach—nor would Geoffrey or Mary herself. With the help of the nannies and a regular cleaner and gardener, Mary ran an orderly household with regular meal-, bath- and bed-times for the children, a sleep in the afternoons when they were young, good meals, regular sheet-changing days and plenty of planning and respect for the nanny's day off. As the children grew up, twice-daily music practice would be expected and there were family outings on Sundays for country walks, blackberrying or watching Geoffrey play cricket, according to the season. At home, the children's lives were kept fairly separate from the adults,' even on holidays, with their own playroom (as far away from the adults' sitting room as possible), separate evening meals (though Mary presided over these), and an expectation that adults should not be disturbed in the evenings. 'The children,' Mary reported, 'always thought that coffee was called "peace" because after lunch we'd say now the grownups want some peace and they would have to go upstairs for half an hour while we had our coffee.'[23] A downside to this orderliness was that friends sometimes took advantage of it, dumping their children into the care of the Warnock's nanny when they wanted some child-free time. Mary always said she did not mind, but the nannies did.

This regime, modelled on her own childhood, was already old-fashioned by the 1950s. No doubt it enabled Mary to get more work done herself, but she justified it in part by her wish to protect Geoffrey from disturbance. The children recollect Mary as constantly concerned that the children would disturb him and highly protective of him in this respect. He was not, he admitted himself, 'a great fancier of young children [...] I'm a fanatically neat and tidy person,' he said.[24] According to Maria he 'very rarely lost his temper, but when he did it was terrifying—he would go white and silent—no shouting and screaming, just ominous and horrible silence.'[25]

Fig. 4 Mary with baby Fanny (1957), provided by the Warnock family, CC BY-NC.

Like her own mother, Mary was not particularly cuddly but was, as her mother had been to her, extremely supportive to her children. Within the framework of order and discipline, she had her own ideas of child development. 'I think,' she later said of children generally, 'their personalities are developed very early in life.'[26] Felix, her second-born, confirms this was the way his mother had perceived her children. 'I think we were all a bit type-cast,' he said. 'Kitty was the independent one. I was good at games, but stupid. James was the clever one. Fanny was sensitive and the most needy. Boz, as the youngest was inevitably cast as the clown.'[27] Mary's views on the significance of the individuality of children's personalities were, as it happened, ahead of her time. In the

1950s, two American psychiatrists, Alex Thomas and Stella Chess, and a psychologist, Herb Birch, were collecting evidence on the way children differed from each other from shortly after birth, such differences persisting at least into their teens. In *Your Child is a Person*, published in 1965,[28] they advised parents to tailor the upbringing of their children to their personalities, an approach Mary had discovered for herself.

The only way her children could really irritate her was by saying they were bored. She could not bear the thought of her children not being able to amuse themselves. When they were young, as we have seen, there were certain rules that had to be obeyed. The children had to have a sleep in the afternoons and were not allowed to disturb the adults after seven p.m. This separation or compartmentalisation between her roles as wife, as mother and as an academic is surely one of the reasons for her degree of success in all her roles.

The children's school careers were not as straightforward as Mary would have liked. Kitty recollects not being a very happy child, either at school or at home. She tried to be good and work hard as she was expected to but often without much enjoyment. She attended the Oxford High School until she was sixteen when her mother was appointed the school's headmistress. At this point, Mary asked her to move to another school as, according to Kitty, she could not bear the thought of her daughter mocking her when she was taking assembly. Kitty was happy to leave the High School and chose to go to Prior's Field, the boarding school her mother had attended and of which she was now a governor. She went on to study English at St. Hugh's, trained as a teacher, and worked for a while in a Palestinian university. While there, she wrote a book about the lives of Palestinian women in the Occupied Territories. Mary saw Kitty as 'independent and bolshie even as a tiny baby.' Mary always felt she had given Kitty 'the hardest deal of all being the eldest of them, shoved out of the cot for the next one.'[29]

Felix was happy at the Dragon School, the private preparatory school near the Warnocks' home in Oxford. He excelled at cricket and rugby, being captain in all the sports. He won a music scholarship to Winchester College but there he was not happy. The only things he enjoyed were games and music and he left early with poor O and A levels. After re-taking A levels at Oxford Technical College and with private music tuition at home, he went on to a degree course at the Royal College of

Music and a career first as an orchestral musician and then in orchestra management, neither of which were roles for which his mother had cast him earlier on. He told his mother later that what he liked most about his childhood was supper. Why was this, she asked? 'Because I never listened to the book you were reading, it was just that nobody could speak to you, so you didn't have to think about anything at all.'[30]

James, seen as the 'clever one' by Mary, was able to read the headlines of *The Daily Mirror* (a rather surprising newspaper for the Warnocks to take alongside the more predictable *Times*) by the age of three. Like his brother, James started off at the Dragon School where his poor performance in sport disappointed his father, though not his mother. He won a scholarship to Winchester, but then things started to go wrong for him. For reasons that are not clear, he did very little work, his termly reports got worse and worse and he found himself active only in activities that were at best non-curricular and often against the rules. Finally, at the age of fifteen, just a few weeks before he was due to take his A levels, he was summarily expelled in a brutal manner, being dumped at the railway station by his housemaster who had phoned his parents beforehand to tell them he was on his way home. Mary later recalled that it was because he smoked cannabis but, according to James, it was other misdemeanours that got him into such trouble. Mary and Geoffrey were remarkably supportive to James during this episode. Mary's former high opinion of the school had already been shaken by the way it had treated Felix, and now she blamed the college rather than James. Geoffrey wrote a stiff letter to the school, also blaming the staff for what had happened. James did his A levels in Oxford and then took more in different subjects at a grammar school in Thame, not far from Oxford. He went on to the University of East Anglia and a career in the civil service and local government.[31]

Fanny, early on designated as the 'sensitive and needy one,' sadly fulfilled Mary's expectations. As a young child, she suffered from night terrors, waking terrified in the night and needing to be comforted before she could go back to sleep. Although James was nearer in age to Felix, he was closer to Fanny with whom he recalls playing imaginative games, involving songs and playlets and performances. Fanny grew out of night terrors, but they were replaced by an anxious personality with occasional episodes of extraordinary tantrums, during which she seemed to lose track entirely of where she was. These episodes were extremely painful for Mary. She found it impossible to let them blow over on their own while Geoffrey was less sympathetic. Fanny had considerable musical talent and it was clear from an early age that she would aim for music college and perhaps a career as a pianist or cellist. In her teens she went to board at Downe House School. Here she had very good teachers, but by this time she was suffering great stress and anxiety about her failure, as she felt it, to live up to their expectations. She returned to Oxford for her sixth form at the OHS, after Mary had stepped down as headmistress. Here she played one of Beethoven's piano concertos at a school concert though she found such performance highly stressful. She won a place at the Guildhall School of Music and Drama and did well there, but after she graduated her self-confidence collapsed and she did not pursue a career in music to Mary's enormous disappointment. She worked instead in a variety of jobs, never really settling to anything.

Mary's last-born child, Maria, nicknamed Boz, arrived after a five-year gap. She was born with an intestinal obstruction, caused by a rare anatomical anomaly—an annular pancreas. Operated upon within days of her birth, she needed a great deal of medical attention in her first few months and had other medical problems later on. The first affected the muscles in her legs, so she had to have surgery on her left knee when she was three years old and was in a plaster from toe to hip for several months. A recurrence of stomach problems when she was twelve required another lengthy stay in hospital and, in her twenties, she had to have further leg operations. These were carried out in an orthopaedic hospital in Surrey. Mary often came to visit her and, Maria recalls, used to smuggle in gin and Martini.[32] Although she missed a great deal of school, her parents remained remarkably relaxed both about her illnesses and about her academic progress. Despite her medical problems, Maria was not at all over-protected. She spent several summer holidays away from her family with an organisation called Colony Holidays which she loved. Later this organisation was reborn as Active Training and Education (ATE) with Maria as one of its directors and holiday organisers and Mary as the Chair. After leaving the OHS, Maria went to the West Surrey College of Art and Design. She trained as a teacher and was Director of Art at Dulwich College for twenty years before moving to other schools abroad.[33]

In March 1952, shortly after the birth of Felix, the Warnocks bought
a four-storey semi-detached Victorian house in Fyfield Road nearer
the centre of Oxford. It was an inconvenient house but they loved it.
According to Mary, it was now that she stopped caring about housework.
'As long as things were reasonably tidy, the mice in the larder kept more
or less under control, and the water hot, we were content,' she said.[34]
As happens, the children began to make friends of their own. Mary
remembered Kitty, aged five, sitting on the wall in front of the house
reading aloud 'to an awestruck group consisting of her brothers, Felix
and the infant James, and a slippered girl from across the road and her
siblings.'[35] At this period, the streets in North Oxford, as elsewhere, were
much safer than they are now, and quite young children were allowed to
play in them unsupervised. From five years, James was expected to walk
to school by himself.

In late 1949, Geoffrey's general practitioner father, James Warnock,
despite being a lifelong socialist, became disillusioned with the recently
established National Health Service and retired. He and his wife
Kathleen left Leeds and bought a house in Sutton Courtenay, a village
not far from Oxford. However, James only survived three years there,
dying in 1953. Geoffrey's mother was lonely living by herself and in 1956
she helped her son and Mary buy a larger house in North Oxford and
moved in with them.

Geoffrey and Mary were generally able to live at a somewhat higher
standard than other academic families, with his mother's contribution
to the household bills and Mary's modest inherited wealth. They owned
their houses outright and had a nanny and a one-day-a-week cleaner
and gardener. Groceries were delivered to the door. They were able
to afford music lessons for the children and, most expensively, public
school education for the four older children (although Felix and James
were academic and music scholars respectively which reduced to some
extent the pressure on family finances). Holidays were mostly not
extravagant; three relatively expensive holidays in Italy required careful
planning and were paid for by Geoffrey's lecturing semesters in the
US. Geoffrey's personal expenditure was extremely modest and Mary's
equally so apart from the occasional purchase of expensive clothes
or furnishing. She did love shopping for clothes, and Maria recalled
that, for a few months, when Mary was taking part in a regular radio

programme, she would come up to London with her mother who was
in a talk show in Broadcasting House. After the broadcast, they would
go shopping together for clothes with Mary making, in Maria's eyes,
extravagant purchases. But generally, Mary spent extremely little on her
own appearance. Given the frequently remarked upon undisciplined
state of her hair, it is not surprising to learn that Mary did not visit a
hairdresser regularly. When Mary had a second car, it was always
something small, cheap and striking—a Heinkel bubble car, a rare
Citroen Bijou made of fibreglass (of which only 210 were built) or an
open-topped Triumph Herald.[36]

The presence of Geoffrey's mother in the house meant there was
a good deal of tension, especially between Geoffrey and his mother,
generally due to their very different political views. Disagreements
became acute during the Suez Crisis towards the end of 1956. Mary's
brother, Duncan Wilson, was in the Foreign Office. He refused to defend
his government's conspiracy with France and Israel to attack Egypt over
its nationalisation of the Suez Canal, even though this put his career
on the line. Mary and Geoffrey strongly supported his position, but
Geoffrey's mother, for whom Prime Minister Anthony Eden was a hero,
regarded Duncan as a traitor to his country.[37] She took Geoffrey aside
and told him she had always known that Duncan was a Communist.
Why else would he be so interested in the Soviet bloc? (His subsequent
postings included Yugoslavia and Moscow). The house had not yet been
adapted to create separate rooms for Kathleen, so they were sharing
the same living room and Mary couldn't escape from these attacks on
her beloved brother. This particular situation was resolved when Eden
resigned, Duncan was promoted, and Geoffrey's mother moved into her
own living room.[38]

The Chadlington Road house where the Warnocks lived for the next
fifteen years was ideally suited to their needs. It was a large, sunny,
Edwardian house. According to Mary, 'the garden was large, with
a huge lawn that had been a tennis court, but soon became a cricket
pitch, football ground, space-hopper race-course for the numbers of
children who used to drift in and out. My mother-in-law happily took
charge of the rest of the garden with the help of an ancient gardener
who came with the house, and I reverted to childhood, enjoying the
garden but taking virtually no responsibility for it.'[39] The road was

quiet and peaceful, ideal for bicycling and other children's games with neighbouring children. The Dragon School which both the Warnock boys attended was close by, and the Oxford High School only a few minutes' walk away. Geoffrey's mother had her own kitchen, bathroom and living room. Mary found her mother-in-law's lack of independence extremely irritating, being used to her own mother managing perfectly well for many years without a husband. The antipathy was reciprocated. Mary thought her mother-in-law never liked her, seeing her as too clever by half, neglectful of her duties as wife and mother and a crypto-communist 'with dangerous connections through Duncan to a world of plots and spies.'[40] But Kathleen Warnock's presence had many advantages as well as providing some financial assistance. She had the only television in the house in her living room and enjoyed having the children in to watch selected programmes. They chatted easily to her, feeling her to be a constant, amiable presence. Further, she was always pleasant to the succession of nannies and the cleaner and was available to let in plumbers or answer the door to the postman. As a doctor's wife she was accustomed to answering questions about medical matters, so she was always there when one of the children was ill to decide if there was a need to consult a doctor. She never got used to the Warnock family lifestyle, occasionally muttering to herself 'What a way of life.'[41] Mary and Geoffrey found this phrase amusing and often used it of themselves.

In 1958, the Warnocks were well off enough to buy a rather ramshackle holiday house perched on the side of a steep little valley in the village of Sandsend, three miles north of Whitby on the Yorkshire Coast where Geoffrey had come for holidays as a child. The purchase was, in Mary's words, 'a huge success.'[42] The family went there two or three times a year. The house had two sitting rooms, one for adults and one for children. It had been a bungalow and then the roof space had been opened up to form bedrooms under the eaves with sloped ceilings and dormer windows (two large ones for grown-ups, four small ones with bunk beds for children, and one downstairs room for the nanny), so there was plenty of room for guests. The long dining room, once it was furnished with refectory tables and benches from a prep school's closing down sale, could accommodate large numbers of people for meals as well as games of table tennis. The house was close to a golf course where Mary and Geoffrey played, and not far from Ripon where Mary's sister,

Stephana and her family lived. A piano in the hall and a gramophone in the nursery provided constant music. It was not luxurious. The kitchen was primitive, and Mary's children still have bad memories of the dark, damp and cold downstairs bathroom they had to use.[43] Geoffrey's mother used to come to stay sometimes; this made for more work, but it gave her pleasure as she was able to visit old friends in Leeds.[44] As we have seen, Mary took work away on holiday, but she managed her time efficiently and it was she who did most of the cooking; one young visitor remembers a particularly delicious fruit cake.[45] Visitors invited to join the Warnocks for their holidays included adult friends, families with children, cousins, or the children's school friends. Stephana would come over from Ripon for a day with four of her children. Guests reported finding these holidays great fun, with Mary constantly energetic and finding new things to do. When the Warnocks later spent three family holidays in Italy, they also went with other families. Geoffrey loved life on the beach at Sandsend—French cricket, building sandcastles against the incoming tide, and particularly damming the streams.

Back in Oxford, Mary resumed her busy life. After preparing breakfast with an ear open for someone's piano practice on the kitchen piano, she would see the children off to school, then leave the younger ones in the care of their nanny and start her day of lectures, supervisions or other college appointments, or work either at home or in her college room, reading undergraduate essays, preparing lectures or working on whichever book she had in progress. By early evening, she was at home again to prepare supper for the children and read to them while they ate it. During much of their childhood, Mary regularly reviewed children's books for *The Times Literary Supplement*, so there was always plenty of suitable reading material around. She later recalled some of the books she read: '*Lord of the Rings* and *The Secret Garden* and *The Little Princess*, and all of the C. S. Lewis *Narnia* books, which in many ways I don't approve of, but the rhythms of the prose are so perfect. I remember when we got to *The Last Battle* all of us were in floods of tears, including me.'[46] Then, with the nanny, she put the children to bed and cooked supper for herself and Geoffrey. She would often also prepare dinner for Geoffrey's mother, taking it in to her on a tray. She and Geoffrey would have dinner together, the rule being, as we have seen, that the Warnock parents did not expect to see their children after seven or seven thirty p.m. The nanny was usually free to spend the evening in her own room or go out. After dinner, Mary would carry on working sometimes to Geoffrey's exasperation. He might ask her if she couldn't 'knock off now,' to which she would reply 'What do you expect me to do? Twiddle my thumbs?'[47] This frenetic pace of life continued as the decades went by. Kitty, interviewed in 1995 when her mother was over seventy years old, reported: 'She's one of those people who can get up at six in the morning, start working or drive to London, do an interview, then come back and write a book, then go off to dinner, come back at two in the morning and start again at six the next day.'[48]

Mary is recalled by her children as a good cook, who served up traditional Sunday lunches every week, with perfectly cooked roast beef being a favourite. She was adventurous, cooking curry, which at that time was quite exotic, and Italian ingredients available from a delicatessen in Oxford market. She was not above serving convenience foods—dried 'Surprise' peas, or a powdered pudding called 'Angel delight.' Maria recalled later that 'some things acquired new names— Heinz salad cream was called 'false' to distinguish it from home-made mayonnaise; when Hellman's mayonnaise appeared we called it 'real false'—and any salad cream not made by Heinz was called 'false false,' and so on. I still call golden syrup 'beastly,' having been told as a child 'don't eat that, it's beastly.'[49] Except when they were on holiday in Italy, they never went out to eat in restaurants; this would have been regarded as a ridiculous waste of money.

Mary's intelligence, level of energy and intensity of activity were found intimidating by some of her friends. Ann Strawson recalled that Mary 'was a great character and had a huge force of personality.'[50] Though an Oxford graduate herself, Ann admitted to being rather frightened of her and feeling she had nothing to say to her, despite the fact that Mary was 'terribly nice' to her and gave her books to read. Ann thought that Mary was good at setting people at their ease though she could be caustic about them behind their backs. She was not alone in noticing that, in her thirties, Mary seemed very attractive to men, who often made 'passes' at her.[51] One of Mary's favourite memories gives credence to this suggestion. On one occasion, when Geoffrey was lecturing abroad, she was invited to lunch by the Editor of *The Daily Telegraph*. The only other guest was Hugh Gaitskell, then Leader of the

Opposition. Gaitskell, though just fifty-six years of age, only had a few months to live. He clearly took to Mary and was reminded by his host that Mary was the sister of Duncan Wilson, with whom he had been a pupil at Winchester. In Mary's words, Gaitskell turned to her with an intense and piercing smile and said, 'I don't need to know whose sister you are.'[52] Ann remembered Geoffrey as lovely, very witty, though a controlled person. He was athletic. Ann showed the author a small table in her living room and claimed Geoffrey could stand on his head on it. She thought he was very good at entertaining young children.[53]

In 1972, when Geoffrey was appointed Principal of Hertford College, the Warnocks moved into the Principal's lodgings, a large house that formed part of the college building in central Oxford. Mary was very fond of Hertford and of their house. She loved the view from their bedroom overlooking Radcliffe Square, with the Bodleian Library just across the road. It had the disadvantage of being noisy. 'In the summer,' she wrote, 'both tourists and undergraduates swarmed like flies most of the night, sometimes playing guitars or kicking empty coke cans down the road outside our window.'[54] The bedroom had another disadvantage: accessibility to the outside world. On one occasion, an undergraduate who had climbed up a drainpipe, looking he said, for a friend, came into their bedroom where the Warnocks were asleep. On Mary's account, 'Geoffrey, by threats of the police, got him to give his name and college, and escorted him out of the front door. The next day he sent a large cheque for the college appeal, and an apology. But he was a bright chap, and he also sold his story to one of the tabloids, claiming that he had surprised us in bed discussing the philosopher, Kant.'[55] Geoffrey's main concern was that his children, especially his daughters, should behave themselves in the college buildings. On one occasion, he turned up in his pyjamas in the college bar, to extricate Fanny from the company of Hertford undergraduates and take her back into the lodgings.[56]

Despite having a family and teaching duties, Mary was very sociable and generous and there were often guests staying in the house—friends, relatives or young people needing shelter during some sort of difficulty. Sometimes a whole family would come and stay for several weeks. The three-child family of her school-friend Imogen visited from Washington DC, the two-child family of Geoffrey's sister Jocelyn visited from Southern Rhodesia (now Zimbabwe), the two sons of a visiting academic colleague stayed while their parents looked for accommodation. Jeannie Simpson, a school friend from Prior's Field, was a frequent visitor, sometimes leaving her two children with the Warnock nanny while she went off elsewhere. Jeannie was a great favourite of Geoffrey who objected when other parents dumped their children with the nanny, but not her. It was through Jeannie that Mary met Kingsley and Hille Amis in the early 1950s, before and after Kingsley published his enormously successful novel, *Lucky Jim*, in 1954.

The Warnocks' closest friends at this time were two couples, Peter and Ann Strawson and Marcus and Cecilia Dick. Both the men were philosophers and both the wives Oxford graduates. Both families had children roughly the same age as the Warnocks,' so the children could be relied on to go off and play or chat together, leaving their parents in peace. Mary and Ann Strawson had their first children within a few weeks of each other and thereafter, with one exception, whenever one gave birth, the other did too. Thus Kitty, Felix, James and Boz all had a same-age friend in the Strawson family. James was also particularly close to Sophie Dick who was in the same class as he in primary school. Fanny Warnock complained to Ann that it was unfair that she had failed to produce a playmate for her.[57]

Despite seeing themselves as the reverse of smart, the Warnocks were frequent attenders at parties, sometimes quite smart ones. One host was Anthony Quinton, an unusually wealthy philosopher who, later, like Mary, was made a life peer by Margaret Thatcher, to whom he was an adviser. At his lavish events, guests were asked to write down the name of the most attractive person in the room. It was said that Mary and Geoffrey always wrote each other's names down on the grounds that if they didn't, they wouldn't get any votes at all.[58] Another wealthy host was Ian Little, an economist with whom Geoffrey had shared tutorials with Herbert Hart at New College. Ian and his wife Dobs lived in Sutton Courtenay, the village where Geoffrey's parents lived when his father retired. Mary and Geoffrey would sometimes leave the children with the Littles' nanny and go for a round of golf with the Littles. When the Littles moved to a larger house in Clifton Hampden on the Thames, they used to give parties there for the so-called 'dancing economists.' The Warnocks were not the only non-economists invited. There was at least one developmental biologist, Geoffrey Dawes, and several front-bench

Labour politicians. Nor was dancing the only activity. Mary reports that if one ventured upstairs and was unwise enough to open a bedroom door, one was quite likely to encounter Labour politicians, 'Gaitskell or Douglas Jay in bed with the girl of their choice.'[59]

Towards the mid-1950s, although the friendship with the Strawsons continued, the Warnocks developed a closer and much more intense relationship with Marcus and Cecilia Dick. Marcus, after a brilliant undergraduate career, was offered a fellowship at Balliol even before he had taken his Finals examination. Cecilia had taken a resoundingly successful first-class degree in history and was offered a lectureship at Lady Margaret Hall. They were a 'golden pair' and Mary was surprised that she and Geoffrey should be chosen by them as sufficiently interesting to be friends.[60] When Marcus and Geoffrey developed the habit of dining in their own colleges on Wednesdays, Cecilia and Mary started to spend those evenings together. The families began to go on holidays together and the two sets of parents would often go as a foursome to the cinema. Other friends, apart from the Strawsons, were relatively neglected. As time went on, it gradually became clear that both Marcus and Cecilia had major problems. According to Mary, Marcus was compulsively unfaithful and more and more dependent on alcohol. Cecilia, whose lectureship at Lady Margaret Hall was not renewed, felt paranoid hostility to her college and developed an obsessive hatred of her husband.[61] In 1963, Marcus left Oxford to become Professor of Philosophy in the new University of East Anglia. He was successful there, became involved in university administration and was appointed Dean. But his drink problem persisted and he died in 1972.[62] Cecilia, who had started divorce proceedings after he left Oxford, became more and more dependent on Geoffrey for emotional support. This precipitated the greatest crisis in the Warnocks' married life, but the three of them gradually established 'a new but never an easy relationship.'[63]

Whether Mary herself had any extra-marital relationships is an open question. In her memoir she described how Oxford was 'a place for extraordinary friendship, and indeed for adultery (though gossip and the grapevine were for most people partially inhibiting factors in this field).'[64] Every fellow had a private room and a telephone. 'There can be no other profession,' she wrote, 'so well suited to friendship or, as I have said, to extra-marital flings.'[65] Reviewing Mary's memoir, published in

2000, John Bayley, Iris Murdoch's husband and a Warnock friend, while finding much to praise was evidently disappointed at the absence of titillation or revelation. One might surely have expected, he writes:

> that a memoir of contemporary Oxford High Life by such a forthright, strong-minded and fearless woman as Baroness Warnock would have contained a good mouthful at least of juicy gossip, all the more so because the Baroness has an excellent sense of humour and can be extremely funny at her own expense. Unfortunately, she is invariably kind to enemies and to the foolish, as well as unswervingly loyal to friends.

Why, John Bayley asked, was there 'no mention of the well-known Oxford story of the don, deeply smitten, who went to bed in one of Mary's nightgowns (how did he get hold of it?) to the amusement rather than indignation of his own wife?'[66] Was he the only philosopher who had an intimate relationship with Mary? Possibly not. Certainly, Ann Strawson, the widow of Peter Strawson, the distinguished philosopher, believed that her husband and Mary had had what she called a 'brush.' Ann described how, at one point, her husband had left his gloves behind after seeing Mary. Geoffrey went to Peter's rooms at University College with the gloves and said to Peter 'I think these are your gloves, Peter, that you left behind.' Without another word, he walked out.' Ann commented on this episode—'You know how it is when you're young.' When asked if any of these extra-marital relationships became 'serious,' Ann replied 'Oh no. We knew on which side our bread was buttered.'[67] Ann Strawson's daughter, Julia, reported that her mother thought that Mary had had a similar 'brush' with Marcus Dick.[68] It seems possible that Mary did have a number of such relationships and that these were known to some, but well concealed from others.[69]

After the end of World War Two, Mary's brother Duncan was posted by the Foreign Office to China, then as Ambassador to Yugoslavia and in 1968 to Moscow. In April 1971, he invited Mary and her music student son, Felix, to spend two weeks in the Embassy in Moscow to attend some Days of British Music that Duncan (by now Sir Duncan Wilson) had organised.[70] This was a memorable occasion. Duncan had invited Benjamin Britten, Peter Pears, William Walton and the whole of the London Symphony Orchestra. For Mary, highlights of this visit included hearing Sviatoslav Richter playing some of Britten's music for the piano in Leningrad and being introduced to Dmitri Shostakovich.

Another memorable encounter was with a class of English students at Moscow University. Duncan's wife, Betty, invited Mary to take a session of a seminar she regularly taught there.[71] It was not revealed to the students that Mary's field was philosophy for if they knew they would have expected her to talk about Marxism and Communism. Instead, she had a free-ranging discussion about images and icons. The students revelled in the freedom they were given to discuss anything they wanted to. When they eventually extracted from Mary the confession that she was a philosopher, they were delighted and asked her incredulously 'Is this how you are allowed to teach in Oxford?'[72] The idea of such freedom amazed them.

After he retired from the Foreign Office, Duncan served for six years as Master of Corpus Christi College, Cambridge. His major contribution while he held this position was fundraising for a new University Music School.[73] He then retired with Betty to Islay, the southernmost island of the Inner Hebrides where he had long owned a house. In his last years he frequently visited Oxford and stayed with the Warnocks while he was researching in the Bodleian Library for a biography of Gilbert Murray, the early twentieth-century Oxford classical scholar.[74] Geoffrey greatly enjoyed these visits, frequently playing golf with his brother-in-law. When Duncan died suddenly, two years after retirement, he had not completed his book but had left sufficient notes for Mary and Betty to finish it.[75]

The title of Valerie Grove's book, *The Compleat Woman: Marriage, Motherhood, Career: Can She Have It All* accurately sums up Mary Warnock's life. She did indeed 'have it all.' But her life contained more than that. In her diary entry for 4 February 1944, when she was nineteen, one of the resolutions she made for her future life read: 'My life to be balanced with riding and poetry and the utmost energy and generosity towards my friends.' Riding she gave up fairly soon, but poetry remained an abiding love; energy and generosity were absolutely the hallmarks of her life with friends and then with her husband, children and then grandchildren as well as her siblings. Even given her superabundant energy, she had to prioritise. When there was a choice between family and work, if her family needed her, she was always there. But when family life was apparently going smoothly, she had no hesitation in ignoring the family to concentrate on her work. Mary's own view of her success

in combining family and work was pretty negative. She told Valerie
Grove 'I do think I have partially failed as a wife and partially failed as
a mother.'[76] This emphasis on failure rather than on success a great deal
better than 'partial' is not a view shared by her family, particularly her
children or by her professional colleagues. For her children, her wider
family and her friends, she was always there with her support when
they needed her while her professional colleagues accurately judged her
to have had an admirably productive career.

Notes

1   As will be apparent, in writing this chapter, I had an enormous amount
     of help from Mary's surviving children, Kitty, Felix, James and Maria.
     They all gave most generously of their time to provide vivid and detailed
     accounts of their childhoods. I have only attempted to attribute information
     infrequently as there was much unanimity between their accounts. Any
     inaccuracies are entirely my responsibility.

2   Valerie Grove, 1988.

3   Valerie Grove, personal communication.

4   Unpublished autobiography (UA), 6, p. 1.

5   Ibid., pp. 3–4.

6   Ibid.

7   Ibid.

8   Ibid.

9   Mary Warnock, 2000, pp. 197–201.

10   Strawson, 2004.

11   UA, 6, p. 5.

12   Private correspondence, JW to MW

13   Valerie Grove, p. 48.

14   Mary Warnock, undated typescript.

15   UA, 6, p. 2.

16   Ibid.

17   Ibid., p. 3.

18   Ibid.

19   Grove, p. 44.

20   Ibid., p. 43.

21   Ibid., p. 45.

22   Spock, 1946.

23   Grove, p. 47.

24   Ibid., p. 48.

25   Maria Jenkins, personal communication.

26   Grove, p. 471.

27   Felix Warnock, personal communication.

28   A. Thomas, S. Chess and H. Birch, 1965.

29   Grove, p. 47.

30   Ibid., p. 46.

31   James Warnock, personal communication.

32   Maria Jenkins, personal communication.

33   Ibid.

34   UA, 6, p. 11.

35   Ibid.

36   Kitty Warnock, personal communication.

37   UA, 6, pp. 32–34.

38   Ibid.

39   Mary Warnock, 2015, p. 33.

40   UA, 6, pp. 32–34.

41   Ibid., p. 34.

42   Ibid., p. 33.

43   Ibid.

44   Kitty Warnock, personal communication.

45   Julia Lloyd, personal communication.

46   Grove, p. 46.

47   Ann Strawson, personal communication.

48   Malu Halasa, 1995.

49   Maria Jenkins, personal communication.

50   Ann Strawson, personal communication.

51   Ibid.

52   Warnock, 2000, p. 160.

53   Ann Strawson, personal communication.

54   Warnock, 2000, p. 28.

55   Ibid.

56   Maria Jenkins, personal communication.

57   Ann Strawson, personal communication.

58   Personal communication to author.

59   Warnock, 2000, pp. 158–159.

60   UA, 6, p. 23.

61   Ibid., p. 25.

62   Ibid.

63   Ibid.

64   Warnock, 2000, p. 122.

65   Ibid.

66   John Bayley, 2000.

67   Ann Strawson, personal communication.

68   Julia Lloyd, personal communication.

69   In the account of the meetings of the Committee on Special Educational Needs in Chapter Seven, the author describes how Mary reports (accurately) that he had been 'though not a lover, a great friend and support (and probably all the better for not being a lover).' It might be thought that this remark suggests that Mary was more open to taking lovers than many people thought possible. When the author delicately broached the possibility of affairs with some of his interviewees, the response from most was along the lines of 'Goodness me, no. She was far too busy for any of that.' Others were less certain.

70   Warnock, 2000, pp. 219–230.

71   Ibid., pp. 228–229.

72   Ibid.

73   Ibid., p. 233.

74   Ibid., pp. 237–238.

75   Ibid., p. 236.

76   Grove, p. 47.

6. What Are Schools For?

After nearly a decade at St. Hugh's, Mary had begun to feel frustrated and bored with her life as an Oxford philosophy don, limited as it was by the demands of teaching a rather rigid curriculum and by the parochial concerns of college politics. She was not sure what new directions she could take but was at least certain that she should seize any opportunities which arose. In this spirit, she accepted, in 1956, the appointment as Editor of *The Oxford Magazine*,[1] a weekly periodical for senior members of the university covering academic matters, book reviews and obituaries. She had served as a member of the editorial board, but now, as editor, she had to write a 1,000-word editorial every week in term time. She also found herself with a hands-on executive role, one of her duties being to set up the magazine at the printers. This experience served her well when she later embarked on what virtually amounted to a second career in freelance journalism. Over the years she wrote opinion pieces and book reviews for, among others, *The Sunday Telegraph*, *The Telegraph*, the *Times Educational Supplement*, *The Times Higher Education Supplement*, *New Society*, *The Listener*, *The Oxford Quarterly Magazine*, *The New Republic*, *The London Review of Books*, and *The Glasgow Herald*.[2]

In the post-war period *The Oxford Magazine* had moved away from its more literary origins but it still maintained a focus on poetry alongside its newer role as a forum for commentary and discussion of university affairs. J. R. R. Tolkien and C. S. Lewis had both been contributors in the pre-war years as had Dorothy Sayers and a young W. H. Auden. It was perhaps this aspect of the magazine's history which attracted the interest of the publisher, Robert Maxwell, who approached the new young editor with a takeover offer.[3] To protect the magazine's independence, Mary successfully resisted the proposal, but she was fascinated by the power of Maxwell's personality and his drive to dominate. She got on

  https://doi.org/10.11647/OBP.0278.06

well with Elisabeth, Maxwell's wife and on discovering that she wanted
to study for a degree in French arranged a place for her at St. Hugh's.[4]

Around this time she joined the Board of Governors of Littlemore
Grammar School which always co-opted a fellow of St. Hugh's. In the
early 1960s, there was a move to abolish the tripartite system set up in
1944 of grammar, secondary modern and technical schools, merging
the three types into a single 'comprehensive' system. Littlemore was
an ideal candidate for such rationalisation as it already shared its site
with Northfield Secondary Modern. The two schools merged to become
Oxford's first comprehensive school. The moving spirit behind the
merger was Jack Peers and the new school was named after him—the
Peers School. He became a friend. Mary was swayed by the arguments
for the comprehensive system and briefly became an advocate for them,
though she was soon strongly opposing the abolition of grammar
schools which, it seemed to her, provided a valuable pathway for the
clever children of working-class parents to access higher education with
all the subsequent career benefits that could offer.

Peers was Chairman of the Oxfordshire Education Authority and
Mary soon found herself a member of that body too.[5] She decided the
teaching of music in the local authority would be her main focus. She
had always been passionate about music and was determined that all
children should have the opportunity to share her enthusiasm. The
County Education Officer was willing to support her, but, a shy man,
he could not cope at all or communicate with his eccentric Director of
Music, Constance Pilkington. After Mary had tried and failed to act as a
liaison between them, it was agreed that a Music sub-committee should
be set up and she should chair it.[6] Mary described Miss Pilkington, as
she was known, as having brilliant, short white hair and bright blue
eyes and wearing 'impeccable pleated skirts and striped Macclesfield
silk blouses and extremely elegant pointed brogue shoes.'[7] When Mary
asked her where she bought these shoes, she replied with withering
scorn, mingled with embarrassment 'They were made for me, of course.'
Miss Pilkington was hopeless at any sort of organisational development
but had an unerring eye for unusual ability and would identify and
encourage any really talented child musicians, setting many of them
on the path to a professional career. Mary provided the organisational
touch as well as advocacy for music within the local authority and soon

music teaching began to flourish. There seemed to be limitless money for new premises and instruments. New school orchestras were encouraged throughout the county and a new county youth orchestra was launched with professional guest conductors. Notable amongst these were Muir Matheson, a successful composer and conductor of film music and a young Hungarian refugee, Laszlo Heltay, who went on to found the Brighton Festival Chorus and the chorus of the Academy of St. Martin in the Fields.[8]

Mary's tentative explorations of opportunities outside university life took an unexpected turn following a chance meeting in Oxford's Broad Street with Dame Lucy Sutherland. Dame Lucy was the Principal of Lady Margaret Hall and Chair of the Girls' Public Day School Trust, the governing body responsible for a number of independent girls' schools, including the Oxford High School (OHS). She told Mary that the head of this school was leaving and suggested that she should apply for the vacancy.[9] The suggestion appealed to Mary more than Dame Lucy probably expected. Mary felt that she had been pigeonholed as a specialist in existentialism and she was being asked to supervise every postgraduate who showed an interest in the subject. She found some of these students 'rather dim' and teaching them unrewarding.[10] 'Each was more terrible than the last,' she felt. They would hang around after the usual hour was over and, unlike undergraduates, expect to be supervised in the vacations. Mary couldn't wait to get away. Her two daughters, Kitty and Fanny, who were at the High School, encouraged her to apply. Geoffrey thought she was mad to want to change her job but didn't discourage her.[11] As for her two sons, they bet her that if she were to apply she would not get the job. This probably only served to spur her on.

Given that her experience in school teaching was limited to six months spent as a school-leaver at the preparatory school, Rosehill, before she went up to Lady Margaret Hall, and two years at Sherborne Girls' School as an assistant teacher while she was an undergraduate, it is indeed surprising that she was appointed. But in February 1966, appointed she was, and she took up her appointment the following September.[12] The OHS was a direct grant school, receiving a grant from central government on condition that it admitted a certain number of children who otherwise would not have been able to afford the fees. The idea of the direct grant was to open such schools to the brightest poor children, but the majority of pupils were fee-paying, and therefore from middle-class families as, in fact, were many of the scholarship girls.[13]

Mary, by now in her early forties, made an immediate impact, not least by her style of dress. According to one ex-student, 'she was always soberly but smartly dressed, yet with a sense of individuality [...] She wore no nonsense pencil line skirts with a blouse or jumper, occasionally a suit with flat shoes. Her gown billowed as she strode on to the stage for morning assembly.'[14] Another former student remembered her, perhaps on more informal occasions, as wearing 'swirling purple capes, hats, big belts, once even an ethnic hammock'[15] (whatever that may have been). It was recalled that 'through her glasses she had a steady gaze. Her voice had a distinctive and rich timbre. She had clear diction with an unmistakeable North Oxford delivery of clear and considered thoughts and ideas. She was forthright, unfussy, calm and direct in her communications.'[16] She was also outspoken in her enthusiasms and extremely energetic.

One of her early priorities was to improve the teaching of music in the school. When she arrived, there was a significant obstacle in the form of the Head of Music who had an unfortunate tendency to turn 'people against the subject.'[17] She had high standards but was 'inflexible and snobbish.' Mary's view was that she really hated teaching and, given that she also seemed actively to dislike her pupils, sometimes throwing a board rubber at anyone who crossed her. The distressing consequence was that her pupils reciprocated with a dislike of her subject. Mary successfully persuaded her that her real talents lay in organisation, 'that she was wasting her time in the lowly company of school mistresses' and that she should change career and become a hospital administrator.[18]

Mary already had her eye on a successor, John Melvin, who was teaching in a preparatory school in Malvern. His initial appointment was part-time but when the position became vacant, he was appointed Director of Music. When Melvin arrived, he found that many of the students viewed music with positive animosity and regarded it as a subject not worthy of serious thought. As one ex-student put it, 'great things were expected of him and great things he gave.'[19] He found his position, one ex-student wrote 'a true baptism of fire but quite soon he had established an orchestra which was gradually able to tackle the symphonic repertoire—an indication of both his leadership and the potential of musical ability there was in the school.'[20] His other great aim was to involve as many girls as possible in musical activities and his warm, enthusiastic personality and humour soon resulted in a high-powered senior orchestra and large senior choir as well as two other orchestras, two choirs, a wind band and other smaller chamber groups. Mary helped him by ensuring that on entry to the school, all girls with musical talent were placed in the same entry form thus facilitating the timetabling of music. She also established the principle that girls were allowed to absent themselves from other lessons if they were required for rehearsals. Mary led by personal example. At one point the junior orchestra needed a French horn player. Mary bought a horn and began to learn to play it from scratch. She bribed the students in her Latin class to play the instrument too by offering a reward of Smarties to any of them who reached a higher standard than she did after a year.[21] Mary's enthusiasm for learning the horn did not last for long but her 'can do' approach and determination to lead by example clearly captured the imagination of the girls. At a more strategic level her most enduring legacy to music at the school was the planning and fundraising for a separate music block which was built and opened in 1975.[22]

Perhaps the trickiest task for new headteachers is deciding what to do about existing members of the staff they have inherited whom they find to be incompetent, obstructive or difficult to work with. As well as the Head of Music, whose redeployment is described above, there were two other teachers who fell into this category. One was a man whose poor teaching combined with unfortunate personal habits such as forgetting to do up his fly buttons. Mary convinced him he would be better off teaching at a boys' school.[23] The other was the teacher responsible for religious education. She was a figure of fun to many of her pupils who mocked her with pranks competing, for example, to see how many lunch boxes they could manage to drop out of the classroom window during a forty-minute lesson. This teacher saw Mary as an ungodly influence. When Mary broached the possibility of her leaving, the response was discouraging. 'Mrs. Warnock,' she replied, 'As long as you are in the school, I feel it is my duty to stay.' Mary eventually enticed her to leave by persuading a friendly don at one of the Oxford women's colleges to offer her a place to read Theology.[24]

The rest of the staff viewed Mary with some reserve but were largely swept along by her enthusiasms. Initially she found staff meetings unnerving because no one volunteered any ideas or responded to hers. Yet almost before she was out of the room, she could hear discontented mutterings about proposals she had made. However, she was fortunate in having two deputy headteachers whom she found energetic, competent and delightful to work with.

One might have thought that, given the school's academic catchment area, the students would all have had a good grounding in basic literacy and numeracy skills. This was far from the case. The prevailing philosophy in British primary schools at that time was that young children should learn reading and basic maths by a process of discovery, preferably through play. This child-centred approach had been developed in the 1920s and 1930s by Susan Isaacs, a psychologist and child psychoanalyst, whose books *Intellectual Growth in Young Children* (1930) and *Social Development of Young Children* (1933) were compulsory reading for teachers training to work in infant and primary schools.[25] Mary had visited a number of primary schools during her time as a member of the Oxfordshire Education Authority and had come to believe that children were being short-changed by educational methods such as these. In one school in Thame she had seen 'children [...] being encouraged to count books by piling them up in lots of four along the walls. They had never heard of the four times table.' For Mary, this meant every child had to be a 'sort of Leibniz, an inventive mathematician. who could discover how to calculate without rules of thumb or rote learning.'[26] Fortunately, her Head of Maths, Miss Jackson, took a similar view and was driven to despair by the students' ignorance of their times tables. It became a common sight to see Miss Jackson 'tramping around in the grounds, often in rain or snow, with one small girl, getting her to recite her tables or repeat formulae whether she understood them or not.'[27]

Unlike many headteachers, Mary took on some classroom teaching herself. All girls had to learn Latin and she allocated herself the lower of two streams containing the girls supposed to be less linguistically competent. Her aim, which she shared with her class, was that by the end of the year they would as a group be achieving better than the top stream. On Mary's account they nearly always won. They learnt their conjugations by heart. Mary wrote later: 'The sheer spirit of competition entered the souls of these children and they mopped up knowledge of tenses, conjugations, parts of speech, the agreement of adjectives with nouns.' Mary drew on the teaching she had received at St. Swithun's as well as her experience of teaching Latin to the Sherborne girls during the war, There was, of course, no nonsense about girls learning to conjugate Latin verbs by a process of discovery; indeed there was much chanting of Latin grammar of the 'hic haec hoc' variety. She again awarded her pupils prizes of packets of Smarties for success in their tests.[28] Doubtless Mary's own competitiveness was infectious.

Fig. 5 Images of Mary during her time as headmistress (1966–72), from Oxford High School Magazine. Photographs provided by Oxford High School with the permission of Mary Warnock's family, CC BY-NC.

As headmistress she had many more arduous duties, amongst which was dealing with parents. Mary categorised the parents, in a rather sweeping generalisation, as either pushy (the academic parents) or indifferent. But there was another group who 'tended to be either rude or patronising or both.'[29] Surprisingly these were often the parents of so-called scholarship girls rather than the fee-paying. Many parents were dissatisfied that the school was not following the new trend of learning through discovery rather than learning by rote but here Mary was implacable. She had little patience with parents like this and found them hard to deal with. Her attitude to parents may have come from a sense of identification with girls whose parents were not allowing them sufficient autonomy. In any event, it was unjust to many parents, and later lost her some allies.

In contrast, Mary was far more positive in her attitude to the older girls in the school. A new Sixth Form block was completed shortly after her arrival. Judy Hague, who was a pupil throughout Mary's tenure as headmistress, recalls

> the Sixth Form block was an important step as it gave generations of sixth formers a place to study and socialize: a half-way house between school and university. There was a common room, library and study area and a kitchen. It was the sixth formers' domain, staff had to be invited in. On the study area walls hung art by Leonid Pasternak, father of Boris, which inspired me as I began to learn Russian. To aid the transition to life after school, sixth formers were allowed to wear their own clothes rather than school uniform.[30]

Under Mary's leadership, the prefect system and position of Head Girl were abolished. Instead, older girls volunteered to be 'part of a changing group who ran the school and ran the School Council.' She regularly had tea with this group and any other member of the sixth form who wanted to attend 'and these teas went on until I had to throw people out to go home to get the supper.'[31] Every aspect of the school was discussed; the curriculum, the narrowness of the A level syllabus, what to do about drugs and other less important disciplinary matters. At times, Mary wrote later, 'I felt myself in danger of discussing things more freely with the sixth form than with staff.'[32]

The mid- and late 1960s coincided with the rise of hippy culture in Britain. Mary herself, like most of the school parents, felt that the use of cannabis was by far the most worrying feature of the societal changes that were occurring at this time. It was widespread. For example, nearly all the 400.000 people, among them a significant number of sixth-formers who attended The Isle of Wight Music Festival held in August 1970, smoked cannabis. As a university town, with large numbers of young people in its population and on a drug circuit stretching from Birmingham to Southampton, Oxford was an epicentre of cannabis usage.[33] Thus, the girls at OHS were exposed to a culture in which the use of cannabis was both normalised and regarded as adventurous and exciting. The main worry, which Mary shared with parents, was that cannabis use might lead to experiments with more dangerous drugs, particularly heroin. Many parents would have known that the issue of drugs had arisen in Mary's own family. As we have seen, in 1971, she was asked to remove her younger son James from Winchester College. Although no reason was articulated, she and Geoffrey were given the misleading impression that the main problem was drugs in some form. James was friends with a number of OHS girls, so his expulsion was widely known about.[34]

Another challenge arose from the fact that the contraceptive pill had come on the market in the early 1960s and was widely available when Mary became headmistress of OHS. Now that it was becoming so safe and easy to prevent pregnancy, the trend towards earlier intercourse, which was already underway, accelerated. The average age of first intercourse for women fell from twenty for women born in the late 1940s, to eighteen for those born in the mid-1960s.[35] Many more girls were becoming sexually active for the first time before the age of 18, something that would have been distinctly less common in their parents' generation and even less so when Mary had been an adolescent. This raised generational anxieties among parents and staff who were dealing with these issues for the first time and who were uncertain how to respond.[36]

There was also the question of clothes. The Upper-Sixth had been allowed to abandon wearing a uniform before Mary arrived and it was hard to resist the pressure from the Lower-Sixth to follow. Dress was a topic always raised at governors' meetings. Governors thought that the girls in the top forms presented an appalling spectacle and Mary could not but agree. On her description, 'their hair was lank and drooped in curtains across their faces. Out of doors they wore blankets with a hole through which their heads appeared. They seldom wore shoes.'

In Assembly one day she told them the school was the opposite of a Mosque: the rule was that you had to put on your shoes when you entered it. The girls often wore 'exceptionally smelly Afghan coats, the dirty-white uncured leather revealing the fur of the animal through the seams. Their skirts were little frills, barely concealing their knickers, and over these, ridiculously, they often had much-prized maxicoats' falling to the ground.[37] But having said they need not wear uniform, Mary thought it would be counter-productive to try to specify what was acceptable clothing. Gradually through persuasion and common-sense, most of the girls settled 'for a kind of cleanish voluntary uniform of trousers and floppy men's sweaters, with no shirts under them,'[38] though the curtains of hair remained.

Before they made their choices of A level subjects, all students had to go and see Mary to discuss them. Judy Hague described her own interview:

> I was apprehensive about the interview as I wanted to study three languages and did not know how the school/Mrs Warnock would view this. I knew I wanted to pursue my love of languages and literature. I had taken my French O level one year early and was already studying German. Having passed my French O level, I took up the opportunity to begin Russian. I was clear where my path lay, I wanted to study languages at university. No-one in my family, at that stage, had attended university. I tentatively asked Mrs Warnock if it was acceptable to take three modern languages. She agreed and I was relieved. Even more tentatively, I asked if I should be aiming high and thinking of applying for Oxford. She fixed me with a steady, encouraging gaze and replied 'absolutely'.[39]

This encouragement to aspire high was characteristic of Mary's approach to students. Judy, who afterwards did indeed go to Oxford, writes

> without her encouragement and the high standards of education at the High School, I would not have had the courage to step out and aim for Oxford. My subsequent career was in the UK public sector, civil service and international development. Growing up in Oxford and attending the High School under Mrs Warnock's leadership gave me a love of learning, a wide angled lens on the world, a cosmopolitan outlook, a passion for the arts, literature and languages and a sense I could make a difference.[40]

Mary took a more personal, continuing interest in girls who were suffering difficult family circumstances. One of these was Ruth Cigman. In the summer of 1967 Ruth had taken her O levels at another Oxford grammar school, Milham Ford. She was then, however, asked to leave as she was seen as naughty and rebellious, leading a group of girls who broke all the rules. Ruth's parents had separated acrimoniously. Her mother had come from London to Oxford to study but had very little money. Needing to find another school for her daughter, she was put in touch with Mary who agreed to admit Ruth to the High School on a scholarship. Ruth wanted to study French, Russian and Music, but there was no Russian teacher. As there was one other girl who wanted to study Russian, Mary hired a Russian teacher for the two of them. Then Ruth didn't get on with the music teacher whom Mary knew was difficult. Mary arranged for her to have lessons in her home with her own son, Felix, who was also studying music from home, following his early departure from Winchester at the age of sixteen. Ruth had a difficult home life, caught between warring parents. She became anorexic and was referred to the Warneford, Oxford's mental hospital where she was given no psychotherapy but prescribed medication she didn't take. To reduce the pressure on her, Mary suggested she gave up French and this seemed to relax the situation. Subsequently, Ruth became an academic philosopher of education attributing her career to Mary's influence. She later commissioned Mary's so-called U-turn *Special Educational Needs: A New Look* (2005, see Chapter Seven) and worked on several further writing projects with her.[41]

Jane Wardle was another pupil Mary took under her wing. Jane's parents were unable to provide a stable home for her. Her father, portrait painter Peter Wardle, spent much of the year in Portugal. Her mother suffered from a chronic mental illness and spent long periods in mental hospitals. Jane and her two brothers were moved from pillar to post during their childhood, even spending some time in children's homes. She attended thirteen different schools before presenting herself to the OHS at the age of sixteen. Typically, Mary took a particular interest in her and, on a number of occasions when the home situation broke down, while permanent solutions were sought, she found room for Jane in her own home. Jane won a place at St. Anne's College, Oxford and went on to train as a clinical psychologist. As an academic, she made important and original contributions in cancer prevention and specialised in the psychological impact of cancer. She herself tragically died of cancer in 2015, not long after her appointment as Professor of Clinical Psychology at University College, London.[42]

While Mary was immersed in the administration and leadership of the High School, Geoffrey's academic career was also moving in an administrative direction. Having been Senior Tutor at Magdalen for many years he had been narrowly defeated (by a single vote) in the 1968 election for president of that college, but three years later he was appointed Principal of Hertford College. This was clearly going to be a challenge: the college was achieving poor academic results, was in financial difficulties and the buildings were in a state of disrepair. After a short period of time, Mary decided that she could not continue as headmistress of the High School while also providing the level of support she felt Geoffrey needed.[43]

There was a second, more complicated reason for her departure: she was becoming increasingly troubled that the direct grant arrangement was under threat. The High School would either have to become fully independent or it would need to merge into the state system and become comprehensive, and neither option was especially palatable to Mary. She felt that the abolition of grammar schools would disadvantage the brightest pupils from the poorest backgrounds. Their access to fee-paying schools would be curtailed, condemning them to remain in the comprehensive state schools which, she thought, would be less academically aspirational. When the High School's governors took the decision to become independent, Mary did what she could to mitigate the damage (as she saw it) by arranging with the headmaster of the local comprehensive, Cherwell School, for some of their sixth formers to attend the OHS for specific subjects.[44] But there was no turning back the tide and the direct grant system was duly abolished in 1976.

Mary left the High School in the summer of 1972. Despite her disagreements over education policy, she did not find leaving easy. Many years later, when she was in her late seventies, her daughter Maria, who was then Director of Art at Dulwich College, London, arranged for her to spend a morning at the school, taking two assemblies and then teaching philosophy to various classes of different ages. Mary wrote of this experience: 'I had forgotten the excitement of teaching a class of perhaps 24 children, all keen to contribute, all eager to absorb new ideas, all articulate and confident. I ended my morning exhausted but exhilarated, thinking "if I had my life again, this and only this is what I would do. Who knows?"'[45]

In truth, Mary knew that assisting Geoffrey in his duties would not amount to a full-time occupation but she did not want to go back to university teaching. Fortunately for her, Lady Margaret Hall was advertising a research fellowship and, although she was more senior than might have been expected for an award of this sort, she applied and was appointed to it. This gave her the time to write her next philosophical work, *Imagination*, published in 1976.[46]

She was also able to contribute to the public debates which were just then beginning on the future direction of education in British schools. These were given a strong impetus by a speech delivered by James Callaghan, then the newly appointed Prime Minister, at Nuffield College, Oxford in October 1976. Callaghan had previously taken little or no interest in educational issues and this speech was, in fact, written by his Senior Policy Adviser, Bernard (later Lord) Donoughue.[47] Much of the public controversy around state secondary education was still centred around the contentious issue of the abolition of grammar schools, but Donoughue, who had four children being educated in the state sector, pointed out that what parents were really worried about was that their children should be protected from bullying and intimidation and that basic standards in educational skills and discipline should be ensured. In a deplorable number of schools, he thought, this was not happening. In a note to the Prime Minister, he wrote 'This is surely an appropriate time to restate the best of the traditional and permanent values—to do with excellence, quality and actually acquiring mental and manual skills; and not only acquiring these qualities but also learning to respect them.'[48] Callaghan's speech echoed these sentiments and concluded with a call for a Great Debate on education. The teaching unions and Her Majesty's Inspectorate were predictably incensed at this political incursion into what they saw as their exclusive territory. The civil servants at the Department for Education and Science were also unenthusiastic and produced a bland Green Paper barely responding to the issues raised in the Prime Minister's speech.[49] But Callaghan had prompted a debate which was to continue for some years both regionally and nationally, and Mary contributed to it.

First she collaborated with an education journalist, Ian Devlin, in writing a book *What Must We Teach* (1977).[50] Devlin attended all the regional conferences that followed the Prime Minister's speech and interviewed large numbers of teachers, parents, children and business leaders about their views. This collaboration with Devlin was the first of a number of books, public lectures and articles in magazines in which she expressed opinions on many aspects of education in schools. Her views were partly an expression of her own experience as a pupil but had been developed most substantially in the various teaching roles and institutions she had been involved in. In fact, her own education, as we have seen, was unusual: she did not go to school until she was nine and so had no personal experience of infant or state primary schooling. From nine to sixteen she attended an independent school with a particularly strong emphasis on the teaching of moral behaviour as the highest purpose of secondary education (at least for girls). She then moved, for her sixth form years to another private secondary school with more rigorous academic teaching. It was as a university teacher that she began to gain a wider experience: her undergraduate pupils came from a range of different secondary schools, so she was able to see for herself the skill levels and diverse value systems which such schools had taught. Above all, though, it was her experience as headmistress of the Oxford High School which had shaped her opinions on educational matters. Another formative experience, on a strategic and policy-making level, was her chairmanship between 1974 and 1978 of a government committee on the education of children with special educational needs (see Chapter Seven). She had not previously worked in special education, but she visited dozens of schools for such children both at home and abroad. Any gaps in her first-hand experience in education were compensated for by her professional background in philosophy; she had learned always to rely on evidence rather than opinion and, especially, to subject received wisdom to the closest scrutiny.

Mary continued to take an interest in education for the rest of her life. Over a period of forty years she wrote on a wide variety of educational matters. In that time there was a number of reforming Ministers for Education and Prime Ministers, notably Kenneth Baker, Tony Blair and Michael Gove, and some major changes to the educational system, particularly the introduction of the National Curriculum as well as some significant changes in teacher training. For the most part, Mary's views remained consistent, but consideration of her published work needs to take account of the changing context in which she was writing.

She was never afraid to tackle the really big questions relating to education, so it is not surprising that she wrote extensively on the fundamental question—what was education for? In *Schools of Thought*, published in 1977, she proposes that education should be judged on whether it improves the life of the pupil in the future.[51] This is an arguable proposition for surely one's time at school is a part of life, not just a preparation for life, but Mary saw the preparation of children for the future as the main purpose of schooling. In order to decide whether an individual's life has been changed for the better by education, one needs to be clear about what we mean by a 'good' life and she examines three criteria: virtue, work and imagination.[52]

Mary draws on the work of three philosophers, Aristotle, Kant and Hume, to suggest that to be judged virtuous or 'good' an individual must behave 'truthfully, loyally, bravely, kindly and fairly.'[53] When teachers consider the ways in which they can encourage 'good' behaviour, they should think beyond mere conformity to school rules. Some rules are clearly necessary, but school rules are largely 'specific regulations with regard to such things as the marking of clothes, the production of explanatory notes in case of absence, the seeking of permission to leave the school grounds during the day and other such matters.'[54] Some rules are clearly necessary to ensure the safety and wellbeing of pupils, but 'so-called moral rules are utterly different [...] in the case of morals, what is wanted is essentially a certain attitude, specifically an attitude towards other people.' This distinction, between behaviour determined by narrow rules and behaviour governed by sympathy for and consideration of others,[55] was an issue she was to return to several times.

At the time Mary was writing some moral philosophers were advancing the view that being moral was primarily a matter of making the right decisions. There were correct moral principles which, if followed, would inevitably lead to moral behaviour. As Mary put it, this view claimed that 'the knowledge in question is knowledge of how to make rational and defensible decisions.'[56] If this were the case, then morality could be taught, like arithmetic. Mary profoundly disagreed with this rationalist view of morality. According to her, while mathematics is an abstract subject that can be taught in the classroom, 'there is no such thing as "doing morality", only behaving well or badly, and behaviour needs real contexts, not merely exemplary ones.'[57] The most effective way for children to learn morality in school is for them to see their teachers behaving well themselves. 'A teacher can be fair or unfair, honest or dishonest (pretending to knowledge he hasn't got, for instance), kind or cruel, forgiving or relentless, generous or mean.'[58] These kinds of qualities allow a teacher when dealing with children's conduct, to be unequivocal in condemning certain types of behaviour such as claiming to have finished work when it hasn't been or taking the belongings of another child, and praising other behaviour, such as being helpful or generous.

Schools of Thought had a mixed reception in philosophical and educational journals. Karen Hanson agreed with Mary that we should all bear more responsibility for our educational institutions. She finds the book 'a passionate and intelligent plea to take up that responsibility and a helpful and interesting aid in the task.'[59] In contrast, Richard Peters, whose ideas are criticised in the book, though he does not mention this, was largely dismissive of the arguments Mary put forward, regarding it as patchy and poorly researched with a misleading title.[60] An American reviewer was disappointed by the absence of any mention of the potentially destructive influence of schools and the neglect of the psychological and political factors that bear on the problem of inequalities.[61]

Mary expanded much later on some of her views on the teaching of moral behaviour in a sermon, titled *Education and Values*, delivered in February 1995 in the University Church in Oxford.[62] Her views as expressed in this sermon are not far from those espoused by her High Anglican school, St. Swithun's, sixty years earlier (although without the emphasis on guilt and remorse). Children have to learn, she claimed, 'that they have such natural passions, that they may be led by them into doing what they immediately want, rather than what they ought to do; that is to say they can be tempted.'[63] According to Aristotle and Christian teaching, overcoming temptation is powerful in contributing to a positive self-image. In contrast, determinism, the belief that one is fated to behave in the way one does, undermines self-belief. Determinism, she wrote, 'is the most hopeless philosophy if taken seriously. It removes all will to fight, whether for intellectual or moral improvement.'[64] In her sermon she quotes Bishop Joseph Butler who, in 1726 argued there were two steady principles in human behaviour: benevolence and what he called 'cool self-love.' He was convinced that humans do care for other people, it was part of their nature to do so. But they should also care for their long-term self-interest, realising coolly that it is contrary to their own interests to behave badly, to let people down, to bully them, to prove themselves too greedy or ambitious.'[65]

The school, Mary wrote, is an important, perhaps the most important, place for children to learn values, including the value of behaving well. But other values were taught in school. For example, for many children, 'it may be the only place where aesthetic values can be experienced and discussed.'[66] A powerful medium for teaching morality, particularly to young children, is, Mary believed, the telling of stories with strong moral relevance to their own experience. By way of counter-example, she did not believe that teaching about cutting down rain forests or over-fishing, reprehensible though such activities undoubtedly are, would do much to improve children's moral behaviour—these issues were too remote from children's everyday lives. Instead, the discussion of stories that raised moral problems about children like themselves would be far more effective.

More broadly, Mary sensed that teachers found it difficult to teach moral values. 'Either they say that it is a matter for the family, or, more specifically, they say that of course they are prepared to keep decent order in the classroom and playground, but they raise the question, who are they to dictate morality to their pupils?'[67] Mary thought this reticence arose from moral relativism, a mistaken deference to multiculturalism, when there were 'common elements in humanity [...] the preferences, likes and dislikes, loves and hates, which all

humans share.'[68] These universal human values *must* be taught. It
followed that schools should not base their teaching of such values
on any particular set of religious, including Christian beliefs. On the
other hand, there are some kinds of values which are not universal,
such as sexual mores for example, and in these cases, Mary recognised
a valid place for instruction according to religion if this accorded with
the ethos of the particular school.

The second ingredient of a good life for which school should prepare
children was work, which included practical skills training as well as
what might be described as a 'work ethic.' 'Children should learn at
school what will help them to work for the rest of their lives,' she wrote
in *Schools of Thought*, although she made it clear this should dictate only
part of the curriculum.[69] She realised, too, that there is hostility in some
circles to the idea that 'one should teach children with an eye to what
they will do, how they will work, when they leave school.' This might
suggest working-class children should only be prepared for working-
class jobs. Preparing children for work does not mean preparing them
for particular types of work; they should be prepared for a wide range
of work situations. Mary accepted that some work is by its nature boring
but 'even where a job is bad in all kinds of ways, it is better to have it
than not, and probably better to work hard at it than less hard.' School
is a place where one learns that it may be necessary to work really
hard, overcoming boredom to achieve a worthwhile academic goal.[70]
She noted that most people find hard work surprisingly enjoyable, and
that money earned is better than money 'handed out.' But schools, in
determining what they should teach, should listen to what the outside
world is demanding.[71] This does not, as is sometimes implied, diminish
the subject in question. 'To know that arithmetic will be useful to you
later does not mysteriously reduce the value of learning it or render it
impure.'[72]

Mary concludes the section on work with a list of subjects that
children should be taught.[73] She begins with reading and writing and
mathematics, especially arithmetic, to a standard of competence. The
pupil will need to gain understanding of what adult society is and this
will lead, depending on interests and ability, to a branching out into
economics, geography, history and sociology, together with at least one
foreign language. The pupil must also have a certain understanding,

part practical, part theoretical, of the physical sciences and technology.[74] Looking back at Mary's list it may nowadays seem uncontroversial, even banal, but her point was that these were subjects which all schools should teach. Of course, they would also be expected to add numerous other subjects in response to demand from their pupils.

Finally, after discussing virtue and work as components of the good life for which schools should prepare children, Mary considers the third and, in her view equally important component—imagination. Imagination, or the capacity for 'image-making,' is essential for the construction of memories of the past and visualisations of the future: 'Educating a child's imagination, then, is partly educating his reflective capacity, partly his perceptive capacity; it may or may not lead to creativity; but it will certainly lead to his inhabiting a world more interesting and understood, less boring than if he had not been so educated.'[75] Of the types of educational activity that stimulate the imagination, she considers the vital importance of play in younger children who, as they grow older, begin to find in work the fun they enjoyed in play. Indeed, a recurring theme in Mary's writings on education was that one of the many purposes of education should be 'pleasure.' To increase the chances of enjoyment, the curriculum should allow the child to choose some of the subjects studied. This would reduce the possibility of boredom. She believed also that a pupil's imagination would be more stimulated by specialisation in some subjects than by learning 'a little bit of everything.'

Mary very much believed in the vital place of the arts as part of every pupil's education, but she rejects the idea that offering students endless opportunities for self-expression is the only or even the best way to educate the imagination. Nor should art education be seen as therapy for which most children have no need. Such an approach might result in children missing out on the appreciation of great art. 'While teachers are flogging their pupils into original compositions, may not masterpieces of music or painting or literature go unobserved [...]?'[76] If Mary was sceptical of the excessive value sometimes attached to 'self-expression,' especially in music, she was clear that time and space should be available for 'solitary reflection' and for contemplation of the beauty of the natural world, and that such opportunities were often undervalued. Of course it is difficult for schools to find time when such reflectiveness can occur, but teachers should provide moments when the child's mind can 'wander, for him to think and feel as he likes.'[77] Mary was writing this nearly fifty years ago but it seems relevant in the twenty-first century when the 'crowding out' of solitude and reflection by children's constant exposure to screen-based activities such as television and video games, is a source of growing anxiety amongst present-day parents and educationalists.

While Mary stopped short of advocating a national curriculum as a legal requirement, in *What Must We Teach* she strongly encouraged the then Secretary of State for Education (Shirley Williams) to 'intervene now to restore a sense of direction to teaching in schools which is so badly lacking.'[78] She should, through the national inspectorate and local advisers, 'issue positive guidelines by altering the examination system, by the use of specific grants to encourage the teaching of compulsory subjects.'[79] In fact, the Secretary of State did nothing, and it was to be a further eleven years before a reforming Conservative minister, Kenneth Baker, introduced a compulsory national curriculum.[80]

The political debate around Baker's Education Reform Bill 1988 spurred Mary to make a further significant contribution. Except in the field of special needs education, she did not intervene in the debates on the Bill in the House of Lords, but she wrote a book, *A Common Policy for Education* (1988), in which she discusses the issues raised in the Bill. The book was greeted in the press in rather sensational terms, described by the *Morning Star* as a 'new broadside for Baker— the latest missile to be fired is by a formidable educationalist' and by the *Financial Times* as containing 'a string of proposals of breath-taking boldness,'[81] but in truth it is no more than a measured contribution to the debate and contains proposals that, had he read them, would have been largely acceptable to Baker. A review in *The Spectator* was more accurate, describing the book as 'one of the most lucid contributions to the "great debate". It merits the widest possible readership.'[82] Mary agrees with Baker, against the views of many teachers, that competition is necessary in education, provided it is fair competition with all students given a fair chance of success, and she also recognises the inherent risks in the imposition of a centralised and paternalistic curriculum. But, she claims, paternalism that works for the common good is by no means necessarily harmful.[83]

Despite the dangers of over-rigid centralisation, Mary was by now clearly in favour of a national curriculum, but she was understandably concerned about what it would contain. Her greatest concern, just as it had been a decade earlier, was that a prescriptive curriculum would discourage the development of the imagination, which should not be seen as an optional extra but as an essential part of all levels of education,.[84] She also draws an interesting and important distinction in the teaching of English, between the 'two great arms of the educational system.'[85] Students must learn the 'practical' skills such as how to construct a letter, write grammatically and spell correctly. They should also, if possible (and it will not be possible for all students) study English literature, a 'theoretical' subject. The curriculum and the examination system must give equal weight to both arms. This distinction between the practical and the theoretical holds for all the humanities as well as for the sciences and mathematics. In her view, the 'theoretical' should become more philosophical and more critical than it is at present.[86]

In *A Common Policy for Education*, Mary wrote for the first time on the teaching profession itself, its status and training programmes. She had already spoken on this, in February 1985, in the BBC's Richard Dimbleby Lecture, titled *Teacher, Teach Thyself*,[87] but in her book, she was able to give more considered views. Her lecture had been criticised for containing some patronising attitudes to parents, whom she categorised as either pushy or indifferent, but the book recognised the fundamental importance of a more collaborative relationship between parent and teacher, a stance that had been taken up strongly in the *Report on Children with Special Needs* nearly ten years earlier.[88] In *A Common Policy for Education* she discusses the low standing of teachers among the general population. The stereotypical teacher had for long been viewed either as a frustrated spinster or as a man who has failed at some other profession, but she felt there were two further reasons why teachers had fallen even lower in public estimation. A long teachers' strike had just ended. The strike appeared to have achieved little in terms of teachers' demands but had undoubtedly been highly exasperating for hard-pressed parents unable to send their children to school. The reluctance of teachers to return to the classroom had, in Mary's view, damaged the standing of the teaching profession. Indeed, it raised the very question that Mary had addressed in her Dimbleby Lecture: can we speak at all of teaching being a 'profession' when one of the essential characteristics of 'professionals' is that they do not withdraw their labour. And her second point was related: she described what she saw as the increasing politicisation of teachers. Inevitably, when teachers discuss unfairness in society, they risk encroaching on political territory, but, to the best of their ability, they should avoid taking sides where political controversy exists.[89] Once again Mary was highlighting an issue which remains relevant today.

While the politics of teachers, and of teaching, are matters of general concern for Mary, she sees teaching as primarily a practical task and considers in some detail what teachers need to be taught to do their job effectively. There are some purely practical skills, such as, for example, record-keeping, tracking pupils' progress, marking examinations and marking homework within a reasonable time. Then there are communication skills which may be instinctive in some, but which can also be learned. Amongst these she highlights learning how to respond to abuse from pupils and encouraging parental co-operation. A teacher's relationship with parents is distinguished from that of social workers who, seeing parents as products of their environment, are careful to avoid implying they 'could do better.' For Mary, 'could do better' is a necessary part of a good teacher's approach to children, and they need to convey this to parents. Teachers should strive to avoid preconceptions, based on social background, about their students' potential. Instead, they should nurture the individuality in each pupil and encourage parents to be surprised by what their children can achieve. Lastly, skills of a more personal kind are needed for the trainee to learn how to maintain control over a classroom of children, indeed, to exercise power.[90] This requires self-awareness and self-monitoring to avoid, for example, favouritism or signs of gender or racial preference. Nurturing individuality is vital, in Mary's view, and she returns to this theme again when reminding teachers to be constantly aware of the differences between students in their level of understanding and to tailor their approach accordingly.[91]

To emphasise the practical skills required to teach well and to develop the concept of teaching as a profession of equal status with other professions, Mary proposed the establishment of 'teaching schools,' analogous to the familiar teaching hospitals. Mary was ahead of her time with this idea, and it would be another twenty years before the first 'teaching school' was established in 2010. Also ahead of her time, although this was an idea which was already part of the public discourse on teacher training, she proposed a General Teaching Council (GTC) set up by teachers themselves to achieve common professional standards.[92] Such a council was indeed established in 2000 but was not a success, surviving only until 2012. It was replaced by a less bureaucratic Teaching Regulation Agency, which does not have the powers Mary envisaged for the GTC. Finally, Mary argued for an improved career structure and greatly enhanced salaries, especially for headteachers. 'The top salary they can reach is ridiculously low compared with that of other professions [...] It is not satisfactory if the only people willing to embark on teaching as a career are [...] those who feel themselves incapable of making a living in the competitive world of commerce/ industry or the City.'[93] To some degree at least this has been achieved, but only in the early years of the twenty-first century when the salaries of headteachers were significantly increased and when, in order to attract the brightest graduates, the fast track Teach First scheme was introduced.

So how can we assess Mary Warnock's contribution to secondary education in the last half of the twentieth century? First, she was an inspirational headmistress of the Oxford High School who made a significant impact on many of those who attended while she was in post. Nationally, her thoughtful contributions to the education debate that ran into the early years of the twenty-first century were marked by great common sense and a consistent philosophy. Over this period, education in Britain changed in two very significant ways. The responsibility for the running of schools was increasingly removed from local authorities with central government taking a much larger role. On this matter, Mary had very little to say in public though her unpublished writing reveals she was largely in favour. There was also very significant centralisation of teaching itself through the mechanism of the central control of the curriculum. This had begun with the debate initiated by James Callaghan in 1976 but was only activated by Kenneth Baker in the late 1980s and then carried even further by Michael Gove in the 2010 coalition administration. In the early years of the reforms, she had been greatly in favour of the emphasis on standards in literacy and numeracy and on the retention of a strong academic focus in secondary education. But her advocacy of a broader view of the purposes of education went largely unheeded. Instead, just as she had feared, the curriculum was increasingly determined by the content of examinations which seemingly had little relevance to adult life. Mary was disappointed, to put it mildly, that the increased emphasis on the measurement of academic achievement through testing and exams led to the neglect of the arts and humanities and of the imagination itself, all of which were being relentlessly squeezed from the system. Hopefully, as the twenty-first century unfolds, more attention will be given to the logic and sound common sense of her views.

There was just one area of great educational significance which Mary discussed not at all. The success of a school depends very largely on two factors—first, the quality of classroom teaching, on which she had much to say, and second, the quality of leadership, on which she said nothing.[94] Yet leadership was the quality in which Mary perhaps most excelled. As headmistress of the Oxford High School, she provided a model of academic excellence, discipline, fairness and compassion. In her subsequent writing on education in schools, she provided unique intellectual leadership, combining practical experience with the clarity of thought of a trained philosopher, this combination making her uniquely qualified to contribute to the debate.

Notes

1   Unpublished autobiography, UA, 7, p. 1.

2   Girton Archive, 1/16/2/7.

3   UA, 7, pp. 3–4.

4   Ibid.

5   Ibid., p. 6.

6   Ibid., p. 7.

7   Ibid., p. 8.

8   Ibid.

9   Ibid., p. 10.

10   Ibid., p. 11.

11   Ibid.

12   OHSGA Archive, Oxford High School for Girls Archive, http://oxfordhighschoolforgirls.daisy.websds.net/.

13   UA, 7, p. 13.

14   Judy Hague, personal communication.

15   Ibid., Janet Jones.

16   Judy Hague, personal communication.

17   UA, 7, p. 19.

18   Ibid.

19   OHSGA, John Melvin.

20   Ibid.

21   UA, 7, pp. 18–19.

22   OHSGA.

23   UA, 7, p. 23.

24   Ibid.

25   Graham, 2009.

26   UA, 7, p. 16.

27   Ibid., p. 15.

28   Ibid., p. 18.

29   Ibid., p. 13.

30   Judy Hague, personal communication.

31   UA, 7, p. 22.

32   Ibid.

33   Warnock, OHSGA.

34   Ibid.

35   Wellings et al., p. 41.

36   Warnock, OHSGA.

37   Ibid.

38   Ibid.

39   Judy Hague, personal communication.

40   Ibid.

41   Ruth Cigman, personal communication.

42   Andrew Steptoe, personal communication.

43   Warnock, 2000, p. 24.

44   OHSGA.

45   UA, 5, p. 15.

46   Warnock, 1976.

47   Donoughue, 2003.

48   Ibid.

49   Ibid.

50   Devlin and Warnock, 1977.

51   Warnock, 1977.

52   Warnock, 1977, p. 129.

53   Ibid., p. 132.

54   Ibid., p. 137.

55   Ibid., p. 138.

56   Ibid., p. 131.

57   Ibid., p. 132.

58   Ibid., p. 135.

59   Karen Hanson, p. 145.

60   Richard Peters, p. 115.

61   Joseph Novak, p. 85.

62   Warnock, University Sermon, 5 February 1995.

63   Ibid., p. 14.

64   Ibid., p. 15.

65   Ibid., p. 16.

66   Ibid., p. 1.

67   Ibid., p. 3.

68   Ibid., p. 8.

69   Warnock, 1977, p. 143.

70   Ibid., p. 144.

71   Ibid., p. 148.

72   Ibid.

73   Ibid., p. 150.

74   Ibid., pp. 150–151.

75   Ibid., p. 152.

76   Ibid., p. 160.

77   Ibid.

78   Devlin and Warnock, p. 154.

79   Ibid.

80   Baker, 1993, pp. 189–209.

81   Warnock, 1989.

82   Ibid.

83   Ibid., p. 176.

84   Ibid., pp. 37–38.

85   Ibid., p. 171.

86   Ibid., pp. 172–173.

87   Warnock, 1986.

88   Department of Education and Science, 1978, pp. 152–161.

89   Warnock, 1988, p. 112.

90   Ibid., pp. 117–118.

91   Ibid., p. 126.

92   Ibid., p. 132.

93   Ibid., p. 134.

94   Leithwood et al., 2006.

Fig. 6 Portrait of Mary Warnock, unknown photographer (1977), provided by the Warnock family, CC BY-NC.

7. All Change for Special Education

After Mary resigned from her post as headmistress of the Oxford High School for Girls in the summer of 1972, she turned her energies to supporting Geoffrey in his new position of Principal of Hertford College. She was involved in his social duties, in improving the college buildings and college arrangements, and in bringing up her younger children, now in their teens, in the Principal's lodgings. She also continued to tutor undergraduates and write philosophical works such as *Imagination* (1976), discussed in a later chapter. In fact, she later gave her wish to spend time on this book as one of her reasons for leaving the High School. In addition, she was sometimes requested to chair or sit on government committees.

In early 1974, she was approached by the then Secretary of State for Education and Science, Margaret Thatcher, to chair a committee of enquiry into the education of handicapped children and young people. The committee met first in September 1974 and presented its report in March 1978.[1] Surprisingly during the three and a half years the committee sat, Mary was only to have one very brief exchange with Margaret Thatcher about its progress and that was a somewhat accidental encounter. In March 1977, she was introduced to Thatcher, by now Leader of the Opposition, at a pre-lunch party in Oxford. Thatcher asked how the committee was going and, without waiting for a reply, said: 'SO important, I always think,' and moved on. Mary added 'I had the chance to notice what I thought was a total absence of warmth, and also that the back of her stiffly bouffant hair (nevertheless not as startling then as it later became) was less impressive than the front, indeed quite ragged.'[2]

    https://doi.org/10.11647/OBP.0278.07

The history of the education of children with handicaps is complicated.[3] The earliest efforts, for deaf children in the 1760s, blind children in 1791, and physically and mentally handicapped in the mid-nineteenth century, aimed at training young people for employment rather than educating them. Compulsory elementary schooling for the general population was introduced in Britain in 1870, and in the following years it was gradually recognised that many handicapped children should and could receive education as well as training. Local education authorities began to provide this, sometimes in special schools, sometimes within or attached to ordinary schools. This provision became a statutory duty following the recommendations of a progressive committee investigating the education of mentally and physically handicapped people which reported in 1898. Behavioural difficulties began to be recognised and addressed as a category of handicap at around the same time. In the 1920s, a principle emerged that established that education for the handicapped should be considered as part of overall education provision and should, as far as possible, be provided within mainstream schools.

The next big milestone was the Education Act 1944, the so-called Butler Act, best known for introducing selection of children at the age of eleven to enter grammar, secondary modern or technical schools. The act confirmed the principle that education of the handicapped should be part of the overall provision of education and the responsibility of local education authorities. These could meet such needs by establishing special day or boarding schools, education within ordinary schools, or support for pupils in private institutions, as they chose.[4] Children who were thought to be 'ineducable' were to be reported to the local authority so that provision could be made for them outside the education system.[5] In 1946, guidance from the Ministry of Education defined eleven categories of disability.[6] To be eligible for special education a child had to be diagnosed as having one of these—epilepsy, blindness, deafness etc. Guidance was given as to where each category should be educated. All children with physical handicap should be educated at a special school. So-called educationally subnormal children should be educated partly in special and partly in maintained schools.[7] The government estimated the number of children with different types of disability who would need some sort of special provision as between 14% and 17% of the total school population (very close to the estimate thirty years later in the Warnock Report).

Over the next thirty years some physical disabilities fell in number as improved social conditions, immunisation and medical treatments virtually eradicated tuberculosis, post-rheumatic fever and post-poliomyelitis conditions.[8] In contrast, there was increased awareness of the degree to which emotional and behavioural disorders or 'maladjustment,' as it was then called, affected school performance, and larger numbers of children were being seen by the rapidly expanding child guidance service.[9] Contrary to the intentions of the 1944 Act, new special schools were established more frequently than new classes within ordinary schools: this was partly due to the lack of buildings and resources in ordinary schools after the war, and the fact that big country houses, suitable for small educational establishments, were easy to find and relatively inexpensive to buy. Large numbers of children were still deemed 'ineducable.' As late as 1970 there were 24,000 children in Junior Training Centres, receiving instruction from untrained teachers, as well as 8,000 children in hospitals for the mentally subnormal.[10] The Brooklands experiment in the 1960s studied severely mentally handicapped children living in an austere, impoverished mental subnormality hospital. Removed to a small country house and given a nursery-school type of programme with much outdoor activity and play, these children made significant progress especially in their language ability compared to children who did not have this experience.[11] The findings from this study transformed views regarding the educability of even profoundly mentally retarded children.

In 1967, a group led by Dame Eileen Younghusband was set up to make recommendations to improve the situation of disabled children and young people. It recommended that there should be equality of opportunity for all children and better help to support them and to help them lead independent lives.[12] The 1970 Education (Handicapped Children) Act deemed that all children were now to be regarded as educable and become the responsibility of local authority education departments. In the same year the Chronically Sick and Disabled Persons Act required local authorities to provide education for deaf-blind, autistic and dyslexic children in maintained or assisted schools. These reports and new legislation combined with strong pressure from the voluntary sector, led by Stanley Segal, a passionate advocate for the education of disabled children and author of an influential book *No Child is Ineducable*,[13] persuaded the government to set up a new enquiry into the subject.

On 22 November 1973, the Advisory Committee for Handicapped Children that existed to advise the Secretary of State for Education on these matters had one of its routine all-day meetings. The committee, of which I was a member, was chaired by Professor Jack Tizard, the psychologist who had carried out the Brooklands experiment. At the end of the morning session, instead of the usual stale sandwiches, we were given an unusually delicious lunch at which, again unusually, wine was served. Immediately after lunch, when we had assembled for the afternoon's session, we were addressed by a civil servant who told us that our committee had been abolished. We were immediately shown out of the building. Later that afternoon, Margaret Thatcher, then Secretary of State for Education and Science, announced in the House of Commons that she proposed to set up a committee to review provision for handicapped children and young people. Thus was the Warnock Committee born.

I was the only member of the previous committee to be appointed to this new one. The first meeting was held on 17 September 1974. Based on her diaries, Mary wrote an account of the deliberations of the committee that was published in 2003.[14] The following account is partly based on her description and partly on my own recollections, not always identical with hers. It has to be said first, that Mary had virtually no experience in the field of special education. As headmistress of an independent girl's school, she had doubtless been faced from time to time with girls with health problems, but these gave her little idea of the range of physical and mental health problems as well as learning difficulties of all levels of severity which were the concern of the committee she was to chair. In fact, she thought this was probably one of the reasons she was chosen for the role of Chair. She had no preconceptions or vested interests. As we shall see, she was a rapid learner.

She took no part in choosing the members of the committee and was shocked to discover that there were twenty-six of us. The civil servants had perhaps been over-zealous in ensuring every interest was represented, though even so there were omissions. When Mary gazed round the room at the first meeting, she felt depressed at the thought that she would 'never learn the difference between one person and another' nor remember everybody's name, let alone why they were supposed to be there.[15] Her diary entry after that meeting read 'not a nice committee: too big, dowdy and full of vested interests. I hate it and probably always shall.'[16] This first meeting was indeed a 'getting to know each other' occasion with not much else discussed. Mary had a better opportunity of getting to know one member whom she met by chance on her return journey by tube and train to Oxford. This was Winifred Tumim, selected to serve because she had two profoundly deaf daughters. She had been highly active in achieving a better education for them and indeed for other deaf children. Winifred was a tall, statuesque, uninhibited Oxford graduate, whose first remark to Mary about the other members of the committee when she bumped into her after the first meeting was 'Well, no lovers for us, I fear.'[17] She and Mary found many other matters to talk about on their journey. Delighted to have found a friend among the members of the committee, Mary faced subsequent meetings more cheerfully.

In her account of the committee members, apart from Winifred, there was one other person who was given an extended description—myself. She described me as 'by far the cleverest member of the committee.'[18] This was flattering but certainly inaccurate. Besides Mary herself, doubtless the cleverest among us, there were several other members who would be considered 'clever' (whatever that might mean). They included the Vice-Chairman, George Cooke, County Education Officer for Lincolnshire; Moya Tyson, an educational psychologist from Hounslow; Sir Edward Britton, the General Secretary of the National Union of Teachers and many others. Sadly, Mary's view of the majority of the members of the committee as expressed in her recollections reflects an undeserved lack of respect for them. Most likely, the reason Mary saw me as 'clever' was because we found ourselves in agreement on nearly all the important points where there was disagreement among the members. Another reason was that we were both fascinated by the underlying philosophical questions raised by the committee's deliberations. For example, 'Is the purpose of educating children with special needs any different from the purpose of educating all children?' and 'What are the criteria by which to judge the quality of educational provision?' Most other members of the committee were, very appropriately, much more concerned with nitty-gritty practical issues.

Mary was disappointed that most of the members were preoccupied with the roles and status of their own professions or disciplines.[19] She thought that the doctors were dismissive of the social workers and uninterested in the social needs of their patients. The social workers were taken up with fighting the medicalisation of disabilities to the exclusion of concern about the reasons why, for example, children had learning difficulties or behaviour problems. The teachers, understandably, wanted to make sure that children with special needs were taught by teachers as well qualified as those teaching 'normal' children. At one point, the paediatrician on the committee became furious at the thought that he was going to be encouraged to pass on clinical details of babies who might be in need of special education to community doctors and local authorities. His concern for medical confidentiality blinded him to the need to ensure children with special needs received well-informed early intervention by educationists.[20]

Winifred Tumim and I were, I felt at the time, in a sense 'teacher's pets' and Mary always listened to us with obvious respect. But there was another committee member she could not stand. This became so obvious I felt I had to intervene. Mary describes my intervention thus:

> There was a day when we were travelling somewhere on a visit and [Philip] came and sat by me in the carriage, saying 'there is something I must say to you.'[21] My heart sank. It reminded me of when my mother used to say: 'I must speak to you.' (It is amazing what emotive force words like 'say' and 'speak' can have in certain contexts.) Anyway, what he had to say was indeed a reproach. He had noticed that I called all the other members of the committee by their Christian names except one person whom, he said, I manifestly disliked. I did, it is true, find her awkward, reopening a topic when I thought I had wrapped it up, with the words 'One last point....' (How did she know it would be the last point?) Anyway, I said humbly that I didn't even know what her Christian name was, and he told me. I think I managed to use her Christian name once, but no more.[22]

This preference for some members over others did not affect Mary's capacity to take all views into account.

Looking back at the composition of the committee, large though it was, by today's standards there were several omissions. First, there were no members from any of the ethnic minorities, even though, as far as some physical conditions and behaviour disorders were concerned, minorities were over-represented in the disabled population. Second, there were no members who had physical or mental conditions themselves. We had parents of children with disabilities, but no adults who had lived through the 'disability experience' with its frequent risk of painful stigmatising. It was not that we lacked the opportunity of meeting children with disabilities on the numerous visits we made to special and maintained schools. For example, I remember meeting two teenage boys in a special school for the 'maladjusted' who explained to me how it was normal and indeed healthy to be maladjusted to a world that was itself so crazy. We were, however, disadvantaged by not having people with direct experience of disability during their education on the main committee. Finally, and this omission was noted by critics of the report not long after it had been published, we did not include a sociologist among our number.[23] This might not have mattered, for it is not only sociologists who can contribute a sociological perspective to discussions. But, as it turned out, the part that society plays in defining handicap and the importance of the school ethos relating to children in need of special help in creating an inclusive environment were issues neglected in the report.

Committee members made many visits to both special and mainstream schools, hospital units and local authorities. Mary found these visits enormously enjoyable, if sometimes alarming. On a visit to a special school in Liverpool, she was approached and hugged 'by a black boy, about six-foot tall and very strong, who asked, in urgent tones, "Are you Liverpool or Everton?" I felt as if my life might literally depend on my answer, so I managed to breathe out that I was a supporter of Leeds United, and he let me go.'[24]

Some visits were made abroad to see how other countries provided education for children with disabilities. In January 1977, Mary travelled to the East Coast of the United States with one of Her Majesty's Inspectors (an HMI), a Scottish educational psychologist and me.[25] The HMI and the psychologist went their own way, which left Mary and me to visit special schools and classes separately. One of these visits was particularly memorable. Virginia Wilking, a child psychiatrist based in New York, had previously visited my department in London on several occasions with her husband, Leo, a paediatrician. I contacted her and she invited Mary and me to visit her hospital day units sited in Harlem

Hospital. The hospital was in a predominantly African American part of the city, but largely staffed with white physicians. (That is not the case now.) Guided by Virginia, we saw how behaviour and emotional disorders of varying degrees of severity were managed in this setting. Mary was impressed by her 'humanity, optimism and efficiency.'[26]

We had gone to the hospital by taxi but decided to take the subway back and had to walk a few hundred yards to the station. This was a frightening experience. We walked past several apartment blocks with what seemed to us like threatening groups of African American men standing on the steps of the buildings in the freezing cold weather. As we passed, they stared at us, sometimes moving as if to follow us or, it seemed to us, calling to the next group of men along to stop us. Apparently, Mary found my presence reassuring but in truth I was as frightened as she was. We were told afterwards that our relatively brief walk had been risky and dangerous, though this was, in fact, very probably not the case and, much more likely arose from the racial stereotyping of the people we subsequently met as well as, I regret to say, ourselves.[27]

As it happened, our visit was made at a particularly interesting time in the delivery of education to American children with disabilities. Congress had a couple of years previously passed Public Law 94/142 which had laid down that all public schools accepting federal funds should provide equal access to education and one free meal a day. Schools were required to evaluate children with disabilities and create, with parental input, an educational plan as close as possible to the educational experience of non-disabled students. Visits to schools in Boston made us realise how deceptive the term 'integration' might be. Students who were said to be integrated because they were attending mainstream schools might well be taught in completely separate classes and be let out to have their breaks at different times from other children, so that in reality there was no contact at all between the disabled and the non-disabled.

I had decided that I would like to recapture the experience of immigrants to the United States as they arrived in New York by boat in the nineteenth and early twentieth century. Mary was enthusiastic about this idea and agreed to come along. As our days were fully taken up with visits, we had to make our expedition one early January morning.[28] We got up at five thirty a.m. During our walk to the subway station, although we were well wrapped up, it was so cold it felt as if the exposed part of my face had stiffened with ice. We took the ferry to Staten Island where we had a huge breakfast. During the return journey, accompanied by a boat load of commuters, we passed the Statue of Liberty and indeed, though of course we did not have to go through the anxiety-provoking procedure of immigration controls on Ellis Island, we were able, as I had hoped, to re-live at least partly the immigrant arrival experience. We returned to our hotel in New York well in time for our first meeting.

Most of Mary's visits in the UK were made with John Hedger, the Department of Education and Science civil servant assigned to be Secretary to the Committee. She found him congenial company. He had had virtually no previous experience of special education but rapidly warmed to the task in hand. With young children of his own he was able to relate rapidly to the children and young people they met together on their visits.[29] He also had a sense of humour. I remember him describing to us how he had accompanied an Anglican bishop on a visit to a Church of England village primary school in his diocese. The two of them were asked to sit in a biology class for seven-year-olds. The bishop looked out of the window and saw a small furry animal in the school playground. He beckoned to a boy to come over and look at it. 'What do you think that is?' asked the bishop. 'I think I'm supposed to say "Jesus Christ",' said the boy, 'But it looks awfully like a squirrel.'

Unfortunately, John was removed from us, Mary thought cynically because he was getting more involved in the topics we discussed than a civil servant should be. He was replaced by a young woman Mary found much less congenial. She could not cope with working long hours and so was put out by Mary's wish to work well into the evening. She also had a bad back so when they went on visits together, luckily not a frequent occurrence, Mary had to carry her bags for her. On one occasion Mary had to swap rooms with her as she was intolerant of noise and her room was much noisier than Mary's.

Most of the meetings were held in a room in the Department of Education building, York House, close to Waterloo Station that was too small for the numbers of people on the committee. In the summer it was unbearably hot, so we had to have the windows open, which meant our discussions were interrupted by the station announcer informing us, for example, of the imminent departure of trains to Basingstoke,

Winchester and Southampton.[30] On two or three occasions, however, we spent weekends away in hotels or conference centres. It was at such an away meeting, in the Llandaff College of Education in Cardiff, that there was a breakthrough in the committee's thinking. Up to this point, discussions at the meetings had been on specific topics—under-fives, teacher training, assessment etc. A number of members of the committee now requested we should determine the whole structure of the final report so that, when we discussed a topic, we would know how it was going to fit in to the rest. The civil servants resisted, but Mary was with the rebels. Tackling the final structure meant that we had to reflect on the underlying principles involved in providing special as distinct from mainstream education.[31] This was a fruitful exercise.

The discussion began with a statement by Sir Edward (Ted) Britten that our aim should be the abolition of all special schools, with the placement of all children, however handicapped they might be, in mainstream schools. He was particularly opposed to boarding schools. He accused Mary and me of favouring residential placements because of our own boarding school experience. He saw us and Winifred Tumim as being elitist, and referred to Mary as a 'boarding school product.'[32] It is probably true that the three of us were the only members of the committee who had been both to public schools as boarders and to Oxford or Cambridge. However, this did not mean we were in favour of boarding schools. As Mary pointed out to him, all my children attended day schools. As the argument threatened to become acrimonious, Winifred Tumim intervened to distract us by claiming that many people saw children with severe learning difficulties as little more than 'vegetables.'[33] Why should large sums of money be spent on them?

This led to general agreement that education was a 'good' to which *everyone* was entitled. Ted Britten was inspired by this, according to Mary, to frame an unoriginal but truthful dictum. He drew a line on a blackboard representing a continuum of special educational needs, extending from those children who had no such needs to those whose needs were extremely special.[34] Mary transformed this image into one involving the pursuit of several educational goals which she named Knowledge, Experience, Imaginative Understanding and Pleasure.[35] The civil servants baulked at the idea that the taxpayer should be expected to fund the pursuit of pleasure, and there was no mention of pleasure in the final report. (Perhaps today she would have used the concept of 'quality of life' but this was only starting to come into use in the 1970s). The committee was generally in favour of such a conceptualisation, agreeing that the report should appear under the title of 'special educational needs' with no reference to handicap or disability. This approach led logically to the abandonment of medical categories to decide what sort of education children needed. Another logical conclusion was that the sharp distinction between special and ordinary education was unsustainable and that teachers in mainstream schools should be trained to recognise children with special educational needs and to meet those needs unless they were so great as to require separate educational facilities.[36]

Such an approach, though widely accepted today, was controversial at that time. Teacher trainers and the teaching unions obstinately stuck to the view that special and mainstream education should remain distinct. There were some on the committee who argued passionately for this view, while others, such as myself, were strongly opposed to it. Some years later, Mary wrote that her face 'creaked and ached with the effort to smile and look pleasant when involved in these apparently endless disputes.' 'Some members of the Committee' she reported, 'congratulated me on my patience, after an especially long drawn-out and irritating meeting.' She added that I had interrupted at this point to observe that 'my patience was the "thinnest veneer" he had ever seen.'[37]

The department officials were happy with the abandonment of medical categories probably for the territorial reason that removing them reduced the importance of a health service input into educational decisions. They were distinctly less happy with the argument of some members of the committee that we were in danger of omitting two important issues. There was to be no mention of dyslexia. This offended the powerful dyslexia lobby, but in practice it made little difference as the 'needs' approach meant that, if children needed special help with reading, we were agreed they should receive it regardless of whether or not they were labelled as 'dyslexic.'[38] The second area which Mary and some members of the committee regarded as important was social deprivation. Mary and others, including myself, argued that it was impossible to deny that social disadvantage and deprivation had damaging effects on educational progress. The report should emphasise this fact and discuss what should be done about it. Both social service representatives on the committee and the department officials were deeply unhappy about confusing the roles of different government departments.[39] The final report contained only passing reference to these issues.

The report was published on time in March 1978. It was titled, as agreed at Llandaff, 'Special Educational Needs.' It opened with a consideration of the scope of special education. Noting that as many as one in six children at any one time and one in five at some time will need some form of special education, it conceived of disability as a continuum, ranging from mild and sometimes short-term disabilities to longer-lasting, more complex or multiple and more disabling conditions. The term 'educationally subnormal' should be replaced with the term 'learning difficulties.' The categorisation of handicapped pupils by their type of disability should be abolished and replaced by a focus on each child's educational needs.

Fig. 7 Photograph of the Warnock Committee, taken in Gunnersbury Park, London, 20 March 1978, unknown photographer. Mary Warnock is at the centre front, and the author is in the back row, seventh from the right.

The recommendations were strongly in favour of children with disabilities being educated within mainstream schools wherever possible, with an agreed education plan for each disabled pupil entering a mainstream school and a single teacher within the school given overall responsibility for its being followed. Recognising that for children with some types of disability or particularly severe or complex disabilities, education within mainstream schools would not be feasible, the report emphasised that some separate special schools, including some boarding schools, would continue to be needed. To identify which pupils would need to attend these separate schools, the report proposed a system of multi-professional assessment and recording of these children's needs.[40] (The term 'statement' later replaced the 'record,' so that the ugly term 'statementing' replaced 'recording' to describe the process).[41] Such assessment should take into account the child's cultural and ethnic background. It was noted that there had been concern that 'a disproportionate number of children from West Indian families' had been placed in Educationally Subnormal (Moderate) (ESN (M)) schools.[42] Any assessment would be incomplete without reference to the child's cultural background or what would now be called ethnicity.

The report recommended a greater role for parents, who should be treated as partners throughout the educational process. Parents should be involved in multi-professional assessment; they rather than teachers should be seen as the main educators of children under five, and there should generally be more support for parents, especially for those with children with severe disabilities. One person, usually the health visitor, should be designated as a point of contact for parents to help them navigate around different services. The report also proposed a greater role for nursery education. Nursery education should be substantially increased to cover a greater part of the whole pre-school population. Playgroups and day nurseries should provide facilities for young children with special educational needs, while special nursery classes should be established for children with complex, severe disabilities.

Other recommendations were that *all* teacher training should include learning about children with special needs. More academic posts should be created and university departments should carry out not just teaching but also research in special education. Both ordinary and special schools should provide support for children with special needs at the transition from school to adult life, and continuing education should be available after school leaving in the settings to which children with special needs transfer.

The immediate response to the report both from the broadsheets and from the educational press was very positive. John Vaizey, writing in the *Times Educational Supplement*, called the report 'magnificent and important.'[43] Particularly well received were the recommendations involving multi-professional assessment, the increased role for parents and the idea of parents as partners, the abolition of medical categories and the need for all teachers to be trained in the identification and education of children with special needs. Legislation in this area had continued to be enacted even while the Warnock Committee was deliberating. In 1975 a guidance circular recommended multi-professional assessment for children with special educational needs.[44] The 1976 Education Act made further attempts to insist that local authorities gave special education in county and voluntary schools unless this was incompatible with efficient instruction or unreasonably expensive.

It is uncommon for the recommendations of a committee set up by government to command such universal support. Indeed, the setting up of a committee of enquiry is not infrequently a device (widely known as 'kicking into the long grass') governments use to avoid taking a decision on a controversial matter. Not only were the Warnock recommendations translated into legislation remarkably quickly, but, at the time, everyone seemed to agree with them. For this, Mary Warnock herself should take most of the credit. From the moment I walked into the first meeting in September 1974 and heard her bring the meeting to order so that we could begin, it was clear she was going to be a leader in every sense. The other committee members, like myself, were basically foot soldiers in Warnock's army. She certainly listened to the views of others, but it was she who formulated the key principles and she who achieved consensus when disagreements between committee members threatened to be irreconcilable. She had remarkable energy combined with formidable critical powers of analysis. In her own account of the meetings, she records that I never minded 'ticking her off.' For example, she had insisted on wine being served at lunch and reported that I thought she 'drank too much at lunch and then went to sleep, though he was admiring of how I managed to intervene, usually rather sharply, while apparently in this torpid condition.'[45] I have no memory at all of Mary going to sleep after lunch and suspect she put in this detail more for effect than anything else.

Now, in 1978, government ministers took an immediate interest in the possibility of legislation to implement the recommendations of the Warnock Committee. Civil servants were set the task of drafting a bill. The first meeting of an inter-departmental steering committee to consider the policy implications of the report was held on 18 May 1978, only two months after the report was published.[46] A draft bill was brought to the House of Commons for a second reading on 2 February 1981, less than three years after the publication of the report.

The Education Act 1981 defined the circumstances in which children should be regarded as having special educational needs. It required local authorities to arrange a multi-professional assessment when a child fell into this category and laid down that parents should be involved in the assessment. It made clear that any child under five years who was probably going to need special education later in his school career should be assessed as soon as possible. A formal statement should be made for any child requiring special education giving details of the provision thought to be necessary to meet the child's needs. Parents should have the right of appeal against an authority's decision to make or not to make such a statement.

In introducing the bill, the Secretary of State for Education and Science, Mark Carlisle, acknowledged 'the indebtedness of us all to Mrs. Warnock and the committee for the report. Its observations and the enormous task of gathering evidence that the committee undertook resulted in over 200 recommendations for improvements and a wider dissemination of good practice in all aspects of special education. It has in the report provided what in many ways is a guidebook for the future. It falls to us as legislators to give statutory form to some of the proposals.'[47] In general, there was very little criticism of the content of the bill, except in one crucial respect. Labour's Shadow Secretary of State for Education, Neil Kinnock, having echoed the warm thanks to Mary Warnock and her committee, pointed to the fact that no new resources were to be made available to implement the provisions of the proposed act.[48] Many Labour MPs expressed similar views, perhaps most forcefully Frank Field, who said

What an opportunity was offered by the Warnock report and the Bill—an opportunity of ending the system of educational apartheid between those classified as handicapped and those who are not. What an opportunity lost because, if the resources had been willed, the Bill would have ranked in this century second only to the Education Act 1944. Instead of bringing forward a Bill like a roaring lion, we have a mouse—and a dead mouse at that.[49]

But the Thatcher Government, while supporting legislation, made it clear that no new resources would be found to make the recommendations happen.

Members of the committee themselves had been well aware of the resource implications of implementing the recommendations. Multi-professional assessments are costly in terms of professional time. The production of statements recording the needs of children who require special education inevitably means bureaucratic expense. Training teachers in areas in which previously they have been ignorant cannot be done for nothing. Civil servants advising ministers also pointed out, in an early working paper: 'Since the cost of the full programme of measures advocated by the Warnock Committee would be very heavy, it will be important to determine priorities [...].'[50] In the event, no extra resources were found even for those recommendations with the highest priority. In due course this lack of resources created, inevitably, barriers to implementation, some of which, such as delays in statementing, were seriously frustrating for health professionals, teachers and, above all, parents.

A second government policy that acted later against children with special needs was the 1988 Education Reform Act. This act laid down for the first time that there should be a national curriculum that all schools would be expected to follow. It gave schools more independence from local authority control. The examination (SATs, GCSEs etc.) results obtained by all schools would be published in the form of league tables which would enable parents to choose the most successful among them. This meant that schools with large numbers of poorly performing children whose performance was poor were disadvantaged. Thus the 1988 Act unintentionally gave schools both an incentive not to admit children with special needs and, with increased independence from local authorities the means not to admit them as well as more easily exclude them. Attempts were made to avoid this, but there is evidence that such motivation continues to influence individual school policies towards children with special needs. While this act was going through Parliament, Kenneth Baker, then Secretary of State for Education and Science, was proposing that children with special needs should be exempted from following the National Curriculum which would have meant their performance in examinations would not have counted to a school's disadvantage. But it would also have meant the exclusion of such children from significant learning experiences. The voluntary sector was strongly opposed to such exclusion and successfully resisted Baker's proposal.[51]

Over the decades following the passing of the 1981 Education Act the field of special education gradually changed along the lines it laid down. It became accepted that there should be more integration of children with special needs into mainstream education. The number of special schools, especially those catering for children with mild and moderate learning difficulties was gradually reduced but there remained a substantial number. The term 'educationally subnormal children' was replaced by 'children with learning difficulties.' Statements of special educational need based on a multidisciplinary assessment were now required before a child could be placed in a special school. Children's problems no longer needed to be medically categorised before they could be placed. Communication from paediatricians, especially community paediatricians, to local education authorities about children who might need special education improved. Nursery education places for children with special needs gradually increased. The assessment process ensured that parents became more involved in educational decisions affecting their children and many remained involved after their children had been placed. The number of university departments of special education increased. Though progress in this direction was slow, teacher training now more often included information about children with special needs.

The greatest difficulties in implementing the report's recommendations arose in the so-called statementing process and the delays this frequently involved. Teachers had to trigger the process and, even in the presence of quite obvious need for special education, were often slow to request an assessment by an educational psychologist.

Because of resource limitations there were many fewer psychologists than there should have been. This meant there was a waiting time before the assessment took place; this could be a year or more. The assessment might reveal the need for resources that could be found within the child's existing school but if this was not the case and intervention not available in a mainstream school was required, the educational psychologist then took responsibility for the preparation of the statement. This required input first from the health service, usually from a community paediatrician, from the child's school and from the parents. The educational psychologist then had to summarise and make clear how the child's needs should be met. Finally, the local authority had to agree to provide the necessary resources and its decision could be appealed leading to yet further delay.

Mary was lobbied by parents unhappy with the statementing process. In 2005 she wrote a booklet *Special Educational Needs: A New Look* which expressed strong criticism of this process and regretted that the report had recommended them.[52] She described statements as 'wasteful and bureaucratic,' attacking them on several grounds.[53] First, in line with her objections to labelling, they merely produced an unnecessary dichotomy between 'statemented' and 'non-statemented' children. (At one point it became clear that Mary thought that 20% of children were receiving statements, the total number thought to have special needs.[54] She had to apologise for this, for the fact was that, at the time she wrote, the numbers of children receiving statements had never exceeded 4%.)[55] Then there was the expensive bureaucracy that was built up around the formulation of statements. Thirdly, there was the unhappiness of parents of children with special needs, many of whom felt their children had been wrongly refused a statement and would thus not be eligible for the separate special education they wanted. Such unhappiness was often compounded when the additionally expensive appeals process produced the same result. To some degree, such distress was made inevitable by the fact that the criteria for being in receipt of a statement had never been very precisely formulated.[56] They were meant to be for children with complex, severe and persistent disabilities, but who was to decide what counted as severe and complex? Indeed, it became clear in the first few years after the report was published, that the statement was as much an indication of how much the local authority thought it could afford to spend as a genuine account of what the child in question really needed.[57]

These criticisms were largely rejected by those responsible for statementing policy. It has, to this day, remained widely accepted throughout the education world that some form of multidisciplinary assessment should precede any decisions about a child's educational future. Indeed in 2014 the Children and Families Act extended the scope of the assessment by including the child's care needs and renamed statements as 'education, health and care plans.'

Another issue about which Mary was heavily lobbied and which she discussed in her 2005 booklet was the role and number of special schools. At this time, as a result of financial cuts, a number of local authorities were trying to close some of their special schools. In justifying such cuts, some local authorities cited the 1978 Warnock Report as calling for a reduction in special schools. Further support even for the total abolition of special schools came from bodies such as the Alliance for Inclusive Education which, largely on sociological grounds, campaigned for all children, no matter how disabled they might be, to be educated in mainstream schools.

Mary saw inclusion as a problematic concept, the problem arising from a well-recognised conflict between two sets of good intentions. The first good intention was to ensure that there was protected provision for children who have special needs. The second was to avoid children with special needs and their parents being made to feel different, to be 'labelled' as different from others with the not inconsiderable risk of stigmatisation. The intention of the committee had been, she said, to reduce 'labelling' by abolishing medical categories. However, as Mary pointed out, the recommendations merely replaced one set of labels with another. For example, as we have seen, the term 'educationally subnormal' (ESN) had been substituted by the doubtless less offensive, but nevertheless labelling term 'learning difficulties.'[58] Further, she alleged, using the language of need rather than the language of medical pathology resulted in a failure to distinguish between different sorts of need, so that all children, despite their very different needs, were treated similarly.[59] Medical categories also had the advantage that they could lead to specified funding. They could, in addition, be a source of pride as well as a target of negative discrimination. There was another sense in which the term 'inclusion' was sometimes used which Mary also disliked. In this sense 'inclusion' was understood to mean that all children, whatever the nature of their disabilities, should be educated (included) in mainstream schools. This was a view espoused by some campaigning bodies such as the Alliance for Inclusive Education with which Mary profoundly disagreed. She preferred the view of the National Association of Head Teachers, which referred to the need for pupils to be educated 'in the most appropriate setting' which, of course, might be a special school.[60]

Twenty-five years on from the report, the complex issues, some ideological, some practical, surrounding provision for children with special needs remained hotly debated amongst education professionals and parents. The debate centred mainly on current practices so perhaps it should not be surprising that references to the original recommendations were rare. Whatever the reason, the Warnock Report had come to be associated in the public mind with the abolition of all special schools, and it is unfortunate that Mary, when reflecting critically on her own report, missed the opportunity to correct this common misconception. An extreme, and very disagreeable example of the misconception that the report advocated such abolition was provided by the journalist Melanie Phillips who launched a savage tirade against Mary in the *Daily Mail* for, as she put it, 'first having ruined the educational chances of children with disabilities by insisting they be integrated in mainstream schools and then for blithely changing her mind after the damage had been done.'[61] In a vicious article headed 'A Monstrous Ego Who Has Destroyed So Much of Our Moral and Social Heritage,' Phillips accused Mary of creating a 'classroom revolution, one which has caused chaos and misery for countless thousands of children and their teachers and made many schools all but ungovernable.'[62]

In fact, though there were indeed one or two members of the committee like Sir Edward Britton who did at one point take the abolitionist view, there was a definite statement in the unanimously agreed 1978 Report that there should continue to be special schools. The wording could hardly have been clearer on this matter. It stated 'We are in no doubt whatever that special schools will continue to feature prominently in the range of provision for children with special educational needs.'[63] Now, in 2005, Mary not only agreed with this view but thought there should be more special schools, particularly small schools which she saw as much better able to deal with the bullying to which some children with special needs were exposed in large mainstream schools. Mary's approach was defended by Ruth Cigman who attacked what she called the 'universalist' approach to special education. This proposed, on ideological grounds that failed to respect the wishes of parents and children themselves, that all children regardless of their needs and level of disability, should be educated in mainstream schools.[64]

In 2010, the booklet Mary had written in 2005 was reprinted, this time with a commentary by Brahm Norwich, Professor of Educational Psychology and Special Educational Needs. Norwich took issue with Mary on most of the points she had made. In particular, he pointed to the fact that the concept of 'inclusion' had not existed at the time the 1978 Report had been written when all discussion was around 'integration.' The concept of inclusion was multidimensional.[65] It was important, he wrote, to distinguish between a geographical definition (all under the same roof), with a curriculum definition (following the same learning path). He considered Mary's criticism of statements and the statementing procedure to have some validity but noted her inability to suggest an alternative system of assessing suitability for different forms of provision. He then dealt with other aspects of her negative view of 'inclusion.' He rejected her view that bullying in maintained schools must mean more special schools. There are many other effective ways of dealing with bullying.[66]

Mary wrote a response to Norwich's arguments, but it cannot be said that she did much beyond repeating the arguments she had already made. Nevertheless, she retained her interest in special education until the last months of her life. In July 2018, only nine months before she died, Mary gave evidence to the House of Commons Select Committee on Special Educational Needs and Disabilities. She pointed to the devastating effect the lack of resources put into special education was having on its quality. In its highly critical report, published in October 2019, the select committee echoed her concerns.[67]

These considerations apart, when considering the impact of the 1981 Act on the educational experience of children with special needs, the verdict has to be overwhelmingly positive. It worked extremely well for many individuals. The following is an example with some minor details changed to preserve anonymity:

Peter X. was born in 1980 and is now, in 2020, forty years old. The younger of two children, his father worked in a car factory, north-east of London, and his mother was a shop assistant. His mother had an amniocentesis which revealed that the baby had Down's syndrome, but the parents opted to continue with the pregnancy. After he was born, Peter's motor milestones were passed normally and he was walking by eighteen months, but he was slow to speak. By four years he only had a few words, was very clumsy in his movements and was just starting to feed himself. His development was that of a child a little over half his age.

In addition to the Down's syndrome, Peter had a mild hearing loss partly responsible for the delay in his speech and language skills. He began his education in a mainstream local authority nursery school. He was assessed there by an educational psychologist and a community paediatrician. His nursery teacher provided a report on his development and behaviour and his parents were actively involved in his assessment and planning for his future education. Peter's educational needs were recorded in a 'statement of special educational needs' and the assessment concluded that Peter's needs for support could best be met in a local authority special school. His parents were initially very unhappy with the decision. Although recognising that Peter would need extra support, they had always hoped that he could progress to his local primary school alongside his older brother. However, having visited both the mainstream and the special school, the parents agreed that Peter was likely to do better in the special school, with smaller classes and additional support available on-site for his hearing and speech and language difficulties.

The special school where Peter was placed was three miles from his family home. A school bus picked him up in the morning and delivered him home in the afternoon. The school was in the grounds of a mainstream primary school and the two schools shared some classes and activities. Peter was able to join several school clubs, including music and drama, which he particularly enjoyed. When Peter was ten, his parents decided to relocate to the North of England, primarily because his mother wished to be closer to her own mother, who had become very frail and in need of additional support. Peter's statement of special educational needs meant that the new local authority had a duty to find him a suitable school place and he moved without problems to another school for children with severe learning difficulties.

When Peter was fourteen, his parents and the school began to discuss his 'transition plan' as he moved into adult life. Although Peter had made considerable progress in managing his own personal care and in improving his communication skills, it was clear that he would continue to need support after leaving school and his parents were worried about his longer-term future. Statements of special educational needs covered education up to nineteen and it was clear that Peter would still need and benefit from support with learning after that date. He was fortunate that the Children and Families Act 2014 had replaced statements of special educational needs with 'education, health and care plans' (EHCPs) which could continue to provide education and support up to twenty-five, subject to assessment.

Peter was keen to improve his literacy and to continue to study art, drama and music and he attended classes at the local further education college and also at a community art project. The Children and Families Act 2014 had introduced personal budgets for young people with EHCPs and Peter was able to use his personal budget to support his art classes and pay for membership of a local drama group and join special classes at his local leisure centre to improve his mobility and to lose weight. During his early twenties, Peter, his parents and his social worker discussed where he wanted to live and how he wanted to spend his life. He wanted to move away from home but recognised that he was not independent enough to live on his own. Peter had a comprehensive assessment, as set out in the Care Act 2014, and now has a personal care plan which sets out Peter's wishes, his assessed needs and the arrangements and funding available from the local authority to meet them. It was mutually agreed that Peter should move into a supported living arrangement (a shared flat) with regular support and practical help with daily living. Peter has now made the transition out of the family home, though he has frequent contact with his parents and regularly enjoys home visits. His parents were very nervous about the move to a shared flat, but their own health is now deteriorating, and they are very relieved that Peter is building a life of his own. Peter will have regular annual reviews and notwithstanding his need for support, he thinks, in his own words, that *'life is great.'* His mother, looking back, comments that

> we were upset that Peter couldn't go to the same school as his brother. But now we are pleased that he went to schools which could give him the skills for everyday life. He's been able to make choices, to get a home of his own and when he walks down the street, he seems to know more people than we do! He is really part of his local community and he has got a life.

Since the publication of the Warnock Report there has been an increasing tendency for special and ordinary schools to come closer together, both in geographical and in curriculum terms. What follows is an example of co-location giving opportunities for many shared and integrated academic, but more particularly social activities.

Riverside and Woodside Schools (at both of which the author has served as a school governor) are situated on the same campus in Tottenham, a socially deprived area in the London Borough of Haringey. Riverside is a local authority school for children with special needs, rated 'Good' by OFSTED.[68] It caters for about 140 students with moderate learning difficulties (MLD), profound and multiple learning difficulties (PMLD), and communication and interaction needs: speech and language disorders and autistic spectrum disorders (ASD). Currently, over half the students have ASD, with the great majority of these having learning difficulties as well. Over recent years, increasing attention has been paid to monitoring the academic progress of students.

There is active engagement with Woodside High School. The headteacher of Riverside attends Woodside governing body meetings and vice versa. Although this is unusual, where Riverside students have the potential to take public examinations, they join classes at Woodside. Riverside students are taken on tours of Woodside and vice versa. Students from Riverside who set up a breakfast club joined Woodside students in the Woodside canteen. Riverside/Woodside ran a joint Red Nose Day with shared activities. Riverside's after-school club visited Woodside's open-air Windrush anniversary celebration. Riverside partnered with Woodside in completing the Duke of Edinburgh Silver Award. Students from the two schools worked together to support one another hike and navigate through the planned route. They socialised and played rounders together during the evening times.

Woodside High School is a single school academy rated 'Outstanding' by Ofsted. It has about 1,000 students aged eleven to sixteen years, most of whom are socially disadvantaged. They come from a variety of backgrounds, with 70% not having English as their first language. Their statement of values begins: 'We welcome difference and diversity: learning from and about diversity strengthens our community.' The statement concludes: 'Our starting point is a whole-school approach to making provision for students with SEN/D: we make sure that all staff have the knowledge and skills to support all students with SEN/D (Special educational needs/Disability) in our school.' The school makes provision for a wide variety of students with special cognitive, social, emotional and behavioural, physical and sensory needs. About 3.5% have Education, Health, Care Plans (EHCPs), as statements are now called.

The SEN/D team visits primary schools to assess children with special needs before they are transferred. Subsequently, the progress of students with special needs is regularly assessed. Where there are difficulties, a variety of types of provision is available within the school. Outside agencies are consulted for advice where necessary. The SENDCo is an experienced, qualified teacher, who has undertaken the National SENDCo award training. The Inclusion Department also has three Lead Teaching Assistants with specialisms in autistic spectrum disorders (ASD), literacy and social, emotional and mental health. SEN/D students participate in all lessons, trips, clubs and activities. Students with SEN/D are socially engaged with other students and where possible are involved in the School Council.

* * *

The fortieth anniversary in 2018 of the publication of the Warnock Report was a time not only for reflection, but also, for many, for celebration. The international journal *Frontiers in Education* marked the occasion by commissioning fifteen research papers on issues relevant to special education. These were introduced with a remarkable tribute to the report and the chairman of the committee which produced it.[69] It read:

> Although there had been reports on some disabilities before then, the Warnock Report was the result of the first comprehensive review of the whole range of children with special educational needs. Despite its subtitle echoing previous history, namely *Report of the Committee of Enquiry into the Education of Handicapped Children and Young People*, its main title proposed a new dawn: *Special Educational Needs*. Chaired by Mary Warnock, the Committee produced a review and made a wide range of recommendations that were truly ground-breaking.
>
> This was not just about terminology. Rather, the Warnock Report was responsible for changing the conceptualisation and legislative framework in England, and the Education Act 1981 that followed the report had a totally new system for assessment and determining provision. Also, the Warnock Report recommended elements that in many countries we now take for granted—but at that time were highly original. For example, the meaningful engagement of parents, including their being central *partners* in the assessment of SEN and in making decisions on the appropriate needs, including SEN, of individual children and young people; a greatly updated process of assessment; the inclusion of a chapter on children under five years; the role of special schools; the curriculum; the transition from school to adult life; teacher education; the roles of professionals; the health and social services and voluntary organisations; and—last but not least—research.
>
> The impact of the Warnock Report 1978 for England in particular was substantial. Impact has also been seen internationally, as professional practice and state legislation have developed, not least the policy development towards *integration*, or as we now generally refer, *inclusion*.'

Mary did not live to read this tribute and, if she had, she would doubtless have expressed serious reservations about it. She would have been mistaken; her report had a remarkably positive influence on the education of children with special needs. The recognition she received late in life strongly suggests it may well have been her most important contribution to public life. When she was made a member of the Order of the Companions of Honour (CH) in the 2017 New Year Honours, it was specifically for services to charity and to children with special educational needs. Similarly, when, in 2018, she was named by the *Times Educational Supplement* as one of the ten most influential people in education, this was explicitly in recognition of her work on special educational needs.

Notes

1   Department for Education and Science, 1978.

2   Mary Warnock, 2000, p. 170.

3   J. S. Hurt, 1988.

4   Ibid., pp. 171–172.

5   Department for Education and Science, 1978, p. 19.

6   Ibid., p. 20.

7   Ibid., p. 21.

8   Hurt, pp. 172–173.

9   Hurt, pp. 176–178.

10   Ibid., p. 183.

11   Jack Tizard, 1964.

12   National Bureau for Cooperation in Child Care, 1970.

13   Segal, 1966.

14   Warnock, 2003.

15   Ibid., p. 37.

16   Ibid., p. 40.

17   Ibid., p. 39.

18   Ibid.

19   Ibid., p. 56.

20   Ibid., p. 60.

21   Ibid., pp. 40–41.

22   Ibid., p. 41.

23   Lewis and Vulliamy, 1980.

24   Warnock, 2003, p. 45.

25   Ibid., p. 41.

26   Ibid., p. 42.

27   Ibid., pp. 42–43.

28   Ibid., p. 42.

29   Ibid., p. 45.

30   Ibid., pp. 37–38.

31   Ibid., p. 47.

32   Ibid., p. 48.

33   Ibid., p. 49.

34   Ibid.

35   Ibid., p. 50.

36   Ibid., p. 54.

37   Ibid.

38   Ibid., p. 57.

39   Ibid., pp. 57–58.

40   Ibid., p. 55.

41   Department of Education and Science, 1978, p. 338.

42   Ibid., 4.52, p. 64.

43   Vaizey, 1978.

44   Department of Education and Science, 1975.

45   Warnock, 2003, p. 40.

46   National Archive, ED 285/27.

47   Hansard, 1981.

48   Ibid.

49   Ibid.

50   National Archive, WSC (78) 09: Warnock Report: 'A Common Framework for Policy Analysis'.

51   Philippa Russell, personal communication.

52   Mary Warnock, 2005.

53   Ibid., p. 55.

54   Ibid., p. 13.

55   Mary Warnock and Brahm Norwich, 2010, pp. 118–119.

56   Mary Warnock, 2005, p. 30.

57   Martin Doyle, personal communication.

58   Warnock and Norwich, pp. 125–126.

59   Ibid., p. 19.

60   Warnock and Norwich, 2010, p. 34.

61   Melanie Phillips, *Mail Online*, 9 June 2005.

62   Ibid.

63   Department of Education and Science, 1978, p. 121.

64   Cigman, 2007.

65   Brahm Norwich, personal communication.

66   Warnock and Norwich, p. 80.

67   House of Commons Select Committee Report, October 2019.

68   Doyle, personal communication.

69   *Frontiers in Education*, May 2019.

Fig. 8 Portrait of Mary Warnock in her study, unknown photographer (c. 1980), by kind permission of the Principal and Fellows of St. Hugh's College, Oxford, CC BY-NC.

8. Infertility

1982 was a busy year for Mary. With the passage of the 1981 Education Act, her responsibilities around special education had come to an end, but she continued to be much in demand as a speaker on the topic both at home and abroad. She had already been asked to take up new public roles. In particular, she was chairing a Home Office committee on the use of animals in the laboratory. In September 1981, Geoffrey had been appointed Vice-Chancellor of the University of Oxford. Mary was expected to fulfil the role of the Vice-Chancellor's wife, which involved a great deal of entertaining. Her five children had all now left home and mostly entered on their own careers, but the youngest, Maria, at twenty-one, was still at art college. Mary saw a great deal of all of them, feeling she was 'just about (but no more) keeping [her] head above water.'[1]

So, it was not a reason for immediate joy when, in June 1982, she was telephoned by the Department of Health and Social Services (DHSS) to ask if she would chair a committee that was to be set up to look at the issues surrounding new fertility treatments.[2] Just four years previously, Robert (Bob) Edwards, a physiologist, and Patrick Steptoe, an obstetrician and gynaecologist, had successfully achieved the live birth of a baby by in vitro fertilisation. A husband's sperm had been introduced to his wife's ovum in a laboratory test-tube and had fertilised it. The now fertilised egg had then been transferred into the wife's womb and had developed normally until birth when a healthy baby girl had been born. Now there was an urgent need to consider whether research into the procedure should be regulated, and, if so, in what way. Bob Edwards himself, more than a decade earlier, had expressed a wish that this should at least be considered.[3]

For the first time in her life, Mary was hesitant about taking on a new role. Becoming involved in what was both literally and metaphorically

   https://doi.org/10.11647/OBP.0278.08

a 'sexy' subject, would inevitably bring unwanted publicity to Geoffrey and herself. But they discussed it together, and as they did so, she became increasingly gripped by the moral and philosophical implications.[4] She had always been interested in the interaction between morality and the law and this was a classic example of the nexus between the two. So, when the letter of invitation came from Norman Fowler, the Secretary of State for Health and Social Services, she agreed to chair what was to be called the Committee on Human Fertilisation and Embryology. She was aware this would involve a new way of life, but she was prepared for it.

Infertility has many known causes and sometimes defies medical explanations. Among the more common known causes are male impotence and infections of the female reproductive organs. A less common reason is a low sperm count or even the absence of any sperm at all in the man's ejaculate. This is relatively easily diagnosed by examining the sperm under a microscope. It is by no means always treatable. In the absence of effective treatment, the couple are often faced with difficult decisions. They might opt to remain childless or to adopt. Alternatively, they may choose AID (artificial insemination by a donor). The technique for achieving a successful result by AID was pioneered in the mid-nineteenth century in New York, but the practice did not become available in the UK until the late 1930 and 1940s, when two women doctors, Margaret Jackson in Exeter and Mary Barton in London, started to perform it. Initially this involved obtaining a sample of fresh semen from a donor, often a medical student, who had recently masturbated. The semen was placed just inside the womb or at the opening of the woman's cervix. Occasionally, if the husband did produce some sperm, this was mixed with that of the donor before it was placed in the cervix (AID+H). Margaret Jackson carried out about 500 such inseminations between 1941 and 1971 with a considerable degree of success.[5] Later it became possible to store frozen semen and sperm banks came into existence.

As AID became more widely practised it was realised that there were significant legal and ethical problems associated with it. In 1948 the Archbishop of Canterbury, Geoffrey Fisher, had condemned the practice and recommended it should be criminalised.[6] A government departmental committee under the chairmanship of Lord Feversham eventually advised against the criminalisation of AID but recommended that children born by it should be regarded as illegitimate and the technique itself should be discouraged.[7] A decade later however, in 1973, the Peel Committee, set up by the British Medical Association, recommended that AID should be available in a limited number of NHS-funded centres.[8] What was the government to do?

While the AID debate rumbled on, the possibility of in vitro (test-tube) fertilisation was becoming more real. In December 1972, the Ciba Foundation organised a symposium on the topic 'Law and Ethics of AID and Embryo Transfer.' Bob Edwards and Patrick Steptoe presented a paper, 'Biological Aspects of Embryo Transfer,' which predicted that embryo transfer through the cervix, without the need for surgery, was a procedure which would soon be available to many childless couples.[9] Legal issues were discussed by Olive Stone who pointed out that the birth certificates of AID children were generally falsified to make it appear that the biological father of the child was the husband of the mother who had given birth.[10] As it happened, I attended this symposium and contributed in a minor way. I expressed some concern, which later turned out to be justified, about the distress that might be caused to individuals who learned later in life that their biological fathers were not as they had always assumed. I suggested that children born by AID should be told of their genetic origin before adolescence, during or after which they might discover it by accident with harmful effects to their mental health.[11] During the same symposium, Gordon Dunstan, a Professor of Moral and Social Theology, suggested the need for some sort of register of AID births.[12] Along the same lines, Hilde Himmelweit, the London School of Economics sociologist, suggested the need for practitioners of artificial insemination to be registered.[13] Lord Kilbrandon, the senior judge who chaired the symposium, concluded it with the prescient statement: 'AID is here to stay. This symposium has been about what the law should do about it. The conclusion seems to be that the law has got to consider it not in a prohibitory way and perhaps only in a regulatory way so far as is required to make the technique acceptable to society.'[14] So, many of the issues, including especially regulation, which preoccupied the committee that Mary was to chair, had been under discussion for at least a decade before the committee met.

Following their successful in vitro fertilisation (IVF) in a test-tube carried out in July 1978, Edwards and Steptoe treated a growing number of women with IVF with about a 33% success rate. As the numbers grew so did the public debate around the ethical issues raised by the IVF procedure and the need for an official response to the legal issues raised became more urgent. Media interest in a contentious subject with such obvious human interest was inevitable. For example, the *Daily Mail* initially showed great enthusiasm for the new technique and offered to raise funds for a building to house research facilities but as soon as the morality of the procedure began to be seriously debated, the newspaper withdrew its support.[15] The issue became highly controversial. Hence the call from the Department of Health to Mary Warnock who had become the natural person to turn to when an authoritative view on moral and legal issues was required in the formulation of public policy. As far as is known, no one else was considered. The terms of reference of her committee were presented to her more or less as a *fait accompli*. They were: 'To consider recent and potential developments in medicine and science related to human fertilisation and embryology; to consider what policies and safeguards should be applied, including consideration of the social, ethical and legal implications of these developments; and to make recommendations.'[16]

Mary's scientific expertise in this field was notable by its almost complete absence. Typically for someone who had read Greats at Oxford, she had had virtually no education in biology, even at the most basic level. This was quite usual for women of her generation educated in private schools. It should be remembered however that there were a number of distinguished scientists and physicians in her family, particularly, as we saw in Chapter Two, on her mother's side. The first discussion she and Geoffrey had about the issues raised by the ethics of research focussed on the historical background. With their backgrounds in ancient Greek philosophy, naturally they turned first to the writings of Aristotle, who had opined that the rational soul was added to the body at forty days from conception in male embryos and at ninety days in females. In contrast, Thomas Aquinas, in the thirteenth century, when expressing his doctrine of Ensoulment, suggested that from the moment of conception, the embryo 'is endowed with an immortal soul' and must not be deliberately destroyed. This became the official doctrine of the

Roman Catholic Church, which continued to hold this view into the late twentieth century.[17]

With its Chair's knowledge of the issues dating only up to the thirteenth century, the level of more contemporary expertise among committee members was of great importance. Mary was presented with members suggested by the DHSS and asked if she had any further names to add or whom she wished removed. She did have deep-seated objections to one proposed member, a Catholic psychiatrist, who was regarded by the DHSS as a perfect candidate as he represented two interests. Mary had met this man previously when he had preached a sermon on the joys of sex at Hertford College. She was adamant about not being prepared to work with him. When the civil servant dealing with the matter asked her why, she said he gave her the 'creeps.'[18] As it happens, although I never discussed the matter with Mary, I know exactly who this man, now long deceased, must have been and can confirm that others, including many of his colleagues, felt exactly the same about him. He was replaced by two other doctors, a Catholic neurologist and a psychiatrist.[19]

Fortunately, the proposed members of the committee were of high calibre. The more prominent among them included Anne McLaren, the Director of the Medical Research Council Mammalian Development Unit, Ken Rawnsley, a former President of the Royal College of Psychiatrists, David Davies, a scientist and previous editor of *Nature*, Dame Josephine Barnes, a highly articulate gynaecologist, and John Marshall, the Catholic neurologist referred to above.[20] The Committee was, according to Mary, efficiently served by Jeremy Metters, a senior doctor who went on to be Deputy Chief Medical Officer of Health at the DHSS and the young Jenny Croft, a civil servant, who came from a non-medical background.[21] Although Metters thought that Jenny was out of her depth, Mary thought her good at her job. However, in her recollections of the committee she could not, with her strong sense of appearance, resist describing Jenny as 'generally dressed as a Watteau milkmaid, with huge skirts, beneath which emerged a frilly petticoat and little pointed-toe slippers.'[22] When Mary hosted her and Jeremy Metters to dinner at Hertford College later, she was otherwise attired in 'a scarlet dirndl skirt, an electric-blue satin blouse, strained to bursting over her bosom, and a little scarlet hat perched sideways on her head.'

Jenny's appearance was a distraction when Mary was supposed to be engrossed in more weighty scientific matters.

The meetings of the committee were mostly held in large, windowless rooms in the DHSS Hannibal House building. Mary had a parking space there, but others had to negotiate the bleak, litter-ridden passages leading out of the Elephant and Castle Underground Station next door. Occasionally the unreliable air conditioning failed which gave everyone headaches.[23] All the same, Mary regarded the first meeting a success, largely because the background papers produced by Jeremy Metters were so clear and informative.

In the morning of the second meeting, Anne McLaren gave a lecture on the development of the embryo. She also described the various techniques which were used to deal with infertility. Those members of the committee who, like Mary, had little knowledge of human developmental biology, found this exposition invaluable.[24] Throughout the proceedings Mary turned to Anne for authoritative advice on the biology. Anne described how in the first week or two of life, the embryo is no more than a cluster of poorly differentiated cells and not, as often pictured, a little homunculus curled up inside the womb. In the afternoon, the committee took evidence from Geoffrey Dawes, a physiologist who was the Director of the Mammalian Development Unit in Oxford, and his team. He was a friend of the Warnocks, who since the 1950s and 1960s had been one of the group of young dons, described in Chapter Five, known as the 'dancing economists' because they gave informal dances in each other's houses. At one point, Geoffrey Warnock had been very briefly enamoured of Margaret, Geoffrey Dawes's wife, whom Mary rather liked. Meeting him again, Mary was reminded of how, while they were dancing together, Geoffrey Dawes had explained to her his work on pregnant sheep and their embryos. Giving evidence to the committee on this less romantic occasion Geoffrey Dawes made the case for the vital importance of continuing embryo research if the relatively poor success rate of IVF was to be improved.[25]

David Davies, one of the committee members with a strong scientific background thought that Mary was a 'very good chairman, ran the committee well, though she could be tough at times.'[26] Jeremy Metters thought that she was an exceptionally good chairman.[27] Although, as we have said, she knew little of the medical/biological details at the outset, she was never afraid to take him aside after meetings to elaborate on anything she felt she had not sufficiently grasped. He found her to be remarkably patient, only losing her temper on one occasion when Madeleine Carriline, a social worker member of the committee, accused her of ignoring the social work aspects of the issues.[28] John Marshall, the Catholic neurologist, was also impressed with Mary's chairing. 'There was no dragooning,' he said. 'When a divergence emerged, she would say 'Let's leave that and come back to it later—and you'd think "she hasn't realised"—but she knew very well and when you came back, you'd be surprised at how far the block had melted away.'[29] Mary thought that she herself sometimes got rather too involved in philosophical discussions with the witnesses. For example, in the course of taking evidence from an eminent Jesuit priest, she and he became engaged in a lengthy dialogue on the moral status of the early human embryo, while, she noticed, the rest of the committee looked profoundly bored, twiddling their thumbs and gazing at the ceiling as though they were just waiting for the philosophical argument to end.[30]

The topics which the committee subsequently discussed and on which they had to pronounce were wide-ranging. Throughout, Mary tried to ensure that for every subject, in deciding on their recommendations, the committee had to answer two main questions. First, was the behaviour, technique or procedure under discussion morally wrong? And second, if it was morally wrong, should the law intervene to prevent it happening?[31] She expanded on this approach in the Dixon Lecture given in Queen's University, Belfast in 1989.[32] As a moral philosopher Mary was well placed to lead a discussion on the moral status of a new procedure. But she did not believe that her expertise put her in a privileged position to make moral judgements. Indeed, she rejected the arguments that a small number of moral philosophers, such as Peter Singer, had made at the time, that committees such as hers should be made up entirely of ethical experts.[33]

There were, Mary suggested, two main ways in which people came to judgements as to whether a procedure was right or wrong. The first was to judge according to a pre-existing set of rules which, in Britain, would usually be established according to Christian principles. The interpretation of church leaders might sometimes be required to decide what the teaching of the Bible was on any particular procedure, but nevertheless it was the highest court when it came to moral judgement. Alternatively, people could use the principle of utility. Utilitarianism, Mary wrote, laid down that 'an act is right if it benefits more people than it harms, wrong if the balance is the other way.' However, when it came to the issues on which her committee had to pronounce, Mary found there were serious problems with both approaches. The Bible could not be expected to pronounce on scientific advances which had not been dreamed of in biblical times. What point was there to look to the Bible for answers to questions about in vitro fertilisation? But the principle of utility has its problems too. If it is accepted that an embryo in the earliest stages of development amounts to little more than a cluster of cells, can this cluster meaningfully be said to experience suffering? If not, what is its claim to being an object of moral concern, and if it has no such claim or only a small claim, how does this alter the utilitarian balance of harms and benefits? Clearly a foetus, sitting in the womb in the thirty-second week of a pregnancy and capable of survival, must be regarded as an individual of moral concern. But is that the case thirty-one weeks earlier when it is only a cluster of a few cells?[34]

At this point Mary turned to Hume, the eighteenth-century Scottish Enlightenment philosopher who, in his *Treatise of Human Understanding* (1748), wrote that morality 'was more properly felt than judged of.'[35] Moral sentiment, in the case of the issues the committee had been set up to consider, the *feeling* that a procedure was right or wrong, was crucial. This was not to say that rational, intellectual argument was unimportant. For example, someone might well feel that the donation of sperm by a donor to assist a woman to conceive was abhorrent, undoubtedly immoral. But then, having listened to the predicament of childless women, perhaps in the case of women from some ethnic minorities at risk of divorce if they were seen to be barren, the feelings of such a person might be moved to change. Of course, people's feelings might continue to differ even after they had heard a great deal of rational argument, but Mary was impressed with the degree to which members of the committee shared the same feelings about the issues they discussed.[36] Having said this, Mary's own feelings about a matter were, she readily admitted, not an infallible guide to the moral stance taken by wider society. For example, for reasons that will be discussed later, she had feelings of moral abhorrence about surrogate births. Not long after the report was published, it became clear that her feelings were not widely shared and she admitted it had been wrong, especially as she had been chairing the discussion, for her to take such a firm view against surrogacy.

Agreement that a procedure was wrong by no means necessarily meant that there should be a law to ban it. Here Mary introduced into the debate the arguments that had been put forward by H. L. A. Hart, the Oxford Professor of Jurisprudence. He proposed a clear criterion to help decide whether morally wrong behaviour should be forbidden by law. The question should be asked whether 'the infringement of liberty involved would itself be morally right or wrong?'[37] This might arise on the practicalities of enforcing a new law. For example, if there were a law against AID, because the procedure is relatively easy to carry out with a low level of professional skill, in order to enforce the law it would be necessary to encourage snoopers to inform on people they knew were using it. Most people would think this, itself, was morally objectionable.

As the meetings proceeded, Mary came to see that her insistence on using the language of morality, the constant repetition of 'right' and 'wrong' to characterise procedures, was unhelpful. Indeed, it communicated a rather arrogant approach. Jenny Croft, the secretary to the committee, when she wrote minutes or drafts instead used the words 'appropriate' and 'inappropriate.' Initially Mary hated what she regarded as mealy-mouthed euphemisms, but she gradually realised that inevitably, when legislation was called for, some people would disagree. Such people would be offended if they were told they were morally wrong. It would be easier for them to accept the proposed legislation if they were encouraged to see their views as 'inappropriate' rather than wrong.[38] Elsewhere she pointed to a further complication in evaluating moral choices. She quoted Stuart Hampshire when he pointed out that 'conflict is an inevitable element in morality. We cannot hope to eliminate it.'[39] 'But, given time, consensus may develop out of the apparently beneficial operation of a law.'[40]

The committee's call for evidence elicited a large number of responses (400 in all), mostly from organisations and a few from individuals. Alphabetically these ranged from Action for Lesbian Parents to the Yorkshire Pro-Life Coordinating Committee.[41] All the relevant medical Royal Colleges responded, as did a large number of churches of all denominations and sizes. As Mary wrote, such evidence was 'extraordinarily repetitive' and it was 'hard not to fall asleep over the papers.'[42] It is certainly true that a great deal more effort goes into the preparation of such submissions than the committee to which they are submitted can possibly devote to reading them. It is also unfortunately true that most organisations, being bound to represent the views of their members, become 'single-issue' lobbyists. Such lobbying is often balanced out by opposing lobbies and it is difficult to search out anything genuinely original.

The oral evidence the committee took was more helpful as it could be tested in discussion. This was particularly the case with specialist medical evidence and with evidence from religious leaders. Occasionally there was a farcical element in the way the witnesses presented themselves. Jeremy Metters described how, when evidence was taken in Belfast, representatives of the four major churches (Church of Ireland, Catholic, Presbyterian and Methodist) insisted on entering by four different doors. After giving, in each other's hearing, virtually identical evidence, they then left using the same doors by which they had entered.[43] Some of the members of the committee canvassed opinion on the issues in question on their own account. For example, David Davies, who lived in North Devon, stimulated local discussion at meetings of Women's Institutes, Mothers' Unions and political meetings. He talked to youngsters on youth opportunities programmes about what they thought about the main issues.[44] Others may have done the same.

The first issue on which the committee heard evidence was the significance of childlessness and thus the priority which should be given to childless couples.[45] There were those who argued that the world was already over-populated. This was countered by the more persuasive view that the numbers of children born as a result of medical assistance would always be very small and that childlessness should be seen not as part of a population problem but as a question of individual need. Should such assistance be limited to couples it was thought would make 'good' parents? There was obviously no selection by marital status or by potential for good parenting among those who had children by sexual intercourse though there was considerable selectivity in the approval procedures for adopters. In the end the committee decided it would not lay down any criteria for choosing who should benefit from such medical assistance as was available. It was merely recommended that consultants who declined treatment should provide a full explanation of the reasons. To the anger of some, this opened the door for single women as well as lesbian and gay couples to seek medical help. In the light of the 1967 Criminal Offences Act decriminalising homosexuality, this was, however, a logical decision.[46] Mary later expanded her views on the issue of the right of childless women, including lesbian women, to be helped to have babies in a book, *Making Babies* (2002), to be discussed later.[47]

Despite the fact that AID was already widely practiced in infertility clinics up and down the country, a significant amount of evidence reflected strong hostility to the use of the technique. A few saw it as a threat to the integrity of the family, tantamount even to adultery. The status of the child born by AID was regarded as inevitably ambiguous. The committee recommended that children born by AID should be treated in every way as legitimate offspring with the sperm donor having no legitimate rights over the child.[48] Further, the law should allow the husband of the couple to be registered as the father. The committee articulated a number of additional rules which, it felt, should govern the practice of AID. At the time, it was widely agreed that sperm donors should have the right to anonymity throughout their lives and throughout the lives of any progeny. This was considered appropriate given the possibility of later paternity claims and the fact that the donors were largely acting from altruistic motives. The committee generally agreed with this practice but felt that there should be a limit to the number of children a donor should be permitted to father (a figure of ten was agreed),[49] and that, at the age of eighteen, the child born by AID should have access to information about the donor's ethnicity and genetic health.[50] This recommendation was translated into law. However, over twenty years later, in 2005, after some public pressure, the law was changed so that, at the age of eighteen, to align with the legislation on adoption, those born by sperm donation could find out full details of their biological fathers and contact them if they so wished. Predictably, since this law was passed, it has become increasingly difficult to obtain sperm by donation.

Some members felt that there should be compulsory counselling for all those receiving treatment by AID. In particular, the two social workers, Madeleine Carriline and Jean Walker, the wife of the Bishop of Ely, were determined that counselling should be obligatory. Mary discovered that counselling meant different things to different people. One gynaecologist who gave evidence described how, if a couple wanted treatment and he felt they were unsuitable, he would counsel them and counsel them until they changed their minds. Clearly for him, counselling was a form of persuasion. Others thought that counselling merely involved giving information in a neutral fashion. For the two social workers, however, counselling had a therapeutic function arising from the exploration of the couple's feelings. Mary was sceptical about the benefits of this. One suspects she would not have wanted to have her own feelings explored by someone she hardly knew. At one point, Jean Walker, whom Mary in any case found rather unlikeable, said to her 'I'm sorry you have this problem about counselling.'[51] Mary was unimpressed with the idea she had a 'problem,' rather than possibly well-founded scepticism. In the end, the committee recommended that counselling should always be available to couples seeking treatment for infertility but that it should not be compulsory.

When the committee turned its attention to IVF, it met with many of the same kinds of objection. As with AID, there were those who objected to the procedure largely on religious grounds, with the belief that children should only be born as a result of sexual intercourse. Others, on a more managerial level, were concerned that the technique involved the production of many, so-called spare embryos. It was wrong, in principle, that embryos should be produced with the potential for human life that would never be fulfilled. This was a controversial area. The committee's considered view, expressed in Paragraph 11.9 of the report, was that although human embryos in the early stage of development are alive, they are not yet human persons.[52] On this basis, it recommended unanimously that IVF should be allowed to continue, subject to the licensing of clinics carrying it out and to regulation. The committee received similar objections but made similar recommendations for both egg and embryo donations. IVF should be available within the NHS, an important point as NHS services were patchy and many couples, then as now, had to resort to expensive private treatment or forgo such treatment altogether if they could not afford it.

The issue of surrogacy turned out to be the most contentious of all. Surrogacy takes many forms, but the common feature is that a woman agrees to carry a pregnancy for another couple, handing the baby over when or very shortly after it is born. An egg fertilised in a test-tube, derived from the egg of the wife and the sperm of the husband may be implanted into the surrogate's womb. Alternatively, the husband's sperm may be introduced into the surrogate's womb at the time she is ovulating to give the sperm the most likely chance of achieving fertilisation. The need for the procedure arises when a wife cannot, for some anatomical or physiological reason, sustain a pregnancy herself. Surrogacy had been practised commercially in the United States for a few years at the time the committee was sitting and there were proposals for similar commercial developments in the UK.

According to David Davies the issue was introduced to the committee when Mary

> came into a committee meeting one day flourishing a Sunday newspaper [...] which had got, Mums for Sale, something like that. And she said, 'We can't have this, can we?' And it was about women having children for other women. And the committee on the whole said, yes Mrs Warnock, we agree, we should do everything possible to discourage it, you know, short of making it a criminal offence.[53]

Mary later described endless arguments on this subject which she felt were largely her fault. While on some topics she felt she had been too intellectual or philosophising, on this one she felt she was too emotional. She wrote 'I was so far from being able to imagine handing over a baby to whom I had given birth, so keenly able to remember the bliss of seeing this new life, that I immediately felt it to be morally outrageous that anyone should contract before the pregnancy began that she would hand over the baby.'[54] She was also offended by the sort of language with which people involved were referred to 'agents' or 'surrogates.' She was upset by hearing about women who spoke of becoming a surrogate so that they could 'buy a new carpet for the sitting room.'[55] This was one of the few occasions when Mary's gender clearly affected her contribution to a debate.

In the end, after protracted discussion, the committee followed the majority view that the commercial exploitation of surrogacy should be banned but its practice should not.[56] Professionals who assisted in facilitating surrogate pregnancies should be liable to criminal prosecution and any contracts involving agreements over surrogacy births should be regarded as illegal and unenforceable in law.[57] These were not unanimous recommendations. David Davies and Wendy Greengross (a general practitioner and an agony aunt) signed a minority report opposing criminalisation and taking a much more relaxed view of the procedure.[58] Some months after the publication of the report, Mary began to feel this minority was in the right and blamed herself for bulldozing the majority into holding her view. The view that surrogacy should be permitted has subsequently prevailed in the UK (though not in many other countries), and arrangements for licensing and regulation have gone reasonably well, though it is now felt that further regulatory reform is needed.[59]

Apart from surrogacy, the other major point of disagreement among committee members was the issue of research on embryos. As we have seen, the failure rate of IVF was substantial, and the overwhelming medical view was that the procedure needed to be the subject of more scientific research. It inevitably produced a large number of embryos that were surplus to requirement. Could these be used for such research? Most medical authorities thought they could, but most religious organisations and individuals, particularly the Catholic Church and the Chief Rabbi, deemed such research to be morally wrong. John Marshall was a strong advocate of this view, an inconsistent position for he was not opposed, as some Catholics were, to the fertilisation of an embryo in the laboratory for clinical purposes.[60]

The groundwork in enhancing the committee's understanding in the issues of embryo research and reaching a conclusion on the matter was achieved when Anne McLaren described the early development of the embryo. A crucial meeting of the committee was held on 9 November 1983 when members started to discuss the maturity of the embryo beyond which research should not be permitted. Anne McClaren's paper titled 'Where to draw the line' pointed to the fact that it was at fourteen days that the so-called primitive streak appeared. This consisted of the cells from which eventually the central nervous system would develop.

She argued that until this primitive streak appeared it was inconceivable that the embryo could experience any form of pain or suffering. The committee agreed that the maturity of the embryo should be decided on the number of days after fertilisation rather than on the state of development of the embryo, which was seen to be a more arguable and therefore less satisfactory criterion. Research, they decided, should therefore be permitted up to fourteen days of the life of the embryo but not beyond that point.[61]

Even though the fourteen-day rule seemed eminently logical, it was anathema to the Catholic members who held that pre-fourteen-day embryos were potentially human beings and therefore should not be used for research without their consent which, of course, they could not give. In contrast, some geneticists, such as David Galton, pointed out that fourteen days was an arbitrary cut-off point and it was ridiculous to criminalise scientists who carried out research on, say, sixteen-day-embryos.[62] Mary argued arbitrary cut-off points were inevitably set in much legislation. The 30 mph speed limit in built-up areas is arbitrary; it might be set at 20 or 40 mph as indeed it is in some areas. But 30 mph is widely accepted as an appropriate speed limit in most cities and social consensus was the crucial criterion. It was this issue that persuaded Mary that the language of social appropriateness was more persuasive than the language of morality, with its perhaps high-handed insistence on what was right and what was wrong. Whether or not the fourteen-day rule was arbitrary, the ethical question to be decided was whether such early-stage, pre-fourteen-day embryos are entitled to the same moral concerns as a more mature foetus, or even, as some members claimed, a mature adult. Mary's view, shared by the majority of the committee, was that Anne McLaren had demonstrated that such early-stage embryos could not have rights and that the practical long-term benefits of research in any case outweighed any remaining doubts. In the event, the committee's report reflected the majority view, arrived at finally at its December 1983 meeting, that, with the consent of the couple involved, embryos could be used for research up to fourteen days after fertilisation but that it should be a criminal offence to carry out research on embryos at a more advanced stage of development. A minority report, signed by John Marshall and the two social workers, stated that as the human status of the embryo could not be satisfactorily determined at any point in its existence, experimentation on it should never be permitted.[63]

In resolving this issue, Mary's approach was typical of how she tackled other problems. First, she considered relevant evidence. At the risk of repetition, this can be summarised as follows: IVF was only successful in a limited number of cases. To benefit more women, there had to be research on embryos. Anne McLaren had shown that it was inconceivable that embryos of less than fourteen days' gestation could experience pain or other suffering. Then there was the moral question to be considered: was research on these early embryos morally wrong? Did such embryos have the same right to moral concern as more mature foetuses and human beings. The committee concluded that they did not. So, regulated research on less than fourteen-day-old embryos was morally justifiable. The next question was whether there should be a law to criminalise experiments on more mature embryos. Mary's view was that experimentation on post-fourteen-day embryos was morally wrong and that a law forbidding it would have no harmful consequences. On this basis she decided and her committee (with the exception of the three dissidents) agreed with her that research on less than fourteen-day gestation embryos should, with regulation, be permitted and that research on more mature embryos should be criminalised.

The final set of recommendations made by the committee concerned the mechanism for regulation and monitoring of practice in this field. It recommended that a new independent statutory authority be created to regulate both research and infertility services. To avoid the possibility of this new regulatory body becoming dominated by particular interest groups, whether scientists or religious figures, its membership should contain a majority of lay members and the Chair should always be a lay person.[64] The aim was to ensure that in such a contentious area, the regulator should never stray too far from the views of the general public. Following the publication of the report, the establishment of the Human Fertilisation and Embryology Authority (HFEA), at first on a temporary basis, but soon made permanent, has been widely regarded as a conspicuous success. The HFEA is responsible for licensing all research using human gametes and preimplantation embryos and is generally regarded as providing helpful guidance to research workers and maintaining high standards of practice in infertility services.

The HFEA has, however, no power to ensure that fertility services are available under the NHS. The report had stated that it was important that 'there should be a sufficient level of NHS provision for childless couples not to feel that their only recourse is to the private sector.'[65] Sadly, this is still far from the case. Since the publication of the report, provision has been dominated by the private sector and is often out of reach of childless couples with limited means.

The last meetings of the committee were ill-tempered with disagreements over surrogacy and embryo experimentation coming to a head. Mary recorded details of a meeting in the Holiday Inn in Cardiff in March 1984. There was adequate hot water in the bedrooms and edible food, she noted, but no satisfactory meeting room so the last session was held in the hotel bar. Further, although the hotel had a photocopier, there was a problem with the production of drafts for discussion. No one in the so-called DHSS secretariat could type. Ken Rawnsley, the Cardiff professor of psychiatry, went to his office and came back with a typewriter so that Mary herself could type out the drafts. Mary reported it was 'the most disastrous meeting,'[66] though Jeremy Metters, who was partly responsible for its organisation, understandably did not have such a negative recollection of it.[67]

In any event, the discussions led to the production of three minority reports. Wendy Greengross and David Davies produced a cogent argument against the criminalisation of surrogacy, with which Mary later came to agree. John Marshall and the two social workers dissented from the view that human embryos could be used for research purposes. Four members of the committee dissented from the view that embryos could be brought into existence solely for the purpose of carrying out research. If one adds John Marshall and the two social workers who took this view, this means that nearly half the committee disagreed with one or other of the recommendations.

The report was finally signed off with its three notes of dissension on an afternoon in July 1984. Mary only arrived in the nick of time for the occasion, having been entertained to a magnificent lunch given by Norman St. John Stevas.[68] Norman Fowler, the Secretary of State, to whom the report was personally presented, appeared pleased and asked to be briefed by Mary on its contents on a subsequent occasion. Mary records that after he had left 'we all shuffled off, probably glad to be rid of each other.'[69] This gloomy view of the relationships between the members of the committee was not shared by others who had sat on it; they continued to view it as a largely pleasurable learning experience. Mary remained very much in contact at least with Anne McLaren, with whom she often shared a platform until Anne's death in a car accident in 2007.[70]

While there certainly were differences of opinion among committee members reflected in the minority reports, the achievement of consensus owed everything to Mary. Throughout she had led the discussions and from the point of view of the members had been a most effective chair. The focus was always on the issues under discussion with Mary particularly keen to tap the expertise, especially that of Anne McLaren, available round the table. Her background as a moral philosopher, in the view of David Davies, proved invaluable when, as was often the case, conclusions relating to the right and wrong of behaviour were in question.[71] Government reports of this nature are frequently drafted by civil servants with committee members making major or minor changes and approving the final version. This was not the case on this occasion. The civil servants did produce briefing drafts, but Mary took responsibility for most of the writing. Her characteristic style is present on every page. Others, such as David Davies, with his journalistic experience, took on some editing tasks, but it was Mary who drafted all the difficult sections.

The interim Human Fertilisation and Embryology Authority was set up very rapidly. Translation of the other main recommendations of the committee into law was a much more problematic and protracted affair than had been the case with the report on special education. To begin with, whereas the previous report had almost immediately enjoyed near universal support, many of the recommendations of this report proved controversial, some of them even highly objectionable. When its contents were debated in the House of Lords in October 1984, the large number of bishops who were members of the House condemned the report's acceptance of AID, though they were prepared to agree to AIH. They were horrified at the thought of experimentation on embryos at any time from the moment of fertilisation.[72] Donald Soper, a progressive Methodist minister, was the only religious leader to speak in favour of the report. It was not just the bishops who were critical. Leading lawyers such as Lord Denning were equally scathing on the embryo experimentation issue, as were many other peers.[73] Mary was not made a life peer until the following year, so she was not able to respond directly in the debate.

Following an outcry about commercial surrogacy, the Surrogacy Arrangements Act 1985 to regulate the procedure was rushed through Parliament. As a result of the controversies surrounding the area, it took several years before a bill implementing the other recommendations was put before Parliament, Meanwhile, Mary was much in demand as a speaker to discuss the issues in the report. She recalled an improbably uncomfortable stay in the luxurious Danieli Hotel in Venice where she lectured.[74] The bestowal of an honorary degree in Melbourne turned into a highly pleasurable two-month visit with Geoffrey to Australia in July and August 1986. Mary gave a series of lectures on bioethics and had the opportunity of discussions with Peter Singer, the philosopher with whom she had taken issue over animal rights.[75]

It gradually became clear, partly as a result of the responses to a questionnaire in *Women's Own* that Mary helped to draft, that there was popular support for the report's recommendations as well as parliamentary enthusiasm.[76] The civil servants made slow progress, but a white paper was published for consultation in the autumn of 1987 and the bill was finally introduced in November 1989, five years after the publication of the report. On 7 December 1989 at the second reading of the Human Fertilisation and Embryology Bill in the House of Lords, it emerged that there had been a change of attitude among many peers to the recommendations made in the report. Although again most bishops spoke against experimental research on human embryos, even among churchmen there were those who were prepared to be much more favourable. Mary was particularly grateful that John Habgood, the Archbishop of York, who had trained as a biologist, introduced the idea that the gradual development of the human organism from gamete (sperm or egg) to embryo to foetus to baby, child and then adulthood, should result in a similar continuum of moral value being accorded as development proceeded.[77]

Mary was by now a member of the House of Lords herself and could contribute to the debate. She confined her remarks to research issues. Ignorant at one point she might have been, but she was now as well informed as any geneticist about the issues involved. Research on human embryos, she noted, had already been going on for twenty years and had brought great benefits to society. The chromosomal basis of Down's syndrome had been established. The carriers of some dreadful genetic diseases who were concerned they would pass on their conditions could now be assured that embryos implanted by IVF did not carry the genes that were responsible. In addition, of course, it was now possible for a small number of childless couples to have biological children of their own by in vitro fertilisation.[78]

There had already been some attempt to introduce into the debate about the report discussion aimed at changing the age at which abortions or terminations of pregnancy could legally be carried out. Mary pointed out that the question of research on embryos had nothing to do with abortion. She quoted a prayer used in her college chapel to the effect that 'we may be given the grace to distinguish things that differ.'[79] We must learn to think differently, she said, of the pre-embryo compared to the embryo and of the pre-fourteen-day embryo compared to one at a later stage of development. A number of peers had expressed concern that the fourteen-day limit was only the beginning of a 'slippery slope, that, before too long would result in experiments being carried out on embryos at a later stage of development.' Mary dismissed this argument by reminding the House that the establishment of the HFEA would ensure that no such changes could occur without very careful consideration.[80] Indeed, no major changes have occurred in the over thirty years since the HFEA was established.

Again, although the bishops remained largely intransigent, there was widespread support from other quarters for all the provisions of the bill. Mary emphasised the importance of the full consent of all those involved in any procedures, AID, in vitro fertilisation or surrogacy. She reiterated the distinction between issues relating to abortion and those of research on embryos and the importance of continuing to resist the attempts to introduce irrelevant matters into the bill. The existence of a regulatory body meant that there was no need for the fear expressed by many fellow peers that the fourteen-day limit would be the thin edge of the wedge in relation to experimentation on more mature foetuses, babies, children or adults. She made the powerful point that to reject this provision of the bill would be tantamount to going back to the seventeenth century when, as had been the case with Galileo, what was permissible in scientific work was decided by the Church and not by scientists. When an aged fellow peer opined that no Christian could possibly support the bill, Mary cited the Archbishop of York. 'Ah,' said the peer, *'He's* not a Christian.'[81]

After many hours of debate the whole bill was passed in the Lords, but then the House of Commons created difficulties. It introduced amendments relating to abortion. The Lord Chancellor warned that if these amendments were allowed, the whole bill risked defeat. Fortunately, in the end, despite serious uncertainty over whether time could be found to reach a decision, the bill was passed and became law.[82] As for the fears of those who saw the fourteen-day limit as the thin end of the wedge, it is notable that there have been no substantive changes to the regulations since the HFEA was established more than thirty years ago.

Following the 1990 Act, advances in medical and scientific knowledge would regularly give rise to new ethical issues and the demands for Mary to contribute to discussion continued unabated. She frequently spoke in debates about proposed legislation, wrote articles and other books and participated in radio and television discussions. Shortly after the report was published it became clear that it would be possible to carry out manipulation on individual genes or parts of genes with the aim of removing faulty ones and replacing them with healthy ones. In 1991, regulations were passed making it possible to carry out research along these lines using somatic but not germ cells (the latter being cells that develop into sperm or eggs). A major advance took place in 1997 when a sheep was cloned by cell nuclear replacement. This opened up the possibility of creating cloned humans. Not long afterwards, in 2001, an Italian gynaecologist, Severino Antinori, whom Mary described as 'notoriously excitable,' though it does not seem that she ever met him, announced his intention of coming to England to produce a cloned baby. This idea was greeted with alarm by the pro-life lobby and generated sensational press interest, leading the government to take emergency action. The 2001 Human Cloning Bill proposed outlawing cloning in humans. Although Mary broadly supported the bill, she was more relaxed than many others about human cloning, pointing out that identical twins were clones of each other and were not noticeably disadvantaged in any way. She also thought that the government had been panicked into introducing the bill unnecessarily, as the matter could have been dealt with quite easily under existing legislation, presumably by the HFEA.[83]

Another source of public alarm were new developments in stem cell research. There was no doubt that this work had considerable therapeutic potential, but the research was pushing the boundaries of the law. In a House of Lords debate on the proposed new regulations, Mary expressed her irritation that so much time had needlessly been spent on the wrong questions, especially on whether the embryo was a 'person.' She said:

> There is no sense in saying such things as, 'The embryo may possibly be a person', or, 'The embryo is probably, or probably not, a person'. Neither probability nor discovery comes into the question at all. It is a matter of decision—and Parliament did decide in 1990 that the early embryo did not have the right to the protection that presumably belongs to persons.

She regretted that the 1984 Report had used words such as 'respect for the embryo.' That, she said in her usual forthright fashion, 'seems to me to lead to certain absurdities. You cannot respectfully pour something down the sink—which is the fate of the embryo after it has been used for research, or if it is not going to be used for research or for anything else.'[84]

In 2007, it became clear that the 1990 Act needed amendment in the light of recent genetic advances. A bill was introduced to make minor amendments to the earlier act. The new act established that all research on human embryos created outside the body, whatever the process that went into their creation, should be subject to regulation. 'Human admixed embryos,' in which there were contributions from non-human species, should also be subject to regulation. It retained the duty on infertility clinics to ensure that children born by assisted reproduction had their parental needs met but replaced the original wording which had insisted on the 'need for a father' with the 'need for supportive parenting.' The bill recognised both members of a same-sex couple who had children as legitimate parents. Mary, now eighty-three years old, spoke in favour of keeping the Human Fertilisation and Embryology Authority which, not for the first or last time, was under threat by a government seeking economies. She continued to advocate for utilitarianism (weighing benefits and harms) as a guiding principle in making decisions on clinical practice and research. Once again, in this debate, the pro-life group tried to introduce amendments relating to abortion, and Mary deplored such confusing interventions.[85]

Meanwhile other issues in genetics were beginning to arise. The huge project to map the entire human genome was giving rise to ever-growing commercial opportunities, and the question of the ownership of genetic material was demanding urgent answers. Was it the individual from whom a sample had been taken, the scientist who had obtained it or the commercial firm owning the laboratory in which the process had been undertaken? In December 1998, Mary was contacted by a scientist at the University of Reykjavik to ask if she would come over immediately to give a view on the setting up of a privately owned genetic data bank. An Icelandic geneticist, Kari Stefansson, had established a company, deCode, to hold and crucially to own a huge bank of genetic samples from Icelanders. The practical effect would be to deny access to this research material by the wider scientific community, thereby creating a monopoly for deCode.[86]

Mary agreed this would be thoroughly undesirable and prepared her remarks accordingly. While she was delivering her paper, she noticed in the back of the room a man whom she immediately identified as Kari Stefansson. He was 'one of the most enormous men I had ever seen, [...] with piercing blue eyes and fair hair.'[87] It was impossible not to see him, she wrote, except 'in a Viking's helmet, striding the Wagnerian stage.' Unintimidated, she gave her paper, highly critical of commercialisation with its inevitable constraints on the availability of genetic material to those who did not own it. Stefansson strode out at the end, obviously angry, though she was congratulated by the rest of the scientific audience. Unfortunately, the Icelandic Parliament had passed a bill agreeing to deCode's proposals that very morning, so her speech was to no avail.[88] Subsequently, it has to be added, deCode has achieved significant success in advancing knowledge as well as making a significant commercial profit. In 2017, Kari Stefansson was awarded top prize of the American Society for Human Genetics for his far-reaching scientific contributions.[89]

During the late 1990s and early 2000s, Mary spent some time reflecting on philosophical questions arising during her work in this field. She brought together her thoughts in *Making Babies*, published in 2002.[90] The central question she tried to answer was whether people had a right to have children. Why did she write this book? During the enquiry, she had met infertile women who had, she felt, been badly treated by the doctors they had consulted. It is clear from the account she gives of the evidence given by gynaecologists to the committee that she found a number of them arrogant and patronising towards their patients. Certainly, this was how she felt particularly about Dame Josephine Barnes, the doyenne of gynaecologists who was a member of her committee. All the same, when the doctors described the reasons for their negative attitudes towards some of the women who came to them for treatment of infertility, she felt they had a point. There were, for example, women already living at the limit of their meagre financial or emotional resources or those who thought having a child would save their marriages. Some cases raised extraordinarily complex issues. Early on in her book she discusses the case of Diane Blood from whose husband samples of semen were taken while he was in a coma and certain to die.[91] In 1997, the HFEA refused permission for a UK gynaecologist to assist her to have a child using this semen, on the grounds that a posthumous child was bound to suffer psychological trauma. Mary pointed out that the fact that her own father had died before her birth had not meant she suffered such trauma.[92] In the end, Diane Blood found more sympathetic medical care in Belgium where she had two sons who have developed well.

Did infertile women have a right to professional assistance to have a baby regardless of their circumstances or motivation? Did Diane Blood have a right to be fertilised using her late husband's sperm? Mary had always hitherto rejected what she saw as the careless use of language of rights in answer to general questions such as 'does a woman have right to a child.' Her view was that people only have such rights as are conferred by law, and she was suspicious of any talk of 'natural rights.' Nevertheless, her own 'blissfully happy' experiences of giving birth to five babies made her greatly sympathetic to women denied this opportunity for reasons that were no fault of their own. She discusses the changes in the concept of rights and their relationship to the law over the previous half-century. Until the 1960s, she writes, the Benthamite view had prevailed that rights could only exist when conferred by law. More recently, it had become widely held that human rights were the rights of all human beings by virtue of their humanity, regardless of the law, which, if necessary, must be changed to accommodate them. But who was to say what these universal rights were? Rights, she wrote, must be conferred by a higher authority and if this is not the law, who or what is it? There was currently no law that gave women the right to conceive. Mary thought that it was important to keep the language of principle and morality separate from the language of law, but, from 2001, this distinction had been removed in the United Kingdom by the passage of the Human Rights Act which incorporated into UK law the provisions of the European Convention on Human Rights.[93]

Mary then considered the possibility that human rights might perhaps be seen as derived from need. This was certainly the principle behind the policies of the 1945 Attlee Government when it set up the NHS and enacted welfare policies. It could therefore be conceded that people do have a right to certain basic needs, like food, water and shelter, but is the need to have children such a basic need? Clearly people do not need to have children in the same sense that they need water. Although it might be argued that women who cannot have children without assistance have a right to that assistance, it might be that doctors were within *their* rights to refuse treatment if this seemed an appropriate course of action to them? Mary felt this could be a reasonable position for doctors to take, but, if they did, they had a duty to explain their reasons. For example, even though it might be eminently reasonable to refuse infertility treatment to parents with a history of child abuse, the doctor would still need to explain and offer to refer for another opinion.[94] To support her view, she describes the case of a single woman aged sixty years who wanted to have IVF using her brother's semen. Mary clearly thought that any doctor who acceded to such a request would not be acting in the interests of the unborn child and would therefore be entitled to refuse help.[95] She thought cases like these should be decided on their own merits, not on rigidly applied rules. The paramount consideration should be the good of the child.

She goes on to dismiss the idea that any form of assisted conception should be forbidden by law because it is unnatural or against the laws of nature. Here she draws for support on Hume's *Treatise on Human Nature* (1739) in which he affirms that everything that happens must be natural unless it is the effect of a miracle. Having rejected the idea that infertility treatment is unnatural, she goes on to ask whether all such treatment methods should be regarded as legitimate.[96] She expresses doubts about both surrogacy and cloning. Her doubts about surrogacy have by now been reduced to concern about the idea that people should make money out of it. She considers that existing UK law on surrogacy at the time she was writing was ambiguous in relation to profit-making. Expenses were allowed, but these could amount to what was, in effect, an income. She thought it would be better if the process of surrogacy was more tightly regulated.[97] In fact, at the time of writing in 2020, the Law Commission has suggested that, though surrogacy is legal and indeed often carried out with great professionalism in the UK, reform is long overdue to bring greater certainty to parents and the surrogate mother. For Mary, there were more concerns about cloning. Increasingly, she notes, there seemed to be a wish for parents to create 'designer babies' with perfect appearance and brains. But babies are not fashion accessories or possessions. They rapidly develop characteristics of their own. It takes time and experience for parents to realise that they have very limited power over the way their children develop, a view perhaps derived from her understanding of her own children's development. She affirms: 'To allow parents to insist that their babies must be of a certain kind would be a disaster.'[98]

Mary concludes her discussion of rights by suggesting that, rather than thinking in terms of a right for the infertile to be given assistance to conceive by the medical profession, it would be preferable to consider the matter in terms of 'the doctor's professional duty, which is a duty of compassion to his patients, making it obligatory for him to seek as far as he can to alleviate suffering.' She does not think this constitutes a right to have such help. If this were the case, the patient would become a client and the doctor her servant. It would make the doctor like a hairdresser who has to do what his or her customer wants.[99] To suggest there is a fundamental contrast here seems problematic to me. Surely the best sort of interaction between doctors and their patients as well as between hairdressers and their clients is based on discussion. In the end, a hairdresser, exactly like a doctor, can refuse to accede to a client's request, for example, for a bizarre cut or an outlandish dye. In any event, it is clear that Mary would deplore a situation in which a doctor had a contractual duty to carry out a procedure demanded by the patient. We must, she says, beware of the danger of confusing what is deeply and passionately wanted with a right. Further, she thought it would be disappointing if people felt so strongly about their rights that they missed out on the 'astonishment and gratitude' that came with the birth of a child. 'Gratitude is something you do not feel when all you have is what is owed.'[100]

Making Babies was Mary's last contribution to the literature on infertility. Her influence on the field of genetic research and its regulation has, however, endured to the end of the second decade of the twenty-first century and will doubtless continue for years to come. The Human Fertilisation and Embryology Authority, established on the basis of her report, continues to function effectively. It licenses, monitors and inspects fertility clinics, provides information about fertility treatment, clinics and sperm and embryo donation. It collects data about fertility treatments in such a way that people conceived with a donor can learn more about their genetic origins. It also monitors research centres to ensure they comply with the various legal requirements laid down by law. In October 2019, Ewan Burney, a leading British geneticist, described it as 'a model, one of the best in the world, to decide what should be allowable and what not.'[101] Occasionally, as in 2011, there have been attempts by government to shut it down or merge it with other bodies, but these have been strongly and successfully resisted. The positive impact of the Warnock Committee on clinical practice and embryo research is difficult to exaggerate.

In 2003, twenty years after its report was published, Suzi Leather, the Chair of the HFEA, wrote of Mary Warnock:

> Rarely can an individual have had so much influence on public policy. The committee she chaired clearly appreciated the fundamental moral and often religious questions raised by assisted reproductive technology, and yet it produced a coherent set of proposals for their regulation that has stood the test of time. The fact is that almost 20 years later we are still working to the rules suggested by Warnock.[102]

Another sixteen years later, Professor Susan Golombok, Director of the Centre for Family Research in the University of Cambridge, the leading researcher worldwide in the study of children born by AID and surrogacy puts it this way:

> The ground-breaking work of the Warnock Committee set the scene for the HFEA, and a UK regulatory system for assisted reproduction that is the envy of the world. Many of the issues considered in the report,

such as the psychological impact on children of the absence of a genetic connection to a parent, were prescient at the time and relevant to this day. Although the Warnock Report came out against surrogacy, in 2003, Mary Warnock acknowledged that she had been too hostile towards surrogacy, and that the test of time had produced a change of mind. Mary Warnock's far-sighted perspective on assisted reproduction has left a legacy of an ethical and compassionate approach to new developments in the field.[103]

Interviewed for her obituary in *BioNews* in March 2019, Prof. Robin Lovell-Badge, the head of stem cell biology and developmental genetics at the Francis Crick Institute in London, wrote:

> It was her foresight that led to robust but flexible regulations that deal with a sensitive area, and which are often the envy of other countries. She was always determined that 'ignorance and prejudice should not be allowed to dictate the outcome' of legislation. We will greatly miss her clear and level-headed thinking, her wisdom and common sense, and her unfailing support.[104]

Alison Murdoch, Professor of Reproductive Medicine, Newcastle University, considers that the Warnock Report made three highly significant recommendations that have stood the test of time: it affirmed that IVF should be permitted and that the providers and recipients of treatment should be protected by law; that the legitimacy of children born by AID and IVF should be recognised; and that research should be permitted with embryos of fourteen-day maturity or less. Without these recommendations, such vital principles might never have been agreed.[105] Prof. Sarah Franklin, Chair and Head of the Cambridge Sociology Department's Reproductive Sociology Research Group, sees Mary as a pioneer in that she was 'a public intellectual who was able to integrate a profound understanding of ethics and philosophy into a sociological perspective on public policy development, a feat never before achieved.'[106]

Notes

1   Mary Warnock, 2003, p. 73.

2   Ibid.

3   Edwards and Sharpe, 1971.

4   Mary Warnock, 2003, p. 73.

5   A. McLaren, 1973, p. 4.

6   G. Dunstan, 1973, p. 51.

7   Her Majesty's Stationery Office, 1960.

8   British Medical Association, 1973.

9   R. G. Edwards and A. Steptoe, 1973, pp. 11–18.

10   O. Stone, 1973, pp. 69–76.

11   Graham, p. 65.

12   Dunstan, p. 50.

13   Himmelweit, p. 102.

14   Kilbrandon, p. 103.

15   Mary Warnock, 2003, p. 74.

16   Mary Warnock, 1985, p. 4.

17   Mary Warnock, 2003, p. 71.

18   Ibid., p. 76.

19   Ibid.

20   Mary Warnock, 1985, p. iv.

21   Mary Warnock, 2003, pp. 76–77.

22   Ibid.

23   Ibid., p. 80.

24   Ibid., pp. 81–82.

25   Ibid., p. 83.

26   David Davies, British Library, Oral history sound archive, C1379/60.

27   Jeremy Metters, personal communication.

28   Ibid.

29   George Hill, 1985.

30   Mary Warnock, 2003, p. 88.

31   Mary Warnock, 1985, p. xi.

32   Mary Warnock, 1992, pp. 84–101.

33   Mary Warnock, 1985, p. 95.

34   Ibid., p. ix.

35   Ibid., p. viii.

36   Ibid., p. x.

37   Ibid., p. xi.

38   Warnock, 2003, pp. 98–99.

39   Warnock, 1992, p. 95.

40   Ibid, p. 101.

41   Warnock, 1985, pp. 101–105.

42   Warnock, 2003, p. 87.

43   Jeremy Metters, personal communication.

44   David Davies, British Library, Oral history sound archive, C1379/60.

45   What follows is a highly simplified version of the process whereby the committee arrived at its conclusions and, in particular, the fourteen-day rule. For a detailed description based on the original documentation, see S. Franklin, 2019.

46   Warnock, 1985a, p. 12.

47   Warnock, 2002.

48   Warnock, 1985a, pp. 23–24.

49   Ibid., p. 27.

50   Ibid., pp. 24–25.

51   Warnock, 2003, p. 105.

52   Warnock, 2003, p. 91.

53   David Davies, British Library, Oral history sound archive, C1379/60.

54   Warnock, 2003, p. 103.

55   Ibid.

56   Warnock, 1985a, p. 47.

57   Ibid.

58   Ibid., pp. 87–89.

59   Latham, 2020.

60   Warnock, 2003, pp. 92–97.

61   Ibid., pp. 94–95.

62   Ibid., p. 97.

63   Warnock, 1985a, pp. 90–93.

64 Ibid., pp. 75–76.

65 Ibid., p. 33, 5.11.

66 Warnock, 2003, p. 107.

67 Jeremy Metters, personal communication.

68 Warnock, 2003, p. 109.

69 Ibid., p. 110.

70 Ibid., p. 113.

71 David Davies, personal communication.

72 Hansard, House of Lords debate, 31 October 1984, Vol. 456.

73 Ibid

74 Warnock, 2003, p. 114.

75 Ibid., p. 115.

76 Ibid., pp. 113–114.

77 Hansard, House of Lords debate, 2 December 1989, Vol. 513.

78 Ibid.

79 Ibid.

80 Ibid.

81 Warnock, 2003, p. 120.

82 Ibid., p. 125.

83 Hansard, Human Reproductive Cloning Bill, 26 November 2001, Vol. 629.

84 Hansard, Stem Cell Research, House of Lords debate, 5 December 2002.

85 Hansard, Human Fertilisation and Embryology Bill, House of Lords, 19 November 2007.

86 Warnock, 2003, p. 143.

87 Ibid., p. 146.

88 Ibid., p. 147.

89 Mark Daly, 2018.

90 Warnock, 2002.

91 Ibid., pp. 4–5.

92 Ibid.

93   Ibid., pp. 17–26.

94   Ibid., p. 45.

95   Ibid., pp. 47–48.

96   Ibid., p. 73.

97   Ibid., pp. 92–93.

98   Ibid., p. 107.

99   Ibid., p. 110.

100   Ibid., p. 114.

101   Ewan Burney, Radio 4, *Eugenics: Science's Greatest Scandal*, 6 October 2019.

102   Human Fertilisation and Embryology Authority Report, 2003/4.

103   Susan Golombok, personal communication.

104   Rachel Siden, 2019.

105   Alison Murdoch, Progress Educational Trust conference, https://www. youtube.com/watch?v=5b6SEDMflqg.

106   Sarah Franklin, 2019.

9. What Are Universities For?

While the Committee on Human Fertilisation and Embryology was sitting between 1982 and 1984, the members who had university posts were living anxiously through a government onslaught on the finances of their academic institutions. In May 1979, Margaret Thatcher and a radically reforming Conservative government had been elected to power. The Prime Minister saw the universities, particularly Oxford and Cambridge, as anti-business, anti-merit, even, with their cosmopolitan leanings, anti-patriotic.[1] There were some academic subjects to which she was particularly antipathetic, sociology, which had mushroomed in the 1960s and 1970s being foremost among them. Mathematics and the sciences (she herself had studied Chemistry at Oxford) as well as vocational subjects such as law and medicine were more likely to be protected. As was nearly always the case over this period, the country was in an economic crisis. It did not take long for the axe to fall. In 1981, universities were told to expect an 18% cut to their finances over the next three years. They were given a month to decide how to implement the cuts.[2]

Mary's husband, Geoffrey, had been elected Oxford's Vice-Chancellor in 1981. Within a year of his appointment, he attended a meeting of Vice-Chancellors held in London which was addressed by the Prime Minister in uncompromising terms. She relentlessly attacked the universities for what she saw as their elitism and indifference to the economy (see Chapter One).[3] He was astonished that the Prime Minister should assemble a room full of leading academics and university administrators and show no desire to listen to them; indeed they had not been allowed to say a word. He was in the forefront of those at Oxford who had to work out how to cope with a significant decline in funding. Before 1979, universities had been relatively favoured by the Treasury and had seen a gradual but significant expansion over the previous thirty years. Now

 https://doi.org/10.11647/OBP.0278.09

they had to go into reverse. Because of the large endowments of some of the colleges, Oxford was relatively cushioned against the cuts, but even so, between 1981 and 1990 the university lost sixty-nine posts in the arts and social studies and fifty-eight posts in mathematics and the sciences. External funding from research councils and the National Health Service meant that many science posts were retained, but the arts and humanities subjects were badly hit over this period.[4]

The fundamental ideological differences between academics like the Warnocks and the Prime Minister concerned the value to be placed on the arts. Mary and Geoffrey saw them as precious cultural assets that should be supported by substantial public funding. Margaret Thatcher saw them as the preserve of a privileged elite; those who wanted them to survive should pay for them, not taxpayers, the vast majority of whom never went near an opera house. It was not that the Prime Minister dismissed intellectual ideas as unimportant; indeed, her government was ideologically driven to a greater extent than any previous Conservative administration. Unlike any of her predecessors, she was a reasonably regular attendee at a philosophy group, one of whose members was the Warnock's friend, Anthony Quinton.[5] But the neo-liberal, free market ideas discussed in the philosophy group which attracted her were very different from those which influenced the Warnocks and their friends.

While an ideological chasm was opening up between the government and the universities over the purposes of higher education and its funding, Mary herself had become a favoured public figure. The Report of the Committee on Human Fertilisation and Embryology had won widespread praise. In 1984 she was made a Dame of the Order of the British Empire, a high public honour. Lady Warnock was now in demand as a wise woman who could pronounce in the media on virtually every issue in which an element of moral judgement was required. Further, she was good value, speaking entertainingly and often drawing on her own personal experiences as a mother, wife, teacher and friend. She managed to be both profound and funny.

In 1983, there was an unexpected vacancy for the Mistress of Girton College, Cambridge. Brenda Ryman, a distinguished medical biochemist who had been the Mistress for the previous seven years, had died after a relatively short illness. In the spring of 1984, Mary was approached to see if she were willing to be a candidate. She was just coming to the end of her chairmanship of the Human Embryology and Fertilisation Committee. The member of Girton's search committee who went to Oxford to discuss the possibility with her was Gillian Beer, the Vice-Mistress, a distinguished English don and later herself President of Clare Hall, Cambridge. She found Mary to be a delightful, free-spirited woman, interested in a wide variety of topics. She reported back favourably, and, after an extended interview with all the official fellows, Mary was duly offered the post. Gillian Beer recalls that when she telephoned to tell Mary she was to be offered the post, her reaction to the news was to exclaim 'Oh, my Lord' giving the impression she was greatly surprised, having not really thought her candidacy would be taken seriously.[6] In Mary's own honest but rather graceless words: 'I suppose I accepted Girton because I had not got anything particularly urgent on hand in either Oxford or London, and because it felt agreeable to be offered a new job at the age of sixty, when if I had still been a headmistress I would have had to retire.'[7]

Girton College had been founded by Emily Davies and Barbara Bodichon in 1869 to make university education available to women. It was the first women's college in Cambridge and for over eighty years was only joined by Newnham. In 1976, Girton began to admit male undergraduates and by 1984, when Mary became Mistress, there were roughly equal numbers of men and women undergraduates.[8] The fellows, however, were still predominantly female with very small numbers of male fellows, mainly in subjects such as Engineering in which female academics were in a small minority. During Mary's tenure at Girton, there were no controversies regarding the mixed status of the college. When there were vacancies for fellows, men were given equal opportunity and began to be appointed in increasing numbers, no particular concessions being made for women; indeed, Sarah Kay recalls that when she arrived to be considered for a position as a fellow, she was made to leave her baby in the Lodge while she was being interviewed. There was no creche.[9] On the other hand, in contrast to the men's colleges where committee meetings were usually held at five p.m., in acknowledgement of the needs of committee members who were mothers of young children, at Girton they took place at two p.m.

Mary was undeniably a catch for Girton. She was a well-known public figure with a strong academic record who had already received a high public honour. The following February 1985, shortly after joining Girton, she was made a life peer. Indeed, had the life peerage arrived a few months earlier, it is quite possible Mary would not have gone to Girton, making a more full-time career in the House of Lords. As it was, she spent rather little time in the House of Lords while she was at Girton, limiting her attendance to debates about legislation arising from the report on human fertilisation and embryology and a few other topics such as education in which she had some specialist knowledge or opinions.[10]

Mary was already familiar with the complicated governance systems of Oxford; those of Cambridge, though not identical, were very similar. As Vice-Chancellor, with the Chancellor only a titular position, her husband Geoffrey was the administrative head of the University of Oxford. The relationship between the colleges and the university was highly complex, the colleges jealously retaining their independence and autonomy to the best of their ability. Writing in 1964 (and the situation had changed little by the early 1980s), about one aspect of the organisation of Oxbridge, Rose and Ziman claim: 'The organisation of undergraduate education is intricate. Like so much else, it is not the product of straightforward "educational engineering", or indeed planning of any kind. Rather it is a splendid historical growth, rich with complexities and anomalies, positively Burkean in its close intertwining of interests, ancient customs and peculiar practices.'[11] And that was just undergraduate education. Equally complex issues were, for example, postgraduate education, the distribution of government finance between the university and the colleges and between the individual colleges, and the representation of the university to the outside world. While attempting to bring some sort of order into a chaotic situation, Geoffrey had discussed with Mary how to achieve a more logical structure. She was therefore well versed in the problems. Further, by the time Girton approached Mary, Geoffrey had achieved some success in the matter of representation to the outside world. On his retirement as Vice-Chancellor in 1985, he was able to claim: 'We have found ways, while remaining an essentially federal and inevitably complex system, of speaking with one voice when necessary and of acting, when necessary, with respectable decisiveness and celerity; we have found ways of presenting ourselves to government and the University Grants Committee and particularly perhaps to schools as one university and not a disorderly crowd.'[12]

While Mary did not have to deal with politics at a university level, she had thought deeply in the past about the purposes of higher education. To understand her thinking on the aims appropriate for a university, one needs to go back a decade. Although Mary had resigned from her position as headmistress of Oxford High School in July 1972 largely in order to help her husband in his new role as Principal of Hertford College, she also wanted time to write another philosophical book. After appointment to Lady Margaret Hall's Talbot Research Fellowship,[13] over the next four years she dedicated the time available to her after supporting Geoffrey and those of her children still in their teens to writing *Imagination*. This was the first book Mary published putting forward her own original perspective on a philosophical topic. Its content is largely a description of the history of ideas relating to imagination, but the book also makes a passionate plea for the power of imaginative thinking to be valued throughout the education system.

In her Preface, Mary makes clear that she is attempting to follow a thread of ideas about the nature of imagination and imaginative thinking, beginning with Hume's *Treatise of Human Nature*, published in 1739. The sequence of ideas she is to describe links the way we perceive the world to our imaginations. We use mental images in our everyday perceptions but, more significantly, we have the power to use such images to interpret the world as different, sometimes radically different, from the way it is usually perceived. Such creative interpretation may be, in Mary's words, 'inventive, personal and revolutionary.'[14] Our imagination underlies our capacity to think creatively in that it is *'that which creates mental images* [Mary's italics].'[15] She adds that she has come to believe that 'it is the cultivation of the imagination which should be *the* [my italics] chief aim of education.'[16] Ignoring this aim is, she believes, the main reason why current systems of education most conspicuously fail.

She traces the development of the idea of the imagination from the Enlightenment philosophers, Hume and Kant, through to the early nineteenth-century philosopher, Friedrich Schelling. She pauses here to consider the way the Romantic poets, particularly Wordsworth and Coleridge considered the power of the imagination in creativity and our awareness of the infinite. She then moves on to consider how twentieth-century philosophers, especially Wittgenstein, Sartre and her own Oxford colleague, Gilbert Ryle, have explained the function of the imagination. Finally, in her concluding remarks, Mary gives her own characterisation of imagination as follows: 'there is a power in the human mind which is at work in our everyday perception of the world, and is also at work in our thoughts about what is absent; which enables us to see the world, whether present or absent as significant, and also to present this vision to others, for them to share or reject.'[17] She goes on: 'And this power, though it gives us 'thought-imbued' perception (it "keeps the thought alive in our perception") is not only intellectual. Its impetus comes from the emotions as much as from the reason, from the heart as much as from the head.'[18] She approves of Sartre's view that our 'ability to imagine is identical with the ability to detach ourselves from our actual situation and envisage situations which are *non-actual*.'[19]

'One must,' she wrote, 'recognise the universality of the imaginative function, both in that it belongs to everyone and in that it is exercised by each over all his experience.' It is necessarily connected to the emotions and therefore education should include education about the emotions. She believes that 'there is more in our experience of the world than can possibly meet the unreflecting eye [...] a feeling of infinity.'[20] Without this feeling, she believes, life would be boring and, as we know from the horror she had of her own children being bored, this would be one of the worst fates one might have to endure.[21] On the basis of her teaching experience, she claims that children cannot be taught to feel deeply but they can be taught to look and listen in a way that leads them to experience emotions differently.[22] This does not lead her to think that children should necessarily be encouraged to be creative themselves, but more that in looking at art or in reading literary work, they will invent or imagine meanings that give them a sense of infinity.[23] Meanings, she believes, spring up around us from the moment we become conscious and it is the imagination that ascribes these meanings.[24] Thus, the power of the imagination is central to our understanding of the world around us.

The reviews of *Imagination* in the general press were highly positive. The anonymous reviewer in *The Times Higher Education Supplement* wrote

The task [Mrs. Warnock] sets herself—to trace and assess the rise of *Imagination* as a word of power in the eighteenth and early nineteenth centuries—is a formidable one, requiring both acuity of intelligence and a comprehensive literary culture [...]. To read this book is to experience the special pleasure of being taught by a brilliant teacher. It is unlikely to be matched for many years.[25]

Michael Tanner in *New Society* wrote:

Anything that Mary Warnock writes is notable for lucidity and zest, and that is perhaps truer of this book than of anything she has previously written. It is certainly her most ambitious book to date, in that she argues for some views which, if they were taken seriously by educationalists and teachers, would lead to something of a revolution in education.[26]

Frank Kermode in the *New Statesman* wrote: 'One of the charms of this very attractive book is that it disentangles and makes luminous [a] daunting complex of notions [...] [she] has the pertinacious delicacy of Ariadne in the labyrinth.'[27]

The reception by contemporary philosophers was less enthusiastic. Although W. Charlton in the *Philosophical Quarterly* thought that Mary handled the topic with 'a sensitivity and professional expertise which could hardly be bettered,' he felt that she never satisfactorily came to grips with the idea that we [must] have an image-producing faculty if we reject idealism.'[28] Andrew Harrison in *Mind* suggested that Mary's major claim is that 'we need to take something out of the Romantic picture of the imagination (as illustrated by Wordsworth and Coleridge), seriously, but when she comes to the point of saying what that picture is her statement of it becomes curiously insubstantial.'[29] David Carrier in the *Journal of Philosophy* saw Mary as wishing to connect our imagination as an essential part of ordinary perception and imagination as an aesthetic experience. He does not think that she succeeds in linking the two satisfactorily. Further, he does not find her historical analysis of imagination of much philosophical interest.[30]

Imagination may, all the same, be regarded as providing the philosophical underpinning for Mary's views on the purpose of education at all levels. In *Schools of Thought*, the book she had published in 1977, in which she developed her views on secondary education (see Chapter Six), she wrote about Imagination as one of the three components of what she called 'the good life' for which secondary school pupils should be prepared (the other two being Virtue and Work). She was no less insistent on the importance of the development of the imagination when she came to consider the purposes of higher education. In a lecture she gave in 1994, she claimed 'I have argued that the imagination is crucial in the acceptance of shared and continuing values. It is not surprising therefore that I would also argue that the education of the imagination is by far the most important educational goal...'[31]

These then were her ideas of the aims of higher education formulated in the decade before she went to Girton. In addition, while waiting to take up her post, she developed more practical thoughts, mainly expressed in interviews with journalists. In one such interview she cited her interest in women's education. This interest might have seemed misplaced in that Girton, by her time, admitted equal numbers of men and women as undergraduates, but for Mary, this had only led to a number of unanswered questions. 'Mixed colleges at Oxford have not made the faintest difference,' she declared,

> What has been exploded is the myth that girls work harder and do better than boys. In fact, they do worse. Girls never get thirds, but they seldom get firsts. They are less ambitious, more cautious and the fear of seeming to be a clever girl runs very deep. The easiest way for a girl to survive at Oxford is not to compete very hard. If she does get a first or a scholarship, at least some of the men she knows may not be able to put up with it. They may say 'How marvellous' and turn away. They've got to be very careful.[32]

She was depressed and irritated by this. She noted: 'At Girton the previous year, all the first class degrees had been awarded to men—she would like to find out why and how the girls are educated on the way up.'[33] There were other ideas Mary took to Cambridge in the hope of changing minds there. She wanted to broaden the social composition of the undergraduate body, not by making it easier for disadvantaged students to gain entry (she was opposed to any sort of positive discrimination), but by engaging with matters such as the secondary school and especially the A level curriculum, making it broader and more accessible to the whole range of students. She felt the existing, highly focused examination system favoured the candidates from independent schools. She also liked the idea of there being a month-long introductory course before their first term started for students admitted on the basis of their school record, to enable them 'to familiarise themselves with aspects of their subject they would not have covered at school and with the general method and outlook of the university.'[34]

Mary remained at Girton for nearly seven years from January 1985 to the summer of 1991. In many ways these were productive years but, according to her, they were not happy. Although most of the fellows who were on the staff at the time Mary was at Girton do not recall any significant tensions in their relationship with her and find it hard to understand why she should have been unhappy there, she herself wrote later 'the only part of my life that I would not want to live again is my time as head of a college.'[35] For Mary, this was a rather striking admission. Most of us have more than one part of our lives that we would rather not live again. The strong impression from Mary's profuse recollections is that every phase of her life, from her 'blissful' childhood onwards, had been a source of apparently unmitigated delight. For Mary, it was not that the glass had ever been half full or half empty; her glass had always been brimming over. So, her time at Girton was in marked contrast.

The problems, such as they were, probably arose even before she began there. When she arrived, the handsome modern flat built for the Mistress of the College was being renovated, and the temporary accommodation found for her was outside the college, not far away but far enough to make it seem as if she was outside 'the family home.'[36] In addition, when she began at Girton, Geoffrey still had two university terms to run as Vice-Chancellor of the University of Oxford and it was expected that Mary would be beside him when he entertained important guests of which there were many. Further, soon after his retirement from Hertford, Geoffrey began to suffer the early symptoms of the lung disease which led to his death in 1995. Mary's worry about his health and desire to spend as much time as she could with him weighed on her throughout the later years of her tenure at Girton. She got into the habit of driving from Cambridge to Oxford quite early on Friday afternoon. Because she wanted to attend Hertford College chapel services on Sunday evenings, she did not return to Cambridge until Monday, often on Monday afternoon if she had appointments in London on Monday mornings.[37] These various factors meant she had a short Girton week. This might not have mattered. In fact, her predecessor as Mistress, Brenda Ryman, was a more part-time Mistress. She had lived in London where she had a busy medical school job during her seven-year tenure, holding down a four day a week job as Professor of Biochemistry at the Charing Cross Hospital Medical School, only spending from Thursday evenings, when she always attended Formal Hall, until Monday mornings at Girton. When Brenda Ryman was at Girton, however, she made considerable efforts to socialise and mix with the fellows.[38] So, it might not have mattered that Mary was only in Cambridge for part of the week if she had made a serious attempt to mix with the fellows when she was there. In fact, she rarely had lunch in Hall and when she did, she usually arrived late, just in time for grapes and cheese and stayed only a short time.[39] Further, on the grounds that she hated eating dinner as early as seven fifteen p.m. she was only a very irregular attendee at Hall dinners, even at Formal Hall on Thursdays when graduate students joined the fellows at High Table. In her memoir, Mary describes one Tuesday evening, when she did attend dinner in Hall and found it an embarrassing experience. After dinner she went to the Combination Room for a cup of coffee only to discover that this was the evening the scientists got together after dinner to discuss science teaching, so she felt unwelcome.[40] She sometimes gave the impression she was somewhat suspicious of the fellows and Gillian Beer, the Vice-Mistress felt she occasionally had to act as liaison between them.[41] In fact, there is really no evidence that the fellows felt or showed anything but goodwill towards her.[42]

The governance of Girton was mainly in the hands of the Council, consisting of twelve fellows elected by their peers. Decisions made by the Council were passed on to the Augmented Council, formed of all the fellows and lecturers. If there was a matter requiring greater authority it was passed to the College Governing Body for a final decision. The Mistress chaired both the Council which met fortnightly and the Augmented Council which met less often. She also chaired the Education Board, the Academic Policy Committee, the Investments Committee, the committees selecting for research fellowships (one for sciences, one for arts subjects) and appointment committees in general.[43] She was, of course, very fully briefed before all these committees but it is clear she had a heavy administrative load to carry within the college. Further she had to represent the college at university committees. There was a widely held view among the fellows who recollected her time as Mistress that she represented the college most effectively on these university committees, speaking with great authority and experience.

Shortly after her arrival at Girton, Mary was reported to have said at a dinner party that she intended to 'give Girton a taste of strong government.'[44] This may only have been a rumour, but, if true, according to a don who spent her career lifetime at Girton it was certainly never going to work, especially with a fellowship which had found during Brenda Ryman's tenure that it could manage pretty well with a very part-time Mistress. In fact, as far as most fellows were concerned, it had always been a free and easy institution run in a democratic manner. This turned out not to be Mary's style. A couple of examples illustrate her somewhat autocratic manner. It had been a tradition for tea and shortbread biscuits to be provided for the fellows at around four p.m. Fellows in arts subjects tended to finish their supervisions at this time and the science dons who often spent the day in their laboratories in the city two miles away tended to give their supervisions in the late afternoon after tea. So, the tradition of afternoon tea allowed all the dons to get together. Perhaps as an indirect result of pressure for economy from above (from the university and, beyond the university, from the Treasury), in what was seen as a rather petty money-saving measure, Mary, apparently without realising the social importance of the event decreed that afternoon tea (or was it just the shortbread?) would no longer be provided.[45] On another occasion, it was discovered that one side of an avenue of cherry trees was threatening the foundations of a college building. Clearly these trees would have to be removed, but from an apparent desire for symmetry, Mary took the unpopular decision that the trees on *both* sides of the avenue had to be chopped down.[46]

Gillian Beer, who had been so impressed with Mary's openness and charm when she initially discussed with her the possibility of her standing for Mistress, felt she rarely saw this engaging behaviour in her among her peers once established in the college, though Mary was more attentive to the students. Surprisingly, she found that Mary showed very little interest in the academic work in which the dons were engaged. Nearly all the fellows were carrying out research using their imaginations to extend the frontiers of knowledge, activities which, as we have seen, Mary saw as the paramount consideration in academic activity. Yet she seems never to have asked them about their work.[47] Clearly then, Mary was seen as a rather remote figure who was not around very much and when she did appear failed to make much friendly contact with the fellows. Various reasons for this have already been described. At the beginning of her tenure, her flat was outside the college and she was regularly away for quite a large part of the week. But there were other reasons. Mary had never been particularly sociable with her work colleagues. Her family was central to her existence and she and Geoffrey together lived a highly sociable life in Oxford. But neither at St. Hugh's nor at the Oxford High School had she been at all socially friendly with her professional colleagues. This characteristic was particularly marked at Girton although she did regard one of the dons, Gillian Jondorf, as a good friend. Another reason might have been that, even at this relatively early age (she was in her early sixties) she was becoming progressively deaf. Gillian Jondorf, who had to brief her before the committees she chaired, noted that she often had to repeat items of business before Mary grasped them.[48] Deafness, because it makes it difficult for people to know what is going on around them, is sometimes linked to suspiciousness, and this might have been the case with Mary. Further, her sight was also impaired, which meant she sometimes did not recognise fellows when she passed them. Some of them probably mistakenly thought she was 'cutting' them.

One of the dons present while Mary was Mistress, Anne Fernihough, thinks there was a class problem. She thought that Mary regarded all the dons as having the same sort of privileged upbringing she had had herself. At one point, it became clear Mary thought Anne must have had a nanny to help her mother bring her up, whereas in fact she, as well as probably a number of the other fellows, (including Anne herself who came from lower middle-class Manchester) had family backgrounds in whose childhoods nannies certainly did not figure. Anne saw Mary's Oxford background, her smart clothes and her North Oxford voice as setting her apart from the more modest lifestyle of the Girton dons, many of whom prided themselves on their lack of social pretension. She thinks the dons, though not particularly liking these aspects of Mary, were somewhat in awe of her, as indeed, she seemed at times to be of them.[49] Another English don, Juliet Dusinberre, notes that Mary brought a certain aura of Oxford sophistication with her, alien to the more high-minded Girton ethos. Further, Juliet notes, Mary was the first Mistress not to have been an undergraduate at Girton, so was at a disadvantage in being less in tune with the place. According to Juliet, Mary thought Girton was incredibly shabby and was always trying to smarten it up. This got people's backs up, and 'she didn't really handle it quite right, as later Mistresses have managed this without any difficulty.'[50] Juliet thinks Girton has always felt rather gratified by its shabby image, which seemed to guarantee first-rate scholarship. This was noticeable in the dons' clothing.'[51] Mary made some unfortunate comparisons between Oxford and 'the high-minded ladies of Girton' which nobody liked. She also showed lack of judgement in some of her fundraising activities, at one point proposing that Robert Maxwell, the billionaire notorious for financial dealings of doubtful propriety, be approached. This did not go down well.[52] There were also some fellows, such as Frank Wilkinson, the left-wing economist, who were ideologically opposed to Mary's centre-right politics.[53]

Mary may have expected to have more power to make changes than she did. When her husband had been appointed Principal of Hertford College in 1971, academic morale was low, and the buildings were in a poor state of repair. Geoffrey was able, by dint of strong leadership and a hierarchical power structure, to turn things round and Hertford had moved to near the top of the academic table. Cambridge colleges did not work like that, as Mary's brother, Sir Duncan Wilson, had discovered in the early and mid-1970s when he had been Master of Corpus Christi College (see Chapter Five). There may also have been differences in style and academic aspiration between the Mistress and the dons. At least one of the fellows, the Director of Medical Studies, positively disliked the idea of pushing the students towards top grades in their examinations. John Marks wrote: '[...] the Girton attitude to medical studies was to encourage the students to work to a high second-class standard, rather than a starred first, and to enjoy the other opportunities through which Cambridge life nurtures a broad-based character.'[54] This, as we have seen, was not how Mary thought aspirations should be set.

Not all of these problems were of Mary's making, and it was by no means the case that Mary was universally disliked by the Girton dons. Many admired her, including some, such as Edith MacRobbie, a distinguished animal physiologist, who thought she was good for the college.[55] Those who were critical of her also found much to praise. Anne Fernihough reports that she has 'nothing other than fond memories of her during her time at Girton.'[56] Juliet Dusinberre, reported that, despite her reservations, she herself always got on well with Mary. The English dons worked together very much as a team and Mary was highly approving and supportive of this approach.[57] Further, her contacts in the wider world meant that she brought unusually interesting people to the college to give talks and occasionally to dispense advice.

If relationships between Mary and the Girton fellows were sometimes awkward, she was undoubtedly popular with the undergraduate body. She made a point of having face-to-face interviews with all students shortly after they started their first term and all students in their first, second and third years were invited up to the flat for a buffet lunch during the year.[58] In addition, she tutored a small number of the Girton undergraduates who were studying philosophy. One of them wrote to her many years later after hearing her talk on Radio 4:

> You are unlikely to remember my supervisions with you at Girton, but they are a memory I treasure. You once encouraged me to write an entire essay with my views on the topic in question, rather than simply summarizing the various more distinguished perspectives on it, answering my protestations that it would be the Mickey Mouse guide to the topic with the riposte that you had not read that guide, so to go ahead and write it. It was a very kind piece of encouragement.[59]

Probably Mary's main achievement during her tenure was in fundraising. She was proactive in this respect. Sue Palmer, an ex-Girtonian with strong marketing and communications expertise, writes that, in the late 1980s, she was asked by Mary's son, Felix, whom she knew through the Orchestra of the Age of Enlightenment, to meet his mother. This led to the setting up of a group of business-minded ex-Girtonians who advised not just Mary but her two successors on fundraising.[60] Mary understood that, following the government cuts, fundraising must become a serious and continuous activity. About twenty years earlier, while she was a member of the Oxfordshire Education Authority (see Chapter Four), she had worked with the Director of Music, Constance Pilkington, a member of the wealthy Pilkington family which had previously contributed to Girton. Mary wrote to the family trust, mentioning her previous contact with Constance. She was immediately contacted by a Liverpool solicitor who asked if he could come to see her. The solicitor asked what it would cost to endow a fellowship. Mary nervously named a large six-figure sum and the solicitor replied 'All right. That is what Miss Pilkington would like to give, so long as it is not named after her but after her parents.'[61] Thus, the Austin and Hope Pilkington Trust Music Fellowship was endowed. The first holder of that fellowship, Martin Ennis, a keyboard player, was recruited from Christ's College where he was Director of Music. He was still in post thirty years later. Prior to his arrival, Girton undergraduates had put on musical events, but there had been no encouragement from the top. Martin ran the choir and took over the Music Society. After three years, he was appointed to the Music Faculty of the University of which he was Chair over a long period. Girton music was transformed during Martin Ennis's tenure and this made a major positive difference to the College. During the short period from the time of his appointment to Mary's leaving the college, he found her very supportive, though he thought her hearing impairment probably precluded more active involvement.[62]

Towards the end of her time as Mistress she instituted the Emily Davies Fora perhaps as a gesture towards the history of the college and one of its founders. These were annual meetings held in London for Girton students and alumnae which focused on the position of women in society. Mary's successors continued to organise these meetings. According to Nancy Lane-Perham, these were 'an enormous success. Not only Girton scientists but also graduates and practitioners of other subjects took immense delight in meeting at a central London venue to discuss different aspects of issues that impact on all women, such as the problems associated with ageing.'[63]

Mary was succeeded as Mistress of Girton by Juliet Campbell, a retired diplomat, who was somewhat in awe of Mary, having been supervised by her as an undergraduate at Lady Margaret Hall, Oxford. Mary made a considerable effort to ensure Juliet had a smooth transition into her post. But when she took over, Girton did not seem in good shape to her successor, who came from a more civil service background. According to her, the budgeting system was inadequate, and the buildings were in poor repair.[64] We have seen how Mary herself did not regard her time at Girton as a success, but it should be emphasised that many of the dons themselves took a less negative view. The endowment of the Music Fellowship and the kick-starting of fundraising were major achievements. After she left, Girton remained what Sue Palmer describes as a place where 'the legacy of pioneering and the creation of opportunity blaze through.'[65] Since Mary's time, it has continued as a happy, relaxed college, maintaining high academic standards.

* * *

As we have seen, before Mary went to Girton, the Thatcher Government had already cut university funding. Then, after a year or two, it again began to formulate new policies towards the universities that were a distinct threat to the status quo. In 1981, Sir Keith Joseph, a brilliant but tortured Fellow of All Souls, Oxford, was appointed Secretary of State for Education. In 1985, a year after Mary arrived at Girton, he published a consultative green paper, *Higher Education in the 1990s*, that made some rather anodyne proposals for changes to university funding and organisation.[66] The following year Kenneth Baker, a less cerebral but more decisive character with the same ideological commitment to reform of the universities, succeeded him as Secretary of State for Education. In 1987, Baker published a white paper, *Higher Education: Meeting the Challenge*, which proposed a far more radical agenda for universities over the next five years.[67] The tone of the government's policy was set out in the introduction. Prominence was given to the radical idea that an important role of universities should be to serve the economy more effectively and develop closer links with industry and commerce and promoting enterprise. Less contentious, indeed not contentious at all, was the other aim of pursuing basic scientific research and scholarship in the arts and humanities. In the immediate future, the government would plan for student numbers to increase. The needs of the economy would determine the right number and balance of graduates in the 1990s. The quality of academic work would be enhanced by more selectively funded research, targeted with attention to prospects for commercial exploitation. Efficiency would be increased by improvements in institutional organisation, changes in management and the development and use of performance indicators. The University Grants Committee, the body which had hitherto had the responsibility for the distribution of university finance, would be reconstituted (and, it was later proposed, should be retitled the 'University Funding Council') to include 'a strong element of people from outside the academic world.' The government would provide planning guidelines for the university system as a whole.[68] The government also proposed instituting a system of student loans to help finance the cost of higher education. Overseas students had been paying for their university education from 1981, but the idea that home students should also pay was new at the time. The Conservative Party manifesto for the 1987 election was the first occasion for this idea to be mooted.

While at Girton, in addition to a philosophical book entitled *Memory*, discussed in Chapter Two and below, Mary wrote two books critically engaging with these new government policies. The first of these, *A Common Policy for Education* (see Chapter Six) is largely concerned with her views on secondary schools,[69] but the book also contains a chapter on higher education. In this chapter, Mary discusses in some detail the likely harmful effects of changing the basis of student funding. Nearly one third of the UK population of relevant age was currently in higher education and the great majority of these were supported by Local Authority grants. Mary was shocked at the plans to convert grants into loans, with the inevitable consequence that students would leave university with substantial debts. This, in turn, would mean that they would not wish to enter low-paid employment, such as teaching.[70] The fact that, in her view, there was no alternative to government funding of universities made it particularly important that such funding was seen to be justified.

Mary was particularly hostile towards the new government policies but universities themselves did not escape criticism. The expansion of the universities in the 1960s had been accompanied by the fear in academic circles that standards would drop. Universities had responded defensively by insisting that A level admission requirements must not change. She thought that universities should instead have looked at ways in which they themselves might adapt to meet the needs of students whose earlier school experience had left them less well prepared for higher education than it might have done. They should accept candidates with lower grades on condition they attend pre-entry courses to bring their basic skills up to scratch.[71] Second, university courses for undergraduates should put far more emphasis on the method of acquiring and dealing with information rather than with the content of the information itself. Such transferable skills would be of immense benefit to the graduate when expected to enter new fields of knowledge.[72] More attention should be paid to the needs of overseas students, rather than just their ability to pay high fees. The needs of older or more mature students, likely to enrol in ever larger numbers, should also be considered: they couldn't just be slotted into undergraduate courses. In a concession to government policy, universities should also show flexibility in offering partnerships with employers in industry to meet the needs, for example, of employees who required re-training to fulfil new roles.[73]

In this connection, she discusses what she sees as the failure of polytechnics to devote themselves primarily to 'produce an expert workforce for industry as it emerged into the era of new technology.'[74] Instead, polytechnics had drifted towards providing degree courses of varying quality, blurring the distinction between themselves and universities by meeting the requirements of the Council for National Academic Awards (CNAA). She suggests that, instead, they should become free-standing institutions with the power to determine the nature of their own degree courses. At the time Mary was writing, apart from student fees paid by local authorities, universities were funded by grants administered by the supposedly independent University Grants Committee (UGC). This had become less and less independent and now, as has been noted, the government was proposing that it should be replaced by a University Funding Council (UFC) under much closer government control. Such a system might perhaps work for the applied sciences, Mary thought, but funding for humanities and the more abstract sciences such as mathematics or astronomy would be under constant threat.[75]

She then goes on to discuss academic freedom. This topic had come to the fore because the government was proposing to make funding support to the universities conditional on ending the existing lifelong tenure for university grades even as low as lecturer. This, in Mary's view, would give the government powers to insist that academics whose views differed from theirs should have their contracts terminated. This was, in fact, not what was being proposed but one could see the dangers that government policies might present in the future in this direction. She points to the constraints put on universities in Nazi Germany as well as those exerted by the Soviet Union at the time she was writing.[76] (She does not mention the fact that she had direct experience of the blinkered teaching at Soviet universities during her visit to Moscow in 1971 (see Chapter Five).) Nevertheless, she does not claim that universities must be free to teach whatever they want at whatever cost. Further, she thinks that the principle of tenure should not be applied when, for example, a university teacher is clearly incompetent or there are insufficient students to warrant continuation of a particular course. There will also be cases in which universities might justifiably be asked to merge some departments to ensure they are run more efficiently.[77] Concerns about the level of expense of some university research might be met by setting up research centres of excellence independent of universities but, she notes, there are dangers in removing undergraduate contact with researchers at the cutting edge. She concludes her discussion of higher education with a firm statement of belief. '[...] to fulfil its function, higher education must be the source of questioning, critical and sceptical minds. Students will acquire these attributes only if their teachers are free to pursue knowledge and learning wherever they have the passion to do so.'[78]

During 1988, the year that *A Common Policy of Education* was published, the Conservative government passed its Education Reform Act which, in Mary's view, seriously compromised the ability of universities to pursue their proper functions. Accordingly, she rapidly wrote a short polemic, *Universities: Knowing Our Minds*, as an attack on this legislation.[79] She began by repeating her charge that universities were regarded with increasing indifference by successive governments. Not only is there indifference; the level of academic salaries indicates there is contempt for university teachers. Such contempt, she suggests, may arise from the jealousy of some politicians and ministers for what they perceive as the privileged life of the Oxbridge don.[80]

She then goes on to attack what she regards as the confused ideology underlying the 1988 Act. Universities were clearly seen by the government as commodities whose goods were to be bought and sold. She quoted Robert Jackson, the Minister of State for Higher Education, who declared: 'Because a greater proportion of Universities' income will depend on the attractiveness of what they are offering, they will have to fix on what is attractive and market it effectively.'[81] The government, she alleged, was wrong to point to American universities as successfully applying a commercial model on the grounds they were privately funded. On the contrary, she pointed out, apart from a few liberal arts colleges, most institutions of higher education in the United States were funded either federally or, much more commonly, by the individual states.[82]

She went on to allege that the government clearly thought that the content of courses was less important than how they were paid for. In the past, the existence of the University Grants Commission had ensured that universities were seen as fulfilling needs. Now they no longer had an articulated function. Instead, it appeared that governments would only support universities if they were successful in obtaining funding from external sources. Such external funding would ensure that courses were relevant to the needs of society. This ignored the obvious requirement for universities to remain at the top of the academic pyramid. If, as Robert Jackson was suggesting, governments must stop being the providers of funding, and must be seen as customers, it was of relevance that it was widely accepted that customers do not always know best.[83] On another tack, Kenneth Baker, the Secretary of State for Education, was proposing a division between universities carrying out research and those dedicated to teaching. In Mary's view, research and teaching were inextricably linked. At university level, all teachers must be expected to look critically at received wisdom and are themselves best placed to do this if they are engaged in research themselves. This meant that students should realise that their teachers were as interested in research in their subjects as they were in them. 'The test is,' she wrote, 'students should be conscious, through their teachers, of standing on the edge of a changing and developing world of learning.'[84]

The 1985 Jarratt Committee on the management of universities had outlined the fundamental aims of university education:

1. instruction in skills suitable to play a part in the general division of labour

2. teaching to promote the general powers of the mind

3. the advancement of learning

4. the transmission of a common culture and common standards of citizenship.[85]

Mary broadly endorsed these aims, but also proposed an additional function which she saw as paramount. Universities must attempt, she suggested, reverting to the idea she had expressed in *Imagination*, to lift people out of the limitations, both intellectual and imaginative, in which they had hitherto been bound.[86] To do this universities themselves should place more emphasis on how knowledge is acquired rather than focusing so much on the body of existing knowledge. Information, she pointed out, can quickly go out of date, and it is the mental discipline needed to acquire it which matters. Universities should not just leave it to schools to develop curricula which might or might not be useful. She accepted that schools and universities must aim to teach useful knowledge, but, in reality, they have always done so. Latin was originally taught because it was the language of legal documents, and it continued to be taught because it was thought to hone useful transferable skills. But usefulness is, in any case, hard to define. Governments, in her view, frequently confuse the *use* of technological skills with the *theoretical understanding* of technology. Skills could not improve without theoretical advances, and industry could often not afford to fund theoretical research.[87]

However, Mary confidently asserted that all undergraduates should study the humanities as they are 'language based and offer the chance of practice in clear expression and logical analysis.'[88] Language provides the utilitarian justification for teaching the humanities as it is the basis for acquiring and communicating all knowledge. It enables students to learn that the imagination, insight and the ability to relate one subject to another are the most important attributes of a graduate.'[89] Crucially, it allows 'the possibility of envisaging a future different from either past or present that lies at the heart of the human imagination [...] It must be the expansion of imagination that is the first demand on the universities.'[90]

If, as Mary believed, this was indeed the prime function of universities, then funding could not be left to industry that has profit as its main motive. Universities are a long-term investment in the not necessarily calculable future. The introduction of student loans would be folly, forcing students into debt they might never repay. In fact, student loans were only introduced over ten years later by a Labour administration and their introduction has led to many of the problems Mary envisaged. Although, as before, Mary accepts there can be no such idea as *absolute* academic freedom for universities, they should always retain control of the content matter of what is taught and the subject matter of research and its publication. These cannot be compromised. She writes: 'A philosopher cannot be subject to the judgement of a committee, no single one of whom may have the faintest idea of what philosophy is.'[91] Further, while a national curriculum for schools may be acceptable, there can be no such curriculum for universities. Instead, universities 'must be seen as the source of new knowledge, the origin of that critical, undogmatic, imaginative examination of received wisdom without which a country cannot be expected to have its voice heard, and from which ultimately, all intellectual standards flow.'[92] It is only from universities that such learning can come. She claims that when, in the 1930s, refugee scholars, including her most admired teacher, Eduard Fraenkel, came to Britain, this was well understood. She questioned whether this was the case now.[93]

Mary continued to talk and write about higher education after these books were published. In a lecture titled 'Education with a Moral' in 1991, at a symposium on higher education, she reflected on the importance to the undergraduate of the recognition of the principle laid down by Isaiah Berlin that ultimate values sometimes conflict with one another. At higher levels of education, it becomes more important for students to embrace the 'virtue of non-dogmatism [...] with an imaginative grasp of other possibilities.' For such students, values intrinsic to education become central. By this she means 'the imperative to accuracy, the need always to produce evidence for one's statements, the need to argue, not merely assert and the readiness to listen to critical appraisal.' She sees these values as akin to moral values, or at least part of 'the culture of learning and research into which a student enters when he embarks on higher education.'[94] This view continues to resonate in our own age of fake news and social media distortions of 'truths' unsupported by evidence.

Much of the content of Mary's two books on education while she was Mistress of Girton makes admirable sense. However, her views and the views of the very large numbers of academics who agreed and continue to agree with her, have been consistently ignored over the thirty years since she wrote them. The result is that, despite the heroic efforts of the poorly paid academic staff in UK universities, many of the best academics are still tempted abroad, and students leave universities saddled with levels of debt they will struggle to repay for much of the rest of their lives. The history of British universities over the period from 1985 to at least the second decade of the twenty-first century, despite many notable achievements, has not been a happy one. Mary stood against the forces of largely mindless reform and was among the many who were defeated.

While she was at Girton, Mary also wrote the philosophical book, *Memory* (1987), from which I have quoted at the beginning of Chapter Two.[95] She saw this as a sequel to *Imagination*, discussed earlier in this chapter. *Memory* is largely a history of philosophical ideas about recollection and recall from Locke and Hume to the mid-twentieth century. More significantly, in 1992 she delivered the Gifford Lectures in Glasgow and, in the same year, the Read-Tuckwell Lectures in the University of Bristol. These lectures which were brought together and published under the title *Imagination and Time* (1994),[96] elaborated on the themes she had discussed in *Memory* and integrated them with her earlier work presented in her 1976 book *Imagination*.

Mary begins *Imagination and Time* with the proposal that the eighteenth century was a turning point in understanding the mind. The metaphor of the mind changed from it merely being regarded as a mirror reflecting the external world to that of a lamp, illuminating the world.[97] Her aim in these lectures was to bring together literature and philosophy to consider the nature of the 'I.' She begins by claiming that the paramount requirements of both memory and the imagination are fundamentally the same. They depend on what has been in the past and what might be in the future. Because they have imagination, human beings are able to dissolve the otherwise insoluble problem of the relation between the inner and the outer. This provides them with the capability of grasping and understanding the world of which they form a part.

To support her argument, she cites the writings of philosophers such as Kant who explained how contemplating the wonders of nature could affect the sense of ourselves; scientists including the chemist, Humphrey Davy, who saw the imagination as essential to the discovery of truth; and the Romantic poets, Wordsworth and Coleridge.[98] She found helpful Coleridge's proposition that because creative thoughts can be communicated to others the idea that such thoughts can discover timeless and universal truths is validated.

She then brought together the view of R. G. Collingwood, the historian of ideas, who described the function of the imagination in the understanding of art, with those of Sartre who believed that our imagination allows us to comprehend the significance or meaning of things. Our imaginations do this by acting as a bridge between what we perceive and what we understand about what we perceive. This is facilitated by symbolic thinking, with the shared meaning of symbols enabling us to communicate ideas more effectively.

This argument is followed by a discussion of values, the attributes by which we judge actions or beliefs to be good or bad, nice or nasty, pleasurable or painful, great or mean etc.[99] The central means by which we communicate such values are stories. There are many ways of approaching the truth, including deductive argument and historical narrative. Mary attacks the post-modernist notion that truth can only be relative, pointing to Anthony Quinton's refutation of the argument that truth must be relative because some ideas were once believed to be true and are now known not to be true. She quotes Sartre at length on ways we might know that a particular imaginative reconstruction of the past is 'true,' concluding that the more a historical explanation takes account of the known facts, the more likely it is to be accurate.

She then goes on to claim that it is in autobiography that the connections between our imaginations, our values and our awareness of time are most clearly seen.[100] It is in recollection that the idea of a sharp distinction between mind and body is corrected. She quotes the neuroscientist, Gerald Edelman, in support of the idea that human consciousness evolved over time to enable people to develop individual identities based on their unique experiences. Human identity encompasses both mind and body. Further, the idea of a person who has a discernible identity is social; it involves the belief that there are others in the same boat as ourselves with similar discernible identities, some of which are shared, others not. People may wish to affirm their own immortality by writing an autobiography. They achieve a sense of continuity to their lives by telling their stories. The truth-telling element derives from the fact that what they write derives from personal experience.[101]

The Romantic poets believed that truths about oneself could illuminate general truths about everyone. Similarly, Proust claimed that, through writing a work of art, he could endow with wider significance his own memories of the past, especially if he concentrated on those memories which arose spontaneously.

The only meaningful way of seeing ourselves as immortal is to think of ourselves as somehow linked to the future. We can do this by considering our obligations to people not yet born. To do this, following the philosopher Derek Parfit, she suggests we must establish both continuity with and connectedness to the future.[102] When we act, we should do so on the assumption that others will behave like us. Parfit wanted us to believe, and Mary concurs, that we are part of the future. Further, it is the imagination which 'performs the trick of connecting the momentary and ephemeral with the permanent.' Our sense of connectedness between the past and the future carries with it 'an obscure feeling of eternity.'

Mary then considers, as she often has before, the importance of the imagination in both school and higher education. She re-affirms that 'the education of the imagination is by far the most important educational goal and should be central to any curriculum decisions.'[103] It follows, she claims, that the teaching of history is the most important part of education. It should be made clear that the historical narrative is never closed. Finally, she proposes that moral ideas must be thought of as having permanence. They do not need external validation, but they need to reflect values that are beyond the merely personal. Thus, they must reflect a point of view that can be shared with others. This will result in a consensus morality which should govern our laws. She realises this position is under attack by moral relativists but defends it vigorously. Hostility to the idea of a shared morality makes the task of teachers difficult but they must, according to Mary, not be frightened to use the word 'wrong,' especially when discussing stories. Perhaps children cannot be taught what is right and wrong, but they can have their imaginations stimulated to work their values out for themselves.[104]

Memory was not widely reviewed, but Annette Bauer in *The Philosophical Review* declared that Mary was 'a very good guide on the tour of human self-exploration' drawing on a 'rich treasure-house of literature.' She was 'a less good guide to the purely philosophical debate on the nature, role and varieties of memory' for which, Bauer probably accurately suggests, she had little patience. Bauer thinks the book will be a 'fine start' however for anyone wishing to know more about the fascination that biographies and autobiographies exert on their readers.[105] Geoffrey Strickland in a long and discursive review in *The*

Cambridge Quarterly notes Mary's neglect of painful memories and her concentration on memory in its 'most reassuring forms.' He is impressed by her ability to write movingly 'of the conviction by which we lead our lives; of the inability to believe we are any other, for example, than the person we were many years ago.'[106]

Imagination and Time was reviewed very sympathetically by Anthony Storr, psychoanalyst and psychiatrist, in the *RSA Journal*. After summarising her arguments, he wrote 'Mrs. Warnock is a gifted writer as well as a fount of ideas. Her use of language is both eloquent and elegant. This book is a pleasure to read.'[107] David Jenkins, the then recently retired Bishop of Durham, writing in *Theology*, drew from Mary's book the idea that, 'although we can no longer claim "objectivity" in our thinking and the value we put on things, we are not therefore abandoned to total pluralism, relativism and "truths of many kinds".'[108]

* * *

In writing about Mary's time at Girton I have sought to balance her own account with the recollections of others. Naturally these accounts differ, not so much on the facts themselves, but certainly in their interpretation. What they have in common is their basis in memory, both fallible and personal. It is the task of the biographer to exercise their own imagination in creating a coherent account which, it may be hoped, conveys some truth and insight, based as Mary would have insisted, on evidence rather than opinion. Mary herself, in her various published and unpublished recollections, the fellows and Mary's secretary were, in telling their stories to me using their imaginations as well as their memories. For, as Mary wrote in *Memory*, 'memory and imagination [...] are not wholly to be separated [...] the creative construction of a story involves seeking out what is significant, what is to feature as part of the plot.'[109] If I have been successful in writing a coherent, truthful account, then, again in Mary's ambitious words, I may have achieved '*understanding*, a quite general insight into how things are, not only from my own standpoint, but absolutely universally.'[110]

Notes

1   Hugo Young, 1991, p. 412.

2   Ibid., p. 414.

3   Mary Warnock, 2000, p. 174.

4   Harrison, pp. 677–678.

5   Young, p. 406.

6   Gillian Beer, personal communication.

7   Warnock, 2000, p. 37.

8   Diana Barkley, 2005, pp. 17–18.

9   Sarah Kay, personal communication.

10   Warnock, 2003, p. 118.

11   Rose and Ziman, p. 136.

12   Halsey, p. 733.

13   Warnock, 1976, p. 11.

14   Ibid., p. 10.

15   Ibid.

16   Ibid., p. 9.

17   Ibid., p. 196.

18   Ibid.

19   Ibid., p. 197.

20   Ibid., p. 203.

21   Ibid.

22   Ibid., p. 206.

23   Ibid., p. 207.

24   Ibid.

25   Ibid., back cover blurb.

26   Ibid.

27   Ibid.

28   Charlton, 1977, p. 377.

29   Harrison, 1978, p. 455.

30   Carrier, 1978, p. 41.

31   Mary Warnock, 1994, p. 173.

32   Suzanne Lowry, 1984.

33   Ibid.

34   Valerie Grove, 6 July, 1991.

35   Warnock, 2000, p. 126.

36   Kitty Warnock, personal communication.

37   Jean Smith, personal communication.

38   Gillian Jondorf, personal communication.

39   Anne Fernihough, personal communication.

40   Mary Warnock, 2000, p. 126.

41   Gillian Beer, personal communication.

42   Anne Fernihough, personal communication.

43   Gillian Jondorf, personal communication.

44   Ibid.

45   Gillian Beer, personal communication.

46   Ibid.

47   Ibid.

48   Gillian Jondorf, personal communication.

49   Anne Fernihough, personal communication.

50   Juliet Dusinberre, personal communication.

51   Ibid.

52   Ibid.

53   Sarah Kay, personal communication.

54   John Marks, p. 105.

55   Edith MacRobbie, personal communication.

56   Anne Fernihough, personal communication.

57   Juliet Dusinberre, personal communication.

58   Jean Smith, personal communication.

59 Sophia Robb, personal communication.

60 Sue Palmer, p. 176.

61 Martin Ennis, personal communication.

62 Ibid.

63 Nancy Lane-Perham, pp. 99–100.

64 Juliet Campbell, personal communication.

65 Sue Palmer, p. 176.

66 Her Majesty's Stationery Office, 1985.

67 Her Majesty's Stationery Office, 1987.

68 Ibid.

69 Mary Warnock, 1989.

70 Ibid., p. 137.

71 Warnock, 1989, p. 143.

72 Ibid., pp. 143–144.

73 Ibid., p. 148.

74 Ibid., p. 151.

75 Ibid., pp. 158–159.

76 Ibid., p. 161.

77 Ibid., p. 163.

78 Ibid., p. 170.

79 Warnock, 1989.

80 Ibid., pp. 5–8.

81 Ibid., p. 10.

82 Ibid., p. 11.

83 Ibid., p. 18.

84 Ibid., p. 22.

85 Jarratt Report, 1985, para 2.6.

86 Warnock, 1989, p. 25.

87 Ibid., p. 33.

88 Ibid.

89   Ibid., p. 35.

90   Ibid., p. 37.

91   Ibid., p. 41.

92   Ibid., p. 42.

93   Ibid.

94   Warnock, 1991.

95   Warnock, 1987.

96   Warnock, 1994.

97   Ibid., p. 1.

98   Ibid., pp. 31–34.

99   Ibid., p. 87.

100   Ibid., p. 109.

101   Ibid., p. 129.

102   Ibid., p. 152.

103   Ibid., p. 173.

104   Ibid., pp. 182–186.

105   Bauer, 1990, p. 439.

106   Strickland, 1988, p. 392.

107   Storr, p. 83.

108   Jenkins, p. 140.

109   Warnock, 1987, p. 132.

110   Ibid., p. 133.

10. Art and Nature

In the Introduction to her recollections of her public life, Mary listed the issues that had been particularly important to her: education, art and nature.[1] Her contribution to thinking about education has been discussed in previous chapters. Her involvement in the other two stemmed from intense childhood experiences, which shaped her later thinking and many of her contributions to the making of public policy. She believed that such experiences, and the almost equally intense recollections of them later, were fundamental not only to an individual's sense of identity but also to the capacity to imagine and hence to create, understand and empathise. She often cited Wordsworth, in whose poetry this is one of the central ideas—for example, in his 1798 poem, 'The Pedlar,' later published in Book 1 of *The Excursion* (1814).

> While yet a child, and long before his time
> Had he perceived the presence and the power
> Of greatness; and deep feelings had impressed
> So vividly great objects they lay
> Upon his mind like substances, whose presence
> Perplexed the bodily sense. He had received
> A precious gift, for as he grew in years
> With these impressions would he still compare
> All his remembrances, thoughts, shapes and forms;
> And, being still unsatisfied with aught
> Of dimmer character, he thence attained
> An active power to fasten images
> Upon his brain....'[2]

For Mary, a child's exposure to and participation in art (in her own case, mostly music and poetry) and opportunity to enjoy nature were key elements of a rounded education. This idea underlay much of her thinking and writing about education as well as being expounded

    https://doi.org/10.11647/OBP.0278.10

in philosophical writings, particularly *Imagination*,[3] *Memory*,[4]and *Imagination and Time*.[5]

Mary was surrounded by music at home as a child and responded to it intensely—as she did throughout her life. Her nanny was 'always singing; she had an instant and encyclopaedic memory for music, having to hear a song only once to remember it. Her conversation was constantly interspersed with snatches of song, hymns, music hall hits, Gilbert and Sullivan and sad, mysterious songs like 'All the darkies are a-weeping...'[6] In the holidays when Stephana was home from boarding school, she and Mary used to climb onto the bicycle shed roof to sing through the songs, especially hymns, that Stephana had learned at school. They had a nursery collection of records, and cast-offs from their older brother, Duncan.[7] When he was at home, he used to play the piano for hours on end. Mary remembered she enjoyed most a piano version of *Jesu, Joy of Man's Desiring* and Mozart's Piano Concerto in F Major K132. In her mid-seventies she wrote that 'even writing the names of these pieces of music sends shivers down my spine.'[8]

Her grandfather, as we saw in Chapter Two, was also a very good pianist. Mary describes how, on holidays at his house in Sussex, in the mornings, she and Stephana

> sometimes had to go down to the library where two grand pianos were housed. Poor Stephana had to play her pieces to Grandpapa. I was mercifully thought too young and incompetent to face such an ordeal. I remember one time when she played a hornpipe by Purcell (very well, as I thought) and his response was 'there are only three composers to play: Bach, Beethoven and Brahms. He then played us a Beethoven sonata (opus 31, no. 2) which I still hear him playing every time I hear it, and I was overcome with emotion when, years later, my son Felix was given it to learn when he was at school.[9]

She describes her grandfather as 'a powerful and extremely expressive, melancholy pianist, tragedy in every line of his face, every gesture of his shoulders.'[10]

While she was at St. Swithun's School, the opportunities for playing music were very limited and, in Mary's view, the teaching of music was poor. She started to learn piano and flute at home, and played with Stephana, but didn't experience playing with other people until she was fifteen. Then, on holiday in Lymington in the New Forest, she and

Stephana signed up to an orchestral course which they discovered at a nearby school. It was the first time Mary had played in an orchestra and she found 'the pleasure of playing proper symphonies with a proper conductor was extreme.'[11] At Prior's Field the following year, she joined the school choir and had a wonderful piano teacher she remembered all her life. Occasionally, there were opportunities to hear top-class pianists play in nearby Guildford. She heard Myra Hess playing César Franck's *Symphonic Variations*, which were 'heavenly and stirring,' as well as 'the peculiar, not very good orchestra playing the Vaughan Williams *Pastoral Symphony*, FOUR slow movements, deadly' (26 June 1941). On another occasion (18 October 1941), she heard the Russian-born British pianist, Moiseiwitsch there: 'marvellous. By far the best pianist I've ever heard. Tremendous energy and passion. Too much Chopin for my taste, some making one nostalgic for the ballet. But the Brahms *Paganini Variations* utterly superb.' Later that year (22 November 1941) she went with a friend to the Albert Hall, where she once again heard Moiseiwitsch this time play Rachmaninov 'simply heavenly (except for the acoustics).'

It was also at the Albert Hall that she first heard Bach's *St. Matthew Passion*, a work that inspired her throughout her life. On hearing it again two years later, she wrote in her diary:

> I wonder if I shall dare to (listen) to the *St. Matthew Passion* again after today. There were moments in it no words could reach. I suppose the sublime melting, for instance, into a chorale, the different harmonies in the chorales, the tenor and soprano, solos, Leon Goossens, the last chorus. It was I who should have born (sic) the burden, it was I who crucified Christ, I never realised how urgently that was said in this particular work before.

Nearly seventy years later, in her book *Dishonest to God* (2010), in which she castigated church leaders for interfering in politics, she discussed the meaning of the *St. Matthew Passion* in terms not just of the betrayal of a friend, but the betrayal of the son of God and claims that 'however sceptical or atheistical one may be,' (and by this time Mary herself had become an atheist) 'one cannot understand the story or the music without understanding that this conviction was what the Gospel writer, looking back, was striving to convey.'[12]

During her first two years at Oxford, as we have seen, she joined the Bach Choir,[13] and while she was teaching at Sherborne between her two spells as an undergraduate (see Chapter Three), she met Rachel Drever Smith, the witty Scot who became a lifelong friend and they played flute and piano sonatas together, 'practising with great conscientiousness.'[14]

Once professional and married life began, Mary's own performance of music was limited to nursery rhymes for the children and other family musical activities such as singing rounds during long car journeys, and mini-orchestras, usually organised by Stephana, when the two families met. Later, following her appointment as a life peer, she took great pleasure in active membership of the Parliament Choir. But she was always a keen listener, sharing Geoffrey's love of opera, and very actively fostered her children's musical education and experiences. Two of her children, Felix and Fanny, went on to train as professional musicians. Throughout her life she found opportunities to encourage other people's music making. Her first public policy role in the early 1960s was as Chair of the Music Sub-Committee of the Oxfordshire Education Authority and at the Oxford High School the integration of music into the curriculum was a priority.

Mary's introduction to the natural world came, as did many of the good things in her early life, from her nanny. The family home, Kelso House, was in the outskirts of Winchester. It was close to Weeke Down, part of the South Downs, beautiful hilly country with many paths and bridleways. Nearly every day, Mary and Stephana would go for a walk with Nan, who talked all the time and 'pointed out all kinds of objects for us to look at or exclaim about.'[15] They learned about flowers, birds and bird song. Mary had nightmares about Nan falling over a cliff along a path that was on one of their walks. She became so terrified of this path that she refused to go on it but there were plenty of others. From the age of seven or eight, she and Stephana were given a great deal of freedom to explore by themselves for hours at a time. They used to enjoy themselves climbing trees and bird nesting for eggs, forbidden now, but acceptable then.[16]

For the Easter holidays, their mother used to rent a house in Woolacombe on the North Devon coast. Years later, Mary remembered 'rock-climbing, the sea, food, the smell of gorse and primroses' but best of all was horse riding with Stephana at a local riding school.[17] An hour's ride took them along the Marine Drive, between banks of gorse and back along the sands. A two-hour ride took them further into the country. Later they went, 'terrifyingly,' drag-hunting, (hunting the trail of an artificially laid scent), along precipitous North Devon valleys, with banks to jump and trees that 'threatened to knock one out of the saddle.'[18] They spent hours at the stables, grooming, mucking out, helping to get the ponies ready for the next ride or bringing them in, giving them water, cleaning the tack. It was at Woolacombe that Mary first became aware of what she later called a Wordsworthian passion for certain aspects of the countryside. She asked herself: 'why did I feel such a desperate, frightening longing, a kind of thirst, looking at the sea from Baggy Point? Why did I so much adore the tactile properties of the smooth, slate rock, interspersed among the shell-encrusted rocks that were so hard on one's hands and knees?'[19] She describes how she began dimly to get a sense of what she later thought of as 'natural symbols, aspects of the world with a meaning beyond themselves.'[20]

A fortnight of the summer holidays was spent at Verdley, her grandfather's estate in West Sussex. The tone was set by the style of their journey to Verdley from Winchester. Newman, the Schusters' chauffeur, would arrive at Kelso House in the 'new Rolls' to drive Mary, Stephana and their Nan to their destination. Mary hated the rough covering of the seats and the smell of stale cigars and was regularly sick shortly before they arrived.[21] She described the house itself as 'an extraordinary architectural monstrosity of Victorian origin, with turrets and castellations and mock-Gothic windows....'[22] The two sisters lived with Nan in the nursery suite, their meals being brought up by a maid. The food was delicious. Mary describes 'age-old crab-apple jelly, yellow cream in brown jugs from the farm, and a marvellous pudding called mushroom meringues, small meringues with a pinkish filling and marzipan stalks growing out of an earth-bed of chocolate cream.'[23] The sisters' walks often took them to the farms on the estate,[24] possibly giving them a rare insight into the living conditions of children less fortunate than themselves.

It was at Verdley that Mary and Stephana began to invent together a game called Talk-talking—a long-continuing serial of stories about a school that had as pupils and staff all the ponies and horses they had ever ridden. The headmistress was a mare. According to Mary, 'many terrible dramas took place in this school: fires, floods, burglaries, epidemics, ponies running away, police searches for escaped prisoners, the poisoning of the water supply and there were, of course, never any holidays.'[25] Gradually it became less important to the sisters that the characters were horses—they were humans who just bore the names and had the characters of the horses they knew. Talk-talking continued until well into their teens when it became transformed into new productions of operas, with important decisions to be made about casting and plot. Years later, when Mary was headmistress of the Oxford High School and Stephana was Director of Music at the Ripon Cathedral Choir School, they realised that what for years they had been doing in fantasy, they were now acting out in real life.[26]

From 1934, Mary, Stephana, their mother and Nan would often travel to Elie, in Fife, for part of the summer holidays, when they rented a cottage near the harbour. The countryside around Elie is featureless and somewhat dull, but Mary and Stephana found plenty to do, sometimes taking a rowing boat into the harbour or going with their mother on longer fishing expeditions. The two elderly women who kept house for them taught Mary how to cook. She acquired a cookery book full of recipes from the Scottish Women's Institute, full of wonderful cakes and gingerbreads which she used for many years afterwards. Much of the time, however, they played golf, having their first golfing lessons. Mary became a competent golfer, leaving Elie in triumph on the last occasion, having come second in the under-fourteens competition.[27]

Stephana was given a pony when she was fifteen and a year later, Mary also acquired one. Stephana's was a 'beautiful grey called Charles Aloysius Gull or Charlie Gull for short.' Mary's was called Daniel.[28] The ponies were stabled at Headbourne Worthy, on the outskirts of Winchester and Mary continued to ride in the country with Dan until well into her Oxford undergraduate days. Just before she went up to Oxford for the first time, she records in her diary entry for 14 August 1942 having ridden Stephana's horse, Gull, while she was away. Then, on 17 August, she describes a 'very hot and lovely ride. Went a short way only. Dan superb.' Nearly a year later she records on 20 July 1943 chasing Dan who had got out through a gate with another horse, eventually catching them both and having a 'lovely ride' on Charlie until his feet got too sore. Regular riding was an interest that did not survive graduation, academic responsibilities, marriage and bringing up a family, but her feeling for and knowledge of horses, particularly the importance she attached to their intelligence and character, strongly resonated in some of her later public policy work.

Fig. 9 Stephana (left) and Mary (right) in Achiltibuie, unknown photographer (2002), provided by the Warnock family, CC BY-NC.

Mary continued to draw sustenance from nature all her life, on holidays and from the Wiltshire downland country where she lived for over twenty years. She took her young children for holidays in Woolacombe, the scene of her earliest experiences of the power of nature, and then for years to the coast of Yorkshire, which was in many ways similar. After Geoffrey died, she made frequent visits to Scotland to stay with Stephana in her house on the island of Mull or to revisit places she had loved in her teenage years. With Stephana or with her life-long friend, Imogen, she continued to take quite challenging walks: to celebrate Stephana's eightieth birthday, they walked up Stac Pollaidh near Achiltibuie, in north-west Scotland. Stiffness and failing eyesight eventually made such walks impossible and in 2010 she moved to live in London near her daughters and began to get her nature 'fix' from gardens. She enjoyed gardening and was knowledgeable about garden plants. Now she made visits to large gardens open to the public, accompanied by her daughter, Kitty, and sometimes by a friend of Kitty's, Hilary Maxwell-Hyslop, who had known Mary since she was a pupil at the Oxford High School.

According to Hilary, Mary

brought an extraordinary energy to her passion for garden visiting. She
appreciated all aspects of gardens: the planting, the scents, the varieties
of shrubs, the design of a bed, the direction of a path. Her enthusiasm
was infectious, and we would often return home with plants that we
could not wait to install in our respective gardens crammed into the car
alongside us. I remember walking for most of a day around Petersham
in south-west London, visiting a number of private gardens open to the
public. It was hot and crowded but, as always, she was determined to see
as much as possible. We went to Wisley (a Royal Horticultural Society
garden) only a few weeks before she died. It was a cold day in February,
but she seemed impervious to the weather. She had done her research
and wanted to visit parts of the garden that happened to be furthest from
the car park so off we went in the chill spring wind—slowing only so that
she could stop and examine a particular snowdrop variety, or marvel at
the myriad crocus colours. Looking back what I remember was the fun
we had. I loved our excursions and learned a great deal about gardening
from her.[29]

***

Mary's experiences and responses to music and to nature were
unusually intense, and, particularly in the case of music, well-informed,
but of course it was not as an expert or practitioner in these fields that
she was asked to contribute to and often to chair public committees
and commissions of enquiry. It was as a philosopher, able to bring an
analytical mind and powers of clear explanation to ethical questions in
public policy. Her common-sense approach and her skill in bringing
resolution to often difficult and emotive debates meant she was often
in demand.

In 1973, after resigning from the Oxford High School, she was
invited by Brian Young, the Director-General, to become a member
of the Independent Broadcasting Authority (IBA).[30] She knew Young
through his connection with her old school, Prior's Field, of which she
was a governor. She joined the IBA in December 1973 and remained a
member until December 1981.[31] The IBA had been formed in 1972 when
the existing Independent Television Authority took over responsibility
for independent radio, becoming the regulatory body for all commercial
television and radio in the UK. Its powers included awarding licences to
television and radio companies and directing programme contractors

over schedules. Brian Young, a former headmaster of Charterhouse School, was trying to move independent broadcasting away from what he saw as its predominantly entertainment function towards a more educational role. Mary joined a group of forceful members, chaired by Lady Plowden, who had previously chaired an influential government committee on primary education.

Mary described her appointment as 'absurd' as 'I hardly ever watched television and had not listened to commercial radio since the days of Radio Luxembourg in the nursery.'[32] But, she continued, it was 'by far the most enjoyable job I ever did on the side, and I found for the first time what fun it is to learn new things in an environment of work, with knowledgeable people to teach one.'[33] Mary recalled with great pleasure lunches that were held every other Thursday to which distinguished guests were invited. Halfway through the meal the Director-General would introduce a topic and the lunch turned into an informative seminar.[34] The only occasion when this event was singularly unpleasant, described in Chapter One, was when Margaret Thatcher, then Prime Minister, was a guest at the lunch.

Later, Mary took the view that she had made virtually no impact on the IBA. This is not the view of Kenneth Blyth, the Secretary to the IBA and the Director-General's chief assistant.[35] When Mary was appointed, Brian Young described her to Blyth as 'extremely intelligent, highly academic and surprisingly emotional.'[36] Blyth recalled her as having talked a lot, and 'when she talked, people listened.'[37] She was prepared to enter into discussion on any topic regardless of her level of knowledge in it. The staff of the IBA regarded her as a definite asset because of her willingness to speak her mind.[38] Kenneth Blyth acknowledged her clear, philosophical approach by asking her to write a paper drawing a distinction between the IBA's accountability and its responsibility. This paper was soon found valuable by the Annan Committee on The Future of Broadcasting, which quoted it at some length in its report.[39]

Towards the end of her tenure as a member of the IBA, Mary was involved in the establishment of two new channels. One was Channel Four: the IBA set up a board that chose Jeremy Isaacs to be the channel's Chief Executive. The other was to be a breakfast-time television channel and for this the IBA needed to select a company to run it. Applications were received from eight consortia.[40] One was TV-AM, headed by Peter

Jay, an economics journalist and former British Ambassador to the United States, who, according to Mary, had been her brightest pupil when he was an undergraduate at Oxford.[41] Mary supported another consortium, but was happy to go along with the majority view that the contract should go to TV-AM. This turned out to be a bad decision because the organisational structure of the company was inadequate—as the IBA staff had warned IBA members to expect. Eventually TV-AM had to be rescued by an Australian, Kerry Packer, to whom the IBA would never have awarded the contract if he had been an initial bidder.[42]

After Mary left, having served three terms as a member of the IBA, she wrote little about the media, but in 1985, she gave the Eleanor Rathbone Memorial Lecture (a lecture given annually since 1949 in memory of Eleanor Rathbone, an early twentieth-century MP and campaigner for women's equality) with the title 'Social Responsibility of the Broadcasting Media.'[43] She begins by considering the educational function of the media, noting that both the BBC and the IBA are charged with ensuring that broadcast programmes inform, entertain and educate. She suggests that it is widely assumed that programmes fail in their duty to enhance public morality and are often positively harmful in their effects, a concern that persists to this day. The most pressing question was whether screen violence facilitated violence in real life. With so many variables to take into account, Mary claims, it would never be possible to use the methods of social science to answer this question.[44]

More generally, Mary writes, children learn by seeing and hearing stories, affirming the importance of story-telling in the encouragement of moral behaviour. She suggests that teachers could increase awareness of moral issues by showing footage from contemporary television dramas and then initiating discussions about the moral issues they raised.[45] She can think of no better form of moral education than 'to analyse and discuss the motives of those who watch and take part in the competition programmes, those who hope to flog their old aunt's teapot, and indeed those who would sell gossip or secrets to the media, newspapers or TV. I do not think that teachers should regard such material as beneath them.'[46]

Though she dismisses concerns that some television programmes encourage greed for material possessions, (pointing out that greed has always been part of human nature), she has serious worries about the way television influences attitudes towards women. 'Many television programmes,' she writes, 'to say nothing of most advertisements, still convey a view of women that is stereotyped, derogatory and conservative.'[47] Her response is to encourage the idea that we should all, but particularly teachers, 'be our own radio and television critics, alert to presuppositions and unexamined assumptions in the programmes of which we are the audience, ready to complain and argue if need be.'[48]

In 1987, while she was at Girton, the trustees or 'syndics' of the Fitzwilliam Museum in Cambridge were unhappy with the way the director, Michael Jaffé, was running the museum and Mary was asked to chair an internal enquiry.[49] According to Mary, Jaffé's exasperating and domineering manner made it virtually impossible for the committee to carry out its work efficiently. A report was written, but, as it happened, Michael Jaffé became ill and resigned so that its recommendations were never properly examined. Besides, wider considerations, especially cuts to university finance, came into play, which led to other reforms being instituted.[50] In the event, since then, the Fitzwilliam has thrived.

In December 1988, when she was sixty-four, Mary was featured in *Desert Island Discs* on Radio 4. This programme, broadcast continuously since 1942, was rated 'the greatest radio programme of all time' in 2019 by a panel of broadcasting experts. At the time Mary took part it had around two million listeners, surely the largest audience she ever had. In *Desert Island Discs* well-known public figures are interviewed. Each week's guest is led through a review of her life and achievements, interspersed with short excerpts from the eight recordings which she would like to have with her in the highly improbable event that she was 'cast away' on a desert island with the means to play CDs.[51]

The interviewer, Sue Lawley, began by summarising Mary's career and then asked her if she could be described when she was a teenager and young woman as a bluestocking. 'Not entirely,' replied Mary, citing listening to Radio Luxembourg and her love of riding horses as non-academic pursuits. Radio Luxembourg was a commercial channel beaming popular music to Britain from the mid-1930s onwards and she probably only listened to it with her children in the late 1950s and early 1960s though certainly she adored horses during her adolescence and early adult life. Mary was then asked about her reputation for being a smart dresser and happily acquiesced though she claimed she was now too old to wear floppy hats. Having established that she had a 'normal' adolescence, which, of course, in most respects, she certainly had not, Mary's first choice of music is the Albion Ensemble playing a Mozart serenade.[52] She gives her reason for this piece of music as the fact that her son, Felix, is one of the players. It was altogether appropriate that her first choice should relate to her family, so central to the whole of her life.

Mary goes on to describe to Sue Lawley her pleasure in being a philosopher as it involves finding out about other people's fields, something she finds immensely rewarding. Her second piece of music is from Brahm's Requiem, *Alles fleisch*, which she says she has chosen because she constantly needs to be reminded of her own mortality. Certainly, the words of this part of the Requiem are chilling—'alles fleisch es ist wie gras' or 'all flesh is as grass' and goes on 'and all the glory of man as the flower of grass.' The choice confirms Mary's view of music as a source of transcendental reflection.

Most of the interviewees on *Desert Island Discs*, however solidly classical their musical taste, manage to insert one example of popular music and Mary was no exception. She chose *Bye Bye Love*, sung by the Everly Brothers, the country-influenced rock and roll duo. Mary claims she listened to a lot of pop music and bought a lot of singles earlier in her life. Now the Everly Brothers had their first hit single in 1957, when she was thirty-three years old. This selection probably reflects both her own children's choice of music as well as the fact that she and Geoffrey were part of a social group which found relaxation from intensely serious academic work in cinema and dancing in each other's homes (see Chapter Five). It was at this point too, or only a little later, that Mary's children started to experience the sort of adolescence Mary had missed and popular culture pervaded the Warnock home. Before their adolescence, Mary had bought pop records for their nursery collection and some of these songs became great favourites of hers.

The record that Mary said she would choose above all the others she had selected to take with her to a desert island was Henry Purcell's *My Beloved Spake*,[53] the words of which are drawn from the *Song of Solomon*. Her other choices were all solidly classical, works by Schubert, Handel and other baroque composers and, of course, Bach, though surprisingly she chose a Bach cantata rather than a section of the *St. Matthew Passion*.

Her capacity for combining the secular with the sacred was well reflected throughout and this was also the case when she came to choose the book she would take with her. *The Chronicles of Barset* by Anthony Trollope is a series of six novels permeated with the politics of the Anglican Church. Mary's choice of luxury was 'a lot of biros and a lot of paper'[54] reflecting just how central to her life her writing was to her.

Her next task was presented to her in October 1990, a few months before she left Girton. She was asked to chair an Arts Council working party to enquire into the management and financing of the Royal Opera House (ROH).[55] The Arts Council is the main conduit for government funding of the arts. Mary was not a member of the council but was brought in as an independent voice to deal with the difficult situation that had arisen over its grant to the ROH. Under its General Director, Jeremy Isaacs, who had then been in post for two years, it had become increasingly demanding of financial support. Jeremy put in a wider repertoire of opera and ballet with more experimental productions than had his predecessor, Sir John Tooley. This was expensive. Annual losses were mounting, and the Arts Council and its staff were unhappy at the new direction the ROH was taking. Hence the invitation to Mary to sort things out.[56]

By any standards, the financial situation of the ROH was dire. It had four sources of income: ticket sales, donations from wealthy opera-lovers, corporate sponsorship and government funding. Ticket sales were substantial and remained reasonably secure providing the repertoire was confined to popular operas and ballets, but Isaacs's policy was to venture beyond the familiar and audiences did not always follow him. Income from donations and sponsorship was also at risk from over-ambitious programming. As for the Arts Council, its grant to the ROH was already much larger than to any other national company and it could not meet ever-growing annual shortfalls; indeed, there was already criticism that the council's funding was excessively focussed on London and growing political pressure to re-balance its support in favour of the regions.

Another looming crisis was the dilapidated state of the ROH building. The plan was to close it in 1993 for rebuilding, but it was unclear how the money would be found for the construction, an issue made more difficult by the need to make up for the lack of ticket sales during the two-year closure. One idea was that the necessary income would come from the commercial development of a neighbouring site belonging to the ROH. However, the local authority and various community groups were opposed to this scheme and it was far from certain to materialise.[57]

Mary liked and admired Jeremy Isaacs. He had a brilliant track record, first as the producer of inquisitorial television documentaries for the BBC's *Panorama* programme and then as the founding director of Channel Four which had been an outstanding success. But he had an uncompromising style of leadership and left-wing views, which meant that, after twelve years of a Conservative administration, he had few friends in high places.[58] In particular, David Mellor, the Secretary of State for the National Heritage and hence the Arts Minister, made it clear to the Chairman of the Board of the ROH that there would be no additional government money while Isaacs was General Director.[59]

Mary's admiration for Jeremy was only partly reciprocated. He described her as having a 'keen mind and a spry, tough persona.'[60] But, he added, 'she knew nothing of opera or ballet.' This was irrelevant and, in any case, he under-estimated her on three counts. First, though she was not a great opera-goer, she was, as we have seen, intensely musical and capable of an informed view of musical performance of any type, though generally she abhorred modern-dress productions. Indeed, in July 1991, she attended an ROH performance of *Orfeo ed Eurydice* which she described as 'pretty dire, with the chorus on their last legs.'[61] Though she did not record this, it is likely that she was unsympathetic to the production of this eighteenth-century work with the countertenor playing the title role dressed in leather jacket and jeans and carrying around an electric guitar. Second, she was a rapid learner. Finally, as Mistress of Girton, she had been responsible for running a large organisation within a budget and was fully aware of the vagaries of reliance on rich donors. Mary was well-supported by other members of her working party. Among them were Dennis Stevenson, a businessman with arts management expertise, and Hans Landesmann, Commercial and Arts Director of the Salzburg Festival.[62]

She and the other members of the working party spent June and July 1991 interviewing members of the ROH staff, ballet as well as opera, meeting nearly every day, writing their report in August, and presenting it in September. According to Mary, they interviewed people from all sides of the business and all the senior staff more than once. They were seriously unimpressed. Mary later wrote: 'Nobody we spoke to seemed to know how many people were employed on the premises, or how long they had been there or what was in their contracts—if they had contracts.'[63] Members of the orchestra, which had recently been on strike, were the most discontented. They complained they were paid less than other orchestral players and could not earn extra money on the side. Members of the chorus complained they had the worst time and hated many aspects of their work. There seemed to be no retiring age and the working party members met people painting scenery apparently well into their eighties. They were disappointed with the Director of Opera, who 'seemed to have limitless powers' to commission new productions without thought for their cost.[64] According to Mary, Isaacs seemed to have nothing to express other than an uncompromising demand for more government money. She wrote 'There was one day, in July, when we saw Jeremy Isaacs for three hours. We could not stop him; he simply ranted on about how government must produce more money.'[65]

The report recommended that fewer new productions should be commissioned. The building should be closed sooner rather than later as it was manifestly unsafe, but the idea of a complete rebuild should be dropped as there was no way it could be financed. A comprehensive refurbishment would have to suffice. There was criticism of the personnel management such as the absence of job descriptions and performance reviews, and union agreements needed to be renegotiated. The report was critical of the ROH management, but it was more critical of the board members who had not exercised financial scrutiny as they should, nor taken their other oversight responsibilities seriously enough.[66]

The report, which was unanimous, was presented to the members of the Arts Council one morning in late September. The meeting went off reasonably well, with no serious objections raised to the recommendations. Unexpectedly, however, Mary was asked to stay for the afternoon to present the report to the ROH Board. She was told this would take about fifteen minutes. This turned out to be an extremely unpleasant occasion.

After Mary had briefly presented her report, the Chairman asked each of the directors in turn to ask questions. These fell into two categories and were uniformly hostile. Why had the report failed to acknowledge the quality of the productions over the previous years? And what was the evidence for the damning comments made? To the first, Mary had to reply that the working party had been set up to appraise the management and finances, not to make aesthetic judgements. To the second, she merely referred to the pages of the report which provided ample backup for the statements made. It was not surprising that the members of the board were angry. They had indeed failed in their responsibilities as trustees. Further, many of them had been appointed to the board because of the generosity of their donations and it must have been unpleasant to be told that their money had been inefficiently spent. After two and a half hours' grilling, Mary was allowed to leave. She wrote afterwards that she was left 'feeling a complete idiot and [...] should not have been subjected to such bullying without warning.'[67]

The outcome of the financial mess in which the ROH found itself was a great deal better than might have been predicted. The ROH Board had commissioned its own report from the accountants, Price Waterhouse, concurrently with the Warnock working party. Much preferred by Jeremy Isaacs, this came up with very similar conclusions, although couched in more palatable terms and with one or two more constructive suggestions such as the abolition of overtime. In fact, over the next two years, most of the recommendations of both committees were implemented. The Director of Opera and the Director of Administration responsible for personnel left and were replaced. Employment contracts were introduced, and some redundancies were made. Rehearsals were reduced to save money. Despite these cuts, quality was maintained. Indeed in 1993, the ROH won all eight Lawrence Olivier Opera Awards, four for outstanding achievement in opera and four for best new opera productions.[68]

In his recollections, Jeremy Isaacs claimed that the Warnock Report was 'a dead letter' because it had preferred refurbishment of the opera house to a complete rebuild.[69] Hindsight is a wonderful thing. In 1991, there was no realistic plan as to how rebuilding could be financed. Fortunately for the ROH, the Major Government instituted the National Lottery in 1993 and two years later, £78.5 million was awarded for the rebuilding from Lottery funds.[70] *Deus ex machina* indeed. The ROH closed for rebuilding from July 1997 to December 1999. Isaacs had left in January 1997 with thoroughly deserved plaudits for the quality of the productions he oversaw, but some questions over his management. More than twenty years later, he admitted, 'Of course, Mary was absolutely right. We didn't have the right structures in place to make sure the place was run efficiently.'[71]

In many fields of social and cultural activity, there was a feeling in 1999 that the arrival of the new millennium required an appraisal of past achievements and failures and a need for new directions. PEER, a voluntary organisation dedicated to embedding visual arts into everyday life, decided this was the time for a new look at the relationship between artists and public policy-making and funding for the arts. It made a nationwide call for submissions from both artists and people involved in the arts in other ways, such as curators, critics, politicians and art teachers, to contribute to a debate on the subject. They invited Mary, as a philosopher, and the sculptor and conceptual artist Mark Wallinger to edit a book bringing together the most interesting submissions. The result was *Art for All? Their Policies and Our Culture* (2000).[72]

Mary invited Mark Wallinger, PEER trustee Andrew Brighton and its Director, Ingrid Swenson, to a preliminary meeting in the House of Lords, after which she and Mark met frequently to select from the hundreds of submissions.[73] Mark found the experience enormously enjoyable. He was reassured to be working with a co-editor who spoke with such ethical authority.[74] When the book was finished, Mary invited Wallinger and three members of PEER to her house in Wiltshire. Greatly impressed by her array of 'quart' bottles of gin, he went for a walk with her and found her wonderful company. They shared an enthusiasm for horses, Mark having on one occasion submitted a horse as an exhibit.[75] Twenty years later, Mark talked of Mary with great fondness—'it just makes me happy thinking of her,' he said.[76]

The book that emerged, as well as being of considerable historical and political interest, is also informative, occasionally sad and extremely funny. The editors wrote thoughtful introductions. Mary wrote about the impossibility of combining so-called accessibility with high quality. Wallinger derided the recent appearance of 'a new apolitical orthodoxy [which] gave the opportunity of power and influence to a swill of artists/curators who might previously have found employment in PR.'[77]

Mary had insisted on the inclusion of historically important statements such as that by Maynard Keynes, the founder of the Arts Council, at the time of its inception in 1945. Artists Bob and Roberta Smith submitted a postcard which concluded 'What on Earth does Baroness Warnock know?' Janette Parris sent in a rejection letter from the Arts Council with photocopies of unpaid bills from British Telecom, London Electricity and British Gas. A lecture given to the Royal Society of Arts by Chris Smith, the Secretary of State for Culture, Media and Sport, described the first challenge for policy-makers as 'to demonstrate very clearly how art and artistic activity can transform the lives and hopes of those who are socially excluded or marginalised.' This lecture concluded with a poem written by James Oppenheimer who had been moved by seeing banners carried by striking American women millworkers:

> Smart art and love and beauty their drudging spirits knew
> Yes, it is bread we fight for, but we fight for roses too![78]

Art for All? retains considerable contemporary significance. A number of contributors had raised the dangers of what they called 'elitism.' Mary elaborated on her views on the word 'elitism' which she called 'the most noxious' in the political vocabulary. She wrote 'The aim of 'accessibility' ought to come second, subordinate to the aim of high standards, whether in the academic or artistic worlds.'[79] She responded to the question 'Who are you to set up a standard of taste?' by claiming that education can teach you to hear or see excellence. There is a second, more primitive way, she asserts, 'it is the shiver that goes down your spine (or in my case, my legs) when I read something that is really poetry.'[80] Other than education, she does not explain how to arrive at a judgement of quality in the absence of such shivers but nor, arguably, has any other philosopher, and many might agree that, given the intractability of the concept of taste, Mary's thoughts were refreshing and insightful.

The year 2000 saw Mary become a member of the Spoliation Advisory Panel, a body set up to consider claims to ownership of cultural objects during the Nazi regime and now held in a UK institution, and to advise the claimant and the institution on the appropriate action to take in response to such claims.[81] The panel was chaired by David Hirst, a former Lord Justice of Appeal, and included Richard Evans, a historian, Terry Heiser, a retired Permanent Secretary, Martin Levy, a specialist in antique furniture and works of art, and Peter Oppenheimer, an economist. All the members of the panel were highly distinguished in their own fields. While the panel had no power to order restitution of a work of art to its original owner, its recommendations in this respect carried great moral authority. According to Martin Levy, Mary was sparing in her contributions to the discussions, but when she spoke, her views were always crystal clear and commanded the room.[82] She was also, he says, very good company when, periodically, the panel lunched together to discuss matters of mutual interest.[83]

Its reports reflect the care the panel took in considering each claimant's case as well as the complexity of the issues. It was often difficult to know what had happened to the object in question after it had ceased to be the property of the original owner. In addition, and it is here that Mary's clarity of thought and philosophical training were relevant, there were moral questions to be considered. For example, to what extent was a claim enhanced if the original owner had sold the object under duress at below the market price? Or, where the original owner had died, was the moral strength of the descendants' claim weakened by their delay in making it? What was the moral obligation of the institution that now owned the object? Had it taken sufficient care to investigate its provenance? The panel considered such questions before making recommendations about whether there needed to be restitution or compensation and, if so, what form this should take. Mary found this panel very interesting and only resigned from it in 2014 when she was ninety years old and her hearing loss made participation difficult.[84] It was to be the last public position she held.

Before this point there had been many other smaller-scale public activities—judging essay competitions, for instance, or speaking at school prize-giving ceremonies. In 2005, she chaired a panel of judges set up to make the Sandford St. Martin Trust Award for the best religious programme of the year. The awards organiser, Michael Barton, formerly Controller of BBC Local Radio, recalls that the first meeting was held in Lambeth Palace, the official home and workplace of the Archbishop of Canterbury.

[Mary] had driven up from Oxford in an elderly car—every seat covered in loose papers, carrier bags, reference books and a scattering of DVDs which were the entries. A brilliant Chair, she never led the conversation and always got full value out of her panel of judges. Few could match the clarity of her summing up—leading to a decision.[85]

The main award was given to a documentary on the bombing of the World Trade Centre made by a small production company, the Centre for Television Communication (CTVC). She presented the awards at a ceremony in Bristol 'with shrewd observations about each entry, laced with good humour.' At the end of it all, Michael Barton concluded, 'Mary had to dash away for another engagement in Oxford, thanked me profusely, grabbed me in both arms and gave me a long "full on" embrace. Why wouldn't I remember that for the rest of my life?'[86]

* * *

Throughout her life, Mary derived as much pleasure and interest from nature as she did from music and other arts. Her enjoyment of nature, and her belief that enjoyment of nature was a fundamental part of a full human life, informed her various roles in public policy-making. In 1978, she joined a Home Office committee to consider a test, LD50, that was used on animals to ascertain if a particular substance, perhaps a drug or a new cosmetic, was safe for human use.[87] The purpose of this test was to determine what dose of the substance was required to kill 50% of the animals, usually mice or rats, on which it was tested. The test usually required sixty to eighty animals and there was no upper limit on the dose to be used. Many of the animals suffered a painful death and the committee eventually recommended that the LD50 test was inappropriate on both scientific and cruelty grounds. An alternative, the so-called 'fixed dose procedure' (FDP), required that only ten animals should be used instead. The dose administered was determined beforehand on the basis of available knowledge and the experiment was terminated as soon as an animal showed signs of toxicity. The Home Office quietly dropped the LD50 test and over the next few years, the FDP became the internationally recognised standard procedure for assessing toxicity.[88]

When Mary joined the advisory committee, there was almost no statutory regulation of the laboratory use of animals. The relevant law was the 1876 Cruelty to Animals Act which concerned the maltreatment of animals by the general population and did not cover laboratory-based research. A private members' bill had been debated in Parliament without reaching the statute book, but there was a consensus that existing provisions were no longer adequate. In 1979, the Chairman resigned and Mary took on the chairing of a reconstituted committee with an extended brief to make recommendations for new legislation.[89]

Public opinion clearly favoured the continued use of animal testing before new drugs were introduced for human use, but the case for better regulation was overwhelming. Only licensed research should be permitted and licenses should be granted only when strict criteria were met, limiting pain and suffering, ensuring appropriate use of anaesthetics and eliminating long-term suffering arising from the experiment.[90] The question of the number of animals that might be used proved more difficult to decide. Most members of the committee took the view that the legislation should stipulate that as few animals as possible compatible with a scientifically acceptable result should be used. Mary herself thought that the priority should be the optimum scientific outcome and this should determine the number of animals used but she was over-ruled. A majority of the committee, and Mary was amongst them on this issue, felt that public opinion would demand that the licensing procedures should place a heavy burden on applicants to justify their work. However, a lighter, less bureaucratic touch was eventually recommended.[91]

Mary found the other members of the committee well-informed and supportive. Richard Adrian, the Master of Pembroke College, Cambridge, a laboratory scientist who had held a licence in the past, became Vice-Chairman and was particularly helpful. Some difficulties were caused by the RSPCA representative, who had a tendency (convenient for herself but inconvenient for everyone else) to 'pass out in a faint whenever she was losing an argument.' This caused 'such a distraction that by the time she had come round and we had all settled down again, it seemed impossible to go back to where we had left the debate, and we moved on to the next point.'[92] A daunting feature of the committee meetings was the presence of a phalanx of Home Office inspectors at the back of the room who seemed deeply suspicious of any new safeguards that were proposed. Mary understood this better when one of them pointed out to her that they felt that the need for safeguards reflected or implied criticism of the way they had carried out their work hitherto.[93] The committee produced its report in 1982, but it was not until 1986 that the Animals (Scientific Procedures) Bill, incorporating most of its recommendations, was passed into law.[94]

Over the next fifteen years, the legislation seemed to work reasonably well. However, the animal rights movement, founded in the 1960s, was becoming increasingly violent. For example, Colin Blakemore, the Oxford Professor of Physiology, who had previously carried out experiments with kittens resulting in improvements to the care of people with visual impairment, was seriously attacked. His wife and children were also threatened. They received envelopes with razor blades in them, fake bombs, even real bombs. His car tyres were slashed and his car had paint thrown over it.[95] The issue of animal rights had gradually risen up the political agenda and in 2001 Mary became a member of the House of Lords committee set up to review the provisions of the 1986 Act.[96] The committee reported in 2002, its main recommendation being that there was a continued need for animal experiments in applied and non-applied research, but that higher priority should be given to non-animal research.[97] The framework that Mary's committee had recommended in 1982 remained unaltered.

At the heart of all these issues was a series of philosophical questions which Mary discussed in some detail, both in her account of the meetings and in other books, notably in a chapter titled *Man and Other Animals* in *The Uses of Philosophy* (1992)[98] and in a chapter titled 'Rights' in *An Intelligent Person's Guide to Ethics* (1999).[99] The fundamental question was whether it was ethically justifiable to treat non-human animals differently from human animals. As Mary pointed out, the theory of evolution had radically changed the way animals were considered. Before Darwin there was an automatic assumption that animals were qualitatively different from us.[100] But Darwin's discovery of the close biological affinity of animals to humans, an affinity that has been amply confirmed by DNA studies showing the high percentage of shared DNA, suggested such a qualitative difference could not be taken for granted. Though others, such as Mary Midgley, Mary Warnock's Oxford contemporary, had earlier expressed similar views in *Beast and Man* (1979),[101] it was Peter Singer, an Australian philosopher, whose radical ideas in this field gained greatest publicity. Mary and members of her committee interviewed him in the United States where he was then working.[102]

Singer accused the non-vegetarian general public and especially scientists who experimented on animals of what he called speciesism. He claimed 'There is no ethical basis for elevating membership of our particular species into a morally crucial characteristic. From an ethical point of view, we all stand on an equal footing, whether we stand on two feet or four or none at all.'[103] To argue against this view, Singer claimed, was 'speciesism, pure and simple, and it is as indefensible as the most blatant racism.' Singer justified his views on the grounds that there are no characteristics to which we can point that would mark off humans from other animals. In conversation with members of Mary's committee he was less radical. He conceded that one could draw a distinction between 'persons' and 'non-persons.' Persons were those 'who take a conscious pleasure in their lives and therefore should not be prematurely deprived of life.'[104] But he shocked many people by the rigour with which he applied this logic: he excluded new-born babies and the severely mentally incompetent from the category of persons with a right to life, while including chimpanzees, dolphins and possibly pigs. To Mary's puzzlement he excluded horses, although she knew from her own experience that horses had personalities and often 'when fox-hunting or racing, appear to enjoy themselves.'

In response to Singer's views, Mary drew what she regarded as a crucial distinction between two sorts of objection to the eating of meat and the use of animals for experimental purposes. For some, the main issue is the avoidance of suffering. It does not matter if the animal dies, providing death is not painful. Mary saw this position as 'animal welfarism.' The second kind of objection, closer to Singer's views, holds that the premature death of any animal is a cost always to be taken into account regardless of any suffering caused. Mary contended that 'we simply do think of ourselves as importantly different from other animals.'[105] In the case of animals, we assume that if one dies, it can easily be replaced with another. But in the case of humans, we do not, for one moment, think that one can replace another. She argues that speciesism is

not the name of a prejudice we should try to wipe out. It is not a kind
of injustice. It is a natural consequence of the way we and our ancestors
have established the institution of society within which the concepts of
right and wrong, and the law have their meaning. The myth of Creation,
with man as the dominant species in charge of the rest, did not form our
attitudes. It is rather a storybook expression of existing attitudes, as is the
way with myths.[106]

Similarly, she has little time for the concept of 'animal rights.' In line
with her view on other 'rights' claims, she sees those who advocate for
the rights of animals as pointing to acts of *injustice*. Clearly there should
be legislation to deal with cruelty to animals, but where more extensive
rights are claimed for animals, these are likely to remain aspirational.
She points to the inconsistency of those animal rights activists who
claim that no animal should be hunted, when it is obvious that, in the
wild, animals hunt other animals with no thought to the rights of those
they hunt.[107] We instinctively assume, rightly in Mary's view, that our
domestic animals do not have the same rights we do.

> I may give my cat the right to come and go as he pleases by putting in a
> cat-flap; but I do not extend his freedom much beyond this. I am just as
> ruthless as before in throwing out the half-dead mice and birds that he
> may choose to bring into the kitchen, and I never even wonder whether I
> am infringing a right. We live on my terms. He is my property. If I get too
> poor to keep him, I give him away or put him to death.[108]

At the same time as she was chairing the Home Office Committee on
Animal Experimentation, Mary was also, from 1979 to 1986, a member
of the standing Royal Commission on Environmental Pollution.[109] The
task of this commission was to identify and investigate issues of
environmental concern and make recommendations to government.
During Mary's tenure, one such issue was the effect of lead emission
from petrol on the learning and behaviour of children. In 1983, the
commission published a report, 'Lead in the Environment,' which
recommended a gradual reduction and then elimination of lead from
petrol. The following year's report, 'Tackling Pollution: Experience
and Prospects,' is notable for drawing attention very early on to
the greenhouse effect caused by CO_2 emissions. The report stated
unequivocally that CO_2 concentrations were increasing and that one
could be 'fairly confident that this will result in a warming of the

earth's atmosphere' but it was unclear how serious the implications were at that stage.[110] It recommended that 'all necessary steps should be taken to ensure that there is the best chance of an early resolution of the uncertainties surrounding the effects of increasing concentration of carbon dioxide in the atmosphere.'[111] Mary was a signatory to both these reports.

The other members of the commission were mostly eminent scientists but there were also a few 'lay' members: an economist, a public health academic, a lawyer and herself, a philosopher. Mary found the meetings of the commission 'immensely enjoyable' and describes them as like the best sort of Oxford or Cambridge college dinner-table discussions but with the advantage that there was a marked absence of local politics, grudges and antipathies that marred real college high table talk.[112]

She also enjoyed what she learned on the research visits. Oil pollution interested her particularly and this involved travelling to the Shetlands and landing on an oil rig in thick fog. Now in her late fifties, she had to try to conceal her terror 'at climbing up and down slippery ladders out over the sea, where falling would have meant certain death,'[113] (sic) but she gained more from these visits than passing fear or pleasure: she recorded that participation in this commission made her for the first time seriously consider 'whether "the environment" or "nature" is valued intrinsically, for its own sake, or for the sake of some other more obviously human value, as a "utility", or for its contribution to human well-being.'[114] Why indeed did we value a clean coastline with its marine and offshore fauna so highly?

The economist on the commission argued that a clean coastline was an 'amenity' to which a precise economic value could be attached on the basis of a cost-benefit calculation. Based on such a calculation, he considered that cleaning up the Shetlands was too expensive to be justified.[115] Mary objected to the notion that an area of such great natural beauty could be treated as an 'amenity,' especially if that meant taming it and making it universally accessible. For her, in the tradition of the Romantics, part of the value of nature is what we can experience of its wildness and sublimity. She recognised however that there was some truth in the accusation of 'a kind of snobbishness' in the view that she did not want *her* countryside experiences to be spoiled by 'a lot of ramblers' with the 'right to roam' trampling up her mountain path 'especially if they demand a car park and a lavatory and a seat for Granny in the Picnic Area.'[116] One had to understand, she thought, that what might be in the interests of ramblers and industrial farmers might conflict with the interests of the natural world.

On the other hand, she was not opposed to human interventions in nature *per se*. Some people object to genetic modification of crops, for instance, on the grounds that it is 'against nature.' Mary pointed out that medical interventions are also generally against nature, but people do not object to them if they save lives.[117] But there are limits: one area of biotechnology to which she strongly objected was the effort to prevent ageing and prolong human life indefinitely. What gives significance to our lives, she thought, was the contrast, indeed

> sometimes a conflict between what, being mortal and having a more or less precarious hold on life, we can actually do, and what we can aspire to or imagine. The creative imagination it seems to me, feeds on this contrast, allowing us to grasp, or partly grasp, what is beautiful or what is tragic, or what is in some other way, inspirational. Being mortal, we know that there is an urgency in our lives.[118]

Mary developed her thinking on the complex and often contradictory tangle of reasons for valuing nature in the last book she published: *Critical Reflections on Ownership* (2015).[119] Part of a series of reflections on human rights and the environment, this appeared in her ninety-first year. Characteristically, the book brings together philosophy and her personal experience. In the words of the series editors, it is 'refreshingly intimate [...] lyrical [...] insightful.'[120] She had decided that this would be her final book, and it is a fitting summation of many aspects of her life. The aim of her reflections is to explore whether and how the feelings of love, pride and responsibility people usually have for a piece of land they own, even if it is just a small garden, might extend to cover the globe and thus form a basis for commitment to protect and conserve the environment.

She begins by showing that private ownership of land and things is natural to humans. Although property ownership is nowadays extensively regulated by law, Mary describes the 'habit of property ownership' as natural because it is a behaviour shared by other animals, for example by birds building and defending their own nests. She traces the history of philosophers' treatment of property focusing particularly on Hume in the eighteenth century and noting that it was he who recognised that the relations between men and their world were not only governed by reason but also by the passions or emotions. Pride is perhaps the passion most commonly aroused in us by our possessions.[121] She tells the story of her own relationship with the gardens she has owned, loved and tended, from the tarmacked playground of a converted schoolhouse she and Geoffrey bought when they were in their early fifties, through several moves, and finally to the back and front gardens of the small house on a 1930s housing estate in south London where she was living as she wrote this. Her purpose in relating this personal history is to suggest that people generally take pride in making their gardens better than they were when they took them over; this she sees as the essence of ownership.[122] In contrast with the care people give their gardens, she says, land which has no owner has no one responsible for it and is open to neglect and exploitation.

Next, she considers the history of proposals and practical experiments with common ownership, of which there have been many, particularly in the wake of the French Revolution. She recognises that these can succeed on a small scale, citing the early years of the Kibbutz movement in Israel as one example, and the John Lewis Partnership as another. But it seems that if a collective grows beyond a certain size, individuals' sense of emotional attachment to it declines.

There is however a paradox: despite our natural urge to cultivate and improve, at the same time what we think we most love is wild nature, nature that is not interfered with by man. From Rousseau in the eighteenth century down to today, there is a rich literary tradition celebrating the wildness of the natural world. Poets and philosophers have sought to understand our emotional responses to nature's beauty and power in terms of our smallness in the face of nature, a sense of ourselves as conscious moral beings, awe and simply fear. For Mary it was above all Wordsworth who captured and gave expression to experiences of the sublime inspired by nature.

The final third of the book is devoted to a discussion of philosophical considerations and practical steps concerning ways that the environment can be protected from commercial exploitation. She considers that treaties between states can only have very limited success because states have obligations to their citizens which produce competing national interests. But she finds hope in a number of changes that occurred after World War Two when, countering the logical positivists, it once again became possible to take 'values' into account. No longer was it assumed that profit and loss, as determined by economists, should alone govern public policy.[123] Another important shift is in our knowledge, in education and in awareness of the environment and how we fit into it. Increasingly, people see themselves as part of nature, interconnected with it and with other people: a real sense of common responsibility for the globe is becoming possible. In case the hope that people will simply learn to behave better is thought too optimistic, Mary claims a possible positive role for what she calls Promethean fear. In the Greek myth, Prometheus was chained to a rock to be tormented for ever by Zeus in the form of an eagle as a punishment for stealing fire and thus introducing technology, skill and thence all civilisation to mankind. Like the fifth-century BC Athenians, we too should be afraid of what, with our technologies and civilisation, we are doing to the natural world.

The critical reception of this book was highly positive. Ceri Warnock (no relation) wrote in the *Commonwealth Law Bulletin* that there are

> not too many books on property theory that you read eagerly from cover to cover; that bring fresh insights and that make you pause for thought, but also make you laugh. This book is stimulating and enjoyable, but it also has a depth and *gravitas* that belies its brevity, posing and attempting to answer one of the most pressing questions of the time.

She thought it would be of particular interest to scholars and students in the fields of law, politics and philosophy, especially those interested in differing conceptions of property and those seeking philosophical underpinnings for environmental law.[124]

Markku Oksanen, writing in *Environmental Values*, saw the book as unusual, comprising personal memoirs and anecdotes and depersonalised analysis of concepts, the history of ideas and current policies. He was impressed by Mary's capacity to move fluently from enduring philosophical problems to current disputes and back but thought the absence of the mention of the environment in some chapters was a weakness.[125]

During the last twenty years of her life, Mary continued to make frequent appearances in the media, especially radio. She was interviewed by Melvyn Bragg on education, took part in the programme, *A Good Read*, talked on surrogate pregnancies on *Woman's Hour*, and reminisced about her early life in programmes called *Meeting Myself Coming Back* and *The House I Grew Up In*. Sometimes the interviews arose from a recent publication, so she did an extended interview with Laurie Taylor on why religion and politics don't mix after the publication of *Dishonest to God* (see the following chapter). She was frequently interviewed by journalists for *The Guardian*, *The Observer* and occasionally other newspapers. In 2003, Andrew Brown of *The Guardian* carried out a particularly revealing interview. He later referred to her as 'the philosophical plumber to the establishment. Whenever some tricky problem arose, she could be trusted to get things flowing again.'

In August 2015, she took part in the Radio 4 series 'Fantasy Festival.' Interviewees were asked to design their own dream Glastonbury Festival. Mary opted to hold her fantasy festival on Tanera Mor, an uninhabited island in the Summer Isles off the West Coast of Scotland, the place she had visited in youth and again in old age. The theme of the festival would be the Romantic experience of the sublime inspired by nature (she was working on her book about the environment, *Critical Reflections on Ownership*, at the time). There would be no more than fifty participants to ensure good discussion. Formal invitations would be issued to Wordsworth, Coleridge, Keats, the pianist Alfred Brendel and her own children. The remaining places would be filled by advertisement. The days would be spent walking in the surrounding countryside and the evenings in discussion and in listening to music. Brendel would play Schubert's Impromptus. A small amateur orchestra whose players would also enter into the discussions would play Haydn's Symphony No. 44 in E minor, the piece inspired by the death of his mother that the composer wished to be played at his own funeral. Vaughan Williams' 'The Lark Ascending' would remind the participants of the decline in bird song. They would be asked to reflect on the way civilisation had destroyed much of the natural world and hopefully, on leaving the festival, would continue to think about how the progress of civilisation might be combined with the preservation, indeed, the recapture of the natural world we had lost. 'Yes,' Mary agreed with the Fantasy Festival interviewer firmly, 'I *am* a romantic.'[126]

Notes

1   Mary Warnock, 2003, p. 28.

2   William Wordsworth, *Collected Poems*, p. 899.

3   Mary Warnock, 1976.

4   Mary Warnock, 1987.

5   Mary Warnock, 1994.

6   UA, 1, p. 9.

7   Ibid., p. 20.

8   Mary Warnock, 2000, p. 200.

9   UA, 1, p. 6.

10   Ibid.

11   UA, 2, p. 6.

12   Mary Warnock, 2010b, p. 156.

13   Warnock, 2000, p. 79.

14   Ibid., p. 3.

15   Warnock, 2000, p. 5.

16   Ibid., p. 6.

17   UA, 1, p. 11.

18   Ibid.

19   Ibid., p. 12.

20   Ibid.

21   Ibid, p. 4.

22   Ibid.

23   Ibid.

24   Ibid., p. 6.

25   Ibid., p. 7.

26   Ibid., p. 8.

27   Ibid., pp. 21–22.

28   Ibid., p. 4.

29   Hilary Maxwell-Hyslop, personal communication.

30   UA, 7, p. 31.

31   Potter, 1989, p. 312.

32   Warnock, 2000, p. 34.

33   Ibid.

34   Warnock, 2000, p. 171.

35   Potter, 1989, p. 95.

36   Kenneth Blyth, personal communication.

37   Ibid.

38   Ibid.

39   Annan Committee, para 4.11.

40   Potter, 1990.

41   Mary Warnock, personal communication.

42   Potter, 1990, pp. 332–334.

43   Mary Warnock, The Social Responsibility of the Broadcasting Media, 1985

44   Ibid., p. 9.

45   Ibid., pp. 11–12.

46   Ibid., p. 14

47   Ibid.

48   Ibid., p. 15

49   Warnock, 2003, pp. 191–196.

50   Ibid., p. 195.

51   Magee, 2012.

52   https://www.bbc.co.uk/programmes/p009mfcb.

53   Ibid.

54   Ibid.

55   Ibid., p. 196.

56   Ibid., pp. 197–198.

57   Ibid., p. 207.

58   Ibid., p. 199.

59   Isaacs, 1999, p. 121.

60   Ibid., p. 120.

61   Warnock, 2003, p. 205.

62   Ibid., pp. 203–204.

63   Ibid., p. 205.

64   Ibid., p. 206.

65   Ibid., p. 207.

66   Ibid., pp. 210–211; Alex Beard, personal communication.

67   Warnock, 2003, p. 214.

68   Isaacs, p. 130.

69   Ibid., p. 126.

70   Ibid., p. 195.

71   Jeremy Isaacs, personal communication.

72   Mark Wallinger and Mary Warnock (eds), 2000.

73   Warnock, 2003, p. 215.

74   Mark Wallinger, personal communication.

75   Warnock, 2003, p. 215.

76   Mark Wallinger, personal communication.

77   Wallinger and Warnock, p. 11.

78   Ibid., p. 15.

79   Warnock, 2003, p. 218.

80   Ibid., p. 221.

81   Department for Culture, Media and Sport, 2000.

82   Martin Levy, personal communication.

83   Ibid.

84   Ibid.

85   Michael Barton, personal communication.

86   Ibid.

87   Warnock, 2003, p. 150.

88   Ibid., p. 151.

89   Ibid., p. 153.

90   Ibid., p. 155.

91   Ibid.

92   Ibid., p. 160.

93   Ibid.

94   Ibid., p. 161.

95   Derbyshire, 29 December 2007.

96   Ibid., p. 164.

97   House of Lords, 2002.

98   Warnock, 1992, pp. 9–23.

99   Warnock, 1999, pp. 66–69.

100 Warnock, 1992, p. 42.

101 Mary Midgley, 1979.

102 Warnock, 2003, pp. 169–173.

103 Peter Singer, 1979.

104 Singer, 1985.

105 Warnock, 2003, p. 174.

106 Ibid., pp. 174–175.

107 Warnock, 1999, p. 68.

108 Ibid.

109 Warnock, 2003, p. 19.

110 Royal Commission on Environmental Pollution, 5, 130.

111 Ibid., 7, 92.

112 Ibid., p. 20.

113 Warnock, 2003, p. 21.

114 Ibid.

115 Ibid., pp. 21–22.

116 Warnock, 2003, p. 24.

117 Ibid., p. 26.

118   Ibid., p. 27.

119   Mary Warnock, 2015.

120   Ibid., p. 10.

121   Ibid., p. 31.

122   Ibid., p. 38.

123   Ibid., p. 105.

124   Ceri Warnock, 2016, p. 154.

125   Markku Oksanen, 2016, p. 374.

126   BBC Radio 4, *Fantasy Festival*, 20 August 2015.

11. The Manner of Our Deaths

From the time of her first excursion into public life in the 1970s until the end of the twentieth century, Mary Warnock had always been at the forefront of progressive liberal thought in Britain. She had been a supporter of the Labour Party until the mid-1960s, when she left the party because of its support for comprehensive schools and especially the abolition of grammar schools. Since then, she had been generally centre-right in her political views but when it came to social issues she always seemed to be on the same side as left-leaning people. She was with them, for example, on socially divisive matters such as the abolition of capital punishment, the abortion laws and the decriminalisation of homosexuality. In particular, readers of *The Guardian* who bought the paper because they knew they would nearly always agree with the opinions it expressed, were used to finding Baroness Warnock quoted as providing moral philosophical support for views they instinctively knew were the right ones to hold. So, in September 2008, it must have been a shock for these same *Guardian* readers to discover that their highly respected philosopher was on the receiving end of harsh criticism, not only from the reactionary right, but from socially liberal people they would normally expect to agree with her. It was the robustness of her views on death which caused spluttering over the toast and marmalade.

Mary's views on death and assisted dying had developed over a twelve-year period, starting in the mid-1990s with the death of her husband, Geoffrey. In 1994, she had been a member of a House of Lords Select Committee on Medical Ethics. Lord Walton introduced the report of this committee in a debate held in the House of Lords on 9 May 1994. He reported that the members were unanimously opposed to voluntary euthanasia. After describing a number of distressing cases in which individuals desperately wanted to be helped to die, supported by distinguished legal opinions in favour of legalising euthanasia, he said:

 https://doi.org/10.11647/OBP.0278.11

ultimately, however, we concluded that such arguments are not sufficient reason to weaken society's prohibition of intentional killing which is the cornerstone of law and of social relationships. Individual cases cannot reasonably establish the foundation of a policy which would have such serious and widespread repercussions. The issue of euthanasia is one in which the interests of the individual cannot be separated from those of society as a whole.[1]

Clearly Mary supported these conclusions at the time, but it seems likely that her views were already beginning to change.

In 1992, Geoffrey had started to show signs of a chest complaint that would take three years to kill him. The condition, cryptogenic fibrosing alveolitis, is one in which fibrous tissue gradually invades the lining of the air passages in the lungs where oxygen replaces carbon dioxide in the blood stream.[2] As the disease progresses, blood leaves the lungs with less and less oxygen. The patient becomes progressively weaker as oxygen is necessary for the creation of energy and ultimately, for survival. There is no cure, although steroid drugs can slow the progress of the disease. When oxygen levels become dangerously low, the patient is connected to a ventilator and breathes in pure oxygen. Eventually this fails to meet the patient's oxygen needs and death ensues.

Geoffrey managed to lead a reasonably normal life until the middle of 1994 when his symptoms became more acute. He was prescribed large doses of steroids but gradually, in the summer of 1995, breathing became more and more difficult even with artificial ventilation. It was increasingly hard for him to cough. Geoffrey feared he might suffocate and was at risk of drowning in his secretions. His terror of drowning stopped him sleeping.[3] According to Mary, who wrote in response to the author of a letter of condolence ten days after Geoffrey died, he was 'stoical, indeed heroic' in the face of his impending death, and finally decided 'he was not going into hospital and not submit to the horrors and indignities of being unable to get out of bed.'[4] He was offered a hospital bed but turned it down, preferring to spend his last days at home, nursed by Mary. He managed to hold off his death in a manner 'typical of his courage and courtesy'[5] so that he could attend the opening of new student accommodation at Hertford, named after him. On this occasion, he 'delighted his friends and colleagues with a witty and eloquent valedictory speech.'[6] He died twelve days afterwards.

On the morning of 8 October 1995, he saw his general practitioner, Dr. Nick Maurice, who prescribed morphine to ease his breathing and reduce his extreme distress. His daughter Fanny, and her daughter, Abigail, visited and Geoffrey enjoyed their company. After they left, he asked Mary to leave him and 'give me half an hour.' She went for a short walk. When she returned, she found him lying on the floor in the bathroom, dead. The ventilator was disconnected. She realised that he had made up his mind he was not going to go into hospital and so he took the action he did. It was, she wrote, 'a cool, rational choice': he had decided to take matters into his own hands and end his life.[7] When Dr. Maurice returned in the late afternoon he found Mary in floods of tears on the doorstep. Geoffrey's body had already been taken to the mortuary. Nick Maurice was in no doubt that Geoffrey had taken active steps to end his life; the dose of morphia he had prescribed would not have been sufficient in itself to cause death.[8]

Throughout his illness, Mary had been the sole carer. Both she and Geoffrey strongly disliked the idea of causing any interference in the lives of their children. Indeed, when he realised how much he had been shielded from the knowledge of the severity of his father's condition, their son Felix was quite angry with his mother.[9]

So ended forty-six years of married life. Geoffrey had been a most remarkable husband. A philosopher whose work was highly esteemed by his academic colleagues, he had gone on to become a highly successful university administrator. As Principal of Hertford College, he had overseen several substantial new building projects and taken the college from near the bottom to a proud position at the top of the Norrington Table, a league table for measuring the Oxford colleges' academic performance according to undergraduate degree results. He is still remembered with gratitude for having rescued the college from the dismal situation it was in when he took over in 1971. He went on to serve for four years as Vice-Chancellor of the University of Oxford. His close friend and professional colleague, the philosopher Peter Strawson, wrote of him after his death that he 'never deviated from the clear and literal truth, and the difficult exercise of cleaving to that path he conducted, in his writings on perception and the philosophy of language, with such an absence of fussiness, with such coolness, urbanity, and elegance, that the result gave (and can still give) not only deep intellectual satisfaction

‿‿at aesthetic pleasure.'[10] Although he gave the impression of an austere personality, this was misleading. According to Strawson,

> he had a great capacity for enjoyment, and a lively sense of the ridiculous, being vastly and delightfully amused by the absurdities which so often cropped up in human speech and behaviour. He was a games player, a keen cricketer and golfer; and all his friends and colleagues found him a charming companion, invariably courteous and considerate, indeed chivalrous, in personal relations. In the old phrase, he was *'a man of feeling'*.[11]

After his death, Mary asked for and received permission to have carved on his gravestone the motto of his regiment, the Irish Guards, the two words 'Quis Separabit' (Who Shall Separate Us). Doubtless, these words expressed her own feelings that their partnership would endure in some way for ever.[12]

Fig. 10 Portrait of Geoffrey Warnock by Humphrey Ocean (1987), with the permission of the artist and of the Principal, Fellows and Scholars of Hertford College in the University of Oxford. Fig. 11 Portrait of Mary Warnock by June Mendoza (1989), with the permission of the artist and of the Mistress and Fellows, Girton College, Cambridge.

Geoffrey and Mary were extremely fortunate to have had Nick Maurice as their general practitioner. He was the last of several generations of medical Maurices who had served as family doctors in Marlborough, Wiltshire, since 1792. After Geoffrey's death, he and Mary developed a strong friendship. Then, in 1997, Dr. Maurice found himself in the national spotlight as a result of a short article he had written in a newsletter for patients in his practice. In it he disclosed that

> we doctors are practising euthanasia all the time and should be proud of it. In the past three months I have induced a quiet and easy death for two of my patients for which the relatives were grateful. That is not to say I have killed two patients. It is simply to say that I have given sufficient quantities of morphine to ensure that the physical and mental suffering of the patient, and the relative also, has been kept to a minimum.

He defined euthanasia as allowing people to die 'peacefully and quietly.'[13] As it happened, one of the patients in his practice was Sir Ludovic Kennedy, a television personality and President of the Voluntary Euthanasia Society. Kennedy read the article and gave his support for Dr. Maurice in a letter to the Wiltshire Gazette and Herald. He praised the doctor's actions as 'admirable for the compassion shown in bringing his patients' suffering to an end.'[14] The letter caught the eye of the national press. In the subsequent furore, Dr. Maurice received much encouragement and positive support from Mary. He was similarly praised by a number of people who supported his practice, especially from his patients, but he also had some hostile criticism, some of it linking his views with those of Mary. One angry correspondent wrote 'I cannot understand why people like you and Lady Warnock go on talking about it publicly all the time!'[15]

About a year earlier, in December 1996, Mary gave an interview about end-of-life issues to a journalist, Peter Millar, that was published in *The Sunday Times*.[16] She said that her husband's death had 'concentrated her mind' on the subject. She was irritated by the attitude of the doctors who gave ever-increasing doses of morphine. 'They always went on about doing it to ease suffering, not admitting it was killing them.' Her argument was not with what they were doing, just with their lack of honesty. Her views on medical attitudes to elderly people who did not want to go on living were expressed with a brutal honesty. 'I can't bear the idea of all that money being wasted on reviving old people who can't be bothered to go on living, who don't want to burden their children or even the NHS.' Her interviewer, Peter Millar, recorded his reaction to such extreme views. 'I look, I realise, stereotypically aghast. [...] perhaps I ought not to be surprised at an old lady [Mary was seventy-two at the time] advocating attitudes that come straight from the ancient world. But this is Mary Warnock, the champion of humanist enlightenment.'[17] It is clear that Mary's attitude towards euthanasia had changed over the two years since the House of Lords Medical Ethics Committee had reported in 1994, and that the manner of Geoffrey's death had been responsible for this shift in attitude.

In 1999, Mary published *An Intelligent Person's Guide to Ethics*. The first chapter, entitled 'Death' begins with two case examples, in both of which a doctor participates actively in bringing about the death of a patient. The first example is clearly based on Geoffrey's final illness, though she changes the gender of the patient. The terminally ill woman she describes is painfully thin as the result of all the weight she has lost. She is too weak to move and is entirely dependent on her husband.

> She is given analgesics, including morphia, which marginally ease her breathing. But she longs to die as she knows she soon will. She longs to release her husband from his terrible life, and she has had enough of her own. She is terrified of dying of suffocation [...] and now she cannot sleep for thinking about it. When she does sleep, she wakes from a nightmare of suffocation.

The doctor tells the husband he is gradually increasing the morphia. Within a few weeks, the woman has died.[18]

In discussing this case, so clearly based on her own experience, Mary points first to the fact that, although some would suggest that the death of the woman has been brought about by 'unnatural' means, in fact, had it not been for the earlier 'unnatural' medical interventions, the woman would have died much earlier. Second, Mary raises the importance of the fact that the couple love each other and so 'can enter into the other's feelings and discern where each other's interests lie.' She describes how the dying woman has always placed a high value on independence and making her own choices. 'She now finds that, though she wants to die, she cannot choose to do so.' These considerations, Mary thinks, guide the couple in deciding what the right thing to do might be, in formulating their 'private morality' derived from a mixture of principle and sentiment.[19]

An Intelligent Person's Guide to Ethics discusses a number of other issues of great ethical complexity. Nearly forty years after the publication of *Ethics since 1900*, Mary was by now full of relevant experience which enabled her to demonstrate how valuable it could be to focus on how people came to moral decisions when formulating public policy and on the making of moral decisions by individuals themselves.[20] The chapter on 'Birth' focuses on her experience of chairing the Committee on Human Fertilisation and Embryology. In 'Rights,' she expresses once again her scepticism regarding the value of human rights that are legally unprotected, as well as her opposition to the idea of animal rights. The chapter titled 'Where Ethics Comes From' considers historically the religious and Enlightenment views on this subject before asserting that 'in a precarious situation, people must assert and share certain values, or perish. It is this realisation, it seems to me, which lies at the root of the ethical.'[21] *The Intelligent Person's Guide to Ethics* was warmly praised in *The Times Higher Educational Supplement*. While criticising what he regards as Mary's over-simplistic dismissal of moral relativism, the reviewer goes on to say that 'this criticism should not detract from the book's other excellent qualities. It is lucid, accessible and brims with humanity. Warnock should be applauded for her achievement.'[22]

* * *

By June 2003, Mary was ready to give her support to a bill on assisted dying in the House of Lords. In her speech in support of the bill, one of many introduced by Lord Joel Joffe allowing health professional assistance to terminally ill, mentally competent people who wish to end their own lives, she cited three reasons why she was in favour of this new law. First, she said, it was time for assisted death to be regulated. It was happening all the time in an unregulated fashion, and this was dangerous. Second, she asserted, it is time for the matter to be considered separately from religious belief. Instead, 'it is the morality of compassion that must be paramount.' Finally, it is time the wishes of the terminally ill were given the paramount importance they deserve. The terminally ill are not concerned about what will happen to them after they die or whether they will die, but with whether they will suffer 'the deterioration—perhaps the inability to breathe, the total helplessness, or the humiliation—that will precede what they know to be their imminent death.'[23]

In May 2006, supporting a similar bill introduced by Joel Joffe, she made different points. She agreed that palliative care should be improved and be made more widely available. Assisted suicide should never be a substitute for good palliative care. The bill before the House, she thought, had very narrow scope to which no one could reasonably take exception. She was not persuaded by those who opposed the bill on 'slippery slope' grounds: this was the argument that any legislation on assisted dying will inevitably be followed by further measures making it ever easier for lives to be taken for reasons of convenience or for the saving of expense, rather than for the relief of intolerable suffering. She argued that the circumstances in which assisted suicide might be permitted were so narrowly defined and carefully safeguarded as to render the slippery slope argument inapplicable. In particular, there was no realistic threat to disabled people. Clearly, she suggested, people who wanted an assisted death could in no way be regarded as immoral. Why, she asked, should it be expected that they should follow 'the morality of religious or medical leaders rather than a morality in which they do believe, not another which would compel them to live against their wish?'[24]

The following year, in 2007, Mary was approached by Dr. Elisabeth (Lisa) Sears who was thinking of writing a book on the management of terminal illness. Dr. Sears (professional name Macdonald) was a recently retired clinical oncologist with enormous experience in the field. She wrote to Mary asking for advice and was invited to tea in the House of Lords. They discovered many mutual interests and talked non-stop until the staff came to lay the tables for dinner. Mary proposed they wrote a book on assisted dying together. She would provide the philosophical background and Lisa would describe the clinical situations in which an assisted death might become desirable to a terminally ill patient. So Mary wrote chapters on the fundamental principles relevant to the debate on assisted dying, on the importance of mental competence and on the 'slippery slope,' while Lisa wrote chapters giving clinical details of relevant cases and describing the methods currently available to ease death.

The title of the book, *Easeful Death*, was taken from the poem 'Ode to a Nightingale' by John Keats which contains the lines: 'Darkling I listen, and, for many a time, I have been half in love with easeful death. [...] Now more than ever seems it rich to die, To cease upon the midnight with no pain.'[25] By coincidence, though the co-authors did not know it, the title they chose echoed the title of a book *A Very Easy Death*, by Simone de Beauvoir, the lover for many years of the existentialist philosopher, Jean Paul Sartre, about whom Mary had written copiously nearly forty years previously. De Beauvoir's book with its ironic title was about the distressing last months of her mother's life, in which she was tortured by pain and humiliating incontinence. When, after her mother's death from cancer, Simone de Beauvoir's sister, Poupette, agonised to a nurse about the suffering her mother had endured, the nurse replied 'But, Madame, I assure you it was a very easy death [une mort très douce].'[26]

In their book, Mary and Elisabeth Macdonald discussed why someone might qualify, under new legislation, for an assisted death. The experience of intolerable suffering unrelieved by palliative care was likely to be the main reason, but the authors added a further, much more controversial reason. They turned on its head the argument of those who objected to a new law on assisted dying on the grounds that some people might want to die because they felt caring for them was posing an intolerable burden on their relatives and friends. Those who objected to legislation usually took the line that no relative or friend would regard such caring as a burden and wish for the assisted death of the person they were looking after unless they had a mercenary reason for doing so. Only greedy relatives, who could not wait to get their hands on the money of the dying person, it was suggested, would think of caring as a burden. Mary Warnock and Elisabeth Macdonald took a very different view. They wrote:

> It is not difficult to imagine feeling that one's children were getting impatient either for their inheritance or simply for relief from the burden of care and that one had not so much a right to ask for death, as a duty to do so, now that it was lawful to provide it. There undoubtedly exist predatory or even exhausted relatives. But it is insulting to those who ask to be allowed to die to assume that they are incapable of making a genuinely independent choice, free from influence. (Indeed, there are people so determined to confound their children, if they see them as hovering over a hoped-for corpse, that their will to spite them by staying alive may outweigh their wish to escape their own pain).
>
> In any case, to ask for death for the sake of one's children or other close relatives can be seen as an admirable thing to do, not in the least indicative of undue pressure, or pressure of any kind. Other kinds of altruism are generally thought worthy of praise. Why should one not

admire this final altruistic act? And it would not be wholly altruistic: the desire to avoid squandering resources, or being a burden is combined, in the cases we are considering, with a sense that prolonging life is both futile and painful. It is idle to try to separate these motives. Part of what makes a patient's suffering intolerable may be the sense that he is ruining other people's lives. If he feels this keenly, and asks to be allowed to die, he is not a vulnerable victim, but a rational moral agent.[27]

The reviews of the book were largely positive. The distinguished philosopher, Onora O' Neill, a former pupil of Mary's at Oxford, but an opponent of a new law on assisted dying, wrote in *The Lancet*: 'The authors set out with exemplary clarity reasons for prohibiting or permitting physicians to "help" patients to die. Their arguments are cogent, illuminating, and in many ways convincing.'[28] Steven Poole in *The Guardian*, wrote: 'An extremely lucid and sympathetic interrogation.'[29] In *The Times Higher Education Supplement* Julia Stone called it a 'sensitive and succinct book [...] This book not only has the power to stimulate informed discussion, but also to shape social policy and inform good professional practice. [...] "Easeful Death" deserves a wide readership, and it should be compulsory reading for politicians and policymakers.'[30] The book stimulated much popular interest. The two co-authors were invited to talk about it at a number of book festivals, including Hay-on-Wye and Cheltenham. On long train journeys they took together, they became good friends and continued to see each other and correspond until, two or three years before Mary's death, communication became difficult and they lost touch.[31]

The argument put forward in the book that people who felt a burden should be able to ask for an assisted death was out of step with most progressive thinking on the subject. The lead British organisation Dignity in Dying, campaigned only for terminally ill, mentally competent people thought to be in the last six months of their lives who were enduring intolerable suffering to have the legal right to health professional assistance to end their lives. Humanists UK, on the other hand, did not see why it should only be people in their last six months who had this right. Anyone terminally ill who was suffering intolerably should also qualify. But the idea that feeling oneself a burden should justify requesting an assisted death was quite new, although it did not go as far as more extreme but poorly supported organisations such as

EXIT International, which campaigned for anyone who had had enough of life, regardless of the reason, to be able to access help to end it.

It might have been dissatisfaction with the lack of notice taken of the new argument in the book that led Mary to go further. In October 2008, in an interview with the Church of Scotland's magazine *Life and Work*, she repeated her view that the terminally ill who felt a burden to others should be given the right to die with health professional assistance. But now she talked of them having a 'duty to die.' She added: 'I'm absolutely, fully in agreement with the argument that if pain is insufferable, then someone should be given help to die, but I feel there's a wider argument that if somebody absolutely, desperately wants to die because they're a burden to their family, or the state, then I think they too should be allowed to die.'[32] This was highly provocative.

Mary also went further than others when it came to dementia. 'If you're demented, you're wasting people's lives—your family's lives— and you're wasting the resources of the National Health Service.' Most of those who advocated for a new law on assisted dying thought it was important that the person requesting to die should be fully mentally competent at the time the final decision was made to go ahead. Of course, in the early stages of dementia, a person would be competent to make this decision, but the expectation was that people with dementia would not wish to die until the disease had advanced to the point when, for example, they did not recognise their close family members. At this point they certainly would not be mentally competent. Those who wished for sufferers with advanced dementia to be allowed to have their lives terminated therefore proposed that people in the early stages could make advance directives stating that once their disease had progressed to a point when their quality of life was unacceptable, they could have their lives terminated.

This time round, there was no lack of publicity for the views Mary had expressed. Not surprisingly, those with strong right-wing and religious views were most forthright in their criticism. Nadine Dorries, a Conservative MP, wrote,

> I believe it is extremely irresponsible and unnerving for someone in Baroness Warnock's position to put forward arguments in favour of euthanasia for those who suffer from dementia and other neurological illnesses [...] Because of her previous experiences and well-known

standing on contentious moral issues, Baroness Warnock automatically gives moral authority to what are entirely immoral viewpoints.[33]

Phyllis Bowman, executive director of the campaign group Right to Life, which was strongly supported by religious organisations, wrote of Mary's interview: 'It sends a message to dementia sufferers that certain people think they don't count, and that they are a burden on their families. It's a pretty uncivilised society where that is the primary consideration. I worry that she will sway people who would like to get rid of the elderly.'[34]

Equally forthright criticism came from organisations with which Mary much more frequently found herself in tune. Neil Hunt, the chief executive of the Alzheimer's Society, said:

> I am shocked and amazed that Baroness Warnock could disregard the value of the lives of people with dementia so callously. With the right care, a person can have good quality of life very late into dementia. To suggest that people with dementia shouldn't be entitled to that quality of life or that they should feel that they have some sort of duty to kill themselves is nothing short of barbaric.[35]

Sarah Wootton, the Chief Executive of Dignity in Dying wrote in *The Guardian* in strong opposition to Mary's view: 'absolutely no one has a "duty to die". Consequently, when the law on assisted dying does change it will include a legal safeguard to ensure that any terminally ill adult who chooses an assisted death is mentally competent: capable of making the decision and understands its consequences.'[36] There was similar criticism from medical ethicists. Nancy Jecker, writing in the American Medical Association *Journal of Ethics* declared: 'Encouraging elderly people to die, or helping them to end their lives, would certainly save money and free up resources. But this approach is neither ethically defensible nor necessary.'[37] Some, such as June Andrews, a registered mental nurse, although they disagreed with Mary's views, nevertheless welcomed the fact that she had opened a debate. She wrote:

> Baroness Warnock is a dignified philosopher who has led an amazing intellectual life. Now, aged 84, she was asked for an opinion and expressed it. She said that euthanasia and assisted suicide are a good idea and that some of us have a duty to kill ourselves when we become a burden. Personally, I do not agree and never have. But I am glad the debate is now in the open.[38]

It should be added that around this time, there were two more prolonged and distressing family deaths which confirmed Mary's developing thoughts on these issues. The first was her sister Stephana's husband, Duncan Thomson, who died a particularly hard death from cancer. Then her older sister Jean Crossley died. Mary maintained she had been unnecessarily kept alive at the age of 101 when she was hospitalised with pneumonia. She wrote about how angry, then depressed, her sister became at her inability to prevent this so-called treatment when she was ready to die. In 2009, at around the time of Jean's death, Mary had a more unexpected and even more painful confrontation with a death in the family. Her daughter, Stephana, (Fanny) died of pneumonia when she was only fifty-three.[39] Mary was naturally deeply upset and repeatedly asked herself how she could have done more to help her daughter.

To return to the assisted dying issue, it is worth considering in more detail Mary's view that people who face a progressive form of dementia ought to be able to stipulate, in advance of the event, their wish to die. If they are not competent to make a decision themselves, their proxies should be able to decide on an assisted death on their behalf once they have reached an advanced stage of the condition. In the Netherlands, it is legal for doctors to end the lives of people with dementia, even if this is at an early stage, if they have previously expressed a wish for this to happen. Polling in the Netherlands suggests that about half the population support this position, but in other countries there is greater reluctance to extend assisted dying criteria to dementia sufferers. A majority want a right to make such a momentous decision for themselves, but not for others to make it for them. Amongst the medical profession even this limited position does not command support although there are strong signs that opinion amongst health professionals is beginning to change.

There are three main objections to the type of legislation currently applied in the Netherlands. The first is that expressed by the Alzheimer Society. Many people with dementia enjoy a good quality of life and there is no reason why they should want their lives to end. Further, much can be done to alleviate the symptoms of dementia so what is needed is not a defeatist attitude but a positive approach. This point of view is, of course, valid for those at an early stage of the disease, but much more dubious, indeed Mary thought ridiculous, for those whose disease has progressed to the point at which they have lost the ability to communicate, need help with toileting and feeding and can no longer recognise their family members or friends.

A second objection is made on the principle that it can never be right to end someone's life without their informed consent at the time the final decision is made. As Professor Ray Tallis, a passionate advocate for assisted dying for the mentally competent, terminally ill patient has put it, 'informed consent at the time a lethal medicine is taken is a totally necessary safeguard against abuse.'[40]

A third objection can be described as pragmatic. In most countries, such as the UK where euthanasia legislation is not in place, it is believed that the general public finds it abhorrent to suggest that people with dementia or other fatal illnesses should be able to end their lives because they feel they are a burden to their families and to society. People with dementia and other terminal illnesses, it is widely thought, should be reassured that their family members and society are happy to continue to look after them for as long as it takes. Many members of the House of Commons who took part in the debate on assisted dying held in September 2015 reported this was the view that had been frequently put to them by their constituents.

Mary vigorously refuted these objections in an unpublished lecture titled 'Easeful Death for the Very Elderly' delivered to the Society of Old Age Rational Suicide (SOARS) when she herself was eighty-six in 2010. She pointed to the neglect of the plight of people with dementia in discussions of assisted dying. It was widely argued that a health-professional-assisted death should not be permitted for people with advanced dementia because they could not give informed consent. Even if people had made advance directives asking for such a death if they became severely demented, they might have changed their minds. But, Mary argued, the concept of a change of mind was meaningless. 'The patient has no mind left to them to change, no settled intention, no powers to foresee the future or consider the course of a whole life.'[41] This made the advance directive a necessity for those who do not wish to continue to live once they have developed severe dementia.

Mary views the protests of organisations such as the Alzheimer Society that people with advanced dementia can be happy and enjoy life to be offensive. She writes 'I simply do not want to think that, in the future, I may be patronised by people pretending to believe my fantasies

[...]'[42] As for the argument that people should not be allowed to take their own lives because they feel a burden, Mary asks, as she had many times previously, why should 'altruism turn out to be the thing that is avoided?' at the end of life.[43] For her this is a moral issue 'of personal integrity, of trying to behave consistently and trying, roughly speaking, to do what is right by other people'[44] It is also a philosophical issue. 'Once the brain has reached a certain stage of tangles and degeneration which cannot be reversed, I believe I am not the same person as I was and I can take no further responsibility as a moral being.'[45] She goes on to note that some people think it is wrong to take life no matter how deteriorated a person is. This thought she sees as coming from the ancient idea of a spirit or essential being surviving the body. Somehow, she maintains, 'we must escape this dualism, this Cartesian separation of mind from body.'[46] Mary recognised the strong resistance to the idea that advance directives should be honoured even in the cases of advanced dementia but, she writes 'I believe that society is moving in this direction.'[47]

Of course, as Mary rightly wrote, societal attitudes may change, as they clearly have in the Netherlands. Further, there have been societies in the past and there continue to be societies today where suicide is not only sanctioned but, in certain specified circumstances, is regarded as the honourable course to take. In ancient Greece and Rome those condemned to death were given the option of ending their own lives and it was regarded as morally desirable for them to do so. It was in such circumstances that Socrates drank hemlock. Today, or at least until very recently, seppuku, or ritual self-disembowelment was practised by some Japanese soldiers at the end of World War II in 1945 as an alternative to dishonourable surrender. The attitudes of British society to assisted dying in advanced dementia are a very long way from these, at least to Western minds, exotic examples, though nearer to those held in the Netherlands.

Mary took part in two further debates on terminal illness in the House of Lords. In December 2013 she spoke in a debate on health at the end of life introduced by Lord Dubs. She reiterated her view that the present state of the law on what doctors might and might not do at the end of life was 'unsafe and intolerable.' She drew attention particularly to the plight of people who were dying and regarded as incompetent to make decisions about their own care. 'I cannot think of anything more humiliating,' she said, 'than to say that I wanted to die and that my life was no longer worth living only to be told that I was suffering from depression.'[48] She thought it was a 'scandal' that so few people made advance directives. General practitioners were the culprits who did not do enough to make sure their patients were informed about advance directives. She said that she often talked to her GP about her own death.[49]

In July 2014, Mary spoke in a debate on a bill introduced by Lord Falconer to legalise health-professional-assisted dying for the terminally ill. At that time, the Director of Public Prosecutions (DPP) had produced guidelines which made it clear that relatives who assisted a terminally ill person to die would not be prosecuted if it could be shown that they did so out of compassion for someone who clearly wanted to die. Mary pointed out that DPPs change, so the policy might be changed, and a more permanent solution was needed. She said that, although opponents of the bill claimed the numbers involved were small, this was not the case. As many as 30,000 people suffered 'bad deaths' each year. Even if the numbers were much smaller, it was wrong for them to have to suffer unnecessarily. She then reverted to the unpopular argument she had previously advanced. 'It is somehow thought to be wrong,' she said,

> that people who are approaching death and are terminally ill should take into account the suffering, expense and misery they are causing to their family as they are being a burden. Of course, they are also a burden to the state. Why is it that this is thought to be a wrong motive, or part of a motive, for wanting to end one's life when it is coming to an end anyway?

Up to that point in time, it was thought that altruism was a good thing: 'why should it be regarded differently now?'[50] Some supported her, but many did not. The bill was passed by the House of Lords by a clear majority, but a similar bill introduced into the House of Commons the following year by Rob Marris was heavily defeated.

At the time Lord Falconer introduced his bill on assisted dying there was a strong groundswell in the House of Lords in support of such a measure. Indeed, there was a team consisting largely of crossbench peers who actively and often successfully canvassed support. Mary was not part of this group. Her view that seeking death was an altruistic act by dying individuals relieving both the state and their families of the intolerable burden of looking after them was not seen as helpful. The team disagreed with her on advance directives and feared that the way Mary expressed her extreme ideas might turn some against their more modest proposals.[51]

* * *

Over the last decade of her life, Mary began to consider her views on the origins of morality and its relationship to the law and to reflect on her own religious beliefs. She was motivated to do this particularly by the need to justify her views on euthanasia against those of the established Anglican clergy. She admitted that in writing about the relationship between morality and the law she was travelling a very well-trodden philosophical path, but she articulated the fundamental problem in a way which remains hard to answer: those who frame laws must do so by drawing on a pre-existing moral framework. Thus morality must precede the law, but where then does such morality come from? She published her conclusions in a book, *Dishonest to God* (2010).[52]

She begins by examining the widely-held assumption that religion is the basis of morality. Obedience to God's will may, for the religious, enable the faithful to lead 'a good life,' but the values of non-believers, now a majority in British society, are derived more from humanity itself than from religious doctrine. Mary recognises the danger that the separation of morality from religion can lead to moral relativism. In this connection she quotes Lord Denning who, in 1953, wrote that 'without religion there can be no morality and without morality there can be no law.'[53] This view she sees as now outmoded in Britain but still extant in the United States where no politician would dare to put his name forward for election unless he subscribed to a particular religious faith. The rejection of this line of argument in Britain has led, she writes, to a reaction by the Anglican Church which *insists* on the relevance of Christian belief to political life. Rowan Williams, for example, while Archbishop of Canterbury, pronounced that 'Christian ethics is relentlessly political.'[54] Some radical Anglicans go further and join with the Catholic Church in maintaining that unless there is some sort of supernatural standard, people can have no meaningful idea of what is good. They assert that democracy can only function properly if it is based on a 'correct' understanding of the human person and this understanding must accord with Christian teaching.[55]

Such involvement in political decision-making by the Church takes many forms. Mary was especially angry at the amount of lobbying in which the clergy engaged at the time Lord Joffe's bill on assisted dying was debated in the House of Lords in 2007. She describes how the Catholic Archbishop of Cardiff announced he was launching the biggest political campaign by the Church in its whole modern history to oppose this bill. The campaign 'culminated in an article published in *The Catholic Times* entitled "Legalising Euthanasia Turns Carers into Killers" which included a photograph of 24 children who had been murdered by the Nazis in the late 1930s.'[56] So successful was the campaign that the bill was defeated at second reading, thus breaking a long-standing tradition that a Private Member's Bill should always be passed to the next stage. This occurred despite the fact that the provisions of the bill were supported by 80% of the population. Mary believed that 'the conflation of religion with morality and the habit of according moral authority to the declarations of religious leaders, directly led to this outcome.'[57]

She goes on to discuss alternative, non-religious bases for moral judgements. She notes that concepts of human rights are often pressed into service as providing a kind of fundamental law, but Mary is sceptical. Rights, she says, are frequently claimed but can only be regarded as true rights if they are enforceable. She refers to the UNICEF *Declaration of the Rights of the Child*, published in 1990, as a 'meaningless proclamation.' The ideals the declaration declares to be the rights of children, such as the right to play and to exercise their imagination in the arts are, she accepts rather dismissively, 'very nice,' but 'nobody has or could have a duty to ensure they are fulfilled.'[58]

So, if one cannot look to religion or to the language of human rights to underpin morality, where can one turn if morality is not to become simply a matter of personal preference? Some believe that among non-religious people, it is only the retention of the vestiges of religion taught to them by their parents or grandparents, that gives them a sound moral sense. Mary disagrees. She notes that Kant and Hume proposed that humans have an interest in sharing moral values if they are to get on together, and Bentham thought that such shared values could also be based on imagined, as well as real, outcomes. Mary's own view was that human beings need a shared morality to alleviate the predicament in which they all find themselves when facing disaster, loss and death.

She sees moral judgement as based on sympathy and feelings for others. The existence of such feelings depends on the imaginative capacity of human beings, the one defining feature that distinguishes them from other animals. Now our imaginations might lead us to different moral conclusions, but Mary believed this did not happen. The central requirement of such moral behaviour is the ability to resist temptation, to overcome the attraction of yielding to immediate selfish interest. 'Thus, the resistance to temptation is at the heart of individual morality.'[59]

She pointed out, following Auguste Comte, the French positivist, that if moral behaviour is only performed in obedience to divine commands because of the promise of reward in heaven, this can hardly be regarded as morally 'good.' In contrast, when such unselfish behaviour arises in a social context, from community, cooperation and love, then morality has been created which even a non-believer can accept. Inevitably, there will be an element of moral relativism in this view, for as times change and values change, so will moral judgements change, but, Mary maintained, the central core of what lies at the heart of such judgements will remain solid and invulnerable.[60]

In the light of these reflections Mary's hostility to clerical interventions in politics becomes much more understandable. She put her feelings into words most powerfully in an interview with Laurie Taylor after the publication of *Dishonest to God* in 2010. 'I find it extraordinarily irritating,' she said,

when people treat the bishops in the Lords, or the Church elsewhere, or the clergy in general, as moral experts. I think that is an outrageous thing to believe, but people still believe it automatically, without thinking. They think that these members of the Church, of any religion, have a special insight. And often that insight is narrowed down to Christianity alone. There was a perfect example in one House of Lords debate when Lord Lloyd of Berwick, who's a former president of the Law Society, suggested, in the aftermath of the Director of Public Prosecutions' guidelines about [right-to-die campaigner] Debbie Purdy, that one very important step forward would be to change the law of homicide so that it became possible for a jury to say to a judge that there were mitigating circumstances in some cases of murder. Because at the moment if it's murder then it's life. And Lord Lloyd wanted to be able to distinguish between gain-induced murder and a mercy killing. Every single person who spoke in favour of this was a lawyer and they all agreed that this would be an enormous improvement on the law. And then up jumped the Bishop of Winchester and said, 'Ah, but this would give the wrong message. This would show that we didn't, after all, care about life, which is sacred.' That was the collapse of all argument. That was it. That was the end of it. It was terrible.[61]

Despite her views on the inappropriateness of the position of bishops in the House of Lords, she never advocated their removal. Indeed, she wrote: 'I even believe it is right that the established church should have a place in Parliament, provided that no one supposes that the Bishop's Bench in the House of Lords has a monopoly of moral authority.'[62] This inconsistency was symptomatic of her deep affection for the Anglican Church.

Mary's beliefs might have resulted in her seeing herself as a humanist, but she explicitly denied this possibility. When she spoke in a House of Lords debate in 2013 on the contribution to society of atheists and humanists, she said

> I am not a member of the British Humanist Association. I consider myself to be a Christian by culture and by tradition. I frequently attend services of the Church of England, and one of my greatest passions is church music, as sustained in the great English cathedrals and colleges, as well as the great oratorios and passions. I do not want the Church of England to be disestablished, and I regard my loyalty to the sovereign as loyalty to the head of the church as well as to the head of the state. Having said that, I suppose I should confess that I am an atheist.[63]

* * *

Following his four-year term as Vice-Chancellor, (or 'four-year sentence' as he sometimes called it), from 1981 to 1985, Geoffrey returned to his position as Principal of Hertford College until he retired in 1988. On his retirement, the Warnocks sold their small house in an Oxfordshire village, Great Coxwell and bought Brick House, in Axford, in Wiltshire. This house was a surprise in the sense that it was a newly built bungalow sitting on the top of a small hill in the middle of what, at the time, could best be described as a building site. But, according to Mary, it 'had a marvellous view across the Kennet Valley to more downs beyond and the edges of Savernake Forest.'[64] It was built on chalky soil, unpromising for a garden, but she and Geoffrey immediately saw its potential and, over the following years, created a wonderful garden of which they were very proud. They both loved it.[65] Geoffrey settled down to a relatively (for him) inactive life, reading, watching television, gardening and what he himself called 'footling about.' He began to enjoy cooking and even shopping. For three years after his retirement, Mary continued to spend the week in Cambridge where she continued as Mistress of Girton until 1991, returning to Axford every weekend. Then, shortly after Mary herself retired, Geoffrey fell ill and looking after him gradually became a more and more time-consuming occupation for her. For about two years before Geoffrey died, Mary very consciously withdrew from all but her most essential public positions. Quite apart from Geoffrey's everyday needs, there was always the possibility of a crisis and she was determined to be on hand to deal with unexpected demands.

Fig. 12 Mary and Geoffrey Warnock in the garden of their Axford home (1993), provided by the Warnock family, CC BY-NC.

Mary's genuine love of their Axford home did not survive Geoffrey's death. She immediately knew she could not continue there and soon began to plan a move away from Brick House. This was the start of a series of moves which perhaps reflected the spirit of restlessness already noted at other times of her life, but which was also a great source of pleasure and creativity. She simply loved having new decorative and gardening projects. She chose to buy a very different characterful house, 4 Church Street, in Great Bedwyn, a few miles from Marlborough, in Wiltshire. One of the drawbacks of the Axford house had been that it had a steep drive which often became hard to navigate by car (or indeed on foot) in winter. In complete contrast, Great Bedwyn had a main-line station from which the trains ran directly to London, Paddington. Following Geoffrey's death, she was determined to take a more active role in the House of Lords, so to have a main-line station within walking distance of her home was a huge benefit.

When she ceased to be Mistress of Girton in 1991, Mary was sixty-seven: she never again held a salaried position. She had been an infrequent attender at the House of Lords while at Girton, but she had bought a flat in Shepherd's Bush which she could use as a London base. However, as Geoffrey's illness progressed her overnight stays became less frequent and she rented a room to use as an office in her youngest daughter, Boz's house in Camberwell. It was only after Geoffrey died that she was free to contribute more to parliamentary business and she was soon serving on a number of committees and attending on most days the House was in session.[66] For some years Mary also had an office of her own in the Palace of Westminster but with the large increase in the number of peers, this was taken away from her. From 2012 until her retirement from the House of Lords in 2015, she shared a room with three other life peers, Molly Meacher, Elaine Murphy and Valerie Howarth, all distinctly younger than her. Molly Meacher and Elaine Murphy describe her as having been incredibly focused. She had no secretary, made her own arrangements for what seemed like an endless number of lecturing engagements around the country and, when not on the phone, was researching and writing her latest article or book. She seemed to have no close friends among her fellow peers and, unlike many of the others, virtually never put in an appearance at the Bishop's Bar or restaurant where people tended to go to meet colleagues for coffee, lunch or dinner. She was definitely not 'clubbable' in any sense of the word. She was, however, not at all unfriendly.[67] When Elaine Murphy first took her seat in the Chamber, she sat next to Mary who whispered to her 'I gather you are a psychogeriatrician.' When Elaine admitted she was, Mary responded 'Ah well, you'll have plenty of trade here.'[68] She prepared carefully for her contributions to debates and, when she did speak, was listened to with great attention and respect, though she herself felt she never performed at the level she wished. Molly Meacher described her as 'a formidable woman. She had an outstanding mind combined with immense humanity. There are lots of people with outstanding minds, but she enhanced justice and fairness in the world. Her reports on excluded children treated unfairly meant their plight was brought into the mainstream.'[69]

She spoke on a variety of issues in which she had some special knowledge, especially matters concerning children, education at all levels, and genetics. Her support on any issue was greatly valued. In 2014, she spoke in favour of a motion on drug reform introduced by Molly Meacher, who was extremely grateful for her support.[70] Mary described how her own experience with her son, James, and the correspondence she had received had changed her mind on the subject. She also described the contents of a letter she had received from a former student of hers with multiple sclerosis, whose symptoms were greatly relieved by cannabis.[71]

When she reached her eighties in 2004, Mary often reflected on the predicament of the elderly and wrote about her own experience of getting old. In an article published in *The Guardian* in September 2007, she wrote: 'For the first time I feel that I am an old woman [...] my knees are stiff, and I am inclined to hobble.' But she finds much compensatory pleasure in recollection of activities she will never repeat. 'Even of the things I truly loved, like riding, having babies, playing in an orchestra or sex, I think with pleasure that I understand them without inappropriate hankering.' She sees herself not in a second childhood, but in a second adolescence.

> People think of adolescents as perpetually miserable, embarrassed and lacking in confidence and of course the aged can feel like that sometimes. But for me, adolescence was mostly a time of blissful solitude and no responsibilities. It was a time of discovery, of poetry and Greek tragedy, music and Wordsworthian sentiments about nature. All these things seem fresher and more intense, now that I have settled for being old, and have again the solitude to enjoy them.[72]

Mary's sense of being old as adolescence without the angst is highly typical of her positive attitude to so many things. It was a standing joke in the family, encouraged by Geoffrey himself, that he 'had a duty' to die before she did as she was one of 'nature's widows' and should live to enjoy this period of her life.[73] Indeed, she did.

She remained extremely active as a public figure and in writing for newspapers. Her interest in seeing life as a woman in no way diminished. As we have seen, at all points in her life, as young don, as headmistress of a girl's school, as Mistress of Girton, she had had a strong interest in clothes and had delighted in shopping for clothes for herself and other members of her family.[74] In an interview with *The Observer*'s fashion correspondent, Mary fiercely rejected the idea that once you are over the age of forty, it doesn't really matter what you wear.[75] She complained that every article about clothes was written for the young. However, when the journalist examined Mary's wardrobe, it revealed that she completely disproved her own theory. Everything seemed to come from the pages of glossy magazines. Her favourite possession was 'a man's black hat, without which no fashion model would have looked completely dressed last winter.'[76] Not only her clothes, but 'her collection of bangles, necklaces and belts would not disgrace the fashion page of a Sunday newspaper.' As her views on Margaret Thatcher's clothes, described in Chapter One, revealed, Mary thought that a woman's choice of clothes reflected her personality. In her own case, the way she dressed reflected her exuberant, energetic, and, above all, feminine persona and *façon de vivre* that would persist almost to the end.

In 2010 she sold the house in Great Bedwyn and bought a small house in Lower Sydenham in south-east London. This was a characteristically bold decision; she was moving to London in her late seventies, an age when many might be contemplating a move in the opposite direction. But her logic was, as ever, clear: she expected her eyesight and her general health to deteriorate as she grew older, and she wanted to live within reasonable access of the best hospitals and to public transport. She chose Lower Sydenham partly because it was affordable but largely because the house was within walking distance of Maria and her family. Maria was, at this time, Head of Art at Dulwich College. Mary greatly improved the property, indoors and especially outdoors: she removed the 'hideous garage' erected by the previous owner and, as with all her homes, re-invented the two gardens, one at the front and one at the back.[77] Mary benefited enormously from being so close to her youngest daughter, and was delighted to take up her husband Luis's willingness to help her tackle some quite major projects round the house. But the cosiness of these domestic arrangements was not to last for long because Maria was offered an irresistible opportunity to launch a new art department at one of Dulwich's overseas schools in Singapore. Shortly before her retirement from the House of Lords in 2015, Mary sold her house and moved 'round the corner' into the modest ground-floor flat which Maria and her family had recently vacated. Here Mary lived and continued to work until her death in March 2019.[78] According to Norma Scott, the retired Jamaican nurse who lived two doors away, if you walked past the flat, most of the time you could see her working in the front room at her computer.[79] Her very poor eyesight made it difficult for her to see the screen, although it is fair to say that her love-hate relationship with computers was not greatly different from her relationship with all other things mechanical. Cars were always rebellious and washing machines and other domestic appliances seemed wilfully uncooperative in her hands. She was not very skilful in the art of word-processing. She continued, however, to write articles, even providing, shortly before she died, a substantial piece for *The Observer* which was commissioned at six p.m. one evening with a deadline of ten a.m. the following morning. She told Felix and his daughter, Polly, who visited her for lunch later that morning, how staying up into the small hours made her feel young again, like an undergraduate with an essay crisis.[80]

Most of the time, she was at home alone, though she never complained of being lonely. She was very much in touch with her children. She had visits from Felix and from Kitty who came around about once a week for lunch which Mary prepared for her. James came to see her when he was down from Liverpool where he lived and worked. Maria, now working in South-East Asia, spent time with her on her visits back to London. Numerous nieces, nephews and occasionally grandchildren and great-nephews came to visit. In many cases she had been very kind and helpful to them in the past and they were all fond of her.[81] Occasionally other friends and relatives came round. She enjoyed holidays with one or more of her children and their families in rented cottages in different parts of the country. Christmas was usually spent in Liverpool with James's family, but she declined to go there for her last Christmas in 2018 and appeared to have spent most of the day in bed.

Throughout these last years of her life, Mary was troubled with poor eyesight and hearing. All the same, she remained active and was able to manage a trip to Tel Aviv in May 2018. In the autumn of that year, now ninety-four, she suffered a number of mini-strokes. For a few days she was weak and a little confused, and the experience frightened her so much that she decided it would be sensible to move into a care home. The possibility of an eventual move into care had been anticipated; the previous year she and Kitty had visited a number of potential homes and identified the one which Mary preferred, or at least disliked less than the others. This was Peasmarsh Place, near Rye in Sussex, and arrangements were hastily put in place for a trial two-week stay. Despite her frailty, she was deeply reluctant and delayed packing until the last possible moment and, when she arrived, driven there by Kitty and Felix, she had to be more or less dragged through the door, repeating all the time 'This is death. This is death.' She was given a beautiful room and received excellent care including, most importantly, a complete review and proper organisation of her medications. This enabled her to make a remarkable return to tolerable good health with the unfortunate consequence that she quickly came to see herself as confined against her will. A week after her admission, Felix and Polly visited her and took her, on a bright but windy day, to the beach near Rye. Walking with Polly on the sands in the teeth of a howling gale, ice-cream cone in hand, she pronounced this to be 'the happiest day of my life.' The return to Peasmarsh Place was a shock after the elemental pleasures of the wild beach, and it was immediately clear that she had had enough of the 'care' experiment. Indeed, she desperately wanted to return home there and then. At last, though, she agreed to remain one more night provided that Felix return as early as possible on the following day having made the necessary arrangements for her rapid discharge from 'care' and for her return to her own home in London.[82]

Mary's brief stay at Peasmarsh House was a turning point. Following her discovery of how much she disliked being 'cared for,' both her mental and physical state improved. She had no more mini-strokes, her mood lightened and she found a renewed determination to manage her own life, for better or worse. Despite the fact that her eyesight was poor, she continued to do her own shopping in the local Sainsbury's supermarket about half a mile away. The route she took to Sainsbury's was along a path away from the road, beside a little river of which she was very fond.[83] On one occasion, she did fall outside her flat grazing her forehead and damaging some fingers. An ambulance was called but she refused to get in. Her neighbours insisted and she went off to Lewisham Hospital, returning the same evening. Norma Scott, her neighbour, offered to help with the shopping and gave Mary her phone number, but Mary never contacted her. Even Norma's offers to carry her shopping for her were turned down. As Norma remembered her, 'She was a remarkable lady. Just *so* independent.'[84] She was indeed determined not to be a burden.

Finally, on the evening of Tuesday 19 March 2019, she went to bed, leaving not for the first time a saucepan on a hob she had forgotten to turn off. During the night, her upstairs neighbour noticed smoke coming from her flat. Without her hearing aids she could not hear the front doorbell or the phone, so the police and fire service were called. Her front door was broken down and a serious fire averted. Once again, she refused, against all persuasion by the police among others, to go to hospital to see whether she had suffered any damage from inhaling smoke. Her neighbours left her to go back to bed at three a.m. but when her gardener, Peter Lawrence, called at eight a.m. the following morning, there was no reply when he rang the bell. He had the key and entered to find Mary lifeless on the bathroom floor. She had suffered a massive stroke and would have died instantly, thus succeeding in her determination to live her life to the end without being a burden to anyone.[85]

Mary's ashes were interred beside those of her husband, as she wished, in the graveyard of St. Michael's Church, in Axford, Wiltshire. An interment ceremony was held beside the grave followed by a service in St. Mary's, Great Bedwyn and a lunch for family members and her few surviving Oxford contemporaries including Susan Wood and Ann Strawson. The service was taken by her niece, Stephana's daughter, the Reverend Canon Celia Thomson, Dean of Gloucester Cathedral. There were readings from Wordsworth's 'Lines Written a Few Miles above Tintern Abbey' and Keats' sonnet 'To Sleep.' Later that year, a well-attended Service of Thanksgiving was held on 22 October 2019 in St. Margaret's Church, Westminster to celebrate her remarkable contribution to public life over a period of nearly half a century.

On 9 February 2019, less than six weeks before she died, she was interviewed by Giles Fraser, an ex-Anglican priest, for a series titled *Confessions*. In this series, Fraser talked to a number of well-known people about matters they did not usually discuss and might be reluctant to make public, particularly their religious views. (Mary was not reluctant in the slightest degree.) She agrees with him that she thinks of herself as an 'atheist Anglican,' resisting when he tries to persuade her otherwise about the existence of God. 'I don't think we need a God,' she says firmly. In her last public words, based on the Epistle of St. John, she claims instead, 'Loving one another is the most important value.'[86]

Notes

1   House of Lords, *Hansard*, 554, 1344, 9 May 1994.

2   Mary Warnock, personal communication.

3   Nick Maurice, personal communication.

4   Mary Warnock, personal communication, 18 October 1995.

5   Peter Strawson, 2004.

6   Ibid.

7   Mary Warnock, personal communication, 18 October 1995.

8   Nick Maurice, personal communication.

9   Felix Warnock, personal communication.

10 Peter Strawson, 2004.

11 Ibid.

12 Mary Warnock, Kitty Warnock, personal communication.

13 Nick Maurice, Marlborough Medical Practice Newsletter, August 1997, pp. 9–10.

14 Ludovic Kennedy, 1997, p. 6.

15 Nick Maurice, personal communication.

16 Peter Millar, 1996.

17 Ibid.

18 Mary Warnock, 1999, pp. 19–39.

19   Ibid., pp. 21–23.

20   Mary Warnock, *An Intelligent Person's Guide to Ethics*, 1999.

21   Ibid., p. 89.

22   Jackson, 1998.

23   Mary Warnock, House of Lords, *Hansard*, June 2003.

24   Mary Warnock, ibid.

25   Mary Warnock and Elisabeth Macdonald, 2008.

26   Simone de Beauvoir, 1990, p. 78.

27   Mary Warnock and Elisabeth Macdonald, 2008, p. 83.

28   Onora O'Neill, *The Lancet*, 2008.

29   Steven Poole, *The Guardian*, 2009.

30   Julia Stone, *Times Higher Education Supplement*, 2008.

31   Elisabeth Sears, personal communication.

32   Jackie Macadam, 2008.

33   Nadine Dorries, quoted in Beckford, *Telegraph*, 2008.

34   Phyllis Bowman, quoted in Beckford, 2008.

35   Neil Hunt, quoted in Beckford, 2008.

36   Sarah Wootton, *The Guardian*, 29 September 2008.

37   Nancy Jecker, 2014.

38   June Andrews, 2008, p. 3.

39   Felix Warnock, personal communication.

40   Ray Tallis, personal communication.

41   Mary Warnock, unpublished lecture to the Society of Old Age, Rational Suicide (SOARS), 2010.

42   Ibid.

43   Ibid.

44   Ibid.

45   Ibid.

46   Ibid.

47   Ibid.

48   House of Lords, *Hansard*, 12 December 2013.

49   Ibid.

50   House of Lords, 18 July 2014a.

51   Molly Meacher, personal communication.

52   Mary Warnock, 2010.

53   Ibid., p. 96.

54   Ibid., p. 100.

55   Ibid., p. 101.

56   Ibid., p. 108.

57   Ibid., p. 109.

58   Ibid., p. 112.

59   Ibid., p. 121.

60   Ibid., p. 123.

61   Mary Warnock, Interview with Laurie Taylor, BBC Radio 4, 10 September 2010.

62   Mary Warnock, 'The Future of the Anglican Church', unpublished, p. 2.

63   House of Lords, *Hansard*, 25 July 2013.

64   Mary Warnock, 2015, p. 35.

65   Ibid., p. 36.

66   Kitty Warnock, personal communication.

67   Molly Meacher, personal communication; Elaine Murphy, personal communication.

68   Elaine Murphy, personal communication.

69   Ibid.

70   Molly Meacher, personal communication.

71   House of Lords, *Hansard*, 2014b.

72   Mary Warnock, *The Guardian*, 2007.

73   Ibid.

74   Kitty Warnock, personal communication.

75   Sally Brampton, *The Observer*, 24 July 1983.

76   Ibid.

77   Ibid., p. 38.

78   Kitty Warnock, personal communication.

79   Norma Scott, personal communication.

80   Felix Warnock, personal communication.

81   Kitty Warnock, personal communication.

82   Ibid.; Felix Warnock, personal communication.

83   Kitty Warnock, personal communication.

84   Norma Scott, personal communication.

85   Kitty Warnock, personal communication.

86   Interview with Giles Fraser, *Confessions*, 9 February 2019.

List of Figures

Chapter Two

Chapter Four

Chapter Five

Chapter Six

Chapter Seven

Chapter Eight

Chapter Ten

Chapter Eleven

Bibliography

Archival Sources

British Library

Girton College, Cambridge, Archive

Hertford College, Oxford, Archive

House of Commons Library

Lady Margaret Hall, Oxford, Archive

Margaret Thatcher Archive

National Archive

Oxford High School for Girls, Archive

St. Hugh's College, Oxford, Archive

Secondary Sources

Addison, Paul, 'The University at War', in Brian Harrison (ed.), *The History of the University of Oxford, Vol VIII: The Twentieth Century* (Oxford: Oxford University Press, 1994), pp. 167–188.

Alcoff, Linda Martin, *Singing in the Fire* (London: Rowman and Littlefield, 2003).

Andrews, June, Leading Article, *Nursing Older People* (20, 9, 3, 2008).

Annan Committee, *Committee on the Future of Broadcasting* (London: HMSO, 1977).

Baggini, J. and J. Stangroom, *What Philosophers Think* (London: Continuum, 2003).

Baier, A., 'Untitled', *Philosophical Review*, 99/3 (1990), 436–439.

Baker, Kenneth, *The Turbulent Years* (London: Faber & Faber, 1993).

Bakewell, Sarah, *At the Existentialist Café: Freedom, Being and Apricot Cocktails* (London: Vintage, 2016).

Barkley, Diana, 'Girton Goes Mixed', in Marilyn Strathern, *Girton: Thirty Years in the Life of a Cambridge College* (London: Third Millennium Publishing, 2005), pp. 17–18.

Beckford, Martin, 'Dementia sufferers may have a duty to die', *Telegraph* (18 September 2008).

Bolton, P., *Historical Statistics* (House of Commons Library, SN/SG/4252, 27 November 2012).

Bolton, P., *Education Statistics* (House of Commons Library. Briefing Paper 1398. 29 June 2016).

Brine, J., 'Tales of the 50-somethings: selective schooling, gender and social class', *Gender and Education*, 18/4 (2006), 431–446, https://doi.org/10.1080/09540250600805146.

British Medical Association, *Annual report of the council appendix V: Report of the panel on human artificial insemination* (Chairman: Sir John Peel), *British Medical Journal* II (1973), 3–5.

Brooke, Stephen, 'Class and Gender', in Francesca Carnavali and Julie-Marie Strange, *20th Century Britain* (London: Pearson Education, 2007), pp. 42–57.

Brown, Andrew, 'The Practical Philosopher', *The Guardian* (19 July 2003).

Carrier, D., Untitled, *Journal of Philosophy*, 75/1 (1978), 40–44.

Charlton, W., Untitled, *Philosophy Quarterly*, 109 (1977), 375–377.

Cigman, Ruth, 'A Question of Universality: Inclusive Education and the Principle of Respect', *Journal of the Philosophy of Education*, 41/4 (2007) 231, https://doi.org/10.1111/j.1467-9752.2007.00577.x.

Connelly, Katherine, 'BBC 100 Women: Who Won Women the Vote? Suffragists or Suffragettes', *BBC* (6 February 2018).

Conradi, Peter, *Iris Murdoch: A Life* (London: Harper Collins, 2001).

Crossley, Jean, *A Daughter of Winchester* (Privately published, 1993).

Crossley, Jean, *The Houses: A Family Chronicle* (Bicester, Oxon: Bound Biographies, 2006).

Daly, M., 'William Allan Award Introduction: Kari Stefansson', *American Journal of Human Genetics*, 102/3 (2018), 350, https://doi.org/10.1016/j.ajhg.2018.01.010.

Davenport-Hines, Richard, 'Schuster, Sir Felix Otto, first baronet, 1854–1936', *Oxford Dictionary of National Biography* (Oxford: Oxford University Press, 2004), http://www.oxforddnb.com/view/article/35.

De Beauvoir, Simone, *A Very Easy Death* (London: Penguin, 1990).

Deledalle, G., Untitled, *Les Etudes Philosophiques*, 1 (1961), 122.

Department for Culture, Media and Sport, *Spoliation Advisory Panel* (London: HMSO, 2000).

Department of Education and Science, 'The discovery of children requiring special education and the assessment of their needs', *Circular* 2/75 (1975).

Department of Education and Science, *Special Educational Needs* (London: HMSO, 1978).

Devlin, T., and M. Warnock, *What Must We Teach* (London: Temple Smith, 1977).

Donoughue, Bernard, *The Heat of the Kitchen* (London: Politico's, 2003).

Dunbabin, J. P. D., 'Finance since 1914', in Brian Harrison (ed.), *The History of the University of Oxford, Vol VIII: The Twentieth Century* (Oxford: Oxford University Press, 1994), pp. 639–682.

Dunstan, G., 'Moral and Social Issues, Biological aspects of AID', in *Ciba Foundation Symposium 17, Law and Ethics of AID and Embryo Transfer* (London: Association of Scientific Publishers, 1973), pp. 47–55.

Edwards, R., and D. Sharpe, 'Social values and research in human embryology', *Nature*, 231 (1971), 87–91.

Edwards, R., and A. Steptoe, 'Biological Aspects of Embryo Transfer', in *Ciba Foundation Symposium 17, Law and Ethics of AID and Embryo Transfer* (London: Association of Scientific Publishers, 1973), pp. 11–18, https://doi.org/10.1038/231087a0.

Edwards, R., and A. Steptoe, 'Current status of in-vitro fertilisation and implantation of human embryos', *Lancet*, 322 (1983), 1265–1269.

Elliott, Margaret, *Prior's Field School: A Century Remembered, 1902–2002* (Privately published, 2002).

Elsner, Jas, 'Room with a Few: Edward Fraenkel and the Receptions of Reception', in C. Pelling and S. Harrison (eds), *Classical Scholarship and Its History: From the Renaissance to the Present. Essays in Honour of Christopher Stray* (Berlin: De Gruyter, 2021), pp. 319–350.

Equality Challenge Unit, *Equality in Higher Education. Statistical Report* (2015).

Equal Opportunities Commission, *Social Focus on Women and Men* (London: Office of National Statistics, 1998).

Ewing, A. C., Untitled review, *Philosophy*, 36/137 (1961), 236–237.

Eyre, Richard, 'Preface', in Jean-Paul Sartre, *Being and Nothingness* (London: Routledge, 2003), pp. viii–x.

Frontiers in Education, Special Issue, Introduction (May 2019).

Forster, Margaret, *Hidden Lives* (London: Penguin, 1995).

Franklin, S., 'Developmental Landmarks and the Warnock Report: A Sociological Account of Biological Transmission', *Comparative Studies in Society and History*, 61/4 (2019), 741–773, https://doi.org/10.1017/S0010417519000252.

Freedland, Jonathan, 'Margaret Thatcher's Legacy: Round Up of the Best Writing', *The Guardian* (11 April 2013).

Friedan, Betty, *The Feminine Mystique* (London: W. W. Norton, 1963).

Gallie, D., 'The Labour Force', in A. H. Halsey and Josephine Webb, *Twentieth-Century British Social Trends* (London: Macmillan, 2000), pp. 281–323.

Gough, B. and M. Lee, 'Editorial', *Professional Development in Education*, 12/1 (1985), 4–5.

Graham, P., *Ciba Foundation Symposium 17, Law and Ethics of AID and Embryo Transfer* (London: Association of Scientific Publishers, 1973), pp. 33–34.

Graham, Philip, *Susan Isaacs: A Life Freeing the Minds of Children* (London: Taylor & Francis, 2009).

Greer, Germaine, *The Female Eunuch* (London: Hart Davis, MacGibbon, 1970).

Grove, Valerie, *The Compleat Woman: Marriage, Motherhood, Career. Can She Have It All?* (London: Hogarth Press, 1988).

Grove, Valerie, 'The Hard Schooling of Warnock', *Times Saturday Review* (6 July 1991).

Halasa, Malu, 'Relative Values', *Sunday Times Supplement* (6 August 1995).

Hall, Anthea, 'Philosopher of Fertilisation', *Sunday Telegraph* (17 June 1984).

Halsey, A. H., 'The Franks Commission', in Brian Harrison (ed.), *The History of the University of Oxford, Vol VIII: The Twentieth Century* (Oxford: Oxford University Press, 1994), 721–738.

Halsey, A. H., 'Further and Higher Education', in A. H. Halsey and Josephine Webb, *Twentieth Century British Social Trends* (London: Macmillan, 2000), pp. 221–253.

Hansard, HC Deb, vol. 998 cols 27–102, 2 February 1981.

Hanson, K., Untitled, *Philosophical Review*, 88/1 (1979), 436–439.

Hardyment, Christina, *Perfect Parents* (Oxford: Oxford University Press, 1995).

Harman, Harriet, *A Woman's Work* (London: Penguin, 2018).

Harris, José, 'The Arts and Social Sciences, 1939–1970', in Brian Harrison (ed.), *The History of the University of Oxford, Vol VIII: The Twentieth Century* (Oxford: Oxford University Press, 1994), pp. 217–250.

Heath, A., and C. Payne, 'Social Mobility', in A. H. Halsey and Josephine Webb, *Twentieth Century British Social Trends* (London: Macmillan, 2000), pp. 254–277.

Hill, George, 'Schoolmistress to the Nation. Times Profile', *The Times* (21 May 1985).

HMSO, *Report of the Departmental Committee on Human Artificial Insemination* (London: HMSO, Cmnd. 1105, 1960).

HMSO, Royal Commission on Environmental Pollution. *Ninth Report. Lead and the Environment* (London: HMSO, 1983).

HMSO, Royal Commission on Environmental Pollution: *Tenth Report. Tackling Pollution—Experience and Prospects* (London: HMSO, 1984).

HMSO, *Higher Education in the 1990s* (London: HMSO, 1985).

HMSO, *Higher Education: Meeting the Challenge* (London: HMSO, 1987).

Hooper, Arthur, *No Bed of Roses at Verdley Place* (Fernhurst Society Archive. No. 3, [n.d.]).

House of Commons Select Committee, *Special Educational Needs and Disabilities* (October 2019).

House of Lords, Select Committee on Medical Ethics, *Hansard* (9 May 1994).

House of Lords, *Report: Animals in Scientific Procedures* (London: HMSO, 2002).

House of Lords, Patient (Assisted Dying Bill) *Hansard* (6 June 2003).

House of Lords, Assisted Dying for the Terminally Ill Bill, *Hansard* (12 May 2006).

House of Lords, Atheists and Humanists: Contribution to Society, *Hansard* (25 July 2013).

House of Lords, Debate: Health, End of Life, *Hansard* (12 December 2013).

House of Lords, Assisted Dying Bill, *Hansard* (18 July 2014a).

House of Lords, Drug Policy, *Hansard* (11 December 2014b).

Howarth, Janet, 'Women', in Brian Harrison (ed.), *The History of the University of Oxford, Vol VIII: The Twentieth Century* (Oxford: Oxford University Press, 1994), pp. 345–377.

Howarth, Richard. 'Schuster, Sir Arthur, (1851–1934) Physicist', *Oxford Dictionary of National Biography* (Oxford, Oxford University Press, 2004), https://doi.org/10.1093/ref:odnb/35975.

Hurt, J. S., *Outside the Mainstream* (London: Batsford, 1988).

Institute of Government, *Gender Balance in the Civil Service* (2019).

Isaacs, Jeremy, *Never Mind the Moon: My Time at the Royal Opera House* (London: Bantam Press, 1999).

Issman, S., Untitled, *Revue Internationale de Philosophie*, 14/53 (1960), 455–456.

Jackson, B., 'Morality for the Me Generation', *Times Higher Education Supplement* (25 December 1998).

Jarratt, Alex, Report of the Steering Committee for Efficiency Studies in Universities, *Department for Education* (1985).

Jecker, Nancy, 'Against a Duty to Die', *AMA Journal of Ethics, Virtual Mentor*, 16/5 (2014), 30–34.

Jefferson, L., K. Bloor, and A. Maynard, 'Women in Medicine. Historical Perspectives and Recent Trends', *British Medical Bulletin*, 114/1 (2015), 5–15, https://doi.org/10.1093/bmb/ldv007.

Jenkins, D., Untitled, *Theology*, 88/788 (1996), 138–140.

Kennedy, Ludovic, 'Debate rages on after doctor admits practising euthanasia', *Wiltshire Gazette* (11 September 1997).

Kynaston, David, *Family Britain: 1951–1957* (London: Bloomsbury, 2009).

Lane-Perham, Nancy, 'Initiatives in Science and Technology', in Marilyn Strathern (ed.), *Girton: Thirty Years in the Life of a Cambridge College* (London: Third Millennium Publishing, 2005), pp. 97–100.

Latham, S. R., The United Kingdom Re-visits its Surrogacy Law, *Hastings Center Report* (2020), https://doi.org/10.1002/hast.1076.

Leithwood, K., C. Day, P. Sammons, A. Harris, and D. Hopkins, *Seven Strong Claims about Successful School Leadership* (London: Department of Education, 2006).

Lewis, I., and G. Vulliamy, 'Warnock or Warlock? The Sorcery of Definitions: The Limitations of the Report on Special Education', *Educational Review*, 32/1 (1980), 3–10.

Lowry, Suzanne, 'Birth of a New Ethic', *The Sunday Times* (24 June 1984).

Macadam, Jackie, 'A Duty to Die?' *Life and Work, Church of Scotland Magazine* (October 2008).

Magee, Sean, *Desert Island Discs: 70 Years of Castaways* (London: Bantam Press, 2012).

Marks, John, 'Pleading guilty', in Marilyn Strathern (ed.), *Girton: Thirty Years in the Life of a Cambridge College* (London: Third Millennium Publishing, 2005), p. 104.

Maurice, Nick, 'Euthanasia, Pick Me Up', *Newsletter, Marlborough Medical Practice* (August 1997).

McCloskey, Deirdre, 'Paid Work', in I. Zweiniger-Bargeliowska, *Women in Twentieth Century Britain* (London: Routledge, 2001), pp. 165–182.

McLaren, A., 'Biological aspects of AID', in *Ciba Foundation Symposium 17, Law and Ethics of AID and Embryo Transfer* (London: Association of Scientific Publishers, 1973), pp. 3–9.

Middleton, N., D. Gunnell, E. Whitley, D. Dorling, S. Fraenkel, 'Secular trends in antidepressant prescribing 1975–1998', *Journal of Public Health*, 23/4 (2001), 262–267, https://doi.org/10.1093/pubmed/23.4.262.

Midgley, Mary, *The Owl of Minerva: A Memoir* (London: Routledge, 2005).

Millar, Peter, 'Ready to Play God's Quality Controller', *The Sunday Times* (1 December 1996).

Moberly, C. A., and E. Jourdain, *An Adventure* (London: Macmillan, 1911).

Moore, Charles, *Margaret Thatcher: The Authorized Biography*, 3 vols (London: Penguin, 2013–19).

Murdoch, Iris, *Sartre: Romantic Rationalist* (Harmondsworth: Penguin, 1953).

Murdoch, Iris, *The Sovereignty of Good* (London: Routledge, 1970).

Murdoch, Iris, *Metaphysics as a guide to morals* (London: Vintage, 1992).

National Bureau for Cooperation in Child Care, *Living with Handicap* (1970).

Nicholson, D., 'Demography, Discrimination and Diversity', *International Journal of the Legal Profession*, 12 (2005), 201–228, https://doi.org/10.1080/09695950500246522.

Novak, J. D., Untitled, *Journal of Education*, 2 (1978), 83–85.

Office for National Statistics, *Divorce Statistics* (2014).

Office for National Statistics, *How Has Life Expectancy Changed over Time?* (2015).

Oksanen, M., Untitled, *Environmental Values*, 16 (2016), 373–374.

O'Neill, Onora, 'Questions of Life and Death', *Lancet*, 372 (11 October 2008).

Oxford Open Learning Trust, *Gender Diversity in Schools* (2018).

Palmer, Sue, 'The Girton Brand', in Marilyn Strathern (ed.), *Girton: Thirty Years in the Life of a Cambridge College* (London: Third Millennium Publishing, 2005), pp. 174–176.

Peters, R., Untitled, *Oxford Review of Education*, 1 (1978), 111–115.

Phillips, Melanie, 'A Monstrous Ego Who Has Destroyed So Much of Our Moral and Social Heritage', *Mail Online* (9 June 2005).

Phipps, A., and G. Smith, 'Violence against Women Students in the UK: Time to Take Action', *Gender and Education*, 24/4 (2012), 357–373.

Piaget, Jean, *Language and Thought of the Child* (London: Routledge and Kegan Paul, 1926).

Poole, Steven, 'Last Rights', *The Guardian* (19 April 2008).

Potter, Jeremy, *Independent Television in Britain, Volume 3: Politics and Control, 1968–1980* (London: Macmillan, 1989).

Potter, Jeremy, *Independent Television in Britain, Volume 4: Companies and Programmes, 1968–1980* (London: Macmillan, 1990).

Rose, Imogen, *A Difficult Girl* (Privately published, 2002).

Rose, Jasper, and John Ziman, *Camford Observed* (London: Gollancz, 1964).

Rowbotham, Sheila, *A Century of Women: The History of Women in Britain and the United States* (London: Penguin, 1997).

Royal Commission on Environmental Pollution, *Ninth Report. Lead and the Environment*, HMSO (1983).

Sartre, Jean-Paul, *Being and Nothingness*, trans. by Hazel E. Barnes (London: Methuen, 1957).

Sartre, Jean-Paul, *L'Etre et le néant* (Paris: Gallimard, 1943).

Sartre, Jean-Paul, *Existentialism and Humanism* (London: Methuen, 1948).

Schwartz, Laura, *A Serious Endeavour: Gender, Education and Community at St. Hugh's, 1886–2011* (London: Profile Books, 2011).

Searle, John, 'Oxford philosophy in the 1950s', *Philosophy*, 90/2 (2015), 173–193.

Segal, Stanley, *No Child is Ineducable* (Oxford: Pergamon, 1966).

Siden, R., 'Obituary: Baroness Mary Warnock', *BioNews* (25 March 2019), https://www.bionews.org.uk/page_142095.

Singer, Peter, *Practical Ethics* (Cambridge: Cambridge University Press, 1979).

Singer, Peter, 'Ethics and the New Animal Liberation Movement', in P. Singer (ed.), *In Defence of Animals* (Oxford: Blackwell, 1985), pp. 1–10.

Spock, Benjamin, *Baby and Child Care* (New York: Duell, Sloan and Pearce, 1946).

Stone, Julia, 'Review: Easeful Death', *Times Higher Education Supplement* (2008).

Stone, Olive, 'English Law in Relation to AID and Embryo Transfer', in *Ciba Foundation Symposium 17, Law and Ethics of AID and Embryo Transfer* (London: Association of Scientific Publishers, 1973), pp. 69–76.

Storr, Anthony, Untitled, *RSA Journal*, 143/5457 (1995), 82–83.

Strawson, Peter, 'Sir Geoffrey Warnock', *Oxford Dictionary of National Biography* (Oxford: Oxford University Press, 2004), https://doi.org/10.1093/ref:odnb/60440.

Stray, Christopher, 'Eduard Fraenkel: An Exploration', *Syllectica Classica*, 25 (2014), 113–172.

Strickland, G. R., 'The Philosophy of Sartre', *Cambridge Quarterly*, 1/2 (1965–66), 198–202.

Strickland G. R., 'The Analysis of Memory', *Cambridge Quarterly*, 17/4 (1988), 386–397.

Thatcher, Margaret, 'Women in a Changing World' (1ˢᵗ Dame Margery Corbett-Ashby Memorial Lecture), Margaret Thatcher Foundation (26 July 1982).

Thatcher, Margaret, Pankhurst Lecture to the 300 Group, *The Thatcher Archive* (18 July 1990).

Thatcher, Margaret, *The Path to Power* (London: Harper Press, 2011).

Thomas, A., S. Chess, and H. Birch, *Your Child is a Person* (Harmondsworth: Penguin, 1965).

Thomas, K., 'College Life', in Brian Harrison (ed.), *The History of the University of Oxford, Vol VIII: The Twentieth Century* (Oxford: Oxford University Press, 1994), pp. 189–215.

Tizard, Jack, *Community Services for the Mentally Handicapped* (Oxford: Oxford University Press, 1964).

Tomlinson, E., and J. Stott, 'Assisted Dying in Dementia: A Systematic Review of the International Literature on the Attitudes of Health Professionals, Patients, Carers and the Public, and the Factors Associated with these', *International Journal of Geriatric Psychiatry*, 30/1 (2014), 10–20, https://doi.org/10.1002/gps.4169.

Tomlinson E., A. Spector, S. Nurock, and J. Stott, 'Euthanasia and Physician Assisted Suicide in Dementia: A Qualitative Study of the Views of Former Dementia Carers', *Palliative Medicine*, 29/8 (2015), 720–726, https://doi.org/10.1177/0269216315582143.

Tomlinson, Sally, 'Sociological Perspectives on Failing Schools', *International Studies in Sociology of Education*, 7/1 (1997), 81–98.

Tree, Isabella, *Wilding: The Return of Nature to a British Farm* (London: Pan Macmillan, 2019).

Trickett, Rachel, *The Elders* (London: Constable, 1966).

Trickett, Rachel, 'Women's Education', in *St Hugh's: One Hundred Years of Women's Education in Oxford* (London: Macmillan, 1986), pp. 5–14.

Turner, Graham, 'Why All the Toffs Hate Maggie', *Sunday Telegraph* (10 January 1988).

Van Marter, L. E., Untitled, *Ethics*, 76/2 (1966), 151–154.

Visser, J., and G. Upton, *Special Education in Britain after Warnock* (London: David Fulton, 1993).

Wallinger, Mark, and Mary Warnock (eds), *Art for All: Their Policies and Our Culture* (London: PEER, 2000).

Warnock, Ceri, Untitled, *Commonwealth Law Bulletin*, 4/1 (2016), 151–154.

Warnock, Geoffrey, *Berkeley* (Oxford: Oxford University Press, 1953).

Warnock, Geoffrey, *English Ethics since 1900* (Oxford: Oxford University Press, 1957).

Warnock, Geoffrey, *English Philosophy since 1900* (Oxford: Oxford University Press, 1969).

Warnock, Geoffrey, *Essays on J. L. Austin* (Oxford: Oxford University Press, 1973).

Warnock, Mary, Unpublished diaries, 1941–47.

Warnock, Mary, *Ethics since 1900* (Oxford: Oxford University Press, 1960).

Warnock, Mary, *The Philosophy of Sartre* (London: Hutchinson, 1965).

Warnock, Mary, *Existentialist Ethics* (London: Macmillan, 1967).

Warnock, Mary, *Existentialism* (Oxford: Oxford University Press, 1970).

Warnock, Mary (ed.), *Sartre: A Collection of Critical Essays* (London: Anchor, 1971).

Warnock, Mary, *Imagination* (London: Faber & Faber, 1976).

Warnock, Mary, *Schools of Thought* (London: Faber, 1977).

Warnock, Mary, *A Question of Life* (London: Blackwell, 1985a).

Warnock, Mary, *The Social Responsibility of the Broadcasting Media* (Liverpool: Liverpool University Press, 1985b).

Warnock, Mary, 'Teacher, Teach Thyself. The 1985 Richard Dimbleby Lecture', *The Listener* (28 March 1986).

Warnock, Mary, 'Women's Education and its Future', in Penny Griffin (ed.), *St Hugh's: One Hundred Years of Women's Education in Oxford* (London: Macmillan, 1986), pp. 284–298.

Warnock, Mary, *Memory* (London: Faber & Faber, 1987).

Warnock, Mary, *A Common Policy for Education* (Oxford: Oxford University Press, 1989).

Warnock, Mary, *Universities: Knowing Our Minds* (London, Chatto & Windus, 1989).

Warnock, Mary, 'Education with a Moral', in *The Uses of Philosophy* (Oxford: Blackwell, 1992), pp. 160–174.

Warnock, Mary, 'Towards a Moral Consensus', in *The Uses of Philosophy* (Oxford: Blackwell, 1992), pp. 86–101.

Warnock, Mary, *The Uses of Philosophy* (Oxford: Blackwell, 1992), pp. 9–23.

Warnock, Mary, *Imagination and Time* (Oxford: Blackwell, 1994).

Warnock, Mary, 'Education and Values', Unpublished sermon delivered in the University Church, Oxford (5 February 1995).

Warnock, Mary (ed.), *Women Philosophers* (London: JM Dent, 1996).

Warnock, Mary, *An Intelligent Person's Guide to Ethics* (London: Duckworth, 1999).

Warnock, Mary, 'Existentialism, Education and Ethics', in Andrew Pyle (ed.), *Key Philosophers in Conversation* (London: Routledge and Kegan Paul, 1999), pp. 8–16.

Warnock, Mary, *A Memoir: People and Places* (London: Duckworth, 2000).

Warnock, Mary, *Recollections of Recent Headmistresses, 1966–1972* (Oxford High School for Girls Archive).

Warnock, Mary, *Making Babies* (Oxford: Oxford University Press, 2002).

Warnock, Mary, Unfinished Autobiography (abandoned 2002, unpublished).

Warnock, Mary, *Nature and Mortality: Recollections of a Philosopher in Public Life* (London: Continuum, 2003).

Warnock, Mary, *Special Educational Needs: A New Look* (London: Philosophy of Education Society of Great Britain, 2005), Impact Series, No. 11.

Warnock, Mary, '80s', *The Guardian* (9 September 2007).

Warnock, Mary, Interview, *Church of Scotland Newsletter Life and Work* (September 2008).

Warnock, Mary, 'Three Reasons to Hope in an Age of Austerity', in R. Cigman (ed.), *Could do Better: Education Policies in an Election Year* (London: The Philosophy of Education Society of Great Britain, Blackwell, 2010a), pp. 46–49.

Warnock, Mary, *Dishonest to God: On Keeping Religion Out of Politics* (London: Continuum, 2010b).

Warnock, Mary, 'Should Trees Have Standing?', *Journal of Human Rights and the Environment*, 3 (2012), 56–67, https://doi.org/10.4337/jhre.2012.02.03.

Warnock, Mary, *Critical Reflections on Ownership* (Cheltenham: Edward Elgar, 2015)

Warnock, Mary, and Macdonald, Elisabeth, *Easeful Death* (Oxford: Oxford University Press, 2008).

Warnock Mary, and B. Norwich, *Special Educational Needs: A New Look*, ed. by L. Terzi (London: Continuum, 2010).

Wellings, K., J. Field, A. Johnson, and J. Wadsworth, *Sexual Behaviour in Britain* (Harmondsworth: Penguin, 1994).

Wilkinson, Richard, and Kate Pickett 'Margaret Thatcher's Legacy: Round Up of the Best Writing', *The Guardian* (11 April 2013).

Williams, Barry, *So Many Opportunities: A Historical Portrait of Sherborne School for Girls, 1899–1999* (London: James and James, 1998).

Williams, Bernard, *Morality: An Introduction to Ethics* (Cambridge: Cambridge University Press, 1972).

Wootton, Sarah, 'Nobody Has a Duty to Die', *Guardian Social Care* (28 September 2008).

Wordsworth, William, *Collected Poems* (Ware: Wordsworth Poetry Library, 1994).

Young, Hugo, *One of Us* (London: Macmillan, 1991).

Zweiniger-Bargeliowska, I., *Women in Twentieth-Century Britain* (London: Routledge, 2001).

Index

About the Team

Alessandra Tosi was the managing editor for this book.

Melissa Purkiss copy-edited, proofread, indexed and typeset the book in InDesign.

Anna Gatti designed the cover. The cover was produced in InDesign using the Fontin font.

Luca Baffa produced the paperback and hardback editions. The text font is Tex Gyre Pagella; the heading font is Californian FB. Luca produced the EPUB, AZW3, PDF, HTML, and XML editions—the conversion is performed with open source software freely available on our GitHub page (https://github.com/OpenBookPublishers).

This book need not end here...

Share

All our books — including the one you have just read — are free to access online so that students, researchers and members of the public who can't afford a printed edition will have access to the same ideas. This title will be accessed online by hundreds of readers each month across the globe: why not share the link so that someone you know is one of them?

This book and additional content is available at:

https://doi.org/10.11647/OBP.0278

Customise

Personalise your copy of this book or design new books using OBP and third-party material. Take chapters or whole books from our published list and make a special edition, a new anthology or an illuminating coursepack. Each customised edition will be produced as a paperback and a downloadable PDF.

Find out more at:

https://www.openbookpublishers.com/section/59/1

You may also be interested in:

Towards an Ethics of Autism
A Philosophical Exploration
Kristien Hens

https://doi.org/10.11647/OBP.0261

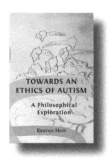

Margery Spring Rice
Pioneer of Women's Health in the Early Twentieth Century
Lucy Pollard

https://doi.org/10.11647/OBP.0215

Beyond Price
Essays on Birth and Death
J. David Velleman

https://doi.org/10.11647/OBP.0061

Lightning Source UK Ltd.
Milton Keynes UK
UKHW020156191221
395834UK00002B/18

9 781800 643383